Complete Cantonese

Hugh Baker and Ho Pui-Kei

First published in Great Britain in 1995 as *Teach Yourself Cantonese* by Hodder Education.
An Hachette UK company.
First published in US in 2006 by The McGraw-Hill Companies, Inc.
This edition published in 2015 by John Murray Learning

British Library Cataloguing in Publication Data: a catalogue record for this title is available from the British Library.

Library of Congress Catalog Card Number: on file.

ISBN: 978 1 473 60082 9

2

The publisher has used its best endeavours to ensure that any website addresses referred to in this book are correct and active at the time of going to press. However, the publisher and the author have no responsibility for the websites and can make no guarantee that a site will remain live or that the content will remain relevant, decent or appropriate.

The publisher has made every effort to mark as such all words which it believes to be trademarks. The publisher should also like to make it clear that the presence of a word in the book, whether marked or unmarked, in no way affects its legal status as a trademark.

Every reasonable effort has been made by the publisher to trace the copyright holders of material in this book. Any errors or omissions should be notified in writing to the publisher, who will endeavour to rectify the situation for any reprints and future editions.

Cover image © Shutterstock.com.

Typeset by Graphicraft Limited, Hong Kong.

Printed and bound in Great Britain by CPI Group (UK) Ltd., Croydon, CR0 4YY.

John Murray Learning policy is to use papers that are natural, renewable and recyclable products and made from wood grown in sustainable forests. The logging and manufacturing processes are expected to conform to the environmental regulations of the country of origin.

Carmelite House
50 Victoria Embankment
London EC4Y 0DZ
www.hodder.co.uk

Illustrations © Barking Dog
Recorded at Alchemy Studios
Voice credits: Sarah Sherborne, Maisy Luk, Oscar Kwan, Catalina W M Chan, Joe Au, Eileen Lee, Jack Ho

Contents

Meet the authors

Hugh Baker taught Chinese (both Cantonese and Putonghua) at the School of Oriental and African Studies, University of London for 36 years until he retired as Professor of Chinese. Hooked on the languages and the teaching, he jumped at the chance of a post-retirement position at the Chinese University of Hong Kong. Ho Pui-Kei also taught Cantonese as a foreign language throughout his working career in Hong Kong and he is equally addicted. Both developed lively interactive styles that kept students amused and took away the pain of classroom study. They certainly do not subscribe to the theory that unthinking repetition is the way to learn, and cannot get their heads round the idea of learning while asleep with a recording playing under the pillow – in their classes students had no chance of a nap.

Ms Helen Ho Kar Yan 何嘉恩 and Ms Patti Tsui Wing Ping 徐詠萍 have both assisted with the production of this revised edition: the authors would like to record their deep gratitude to them for so generously and cheerfully giving their time to make the work go easier. And they are very grateful too to Ms Cheryl Hutty for her thoughtful and meticulous editing work.

Cantonese is racy, rich and highly colloquial, and it is fun – just what you'd expect from a lively quick-thinking people. Here you will not find learned discussion of politics, nor serious philosophy on the meaning of life. Cantonese people tend to talk about matters at an apparently superficial level, emphasizing the living of life rather than analyzing what it is about. Don't be fooled! They face hardship and problems like the rest of us, and the banter and joking don't mean that they don't care or think. The authors have taken the same line. They have aimed to teach the colourful speech that all Cantonese enjoy and they have made the material light-hearted in places, but the intention is a serious one – to teach you the real language as spoken by the real people.

Introduction

Welcome to a new experience. If you have never tried to learn a Chinese language before, you are in for a rare treat.

There are some real eye-openers: have you ever met a language where verbs have only one form? (they don't change according to tense or number or mood); where there are no cases? (you can forget about vocatives, genitives, ablatives and their confusing brethren); where no gender differences are acknowledged? (have you noticed how Chinese people speaking English frequently get *he* and *she* mixed up?); where there are no agreements of anything with anything else? ('singular, third person, feminine' – what's that?!); where there are no subjunctives? (would 'twere so for English!)

yes . ↘↗

And then, have you ever tried a language which has to be sung in order to be understood? Or where word orders are so crucial that if you get them wrong you will be totally unintelligible? Or where you can't count objects without first specifying what kind of objects they are? Or where almost every single syllable has a meaning? (Unlike English where the individual syllables of a word such as *trousers* mean nothing at all.)

Cantonese is a vital living language spoken by upwards of 60 million people in southeast China (including Hong Kong and Macau), as well as by several millions more in Malaysia, Europe, Australia, Fiji, North America and many other parts of the world where the adventurous Cantonese people have settled. It is one of the large family of Chinese languages and retains more traces of its ancient roots than do most of the others. And yet, it is a language which seems unafraid to adopt or adapt, notably from English in the past century or so, and it invents, evolves and discards slang at a frenetic rate. As a result it is a very rich language.

The people who speak Cantonese are lively, quick thinking, direct and fun loving. They are tuned into their language so much that they cannot resist having fun with it – they pun all the time and often with great ingenuity. They love it when foreigners stammer out their first words of Cantonese, because there is bound to be a howler or two which can be punned into something funny or scurrilous. Don't be put off – you are brightening their lives and they will not despise you for it. *↳ I hope so ☺.*

And if you have the chance to get help from a Cantonese you should, of course, seize it. The odds are that he or she will not want to be bothered with the romanized text which you are learning from and it is for this reason that we have supplied Chinese characters for the dialogues and for the new word lists, as well as for the Vocabulary lists at the back of the book. We are not attempting to teach you characters beyond the briefest of introductions. One reason is that the Cantonese that people speak is rather different from what they normally read and write (a bit reminiscent of medieval English speakers reading and writing Latin), and there is no official consensus about what characters to use to represent the spoken Cantonese language on the page. We, for instance, along with others have chosen to use 倒 to stand for the sound **dóu** in one of its meanings, but some people prefer the character 到, and there is no right or wrong here. The other reason is that it takes a great investment of time to master any characters, and you will learn to speak and understand speech much sooner if you ignore the script at first – you can always move on to study it later. That of course is what Chinese people do: they all learn to speak before they learn to read and write.

That's a comfort!

Most of the units of this book follow the same pattern: two dialogues (often humorous, if you think silly jokes are humorous), each with a Vocabulary builder list of the new words used and Language discovery explanations of grammar points, and accompanied by exercises and brain-teasers. Units 7, 14, 21 and 26 are revision units, giving more material based on what has been learned but not introducing anything new. The appendices summarize the most important grammar points, refer you to the units of the book in which they are first explained, introduce you to Chinese writing, and give some tips on how to take your studies further. Also at the back will be found the answers to all the exercises and a two-way vocabulary to help you find your way round the book.

A few points to note:

▶ We do not all learn in the same way. You may feel that before tackling the dialogues you would prefer to read the Language discovery notes that come after them. Why not? Go ahead. Each unit is organized into two clumps of material – consisting of vocabulary, dialogue and notes – how you work on a clump is entirely up to you.

▶ We have supplied translations of the dialogues of the first four units. Thereafter that luxury is denied you, but you should be able to work out the meanings without difficulty or guesswork.

▶ Do not look for consistent characterization of the people who appear in the dialogues: there is none, the Mr Wong of one unit being a totally different person from the Mr Wong who figures in another.

▶ Don't be put off by the fact that in our system of writing Cantonese Mr Wong is spelled **Wòhng**, Mr Cheung is spelled **Jèung**, etc. Rough and ready approximations to the correct pronunciation such as Wong, Cheung, Chan and Yuen may be good enough for use with the English language, but for you the learner who wants to speak Cantonese properly they are not adequate. So when chatting with John or Mary Smith by all means use Wong and Cheung, but to be understood in Cantonese by Mr or Mrs Chan you need the extra pronunciation guidance that is contained in the spellings **Wòhng** and **Jèung**.

▶ You may be puzzled by the numbers of words which are pronounced the same but which have quite different meanings (**daai**, for instance, means both *to bring* and *to wear*). Cantonese, like all the Chinese languages, is full of homophones (words pronounced the same): it is a fact of life that you will have to accept – and it is one of the reasons why punning is so common.

▶ 'Standard Cantonese' used to be defined as the language of the **Sài-gwàan** 西關 area of the city of Guangzhou (Canton), but that status has really moved to Hong Kong over the last six decades, and what we are going to teach you is the version generally accepted in Hong Kong as the speech of educated people who have grown up there. But a large proportion of the population are first, second or third generation immigrants, and they have come from many different parts of China where other Chinese languages or different dialects of Cantonese were spoken. As a consequence, you are bound to come into contact with people who rightly claim to be Cantonese speakers, but whose accents, vocabulary and grammar may be rather less than 'Standard'. There is nothing we can do to help you overcome the extra burden which coping with non-standard Cantonese imposes, any more than we can assure a Chinese person coming to London that everyone he meets on the street will speak 'BBC English'. We can only ask you to bear in mind for the sake of your own morale that this state of affairs is no-one's fault, least of all yours. *Thank you.*

▶ When you first hear Cantonese it sounds rather ugly, and even a normal chat can seem like a hot argument because of the vigour and velocity with which ideas are delivered. *Yeah, I've noticed.* Fear not, you will quickly learn to detect beneath that coarse exterior melodic and beautiful cadences which can be as romantic, heart-warming or soft as anyone could desire. *hope so*

We have had fun writing this. We hope you will enjoy studying it. We know you will get a great kick out of speaking with Cantonese people.

How the book works

You will learn how to identify what you will be able to do in Cantonese by the end of the unit.

Culture point presents an interesting cultural aspect related to the unit theme, introduces some key words and phrases and includes a challenging question for you.

Vocabulary builder introduces key unit vocabulary appearing in the dialogues grouped by theme and conversations, and is accompanied by audio.

Conversations are recorded dialogues of authentic exchanges that you can listen to and practise with a focusing question and follow-up activities.

Language discovery draws your attention to key language points in the conversations, whether a grammar rule or a way of saying things. Read the notes and look at the conversations to see how the language is used in practice and to aid quicker learning.

Practice offers a variety of exercises, including speaking opportunities, to give you a chance to bring it all together and make active use of the language.

Speaking and listening offers additional practice in speaking and understanding.

Reading and writing activities give you a chance to practise in reading and writing everyday items.

Test yourself helps you assess what you have learned. Do the tests without looking at the text.

A system of icons indicates the actions you should take:

 Language discovery

 Listening practice

 Speaking practice

 Pronunciation practice

 Culture

 Reading

 Test yourself

 Practice

 Vocabulary

 Write and make notes

Learn to learn

THE DISCOVERY METHOD

There are lots of approaches to language learning, some practical and some quite unconventional. Perhaps you know of a few, or even have some techniques of your own. In this book we have incorporated the Discovery method of learning, a sort of DIY approach to language learning. What this means is that you will be encouraged throughout the course to engage your mind and figure out the language for yourself, through identifying patterns, understanding grammar concepts, and more. This method promotes language awareness, a critical skill in acquiring a new language. As a result of your own efforts, you will be able to firmly retain what you have learned, use it with confidence, and, even better, apply those same skills to continuing to learn the language (or, indeed, another one) on your own after you've finished this book.

Everyone can succeed in learning a language – the key is to know how to do it. Learning is more than just reading or memorizing grammar and vocabulary. It's about being an active learner, learning in real contexts, and applying what you've learned in different situations. Simply put, if you figure something out for yourself, you're more likely to understand it. And when you use what you've learned, you're more likely to remember it.

And because the essential details, such as grammar rules, are taught through the Discovery method, you'll have fun while learning. Soon, the language will start to make sense and you'll be relying on your own intuition to construct original sentences independently, not just listening and repeating.

Enjoy yourself!

BECOME A SUCCESSFUL LANGUAGE LEARNER

1 Make a habit out of learning

Study a little every day, between 20 and 30 minutes if possible, rather than two to three hours in one session. Give yourself short-term goals, e.g. work out how long you'll spend on a particular unit and work within the time limit. This will help you to create a study habit, much in the same way you would for a sport or music. You will need to concentrate, so try to create an environment conducive to learning which is calm and quiet and free from distractions. As you study, do not worry about your mistakes or the things you can't remember or understand. Languages settle differently in our brains, but gradually the language will become clearer as your brain starts to make new connections. Just give yourself enough time and you will succeed.

2 Expand your language contact

As part of your study habit try to take other opportunities to expose yourself to the language. As well as using this book you could try accessing online radio and television, either live or by using catch-up services to listen more than once, and of course you can order Cantonese language films on DVD. Perhaps you could find information in Cantonese about a personal passion or hobby or even a news story that interests you. In time you'll find that your vocabulary and language recognition deepen and you'll become used to a range of writing and speaking styles.

3 Vocabulary

▶ To organize your study of vocabulary, group new words under:

a generic categories, e.g. *food*, *furniture*.
b situations in which they occur, e.g. under *restaurant* you can write *waiter*, *table*, *menu*, *bill*.
c functions, e.g. *greetings*, *parting*, *thanks*, *apologizing*.

▶ Say the words out loud as you read them.

▶ Write the words over and over again. Remember that if you want to keep lists on your smartphone or tablet you can usually type accented letters (e.g. **à**, **á**, **ā**) by tapping and holding down the base letter (e.g. **a**).

▶ Listen to the audio as many times as you need to.

▶ Cover up the English side of the vocabulary list and see if you remember the meaning of the word.

▶ Create flash cards, drawings and mind maps.

▶ Write words for objects around your house and stick them to the objects.

▶ Pay attention to patterns in words, e.g. tacking **jái 仔** onto a noun shows that it is a small or baby one which is meant.

▶ Experiment with words. Use the words that you learn in new contexts and find out if they are correct. For example, you learn in Unit 6 that **jeui yáuh-méng ge** means *most famous*, so you might wonder whether putting **jeui** in front of any other adjective will also work as a superlative – yes, it does. Hooray! And perhaps you could get more adventurous and put it in front of a verb or an adverb – does that work too? You'll find out if you try.

▶ Make the best of words you already know. When you start thinking about it you will realize that there are a few Cantonese words and expressions which are commonly used in English: **typhoon**, **laichee**, **taipan**, **sampan** … not that you can keep a conversation going for long with these, but what's sauce for the goose … almost everyone in Hong Kong has some English, so you can make use of what they know by popping in an English word when you don't yet know how to say it in Cantonese. Chances are your Chinese friend will understand it, and not even notice that you have slipped into English. Cantonese people do it all the time: we have never heard an office-worker use the correct Cantonese word for *file*, they always say 'file'.

4 Grammar

▶ To organize the study of grammar write your own grammar glossary and add new information and examples as you go along.

▶ Experiment with grammar rules. Sit back and reflect on the rules you learn. See how they compare with your own language or other languages you may already speak. Try to find out some rules on your own and be ready to spot the exceptions. By doing this you'll remember the rules better and get a feel for the language.

▶ Try to find examples of grammar patterns in other people's conversations.

▶ Keep a 'pattern bank' that organizes examples that can be listed under the structures you've learned.

▶ Use old vocabulary to practise new grammar structures.

5 Pronunciation

▶ When organizing the study of pronunciation keep a section of your notebook for pronunciation rules and practise those that trouble you.

▶ Repeat all of the conversations, line by line. Listen to yourself and try to mimic what you hear.

▶ Record yourself and compare yourself to a native speaker.

▶ Make a list of words that give you trouble and practise them.

▶ Don't forget, it's not just about pronouncing vowels and consonants correctly. You need to be really strict with yourself in getting tones right too. Above all, remember that every Cantonese syllable has its own rigid tone, and you must not import your English sentence intonation into your Cantonese – it will conflict with syllable tone and you will end up saying things you don't mean to say. You can hear what sentence intonation does to meaning in English if you examine the difference between *I am rich* and *I am rich?!*, where the words are precisely the same. But if *rich* were a Cantonese word it would not be possible to change its tone, so sentence intonation is not really an option.

6 Listening and reading

The conversations in this book include questions to help guide you in your understanding. But you can go further by following some of these tips.

▶ Imagine the situation. When listening to or reading the conversations, try to imagine where the scene is taking place and who the main characters are. Let your experience of the world help you guess the meaning of the conversation, e.g. if a conversation takes place in a snack bar you can be fairly sure of the kind of vocabulary that is being used.

▶ When there are key words you don't understand in a sentence, try to guess what they mean from the context. If you're listening to a Cantonese speaker and cannot get the gist of a whole passage because of one word or phrase, try looking puzzled and repeating the word in a doubtful way – it may trigger them to paraphrase it to help you understand. And if that doesn't work, you can butt in politely with **X haih māt-yéh a?** *What is X?* or **X haih māt-yéh yi-si a?** *What does X mean?*

7 Speaking

Rehearse in the foreign language. As all language teachers will assure you, the successful learners are those students who overcome their inhibitions and get into situations where they must speak and listen to the foreign language. Here are some useful tips to help you practise speaking Cantonese:

▶ Hold a conversation with yourself, using the conversations of the units as models and the structures you have learned previously.

▶ After you have conducted a transaction with a salesperson, clerk or waiter in your own language, pretend that you have to do it in Cantonese, e.g. buying groceries, ordering food, drinks and so on.

▶ Look at objects around you and try to name them in Cantonese.

▶ Look at people around you and try to describe them in detail.

▶ Try to answer all of the questions in the book out loud.

▶ Say the dialogues out loud then try to replace sentences with ones that are true for you.

▶ Try to role-play different situations in the book.

8 Learn from your errors

▶ Don't let errors interfere with getting your message across. Making errors is part of any normal learning process, but some people get so worried that they won't say anything unless they are sure it is correct. This leads to a vicious circle as the less they say, the less practice they get and the more mistakes they make when they do eventually speak.

▶ Note the seriousness of errors. Many errors are not serious, as they do not affect the meaning, and you do not have to lose sleep over making them. Of course you hope to reach a stage where you sound like a native speaker, so you still should try to avoid any mistakes at all. But we recently heard a candidate in an oral examination claim that he 'loved slaughtering people', a simple mistake in tone wrecking his intention to say that he 'loved Chinese people', and that is not an error he would want to repeat. It is necessary to concentrate on getting your message across and to learn from your mistakes.

That's so bad and really funny too

9 Learn to cope with uncertainty

▶ Don't over-use your dictionary. When reading a text in Cantonese, don't be tempted to look up every word you don't know. Underline the words you do not understand and read the passage several times, concentrating on trying to get the gist of the passage. If after the third time there are still words which prevent you from getting the general meaning of the passage, look them up in the dictionary.

▶ Don't panic if you don't understand. If at some point you feel you don't understand what you are told, don't panic or give up listening. Either try and guess what is being said and keep following the conversation or, if you cannot, isolate the expression or words you haven't understood and have them explained to you. The speaker might paraphrase them and the conversation will carry on.

▶ Keep talking. The best way to improve your fluency in the foreign language is to talk every time you have the opportunity to do so: keep the conversations flowing and don't worry about the mistakes. If you get stuck for a particular word, don't let the conversation stop; paraphrase or replace the unknown word with one you do know, even if you have to simplify what you want to say. As a last resort use the word from your own language and pronounce it in the foreign accent. We said that Cantonese office-workers always use the English word *file*: that's true, but they say it with a Cantonese accent, so it sounds like 'fai-lou'.

Pronunciation guide

A note on romanization

This note is about the sounds of Cantonese and how to represent them on paper. It should be read with the audio ready at hand so that you can hear a clear demonstration of what the sounds are.

Cantonese, like all the Chinese languages, is written in characters. As you will discover when you read the appendices of this book, characters are symbols representing ideas, while the letters of our alphabet are symbols representing sounds. Written English reproduces the sounds of speech using an economical 26 symbols, which are quite sufficient to do the job; but the Chinese writing system pays little attention to the sounds of the spoken language and instead tackles the massive problem of providing a separate symbol for each of the ideas which needs to be written.

When you learn to write an English word, you learn how to say it (even if the spelling is sometimes a little erratic). If you were to try to learn the basic Cantonese of this book through Chinese characters, not only would you have the daunting task of learning to read and write around 1,500 different symbols, but even when you had learned them you would be none the wiser about how to speak the language, because the symbols are dumb about how they should be pronounced.

Because Chinese characters offer no help in learning the sounds of the language, generations of foreign learners have struggled to find ways to 'romanize' Cantonese; that is, to represent Cantonese sounds with the Roman alphabet. There are very few sounds in Cantonese which are difficult for English speakers, and this would be a relatively easy task but for one thing: Cantonese is a tonal language; that is, each one of the sounds of Cantonese can be pronounced (or perhaps 'sung' would be a better word) in seven different ways (the tones). Unfortunately, the Roman alphabet does not have any devices for representing tones, and musical notations added to letters of the alphabet would be much too awkward to handle. So, how do we resolve the problem? All romanization systems have to deal with it, there is no escaping that. Some do it more elegantly than others, but basically all of them use the alphabet to represent the sounds and add indicators of some kind to represent the tones.

We have all been exposed to romanization to some extent – think of **Beijing**, a romanization of the Chinese 北京, or **dim sum** for 點心. But these are just rough guides, crude tools to enable us to pronounce the language in some kind of approximation to the original, and they completely ignore tones. And even if it were acceptable to speak without tones, even then the spellings conceal another problem – **Beijing** attempts to represent what the city is called in Mandarin, but **dim sum** is based on Cantonese, they will never actually appear together in one coherent sentence. So romanization is a bit of a minefield, seldom of much use outside the classroom. It is a necessary scaffolding to build your language learning from, a private communication system between us the teachers and you the learner. There is no 'official' or universally accepted romanization of Cantonese, and many different systems are in existence. In *Complete Cantonese* we have chosen to use a version of the Yale system, which we believe to be best for the following reasons:

▶ It distinguishes clearly each one of the sounds of Cantonese, using sensible spellings which come as close as any system using the 26-letter alphabet can to an accurate representation of those sounds.

▶ It clearly distinguishes each of the seven tones, using only three additional symbols (the macron ⁻, the grave accent ` and the acute accent ´) plus a special use of the letter **h** to indicate them.

▶ There are good reference materials available which use the same system, and you will thus be able to expand beyond the scope of this book if desired.

If you intend to go really deeply into Cantonese, you will certainly have to learn Chinese characters, and at that stage romanization will gradually become redundant. Meanwhile, try to familiarize yourself with the principles of the Yale system as quickly as possible so that it becomes a helpful tool and not an obstacle to your learning the language.

The Yale romanization system

THE TONES

Cantonese has seven tones which it is essential to master for fluent and comprehensible speech. Some teachers have been known to claim that it is possible to be understood even if tones are totally ignored, but while it is true that a certain limited communication may be possible given great goodwill on the listener's part, in normal circumstances the toneless speaker would be met by blank incomprehension. The tones occur on all syllables and are located in three pitches (high, mid, low), the voice remaining level or rising or falling within those pitches. The seven tones are:

High pitch	Mid pitch	Low pitch
High level tone	Mid rising tone	Low falling tone
High falling tone	Mid level tone	Low rising tone
–	–	Low level tone

Low pitch words are shown by the addition of **h** after the vowel.

Rising tones are shown by the acute accent ´, falling tones by the grave accent `, and the macron ⁻ shows the high level tone.

The accents are marked on the vowel or (where there is a vowel chain) the first vowel of the syllable.

Thus the seven tones of the sound **ma** would be written:

High level tone	**mā**	macron over vowel
High falling tone	**mà**	grave over vowel
Mid rising tone	**má**	acute over vowel
Mid level tone	**ma**	letters only
Low falling tone	**màh**	grave over + **h** after vowel
Low rising tone	**máh**	acute over + **h** after vowel
Low level tone	**mah**	**h** after vowel

 00.01 **Listen to how these tones are spoken on the audio and do your best to copy them exactly.**

 1 00.02 **Now listen to some two-syllable words on the audio. Try to write down what the tone on each of the syllables is.**

Every now and then a word changes its tone in a particular context: we have pointed it out when it occurs in this course and suggest that you try to accept these occurrences as the oddities they are rather than try to figure out why they change.

THE SOUNDS OF CANTONESE

Consonants

 00.03 The consonant sounds which begin Cantonese syllables are simple for English speakers. They are **b-, ch-, d-, f-, g-, gw-, h-, j-, k-, kw-, l-, m-, n-, ng-, p-, s-, t-, w-** and **y-**. The only minor difficulty here is the initial consonant **ng-**, and that is only difficult because although English does have the *ng* sound it does not have syllables which start with it. You can imagine how it is done if you think of the word *singalong* and try to pronounce it without the letters *si* at the front. If you listen to the audio you should be able to pick up how **ng-** syllables are pronounced without much difficulty. For example:

ngan   nga   ngok   ngai   ngaam

There are very few consonants which can appear at the end of Cantonese syllables, in fact there are only six (**-n, -ng, -m, -p, -t, -k**). Of these, the first three are completely straightforward, just as you would expect them to be if you were reading the sounds off in English. For example:

haan   seun   leng   mong   taam   gam

But the other three (**-p, -t, -k**) are hardly pronounced at all, the tongue and the lips getting into position to pronounce them and then not following through. So your lips should snap together to get ready to make the **-p** at the end of the syllable **sap**, but you should not open them again to release the puff of air which has built up to make the full **p** sound. Similarly with the sound **bat**, the tip of your tongue should make contact with the hard ridge behind your upper teeth, but the air should not puff out to make a full **t**, and with **baak** the flat top of your tongue should go up into your palate but not allow the air to escape to make the full **k** sound. Listen carefully to the audio examples:

sap   jaap   kat   faat   sik   jek

Vowels

 00.04 The vowel sounds of Cantonese are a little more complicated. The following is a guide to the sounds based wherever possible on 'BBC English' pronunciations, but please note that this is only a rough guide. The best way to grasp them is to listen carefully several times to the pronunciation section of the audio. While your ear is getting used to hearing the sounds, your eye will be taking in the system which we use for spelling those sounds. To start with, concentrate on the sound itself without being too much concerned with tone. You will get plenty more pronunciation practice later, because not only are all the Dialogues and the early Vocabulary builder lists on the audio, but at various places in the book you will find extra tone drills and pronunciation exercises. And, of course, if you have the luxury of a Cantonese friend, ask him or her to make the sounds for you as well.

▶ **-aa** is a long vowel sound, rather like the sound of the word *are* in English. It combines with **-i** to make a long vowel **-aai** as in a drawled version of *eye*, and it combines with **-u** to make **-aau** as in a drawn out version of *cow*. If there is no final consonant or **-i** or **-u** the Yale system uses just one **a**, but it should always be pronounced long as if it were **aa** (**ba** is pronounced *bar*). For example:

ba   baai   baau   baan   saam   laang   daap   baak   saat

▶ **-a** is a shorter version of the **aa** sound, pronounced somewhere between the English *b<u>a</u>t* and *b<u>u</u>t*. For example:

jam   pan   hang   tai   tau   sat   gap   dak

▶ **-e** is rather like the English *<u>fai</u>ry*. For example:

che   leng   jek

▶ **-ei** is like the English *d<u>ay</u>*. For example:

bei

▶ **-eu** is in most cases like English *f<u>ur</u>ther*. For example:

leung   geuk   deu

but before **-t** it is more like English *f<u>oo</u>t*:

cheut

and before **-n** it is close to the *-en* in the name *Owen*:

cheun

▶ **-eui** is rather like *h<u>er</u> <u>e</u>mail* (but don't pronounce the *r*). For example:

heui

▶ **-i** is not too different from English *s<u>ee</u>*, except when it is followed by **-k** where it is more like English *s<u>i</u>ck*. For example:

si   tiu   tim   min   ting   yit   yip   sik

▶ **-o** is somewhere between English *th<u>aw</u>* and *g<u>o</u>ne*. For example:

fo   on   bong   hok   ngoi   mou   hot

▶ **-u** is somewhere between English *t<u>oo</u>* and *c<u>oo</u>k*. For example:

fu   fun   hung   juk   mui   wuht

▶ **-yu** is like the German _über_ or the French _tu_. In English you can get close to the sound by saying _see you_ very quickly. For example:

jyu   syun   hyut

Oddities

 00.05 There are two oddities: the sounds **m** and **ng** exist as full syllables without vowels. They do not occur in many words, but two in which they do occur are very common. So **m̀h** means _not_ and **ńgh** means _five_. The idea of vowel-less words may seem strange at first, but these two are not difficult to say, and they are so common that you will quickly become accustomed to them.

Stress

Cantonese syllables all carry virtually equal stress and each therefore sounds more or less discrete; and Chinese characters each represent one syllable and are all written discretely. Our romanization, therefore, could spell each syllable separately, but we have chosen to use hyphens where two or more syllables are so closely associated that they may be thought of as one word or one concept, as with **pàhng-yáuh** _friend_, **jùng-yi** _to like_ and **Jùng-gwok-wá** _Chinese language_.

 2 00.06 **Now listen to some more two-syllable terms on the audio. Try writing down the sounds, and then you will hear them once more so that you can add the tones as well.**

Signs of change

 00.07 Language never stands still, and Cantonese is changing very rapidly. There are four important sound changes which have been developing over recent decades:

a Many people (probably a clear majority of people now) do not use an initial **n-** sound at all, and all the words which appear in this book with an initial **n-** would be pronounced by them with an **l-** instead. So **néih** becomes **léih**, and **nàahm-yán** becomes **làahm-yán**. You are bound to meet lots of native speakers who do this constantly, and you will hear it in some of the voices used on the audio.

b Some people now do not distinguish between initial **g-** and initial **gw-**, pronouncing **Jùng-gwok** as **Jùng-gok** and [**Gwóng-dùng**] as [**Góng-dùng**]. This change is not so common, but you should be prepared to understand it if you do hear it.

c The initial **ng-** sound has been gradually falling out of favour over many years and some people have now dropped it altogether. So you may hear such things as **óh** for **ngóh** or **àuh-yuhk** for **ngàuh-yuhk**. On the other hand, you may hear an **ng-** initial being used where we have not shown it in the book, and even one of our recorded voices (all of whom have clear standard accents) occasionally does this, presumably coming from a background which is changing rather slower than the majority.

d The distinction between the two high pitch tones seems to be much less critical now than it once was, and you will meet lots of native speakers who use only high level or who use high level or high falling seemingly indiscriminately and regardless of which is the 'correct' tone. There are plenty of examples on the audio, and we have made no attempt to force the voices to conform strictly to the tones as written in the text – you will need to accept that these variations are part of everyday speech.

What you hear native speakers say will affect the way you speak, and you may find yourself following some or all of these changes as you go on. Meanwhile, you can be confident that if you speak in the way this book teaches you, you won't be wrong.

見面 Gin-mihn
Encounters

In this unit you will learn about:
▶ *asking questions.*
▶ *countries and nationalities.*
▶ *greeting and addressing people.*
▶ *negatives.*
▶ *using descriptive words.*

CEFR: *(A1) Can use basic greeting and leave-taking expressions; can ask how people are; can introduce yourself.*

Greetings and name order

English speakers often greet people with 'How are you?'; and Cantonese people, when they are being slightly formal, enquire after your health too, as you will see in the first dialogue. But to their friends and in relaxed mood they usually ask about food, something very close to their hearts: **Sihk-jó faahn meih a? 食咗飯未呀?** *Have you eaten?* To which the reply should be **Sihk-jó lak 食咗嘞** *I have eaten.*

Sìn-sàang 先生 *Mr,* **Taai-táai 太太** *Mrs* and **Síu-jé 小姐** *Miss,* as well as other titles, are all given after surnames. Personal names follow the surname too, so someone called *Mr John Smith* becomes *Smith John Mr* in the Cantonese order. It all fits in with the great importance which Chinese people have traditionally given to the family. The surname shows your family line and so it is the surname which is given pride of place.

Mr Wong's full Cantonese name is **Wòhng Gwok Méih Sìn-sàang**. What is his personal name?

Vocabulary builder 1

 01.01 Listen to the new vocabulary and practise saying it out loud. Then complete the missing English expressions.

GREETINGS

早晨	jóu-sàhn	*Good morning*
你好嗎	néih hóu ma?	*How are you?*
食咗飯未呀?	Sihk-jó faahn meih a?	*Have you eaten?*
食咗嘞	Sihk-jó lak	*I have eaten*
有心	yáuh-sàm	*kind of you to ask*

SURNAMES

張	Jèung	*Cheung*
王	Wòhng	_____

TITLES

先生	sìn-sàang	*Mr, Sir, gentleman, husband*
小姐	síu-jé	*Miss, young lady*
太太	taai-táai	_____, *wife, married woman*

PERSONS

佢	kéuih	*she, her, he, him*
你	néih	_____
我	ngóh	*I, me*

BASICS

都	dōu	*also*
好	hóu	*good, well, fine, OK, nice; very*

FINAL PARTICLES

嗎?	ma?	fp: turns a statement into a question
呢?	nē?	fp: repeats a question about a different matter

> **LANGUAGE TIP**
> 'Final particles' (fp) tack onto the end of sentences.

Dialogue 1

 01.02 Mr Wong and his boss Miss Cheung meet in the lift on the way up to the office.

1 Listen out for the three expressions with final particles on the end. What are they?

Cheung	Jóu-sàhn, Wòhng Sìn-sàang.	*Good morning, Mr Wong.*
Wong	Jóu-sàhn, Jèung Síu-jé. Néih hóu ma?	*Good morning, Miss Cheung. How are you?*
Cheung	Ngóh hóu hóu. Néih nē?	*I'm very well. And you?*
Wong	(Ngóh) hóu hóu.	*I'm fine.*
Cheung	Néih taai-táai nē?	*And your wife?*
Wong	Kéuih dōu hóu, yáuh-sàm.	*She's well too, thank you.*

張	早晨，王先生。
王	早晨，張小姐。你好嗎？
張	我好好。你呢？
王	（我）好好。
張	你太太呢？
王	佢都好，有心。

2 Did you notice that Ngóh hóu hóu has been translated into English in two different ways? Can you think of any other possible translations for this expression?

3 In Cantonese, how would you address the person that Miss Cheung enquires about?

(The answers to all tests and exercises are in the Key to the exercises section.)

> **IS IT *WONG* OR *WÒHNG*?**
>
> We don't mean to confuse you. The Yale romanization spells it **Wòhng**, and that tells you exactly how to pronounce it (tone and all), which is what you need in order to speak like a Cantonese. But for everyday use almost everyone spells the name *Wong*, because that's good enough for non-native speakers who do not know or care about tones or proper pronunciation. We have, as it were, translated **Wòhng** into *Wong* for you. We have done the same with other names (*Cheung* for **Jèung**, *Kwok Mei* for **Gwok Méih**, *Hong Kong* for **Hèung-góng**, *Kowloon* for **Gáu-lùhng**, etc).

Language discovery

1.1 IDENTIFYING PEOPLE

Each of these personal pronouns can be made plural by the addition of **-deih** 哋:

Singular		Plural	
ngóh	*I, me*	**ngóh-deih**	*we, us*
néih	*you*	**néih-deih**	*you*
kéuih	*he, she, him, her*	**kéuih-deih**	*they, them*

> **LANGUAGE TIP**
> Please do not assume that you can make everything plural by adding **-deih**. It doesn't work.

1.2 ADJECTIVES OR VERBS? BOTH!

Hóu means *good, nice, well, fine, OK* and so on. Just as in English, such words (adjectives) go in front of nouns – *a good husband* is a **hóu sìn-sàang**. But in Cantonese all adjectives can also act as verbs to describe things, so **hóu** means not only *good, well* but also *to be good, to be well*:

Kéuih-deih hóu.	*They are well.*
Wòhng Sìn-sàang hóu.	*Mr Wong is fine.*

Remember, it is not only the adjective **hóu** which is also a descriptive verb – all adjectives behave the same. So the word for *ugly* means *to be ugly* too, *big* can also mean *to be big* and so on.

 Have you noticed that verbs only have one form? The same word **hóu** was translated as *am well, is well* and *are well* in our earlier examples and it was no accident. **Hóu** only ever appears like that even though the English verb *to be well* takes many guises (*am well, is well, are well, will be well, have been well, was well, had been well*, etc.). Regardless of the tense, the mood, the subject or anything else, the verb will always be simply **hóu**. And, better still, this applies to all verbs, there are no irregularities to make life difficult!

1.3 SIMPLE QUESTIONS

In Mandarin (now usually known as Putonghua, the official common language of China) you can ask a question simply by adding **ma?** at the end of a statement. Some Cantonese speakers have begun to do the same, but it is still not common. However, in one expression you will hear this 'spoken question mark' very often, and that is in the polite question:

Néih hóu ma?	*How are you?*

The practice seems to be extending to asking after other people's health as well:

Jèung Taai-táai hóu ma?	*Is Mrs Cheung OK?*

You will meet the most common way of asking questions later in this unit.

> **LANGUAGE TIP**
> You learned **néih taai-táai** in the dialogue, meaning *your wife*. *Her husband* is **kéuih sìn-sàang**, and a woman refers to her own husband as **ngóh sìn-sàang**.

1.4 TWO FOR THE PRICE OF ONE

When you learned **hóu** you got double value, because it not only means *good, OK,* etc. but *very* as well.

 So what do you think hóu hóu means?

1.5 FOLLOW-UP QUESTIONS

A special kind of shortcut question is formed with the sentence-ending word **nē?** (usually called a final particle (fp)). **Nē?** asks a follow-up question without the tedium of repeating in full what went before:

Jèung Taai-táai hóu ma?	*Is Mrs Cheung OK?*
Kéuih hóu hóu. Wòhng Síu-jé nē?	*She's very well. And how's Miss Wong?*

1.6 DŌU *ALSO*

Dōu means *also, too.* It always comes just before a verb:

Ngóh hóu.	*I'm well.*
Kéuih dōu hóu.	*She's well too.*

 # Pronunciation

 01.03 A tricky one for you. Listen to the two sentences:
Wòhng Sìn-sàang hóu, Wòhng Taai-táai dōu hóu.
Jèung Síu-jé, Wòhng Síu-jé, kéuih-deih dōu hóu.

Now repeat them, copying the speaker as closely as you can, and remembering that every syllable must be pronounced in the correct tone.

 When you have done this several times and are happy with your efforts, sit back and think what the sentences might mean.

Vocabulary builder 2

 01.04 **Listen to the new vocabulary and practise saying it out loud. Then complete the missing English expressions.**

MORE POLITENESS

對唔住	deui-m̀h-jyuh	*I'm sorry; excuse me; pardon me*
貴姓呀?	gwai-sing a?	*What is your name?* (lit. 'distinguished surname?')
再見	joi-gin	*goodbye*

MORE SURNAMES

何	Hòh	*Ho*
李	Léih	*Li* or *Lee*
姓	sing	*a surname; to be surnamed*

> **LANGUAGE TIP**
> Although there are several thousand different surnames in existence, the vast majority of the Chinese share just a few dozen of them. The most common surname of all among Cantonese people is reckoned to be *Chan* (**Chàhn**).

COUNTRIES AND NATIONALITIES

美國	Méih-gwok	*America, USA*
美國人	Méih-gwok yàhn	*American person / people*
人	yàhn	*person, people*
日本	Yaht-bún	*Japan*
日本人	Yaht-bún yàhn	_____
英國	Yìng-gwok	*Britain, UK, England*
英國人	Yìng-gwok yàhn	_____

VERBS

係	haih	*to be*
貴	gwai	*to be expensive; distinguished*
靚	leng	*to be pretty, good-looking, handsome, of good quality*
賣	maaih	*to sell*
要	yiu	*to want*

BASICS

呀?	a?	fp: reinforcing a question
車	chē	*car, cars*
唔	m̀h	*not*
噢	òu	*oh!* (surprise)

Dialogue 2

 01.05 *When she gets to the office, Miss Cheung is surprised to find a visitor waiting for her.*

1 How can you tell that Miss Cheung is surprised?

Cheung	Òu, deui-m̀h-jyuh, gwai-sing a?	*Oh, excuse me, may I know your name please?*
Ho	Ngóh sing Hòh. Néih haih m̀h haih Léih Síu-jé a?	*My name is Ho. Are you Miss Li?*
Cheung	M̀h haih, ngóh sing Jèung. Hòh Sìn-sàang, néih haih m̀h haih Méih-gwok yàhn a?	*No, I am surnamed Cheung. Are you an American, Mr Ho?*
Ho	M̀h haih, ngóh haih Yìng-gwok yàhn. Ngóh maaih Méih-gwok chē: Méih-gwok chē hóu leng. Néih yiu m̀h yiu a?	*No, I'm British. I sell American cars: they're very nice. Would you like one?*
Cheung	M̀h yiu, m̀h yiu. Méih-gwok chē hóu gwai: ngóh yiu Yaht-bún chē. Joi-gin, Hòh Sìn-sàang.	*No, no. American cars are very expensive: I want a Japanese one. Goodbye, Mr Ho.*
Ho	Néih m̀h yiu, Léih Síu-jé yiu m̀h yiu a?	*If you don't want one, does Miss Li want one?*
Cheung	Léih Síu-jé dōu m̀h yiu. Joi-gin, joi-gin.	*She doesn't want one either. Goodbye, goodbye.*

張	噢，對唔住，貴姓呀？
何	我姓何，你係唔係李小姐呀？
張	唔係，我姓張。何先生，你係唔係美國人呀？
何	唔係，我係英國人，我賣美國車：美國車好靚，你要唔要呀？
張	唔要，唔要。美國車好貴：我要日本車。再見，何先生。
何	你唔要，李小姐要唔要呀？
張	李小姐都唔要。再見，再見。

2 Having read Dialogue 2, can you say which of these statements is / are true and which false?

   a Jèung Síu-jé haih Méih-gwok yàhn.

   b Hòh Sìn-sàang m̀h maaih Méih-gwok chē.

   c Wòhng Sìn-sàang maaih chē.

   d Jèung Síu-jé haih taai-táai.

3 Now try to answer these questions (in Cantonese):

   a Léih Síu-jé yiu m̀h yiu Yaht-bún chē a?

   b Méih-gwok chē hóu gwai, Yìng-gwok chē dōu hóu gwai, Yaht-bún chē m̀h gwai: Jèung Síu-jé yiu m̀h yiu Yaht-bún chē a?

   c Hòh Sìn-sàang haih m̀h haih Yìng-gwok yàhn a?

Language discovery

1.7 PLURALS

Yàhn means *person* but it also means *people*. In fact, all nouns in Cantonese are the same whether singular or plural, and you can only tell which is meant from the sense of the conversation. There is usually no problem.

YOUR TURN By looking at the personal pronouns in these sentences, can you tell which yàhn is singular and which is plural?

a Ngóh haih Yìng-gwok yàhn.
b Kéuih-deih haih Yaht-bún yàhn.

1.8 COUNTRIES AND NATIONALITIES

01.06 As you should have discovered, nationalities are shown simply by adding **yàhn** to the names of the countries, so **Yaht-bún yàhn** are *Japanese people*.

Here are a few more countries:

巴西	**Bà-sài**	*Brazil*	德國	**Dāk-gwok**	*Germany*
法國	**Faat-gwok**	*France*	加拿大	**Gà-nàh-daaih**	*Canada*
中國	**Jùng-gwok**	*China*	南非	**Nàahm-fèi**	*South Africa*
澳洲	**Ou-jàu**	*Australia*	新西蘭	**Sàn-sài-làahn**	*New Zealand*

All of these, and all other countries, cities and place names can have **yàhn** added on to say that that is where someone comes from.

Can you guess what Hèung-góng yàhn 香港人 means?

Some other places that you will certainly hear about or visit are:

北京	**Bāk-gìng**	*Beijing (Peking)*	澳門	**Ou-mún**	*Macau*
上海	**Seuhng-hói**	*Shanghai*	台灣	**Tòih-wàan**	*Taiwan*
廣州	**Gwóng-jàu**	*Guangzhou (Canton)*			

1.9 NEGATIVES

The word for *not* is **m̀h**. It always comes in front of the word it refers to:

Wòhng Sìn-sàang m̀h leng	*Mr Wong isn't handsome.*
Ngóh m̀h yiu chē	*I don't want a car.*

1.10 ANOTHER WAY TO ASK QUESTIONS

The most common way to ask a question in Cantonese is by using the positive and negative of a verb together and adding the final particle **a?** at the end of the sentence:

Kéuih leng m̀h leng a?	*Is she pretty?*

What you are really doing is offering your listener a choice of answers (*She pretty? Not pretty? Eh?*) and the answer is going to be either:

Kéuih leng.	*She is pretty.*

or

Kéuih m̀h leng.	*She's not pretty.*

YOUR TURN **What do you think this question means?**

Néih maaih m̀h maaih Méih-gwok chē a?

Cantonese people like to have a comfortable noise to round off their sentences with and they have a large selection of final particles which they use in this way. **A?** has no meaning on its own, it is just used to punch home the question which has been asked in the sentence. **Ma?** and **nē?**, which we have already met, are other examples of final particles which are in themselves meaningless but which serve to change or emphasize the meaning of the sentence they end.

1.11 THE UNSPOKEN *IF*

There are various words for *if* in Cantonese, but quite often none of them is used, the meaning seeming to flow naturally from the context. In the dialogue the sentence **Néih m̀h yiu, Léih Síu-jé yiu m̀h yiu a?** (lit. 'You not want, Miss Li want not want, eh?') would be understood to mean *If you don't want one, does Miss Li want one?*

 ## Tone drill

 01.07 By chance, the words for *Chinese people* **and** *British people* **have the same tone pattern, high falling, then mid level, then low falling. Play the audio now: you should be able to hear the three pitches (high, mid, low) quite clearly.**

Jùng-gwok yàhn	Jùng-gwok yàhn
Yìng-gwok yàhn	Yìng-gwok yàhn

Sounds almost but not quite like the start of the tune of the nursery rhyme *Three Blind Mice*, **doesn't it? Listen again and repeat after the speaker, it is very good practice.**

Now add in the word for *Americans* **and hear how the 'tune' changes, copying the speaker carefully:**

Jùng-gwok yàhn	Méih-gwok yàhn
Méih-gwok yàhn	Jùng-gwok yàhn

Finally, listen hard to the audio and see if you can get your tongue and voice around these combinations:

Méih-gwok yàhn	Yìng-gwok yàhn	Jùng-gwok yàhn
Yìng-gwok yàhn	Méih-gwok yàhn	Jùng-gwok yàhn
Jùng-gwok yàhn	Yìng-gwok yàhn	Méih-gwok yàhn
Gà-nàh-daaih yàhn	Sàn-sài-làahn yàhn	

🔓 Practice

1 **Here's a fine mess! The words have got all jumbled up. Sort them out and make meaningful sentences of them.**

Example: Taai-táai Wòhng leng hóu → *Wòhng Taai-táai hóu leng.*
Mrs Wong is very beautiful.

   a Hóu kéuih-deih hóu
   b Sìn-sàang Wòhng hóu
   c Dōu Jèung hóu Síu-jé

2 **What would you reply?**
   a Jóu-sàhn.
   b Néih hóu ma?
   c Joi-gin.

3 **Complete the sentences with words which will make sense. You will have to think a bit to work out what each sentence must mean!**
   a Wòhng Sìn-sàang _____ yiu Méih-gwok chē.
   b Chàhn Síu-jé leng _____ leng a?
   c Kéuih-deih haih m̀h _____ Yaht-bún-yàhn a?
   d Ngóh m̀h maaih Yaht-bún chē, ngóh maaih _____.

❓ Test yourself

Translate these simple sentences into Cantonese. If you can do so, you can really congratulate yourself on having mastered this unit.

a Japanese cars aren't expensive.
b He isn't nice.
c You are very pretty.
d Do they want cars?
e He is good-looking too.
f They are Americans.
g Mr Wong sells cars.
h British people don't sell American cars.

2 個人財物 *Go-yàhn chòih-maht*
Personal property

In this unit you will learn about:
▸ *classifiers (measure words) for nouns.*
▸ *numbers.*
▸ *possessives.*
▸ *question words.*
▸ *specifiers (this and that).*

CEFR: *(A1) Can handle numbers and quantities.*

The magic of numbers

Cantonese people are very interested in numbers, and many people believe that numbers can influence fate. Everybody loves the number *eight* **baat** 八 because it sounds rather like **faat** 發, which means *to get rich*. By way of contrast, *four* **sei** 四 is considered an unlucky number because it sounds like **séi** 死 *to die*. *Two* **yih** 二 and *eight* are good because **yih baat** sounds like **yih faat** 易發 *easy to get rich*, but *five* **ńgh** 五 and *eight* are bad because **ńgh baat** resembles **m̀h faat** 唔發 *not get rich*. For many years the Hong Kong government auctioned 'lucky' car registration numbers for charity: an astronomical price was paid for 8888, which adorned one of the territory's many Rolls-Royces.

Why do you think a Chinese purchaser recently insisted on paying £280,000 for a house in the south of England rather than the asking price of £279,500?

Vocabulary builder 1

 02.01 Listen to the new vocabulary and practise saying it out loud. Then complete the missing English expressions.

QUESTION WORDS

邊個	bīn-go	*who? which person? which one?*
乜嘢	māt-yéh	*what? what kind of?*
有乜嘢事呀?	yáuh-māt-yéh-sih-a?	*for what purpose? _____?*

POLITENESS

| 唔該(你) | m̀h-gòi (néih) | *thank _____* |

VERBS

帶	daai	*to lead, bring, go with*
去	heui	*to go to, go*
買	máaih	*to buy*
想	séung	*to want to, intend to, would like to*
搵	wán	*to look for*
有	yáuh	*to have*

BASICS

嘅	ge	*'s (shows possession)*
朋友	pàhng-yáuh	*friend*
寫字樓	sé-jih-làuh	*office*
事	sih	*matter, business, affair*

Dialogue 1

 02.02 Mr Ho is working in his office when a woman comes in.

1 In this dialogue you need to watch the tone marks carefully. There are two words with opposite meanings but very similar pronunciations – can you spot them?

Ho	Taai-táai, néih wán bīn-go a?	*Who are you looking for, madam?*
Woman	Ngóh wán Wòhng Gwok Méih Sìn-sàang, kéuih haih Jùng-gwok yàhn, haih ngóh ge pàhng-yáuh.	*I'm looking for Mr Wong Kwok Mei, he's Chinese, a friend of mine.*
Ho	Néih wán Wòhng Sìn-sàang yáuh-māt-yéh-sih-a?	*Why are you looking for him?*
Woman	Ngóh yiu maaih ngóh ge Méih-gwok chē, Wòhng Sìn-sàang séung máaih.	*I want to sell my American car, and Mr Wong wants to buy it.*
Ho	Hóu, ngóh daai néih heui Wòhng Sìn-sàang ge sé-jih-làuh.	*Fine, I'll take you to Mr Wong's office.*
Woman	M̀h-gòi néih.	*Thank you.*

何	太太，你搵邊個呀？
女人	我搵王國美先生，佢係中國人，係我嘅朋友。
何	你搵王先生有乜嘢事呀？
女人	我要賣我嘅美國車，王先生想買。
何	好，我帶你去王先生嘅寫字樓。
女人	唔該你。

2 True or false?
   a Wòhng Gwok Méih Sìn-sàang séung maaih chē.
   b Wòhng Sìn-sàang séung maaih Yaht-bún chē.
   c Hòh Sìn-sàang, Wòhng Sìn-sàang kéuih-deih haih pàhng-yáuh.
   d Wòhng Taai-táai wán Wòhng Sìn-sàang.

3 Now try answering these questions in Cantonese.
   a Wòhng Sìn-sàang haih m̀h haih Bà-sài yàhn a?
   b Wòhng Sìn-sàang ge pàhng-yáuh wán kéuih yáuh-māt-yéh-sih-a?

Tones matter!

 02.03 Now you can hear it for yourself: the only difference between *to buy* and *to sell* is the tones. Listen carefully to the audio:

買 **máaih** *to buy*   賣 **maaih** *to sell*
買 máaih   賣 maaih   賣 maaih   買 máaih

 There is even one word which combines the two as máaih-maaih 買賣. Can you guess what it means?

Language discovery

2.1 QUESTION WORDS

Question words like **bīn-go?** *who?* and **māt-yéh?** *what?* come in the same position in the sentence as the answer to them does, unlike in English where question and answer have different word orders. In the two examples following, note how the English order is twisted but the Chinese is not:

Kéuih sing māt-yéh a?	*What is he surnamed?*
Kéuih sing Hòh.	*He is surnamed Ho.*
Kéuih wán bīn-go a?	*Who is she looking for?*
Kéuih wán Hòh Síu-jé.	*She is looking for Miss Ho.*

Some people say **mī-yéh?** instead of **māt-yéh?**, and increasingly you can hear an even shorter version, **mē?** There is no difference in meaning, you can please yourself which you say, but for clarity you might do best to stick to **māt-yéh?**

> **LANGUAGE TIP**
> The final particle **a?** is pretty sure to pop up at the end of any sentence in which a question word like *who? what? where? which? how? why?* or *when?* appears, just as we saw it do with the positive-negative **leng m̀h leng** type questions in Unit 1. The questions are perfectly understandable without **a?**, but they rarely get the chance to be alone, and in everyday speech where there is a question there will normally be an adoring **a?** tagging along behind.

 So, do **Jèung Taai-táai hóu m̀h hóu?** and **Jèung Taai-táai hóu m̀h hóu a?** both mean *Is Mrs Cheung well?* Yes, of course they do, but look again at **Jèung Taai-táai hóu m̀h hóu** and pick it apart word by word. **Can you spot another meaning?**

2.2 POSSESSION

The little word **ge** shows possession, like the apostrophe *s* ('s) in English. So **Léih Taai-táai ge sìn-sàang** is *Mrs Li's husband*, **ngóh ge chē** is *my car*, and **kéuih ge** is *his* or *hers*.

YOUR TURN Try to complete the Cantonese translations.

a	Wòhng Taai-táai _____	*Mrs Wong's car*
b	_____ sé-jih-làuh	*our office*
c	Chē haih _____.	*The car is Miss Wong's.*
d	Jùng-gwok chē haih _____.	*The Chinese car is his.*

When there is a close personal relationship with someone, **ge** is often left out, but the relationship term must have at least two syllables, as with **taai-táai** and **pàhng-yáuh** here:

ngóh taai-táai	*my wife*	**kéuih pàhng-yáuh**	*her friend*

2.3 M̀H-GÒI *THANK YOU*

M̀h-gòi literally means *ought not*. It is the most common word for *thank you*. If someone holds the door open for you, passes you the soy sauce or tells you your shoelace is undone, you should politely say **m̀h-gòi** to them.

Vocabulary builder 2

 02.04 Listen to the new vocabulary and practise saying it out loud. Then complete the missing English expressions.

NUMBERS

一	yāt	*one*	六	luhk	*six*
二	yih	*two*	七	chāt	*seven*
三	sàam	*three*	八	baat	*eight*
四	sei	*four*	九	gáu	*nine*
五	ńgh	*five*	十	sahp	*ten*

SPECIFIERS

嗰	gó	*that, _____*
呢	nī	*this, these*

CLASSIFIERS (CL)

個	go	cl: *for people and for many objects*
枝	jì	cl: *for stick-like things*

VERBS

估	gú	*to guess, reckon*
喺	hái	*to be at / in / on; at / in / on*
問	mahn	*to ask a _____*

ANOTHER POLITENESS

唔緊要	m̀h gán-yiu	*never mind, it doesn't _____*

BASICS

筆	bāt	*pen, any writing tool* (cl: **jì**)
遲啲	chìh-dī	*later on*
㗎	ga?	fp: = **ge** + **a?**
手錶	sáu-bíu	*wristwatch* (cl: **go**)
同埋	tùhng-màaih	*and, with*
而家	yìh-gā	*now*

Dialogue 2

 02.05 *Miss Cheung has found a watch and a pen on her desk. She asks Mr Ho if they are his.*

1 Listen for the expressions that mean *this watch* and *that pen*. What are they?

Cheung	Òu! Yāt go sáu-bīu, yāt jì bāt … Hòh Sìn-sàang, nī go sáu-bīu tùhng-màaih gó jì bāt haih m̀h haih néih ga?	*Oh, a watch and a pen … Mr Ho, are this watch and that pen yours?*
Ho	Nī go sáu-bīu m̀h haih ngóh ge: gó jì bāt haih ngóh ge.	*This watch isn't mine, but that pen is.*
Cheung	Nī go sáu-bīu hóu leng, haih Méih-gwok sáu-bīu. Néih gú haih bīn-go ga?	*This watch is very handsome, it's American. Can you guess whose it is?*
Ho	Ngóh gú haih Wòhng Sìn-sàang ge.	*I'd guess it's Mr Wong's.*
Cheung	Ngóh dōu gú haih kéuih ge. Ngóh-deih heui mahn kéuih, hóu m̀h hóu a?	*I guess the same. We'll go and ask him, shall we?*
Ho	Wòhng Sìn-sàang yìh-gā m̀h hái kéuih ge sé-jih-làuh.	*Mr Wong isn't in his office now.*
Cheung	M̀h gán-yiu. Ngóh chìh-dī mahn kéuih.	*It doesn't matter. I'll ask him later.*

張	噢！一個手錶，一枝筆 … 何先生，呢個手錶同埋嗰枝筆係唔係你㗎？
何	呢個手錶唔係我嘅：嗰枝筆係我嘅。
張	呢個手錶好靚，係美國手錶。你估係邊個㗎？
何	我估係王先生嘅。
張	我都估係佢嘅。我哋去問佢，好唔好呀？
何	王先生而家唔喺佢嘅寫字樓。
張	唔緊要，我遲啲問佢。

2 Would it make sense to say Gó jì sáu-bīu?

3 Use Cantonese to answer these questions on the dialogue.

    a Gó jì bāt haih bīn-go ga?

    b Jèung Síu-jé chìh-dī mahn bīn-go a?

    c Jèung Síu-jé mahn Hòh Sìn-sàang māt-yéh a?

Tone drill

02.06 Here are some different combinations of tones and sounds to stretch your voice muscles. Listen and repeat as carefully as you can (but don't worry about the meanings):

tìm – tùhng 添同	**jáau – sáu** 找手	**fùi – chà** 灰茶
jyun – sé 轉寫	**wuh – nám** 互諗	**ou – bàan** 澳班
ngóh – néih – kéuih 我你佢	**gòu – sìn – sàang** 高先生	
hàahng – yàhn – hùhng 行人紅	**tái – hóu – dá** 睇好打	
go – leng – sing 個靚姓	**séui – taai – sàm** 水太深	
yàn – gwóng – yaht 因廣日	**dāk – hot – siht** 特渴舌	
yáhn – jùng – hèung 引忠香	**kàhm – síu – yiu** 嚟小要	
yi – tìng – līp 意聽軐	**daaih – maahn – mahn** 大慢問	

Language discovery

2.4 CLASSIFIERS

All the Chinese languages (Cantonese, Hakka, Shanghainese, etc.) have classifiers (measure words), which appear in front of nouns to show the kind of ('class' of) noun that is coming. Pidgin English felt the need for classifiers too, and it devised the word *piecee* to stand for all the dozens of different ones that Chinese uses (e.g. *that piecee house, which piecee dog?, eight piecee book*). Of course that meant that all nouns were in the same class, the '*piecee* class', so nothing was being classified at all, but languages are not always rational. Take a deep breath, you have just met your first classifiers and are about to learn how to use them … and these are real and do classify nouns, so you cannot ignore them.

> **PIDGIN ENGLISH**
> Pidgin English (also known as China Coast Pidgin) evolved spontaneously from the early 18th century on. It was a strange language which was a kind of halfway house between English and Cantonese and therefore was presumed to be equally easy / difficult for both sides to learn and to speak as they transacted 'pidgin' (*business*) together. It used broken English vocabulary but mostly followed Chinese grammar patterns. Some of its expressions have passed into regular English, such as have a *look-see*, *chop-chop*, and *no can do*.

In English when you identify a noun with a specifying word like *this, that* or *which?* you just put it in front of the word (*this man, which pen?*), but in Cantonese you need to use a classifier word as well (*this classifier man, which classifier pen?*). It is not always easy to guess which classifier goes with which noun, although you can expect, for instance, that almost any object which is thin, straight and rigid will be classified with **jì**, as with **jì** for *pen*.

The classifier for *people* is **go**, so:

nī go yàhn	*this person*
gó go yàhn	*that person*
bīn go yàhn?	*which person?*
bīn go Méih-gwok yàhn a?	*which American?*

The classifier for *wristwatch* is also **go**:

gó go sáu-bīu   *that watch*

In fact, if you don't know of a special classifier for a noun, you can always try using **go**, since it is the most common classifier of all. Another 'universal' classifier is **júng** 種, which can be used almost anywhere English uses *kind of, type of, sort of*.

 In the dialogue if you were to substitute júng for go in Miss Cheung's second speech, it would still make perfect sense. But what would it now mean?

If it is clear what is meant, you are allowed to drop off the noun, but the classifier must still be used. Note the question and answer:

Néih yiu bīn júng bāt a?   *Which kind of pen do you want?*
Ngóh yiu nī júng.   *I want this kind.*

 Did you notice how bīn go yàhn? *which person?* is very much like bīn-go? *who?* Well, they are really the same, but when *who?* is meant it is normal to use the shorter form.

2.5 HOW ABOUT IT?

Hóu m̀h hóu a? literally means *is it good?*, but it is also used at the ends of sentences meaning *what do you say?, how about it?, OK?* (And there is **a?** at the end of a question sentence again!)

2.6 NUMBERS

This looks like a very long section, but don't get worried. The Cantonese number system is actually very straightforward and logical.

As you have seen, the numbers one to ten are all single-syllable words:

yāt	**yih**	**sàam**	**sei**	**ńgh**	**luhk**	**chāt**	**baat**	**gáu**	**sahp**
one	*two*	*three*	*four*	*five*	*six*	*seven*	*eight*	*nine*	*ten*
一	二	三	四	五	六	七	八	九	十

 02.07 11 is 10 + 1, 12 is 10 + 2, and so on up to 10 + 9 for 19:

sahp-yāt	11	**sahp-yih**	12	**sahp-sàam**	13
sahp-sei	14	**sahp-ńgh**	15	**sahp-luhk**	16
sahp-chāt	17	**sahp-baat**	18	**sahp-gáu**	19

20 is 2 x 10, 21 is 2 x 10 + 1, and so on up to 2 x 10 + 9 for 29:

yih-sahp	20	**yih-sahp-yāt**	21	**yih-sahp-yih**	22
yih-sahp-sàam	23	… and keep going up to …		**yih-sahp-gáu**	29

30 is 3 x 10, 31 is 3 x 10 + 1, …:

sàam-sahp	30	**sàam-sahp-yāt**	31 etc., etc.

Now you take up the running from here. Once you have memorized the numbers one to ten you have everything you need to know to count up to 99 (and back again if you are really confident).

So, sàam-sahp-yih is _____ and sàam-sahp-baat is _____.

What is 34? 77? 89? 40? 65? 52? 16? 67? 83? 94?

99 of course is **gáu-sahp-gáu** 九十九. Easy, isn't it?

When things are counted (*one person*, *three pens*, etc.) the classifier must be used in the same way as it is with specifying words. So:

yāt go yàhn	*one person*
sei jì bāt	*four pens*
sahp-yih go sáu-bīu	*12 watches*

⋮ **YOUR TURN Here are a couple of tongue-twisters to pronounce and translate:**

sei-sahp-sei go Sàn-sài-làahn yàhn _____

baat jì Bà-sài bāt _____

The whole number system is nice and regular, with one exception: the number *two*. When it is followed by a classifier the number *two* is not **yih** but **léuhng**, so:

yāt, yih, sàam, sei, …	*one, two, three, four, …*

but

yāt jì bāt, léuhng jì bāt, sàam jì bāt, sei jì bāt, …

one pen, two pens, three pens, four pens, …

> **LANGUAGE TIP**
>
> It is only the number *two* itself which plays the trick of having two forms; complex numbers which end in a two are not affected, as you can see from the example of *12 watches* (**sahp-yih go sáu-bīu**). And don't feel too hard done by: English is even crazier about the number *two* – think of *brace of*, *pair of*, *couple of*, *twin*, *dual*, *duo-* and *bi-*!

🔓 Practice

1 **Try to give answers to the questions. You cannot be sure of the answer to the second one, but common sense should help you.**

   a Gwai-sing a?

   b Wòhng Sìn-sàang haih m̀h haih Jùng-gwok-yàhn a?

   c Néih séung m̀h séung máaih chē a? (Answer: *No*)

   d Dāk-gwok sáu-bīu gwai m̀h gwai a? (Answer: *Very*)

   e Bīn jì bāt haih Jèung Síu-jé ga? (Answer: *This one*)

2 **Make up your own conversation. Tell Mr Wong that you want to go to England to buy a British car. He tells you that British cars are expensive. Ask him what kind of car he's got. He says that he has a British car too.**

🎧 02.08 **When you have made up your conversation, you can find our version in the Key to the exercises section or on the audio. If it is different from yours that doesn't necessarily mean that yours is wrong. There are often different ways of saying much the same thing, and you may very well have a different version of Mr Wong's last remark, for instance.**

3 In the picture all the women are American, all the men are Chinese and all the children are Japanese. Try saying in Cantonese how many of each there are, say how many watches Mr Wong is selling and describe what the woman is doing at Mr Pong's stall.

Test yourself

Make correct and meaningful sentences.

a Nī _____ sáu-bīu haih Hòh Taai-táai ge.

b Néih haih m̀h haih Yìng-gwok _____ a?

c Ngóh gú Yaht-_____ chē hóu gwai.

d Wòhng Síu-jé leng _____ leng a?

e Néih séung máaih _____-yéh a?

f _____-go haih Jèung Síu-jé a?

g Kéuih m̀h haih Yìng-gwok-yàhn, _____ m̀h haih Méih-gwok-yàhn; kéuih haih Yaht-bún-yàhn.

h Ngóh _____ Wòhng Sìn-sàang, 'Néih ge Yìng-gwok chē daaih m̀h daaih a?'

3 家人同朋友 *Gà-yàhn tùhng pàhng-yáuh*

Family and friends

In this unit you will learn about:
▶ *coming and going.*
▶ *family members.*
▶ *final particles.*
▶ *the irregular verb* **to have.**
▶ **not very.**
▶ **Why?**

CEFR: *(A1) Can ask and answer questions about personal details such as where you live, people you know and things you have.*

⊙ Chinese families

Chinese culture has always valued the family highly. 'Family' has traditionally meant people related to each other through males, so that your father's parents are real family but your mother's parents are not. Your father's brothers are family, and you call them **a-baak** 阿佰 if they are older than your father and **a-sūk** 阿叔 if they are younger than he is, but your mother's brothers and the husbands of the sisters of either of your parents are not family and are never called **a-sūk** or **a-baak**. It's all rather complicated.

So, how would you translate *uncle* into Cantonese?

Vocabulary builder 1

03.01 Listen to the new vocabulary and practise saying it out loud. Then complete the missing English expressions.

FAMILY

阿妹	a-múi	*younger sister*
爸爸	bàh-bā	*father*
大佬	daaih-lóu	*older brother*
家姐	gà-jē	*older sister*
家人	gà-yàhn	*family member(s)*
兄弟	hìng-daih	*brothers*
姊妹	jí-muih	_____
媽媽	màh-mā	_____
細佬	sai-lóu	*younger* _____
屋企	ūk-kéi	*family; home*

VERBS

返	fàan	*to return, return to*
走	jáu	*to run, run away, leave*
做	jouh	*to do*
住	jyuh	*to dwell, live*
要	yiu	*must, need to*

> **LANGUAGE TIP**
> The verb **jáu** literally means *to run*, but note how closely it mirrors English in that it also means *to leave*: **Ngóh yìh-gā heui Gáu-lùhng, yiu jáu la** *I'm going to Kowloon now, I must run.*

QUESTION WORDS

邊度	bīn-douh?	*where? which place?*
做乜嘢	jouh māt-yéh?	*why? for what reason?*

BASICS

吖？	àh?	fp: *that's right, isn't it?*
大	daaih	*big; to* _____
都幾、幾	dōu-géi *or* géi	*quite, rather, fairly*
噉，噉樣	gám *or* gám-yéung	*in that case, so*
嘞、嗻	lak *or* la	fp: *that's how the case stands now*
睇醫生	tái-yī-sāng	*to see* (**tái**) *the doctor* (**yī-sāng**)
同	tùhng	*with, and (a shorter form of* **tùhng-màaih***)*
屋	ūk	*house* (cl: **gàan** 間)
一齊	yāt-chàih	*together*
一定	yāt-dihng	*certainly*

Dialogue 1

 03.02 *Mr Ho meets Mr Wong on the street.*

1 In Mr Wong's second speech, is there anything you can delete and still leave an acceptable sentence with the same meaning?

Ho	Wòhng Sìn-sàang, néih heui bīn-douh a?	*Where are you going, Mr Wong?*
Wong	Jóu-sàhn, Hòh Sìn-sàang, ngóh fàan ūk-kéi.	*Good morning, Mr Ho. I'm going home.*
Ho	Néih fàan ūk-kéi jouh-māt-yéh a?	*Why are you going back home?*
Wong	Ngóh daai ngóh màh-mā heui tái-yī-sāng.	*I'm taking my mother to see the doctor.*
Ho	Néih tùhng màh-mā yāt-chàih jyuh àh?	*You're living with your mother then, are you?*
Wong	Haih, ngóh tùhng bàh-bā, màh-mā, hìng-daih, jí-muih, chāt go yàhn yāt-chàih jyuh.	*Yes, I'm living together with my parents, and my brothers and sisters, seven of us.*
Ho	Chāt go yàhn yāt-chàih jyuh … gám-yéung, néih-deih gàan ūk yāt-dihng hóu daaih lak.	*Seven of you living together … so your house must certainly be very large.*
Wong	Haih, dōu-géi daaih. Deui-m̀h-jyuh, Hòh Sìn-sàang, ngóh yiu jáu lak, joi-gin.	*Yes, quite big. Excuse me, Mr Ho, I have to get on. Goodbye.*
Ho	Joi-gin, Wòhng Sìn-sàang.	*Goodbye, Mr Wong.*

何	王先生，你去邊度呀？
王	早晨，何先生，我返屋企。
何	你返屋企做乜嘢呀？
王	我帶我媽媽去睇醫生。
何	你同媽媽一齊住吖？
王	係，我同爸爸，媽媽，兄弟，姊妹，七個人一齊住。
何	七個人一齊住⋯⋯噉樣，你哋間屋一定好大嘞。
王	係，都幾大。對唔住，何先生，我要走嘞，再見。
何	再見，王先生。

LANGUAGE TIP

In the dialogue it is clear that Wong and Ho are friends but not close ones: the language is a bit formal, and they are not up to date with each other's news. Make no mistake, Cantonese people can be casual and personal too, the elaborate politeness and concealment of emotions which used to be their image in the West is rarely met with nowadays.

2 Here is the Wong family. How would C address A? How would D address B?
How would D address A? How would you address D? How would you address B?
Which one do you think is the Mr Wong who figures in the dialogue?

a   b   c   d   e   f   g

Language discovery

3.1 WHERE?

Bīn-douh? *where?* works to the same rule as **bīn-go?** *who?* and **māt-yéh?** *what?*: it comes in a sentence where the answer to it comes (See Unit 2).

Néih heui bīn-douh a?	*Where are you going?*
Ngóh heui Ou-mún.	*I'm going to Macau.*

> **LANGUAGE TIP**
> There is another word (**bīn-syu?** 邊處) which also means *where?*, but **bīn-syu?** is now rather old-fashioned and you will not often hear it any more. We will use only **bīn-douh** in this book.

3.2 FÀAN *TO RETURN*

To return is **fàan**. It combines easily with **heui** *to go* as **fàan-heui** meaning *to go back*, that is *to return in a direction away from me the speaker*:

Néih fàan-heui m̀h fàan-heui a?	*Are you going back?*

or in its more commonly shortened form:

Néih fàan m̀h fàan-heui a?	*Are you going back?*

Fàan also means *to go where one routinely goes*:

Wòhng Síu-jé fàan ūk-kéi.	*Miss Wong is going home.*
Ngóh fàan sé-jih-làuh.	*I'm going to the office.*

3.3 WHY?

Jouh-māt-yéh? literally means *to do what?* but it has come to mean *why?* It can be positioned quite freely in the sentence without any change of meaning.

YOUR TURN What do these examples mean?

Néih jouh-māt-yéh yiu maaih chē a?

Jouh-māt-yéh néih yiu maaih chē a?

Néih yiu maaih chē jouh-māt-yéh a?

> **YES AND NO**
>
> There are no words for *yes* and *no* in Cantonese. You should use the positive or negative form of the appropriate verb, so in answer to **Néih heui m̀h heui Jùng-gwok a?** *Are you going to China?* you can reply **heui** *yes* or **m̀h heui** *no*. If it is not the verb itself which is the focus of the question, it is useful to use **haih** *it is the case* or **m̀h haih** *it is not the case*, as in the dialogue. **Haih** and **m̀h haih** come as close to *yes* and *no* as Cantonese gets.

3.4 THE ADVERB YĀT-CHÀIH *TOGETHER*

Yāt-chàih *together, all together* is an adverb, and like almost all adverbs it comes in front of the verb in the sentence. So **yāt-chàih jyuh** is *to live together* and **yāt-chàih fàan Yìng-gwok** means *to return to Britain together*.

3.5 THAT'S RIGHT, ISN'T IT?

The final particle **àh?** comes at the end of a sentence to ask for confirmation that what you have said is correct:

Néih haih Jèung Sìn-sàang àh?	*You're Mr Cheung, aren't you?*
Néih heui Yìng-gwok àh?	*I take it you're going to England, right?*

3.6 THAT'S HOW THE CASE STANDS NOW

Lak (sometimes pronounced **la**) comes at the end of the sentence to state what the current position is. Naturally enough that means that often there has been some change before that position has been arrived at:

Ngóh yiu jáu lak.	*I must be going now. (I didn't see the need just before.)*
Kéuih m̀h séung máaih chē lak.	*He doesn't want to buy a car any more.*

3.7 CLASSIFIERS AS POSSESSIVES

You will no doubt have noticed **néih-deih gàan ūk** in the dialogue and puzzled over why it was translated as *your house*. The answer is that classifiers can act in the same way as the possessive **ge**, so *her pen* can be either **kéuih ge bāt** or **kéuih jì bāt**.

YOUR TURN How would you translate *my Japanese watch*? (give two answers)

> **REMEMBER**
>
> ▶ Always put a classifier between a number and a noun: **sàam jì bāt** *three pens*.
> ▶ Always put a classifier between the specifying words *this, that, which?* and a noun: **bīn go sáu-bīu?** *which watch?*
> ▶ In front of a classifier the number *two* is always **léuhng**: **léuhng gàan ūk** *two houses*.
> ▶ The correct classifier can be used instead of **ge** to show the possessive: **kéuih-deih gàan ūk** *their house*.

Vocabulary builder 2

 03.03 Listen to the new vocabulary and practise saying it out loud. Then complete the missing English expressions.

POLITENESS

請	chéng	*please*
好耐冇見	hóu-noih-móuh-gin	*long time no see* (lit. 'very long time not see')

TRANSPORT

巴士	bā-sí	_____ (cl: **ga** 架)
的士	dīk-sí	_____ (cl: **ga**)

ADDRESSES

地下	deih-há	*ground floor; the ground; the floor*
花園道	Fà-yùhn Douh	*Garden* _____
… 號	… houh	*number …*
樓	láu	*a flat, a storey* (cl: **chàhng** 層); *a high building*
上海街	Seuhng-hói Gāai	*Shanghai Street*

VERBS

坐	chóh	*to sit*
搭	daap	*to travel by / catch / take (public transport)*
嚟	làih	*to come, come to*
冇	móuh	*have not (negative of **yáuh** to have)*
探	taam	*to see, visit*

BASICS

車房	chē-fòhng	*garage* (cl: **gàan**)
多	dò	*many, much*
嘅	ge	fp: *makes a statement more emphatic: that's how it is and that's how it's going to stay*
啫 or 唧	jē or jēk	fp: *only; and that's all*
重	juhng	*still, yet*
啦	lā	fp: *urging someone to agree with you or do something for you*
唔係幾好 …	m̀h-haih-géi / hóu…	*not very (adjective)*
耐	noih	_____
時間	sìh-gaan	*time*

> **LANGUAGE TIP**
> **Chē-fòhng** means *garage* only in the sense of the covered space where you keep your car, it does not refer to a business repairing vehicles.

Dialogue 2

 03.04 *Mr Ho hasn't seen Mr Cheung for a long while. They meet by chance.*

1 How does the order of a Cantonese address differ from an English address?

Ho	Jèung Sìn-sàang, hóu-noih-móuh-gin. Néih hóu ma? Néih yìh-gā hái bīn-douh jyuh a?	*Mr Cheung, long time no see! How are you? Where are you living now?*
Cheung	Ngóh yìh-gā jyuh hái Hèung-góng Fà-yùhn Douh yih-sahp-baat houh sàam láu.	*I'm living on Hong Kong side, 3rd floor, number 28 Garden Road now.*
Ho	Fà-yùhn Douh hóu m̀h hóu jyuh a?	*Is Garden Road a good place to live?*
Cheung	Hóu jyuh. Fà-yùhn Douh yáuh hóu dò bā-sí tùhng dīk-sí daap. Hòh Sìn-sàang, néih jyuh hái bīn-douh a?	*Very good. There are plenty of buses and taxis on Garden Road. And where are you living, Mr Ho?*
Ho	Ngóh juhng jyuh hái Gáu-lùhng Seuhng-hói Gāai chāt-sahp-sàam houh deih-há. Néih yáuh sìh-gaan chéng làih chóh lā.	*I'm still on the ground floor at 73 Shanghai Street on Kowloon side. When you have time you're welcome to come over to visit.*
Cheung	Néih yáuh-sàm. Néih gàan ūk yáuh móuh chē-fòhng a?	*You're very kind. Does your house have a garage?*
Ho	Ngóh m̀h haih jyuh yāt gàan ūk, ngóh jyuh yāt chàhng láu jē. Nī chàhng láu m̀h-haih-géi-daaih, móuh chē-fòhng ge.	*I don't live in a house, it's only a flat. This flat is not very big, and it doesn't have a garage.*
Cheung	Hóu, yáuh sìh-gaan ngóh làih taam néih. Joi-gin.	*OK, when I have time I will come to visit you. Goodbye.*
Ho	Joi-gin.	*Goodbye.*

何	張先生，好耐冇見。你好嗎？你而家喺邊度住呀？
張	我而家住喺香港花園道二十八號三樓。
何	花園道好唔好住呀？
張	好住。花園道有好多巴士同的士搭。何先生，你住喺邊度呀？
何	我重住喺九龍上海街七十三號地下。你有時間請嚟坐啦。
張	你有心。你間屋有冇車房呀？
何	我唔係住一間屋，我住一層樓啫。呢層樓唔係幾大，冇車房嘅。
張	好，有時間我嚟探你，再見。
何	再見。

2 In Mr Ho's third speech chóh is translated as *visit*, but what does it literally mean?

3 Answer haih *it is so* or m̀h haih *it is not so* to these statements.

    a Fà-yùhn Douh m̀h hóu jyuh.

    b Hòh Sìn-sàang jyuh hái yāt gàan ūk.

    c Hòh Sìn-sàang jyuh hái deih-há.

    d Hòh Sìn-sàang ge chē-fòhng hóu daaih.

    e Jèung Sìn-sàang heui Hòh Sìn-sàang ūk-kéi.

4 03.05 **Answer the questions.**

 a Hòh Sìn-sàang jyuh hái bīn-douh a?

 b Jèung Sìn-sàang jyuh hái bīn-douh a?

 c Hòh Sìn-sàang ge láu yáuh móuh chē-fòhng a?

 d Jèung Sìn-sàang séung m̀h séung taam Hòh Sìn-sàang a?

 e Yáuh móuh bā-sí heui Fà-yùhn Douh a?

5 **Suppose in Dialogue 1 that Mr Wong had answered the question *Where are you going?* differently by saying *I'm taking the No. 16 bus to go to Garden Road to visit my older brother.* Sounds complicated, doesn't it, but don't panic, you can translate it. Have a go!**

LANGUAGE TIP
As you discovered when Mr Cheung gave his address in the dialogue, he gave it in the order *Hong Kong, Garden Road, No. 28, 3rd floor* – i.e. in the opposite way to English. Chinese always prefers to work from the general to the particular, from the large to the small. We shall see later that it is the same with dates and times, so that the Chinese would translate *3.18 p.m. on 17 May 2015* in the order *2015, May, 17, p.m., 3.18.*

 ## Pronunciation drill

 03.06 **There are few difficulties for English speakers in pronouncing Cantonese, but you should pay special attention to distinguishing the following pairs of sounds, concentrating on the sounds rather than the tones when listening to and reproducing them:**

gèui	gòi		fan	faan		làih	lèih
居	該		瞓	販		嚟	離
síu	syú		seun	syun		góng	gwóng
小	鼠		信	算		港	廣
máih	máaih		chò	chòu		hèung	hùng
米	買		初	粗		香	空

Language discovery

3.8 THE VERB YÁUH

The verb **yáuh** *to have* is an oddity. It is not made negative with **m̀h**: instead the negative of **yáuh** is another verb **móuh** *not to have*. So while *Are you English?* is **Néih haih m̀h haih Yìng-gwok yàhn a?**, *Have you got an English car?* is **Néih yáuh móuh Yìng-gwok chē a?** and *I haven't got a car* is **Ngóh móuh chē.**

 Find the English translation for Fà-yùhn Douh yáuh hóu dò bā-sí tùhng dīk-sí daap in the dialogue. How has yáuh been translated?

So, another quirk of **yáuh** and **móuh** is that they can also mean *there is / are* and *there isn't / aren't*.

Hái Hèung-góng yáuh móuh Méih-gwok yàhn jyuh a?
Are there any Americans living in Hong Kong?

LANGUAGE TIP
If you know French, you will see a similarity of use of the verb *to have* in **il y a** *there is / are.*

3.9 JĒ OR JĒK

Jē (pronounced by some people as **jēk**) is a very useful little final particle which gives the meaning *only, that's all*:

Ngóh yáuh léuhng jì bāt.	*I've got two pens.*
Kéuih yáuh yat jì bat jē.	*He's only got one pen.*

3.10 NOT VERY

The negative of **daaih** *big* is **m̀h daaih** *not big*, just as you would expect. The negative of **hóu daaih** *very big*, however, is **m̀h-haih-géi-daaih** or **m̀h-haih-hóu-daaih**, both of which mean *not very big*. So you will need to remember that the verb **haih** is slipped into this *not very* construction:

Nī chàhng láu m̀h-haih-géi-gwai.	*This flat is not very expensive.*
Wòhng Síu-jé m̀h-haih-hóu-leng.	*Miss Wong is not very pretty.*

3.11 A RECAP: FINAL PARTICLES

You have now met quite a few words like **jē**, that is, words that are added to the end of a sentence to round it off or to give an extra meaning. These particles or final particles are used a great deal in everyday speech. Before you meet any more of them, here is a reminder of those you already know:

a?	The final particle which is added to sentences which already contain positive–negative-type questions or question words like **māt-yéh?**
àh?	The question particle which expects the listener to be in agreement: *That's right, isn't it?*
ga?	The particle made when **ge** is followed by **a?**
ge	Makes a statement more emphatic: *That's the way it is!*
jē/jēk	*Only.*
lā	The particle you use when you are trying to urge someone to do something for you or to persuade someone to agree with you.
lak/la	The particle which shows that things were different before but this is how the situation stands now.
ma?	A spoken question mark. It makes a statement into a question.
nē?	The shortcut question particle which asks follow-up questions.

Practice

1 **Sort out these jumbled words into meaningful sentences.**

   a bàh-bā yī-sāng Hòh Sìn-sàang haih.

   b jouh-māt-yéh hái ūk-kéi Wòhng Taai-táai a?

   c tái yī-sāng ngóh heui m̀h séung.

   d ngóh-deih sé-jih-làuh yāt-chàih fàan.

 2 **You have just bumped into your old friend Mr Wong in the street in Hong Kong. You haven't seen him for several months. How do you greet him? Ask after his wife and where he lives now. Apologize to him and say that you have to catch a bus to Garden Road now to visit your father whom you have to take to see the doctor.**

03.07 **Now listen to the audio or read the model version of the answer several times and make sure that you understand it.**

Test yourself

Complete the sentences so they make sense.

a Wòhng Taai-táai heui tái _____.

b Ngóh-deih _____ heui Wòhng Sìn-sàang _____.

c Ngóh bàh-bā haih _____.

d Ngóh-deih jyuh hái _____.

食嘢 Sihk-yéh

Eating

In this unit you will learn about:
- ▸ adverbs.
- ▸ Don't!
- ▸ linking adjectives to nouns.
- ▸ location.
- ▸ 'lonely verbs'.
- ▸ more classifiers.
- ▸ the irregular verb to need.
- ▸ verb endings.

CEFR: *(A1) Can ask people for things and give people things.*

◉ Food, glorious food!

By rights the important subject of food should be the first lesson in any book about China, but you didn't know enough language to tackle such a rich subject, and it would be terrible to get indigestion from something which should give you pleasure. This unit looks like a lot to swallow, but think of it as a taster to whet your appetite, and if you come across a food that you don't like, don't learn it! (There's no reason why teetotallers should bother about the word for *beer.*)

Not surprisingly, rice figures large in Chinese culture, e.g. it is offered in religious sacrifices to the ancestors; and it is thrown over newly-weds to bring fertility to them.

English has only the one word *rice*, but Cantonese has many words for it. **Faahn** 飯 means rice only when it is *cooked rice*.

Sihk 食 means *to eat* and **sihk faahn** 食飯 *to eat rice* means *to have a proper meal* (of Chinese food), whereas **sihk chāan** 食餐 *to eat a meal* means *to have a meal* (of non-Chinese food).

Yám 飲 is *to drink*, and **yám chàh** 飲茶 means *to drink tea*. It also means *to have dim sum* because the important part of having dim sum is considered to be the tea drinking and not the delicacies (**dím-sām** 點心), which are eaten with it as incidentals like the biscuit which accompanies a cup of coffee.

So 起筷 **Héi faai!** *Lift up your chopsticks!* and 食飯 **Sihk faahn!** *Tuck in!*

 If you can describe a tasty dish of noodles as **hóu sihk**, how would you describe a nice cup of tea?

Vocabulary builder 1

 04.01 **Listen to the new vocabulary and practise saying it out loud.**

POLITENESS

請	chéng	*to invite*
隨便	chèuih-bín	*as you please, feel free*
客氣	haak-hei	*polite*
唔駛	m̀h-sái	*no need to, not necessary to*
太 … 喇	taai … la	*too …*

EATING AND DRINKING

便飯	bihn-faahn	*pot luck, 'any old food'*
廚房	chyùh-fóng	*kitchen* (cl: **gàan**)
酒樓	jáu-làuh	*Chinese restaurant* (cl: **gàan**)
煮	jyú	*to cook*
餸	sung	*food; a dish other than rice or soup*

VERBS AND VERB ENDINGS (VE)

幫 …手	bòng … sáu	*to help …, give someone a hand*
等	dáng	*to wait, wait for*
信	seun	*to believe*
預備	yuh-beih	*to prepare, get ready*
用	yuhng	*to use, spend*
… 緊	-gán	ve: shows continuing action, *-ing*
… 咗	-jó	ve: shows completed action, *-ed*

BASICS

半	bun	*half*
餐	chàan	cl: for **faahn**: *a meal*
啲	dī	cl: for plurals and uncountable things
都	dōu	*all, both*
附近	fuh-gahn	*nearby*
咁	gam	*so*
好似 … 一樣	hóu-chíh … yāt-yeuhng	*just like …*
真（係）	jàn(-haih)	*truly, really; true, real*
只（係）	jí(-haih)	*only*
鐘頭	jūng-tàuh	*hour* (cl: **go** 個)
哦	óh	*oh, now I understand!*

Dialogue 1

04.02 *Mr Ho invites Mr Wong to his home for a meal.*

1 See if you can catch Mr Ho out in a little fib in the dialogue.

Wong	Hòh Sìn-sàang, néih taai haak-hei lā, jyú gam dò sung chéng ngóh sihk-faahn.	*Mr Ho, it's too polite of you to cook so many dishes and invite me to dine.*
Ho	Bihn-faahn jē, chèuih-bín sihk lā. Yiu m̀h yiu chàh a?	*It's just pot luck. Pick at whatever you fancy. Do you want some tea?*
Wong	M̀h yiu la, m̀h-gòi. Hòh Taai-táai nē? Kéuih hái bīn-douh a?	*No, thank you. What about Mrs Ho? Where's she?*
Ho	Kéuih hái chyùh-fóng jyú-gán faahn, m̀h-sái dáng kéuih la.	*In the kitchen cooking. No need to wait for her.*
Wong	Hòh Taai-táai jyú ge sung jàn hóu-sihk lak. Hóu-chíh jáu-làuh ge yāt-yeuhng. Hòh Sìn-sàang néih yáuh móuh bòng kéuih sáu a?	*Her food is really delicious, just like restaurant food. Did you help her, Mr Ho?*
Ho	Móuh a!	*No.*
Wong	Ngóh gú Hòh Taai-táai yāt-dihng yuhng-jó hóu dò sìh-gaan yuh-beih nī chàan faahn lak.	*I suppose Mrs Ho must have spent a lot of time preparing this meal.*
Ho	Kéuih yuhng-jó bun go jūng-tàuh jē.	*Half an hour, that's all.*
Wong	Jí-haih bun go jūng-tàuh àh? Ngóh m̀h seun.	*Only half an hour? I don't believe it.*
Ho	Haih jàn ga. Dī sung dōu haih kéuih heui fuh-gahn ge jáu-làuh máaih ge.	*It's true. She went to buy all the dishes from a nearby restaurant.*
Wong	Óh!	*Oh, I see.*
王	何先生，你太客氣啦，煮咁多餸請我食飯。	
何	唔好意思，便飯啫，隨便食啦。要唔要茶呀？	
王	唔要喇，唔該。何太太呢？佢喺邊度呀？	
何	佢喺廚房煮緊飯，唔駛等佢嘞。	
王	何太太煮嘅餸真好食嘞。好似酒樓嘅一樣。何先生你有冇幫佢手呀？	
何	冇呀！	
王	我估何太太一定用咗好多時間預備呢餐飯嘞。	
何	佢用咗半個鐘頭啫。	
王	只係半個鐘頭吖？我唔信。	
何	係真喋。啲餸都係佢去附近嘅酒樓買嘅。	
王	哦！	

2 In Mr Ho's last speech we have deliberately given a very free English translation. Try to give a more literal translation which will show that you have understood how the Cantonese sentence works.

3 True or false?

   a Hòh Sìn-sàang chéng Wòhng Sìn-sàang heui jáu-làuh sihk-faahn.

   b Hòh Sìn-sàang jyú-jó léuhng go sung chéng Wòhng Sìn-sàang sihk.

   c Hòh Sìn-sàang bòng Hòh Taai-táai sáu jyú-faahn.

   d Hòh Sìn-sàang, Hòh Taai-táai yuhng-jó léuhng go bun jūng-tàuh jyú-faahn.

   e Hòh Taai-táai m̀h jyú-sung, kéuih jí-haih heui jáu-làuh máaih-sung.

Language discovery

4.1 CHÉNG *TO INVITE*

In Unit 3 we saw that **chéng** means *please*. It has another meaning of *to invite*:

Kéuih chéng ngóh heui kéuih ūk-kéi.   *He invites me to go to his home.*

Chéng, or its slightly more formal pronunciation **chíng**, is of course part of the language of politeness, and it is considered very polite to be apologetic about any hospitality which you offer. That's why Mr Ho says **Bihn-faahn jē** *It's just whatever we've got* – even though he goes on to admit later that it is fancy food from a restaurant. He might well have prefaced that remark with **M̀h-hóu-yi-sì** 唔好意思 *I'm embarrassed to say that*. That would have made it even more polite. **M̀h-hóu-yi-sì** is well worth remembering as a useful politeness word which will cover *I'm embarrassed*, *I'm sorry*, *Forgive me for …*, and so on.

4.2 'LONELY VERBS'

Some verbs feel incomplete if they have no object, so Cantonese will supply an all-purpose object to comfort their loneliness! In English we have no problem with saying *he is eating*, but the Cantonese verb **sihk** is unhappy on its own and if it is not specified what he is eating then the all-purpose object **faahn** *rice* will be added. The normal translation of *he is eating a meal* is thus **kéuih sihk-faahn**. **Jyú** *to cook* is another verb which takes **faahn** for want of anything more definite: **kéuih jyú-faahn** *he's cooking*.

The title of this unit is **Sihk-yéh**, and **yéh** just means *a thing*, *something*, an even more general object which can go with lots of different verbs.

 How would you translate Kéuih heui-jó Gáu-lùhng máaih-yéh la?

> **REMEMBER**
> The negative of the verb **yáuh** *to have* is never formed with **m̀h** *not*. Instead there is a verb *not to have* which is **móuh**. *I haven't got a pen* is **ngóh móuh bāt**.

Heui *to go* shows direction of movement away from the speaker. Its opposite word is **làih** *to come*, showing movement towards the speaker. **Fàan-heui** is *to go back* and **fàan-làih** is *to come back*.

4.3 ADVERBS OF PLACE

The adverb which says where an action is happening comes either before or after the subject depending on the sense, but in any case it always comes somewhere before the verb:

Kéuih hái ūk-kéi chóh.   *She is sitting indoors.*
Hái sé-jih-làuh néih yáuh móuh bāt a?   *Have you got a pen in the office?*

4.4 TWO NEW VERB ENDINGS

-gán is tagged onto a verb to emphasize that the action is actually going on at the time:

| **Wòhng Sìn-sàang tái-gán yī-sāng.** | *Mr Wong is seeing the doctor.* |

-jó is tagged onto a verb in the same way to show that the action has been completed. Usually the final particle **lak** or **la** is added at the end of the sentence to back it up:

| **Kéuih tái-jó yī-sāng lak.** | *He saw the doctor.* |
| **Ngóh máaih-jó Méih-gwok chē lak.** | *I bought an American car.* |

4.5 AN IRREGULAR VERB: YIU/SÁI

Here's a rare treat, another irregularity in verbs. *To need to* is **yiu** but *not to need to* is **m̀h sái**:

Ngóh-deih yiu dáng kéuih.	*We need to wait for her.*
Ngóh-deih m̀h sái dáng kéuih la.	*We don't need to wait for her.*
Ngóh yiu máaih chē.	*I need to buy a car.*
Ngóh m̀h sái máaih chē.	*I don't need to buy a car.*

However, when **yiu** means *to want* its negative is **m̀h yiu**:

| **Ngóh m̀h yiu faahn.** | *I don't want any rice.* |

The question form for *to need to* is **sái m̀h sái**:

| **Ngóh-deih sái m̀h sái dáng kéuih a?** | *Do we need to wait for her?* |

 So, what do you think the question form for *to want* is? And how would you ask *Do you want some rice?*

> **LANGUAGE TIP**
>
> Another way of thinking about the two different negative forms of **yiu** is:
>
> ▶ When what follows is a noun, the negative is **m̀h yiu**, so **ngóh m̀h yiu Yaht-bún chē** is *I don't want a Japanese car*.
>
> ▶ When what follows is a verb, the negative is **m̀h sái**, so **ngóh m̀h sái máaih Yaht-bún chē** means *I don't need to buy a Japanese car*.
>
> In restaurants, **yiu** is used for *to order*, as you will learn from the second dialogue.

4.6 ANOTHER USE OF GE

We saw in Unit 2 that **ge** shows possession: **ngóh ge chē** *my car*. It is also used to link a descriptive phrase to a noun:

hóu gwai ge ga-fē	*very expensive coffee, coffee which is very expensive*
máaih-gán bāt ge yàhn	*the person who is buying a pen*
kéuih jyuh ge ūk	*the house that he lives in*

Note how easily Cantonese just uses **ge** to make the link in each case. English has to think what kind of a noun it is and then use the appropriate link word: *the car which, the professor who, the day when, the street where*, and so on. Makes you glad you aren't having to learn English, doesn't it?

4.7 HAVE YOU DONE IT?

To ask if an action has been completed, Cantonese (like English) can use the verb *to have* (**yáuh**):

Néih taai-táai yáuh móuh fàan-heui a?	*Has your wife gone back?*
Kéuih yáuh móuh sihk-faahn a?	*Has he eaten?*

The answer is a simple **yáuh** *yes* or **móuh** *no*.

4.8 MORE ON CLASSIFIERS

In Unit 2 we met classifiers used with numbers and with specifying words like *this* and *that*. Some nouns are uncountable – think of water and air for instance – and the classifier to use then is **dī**:

Nī dī sung hóu hóu-sihk.	*This food is delicious.*

Dī is also used as the classifier for all nouns when they are 'plural but uncounted'. Compare the classifiers in the following:

nī go yàhn	*this person*
gó jì bāt	*that pen*
gó ńgh jì bāt	*those five pens*
sàam go Yìng-gwok-yàhn	*three British people*
gó dī yàhn	*those people* (plural but not counted)
bīn dī bāt a?	*which pens?* (plural but not counted)

When a sentence starts with a definite noun (*the pen*, *the food*, *the Americans*) Cantonese uses the appropriate classifier where English uses *the*:

Jì bāt hóu leng.	*The pen is very nice.*
Dī sung m̀h gwai.	*The food is not expensive.*
Dī Méih-gwok-yàhn làih m̀h làih a?	*Are the Americans coming?*

4.9 THE ADVERB DŌU AGAIN

In Unit 1 we met the adverb **dōu** meaning *also*. Other meanings are *all* and *both*. **Dōu** must come immediately before a verb and it obeys a further rule that it must come after the noun it refers to. Note carefully the placing of **dōu** in the following:

Néih yáuh bāt; kéuih dōu yáuh bāt.	*You have a pen, and he has too.*
Ngóh-deih dōu yáuh chē.	*All of us have cars.*

Wòhng Sìn-sàang Wòhng Síu-jé dōu fàan-jó sé-jih-làuh lak.
Both Mr and Miss Wong have gone to the office.

Gó léuhng go Yìng-gwok-yàhn dōu m̀h séung sihk-faahn.
Neither of those two British people wants to eat.

Are you hearing correctly?

 04.03 **Listen to the audio and try to write down the romanization (including the tones) for the pairs of sounds you hear. You can check in the Key to the exercises how well you did, but when you have done that, listen to the audio again with the answers in front of you so as to 'burn in' the correct spellings and sounds together.**

Vocabulary builder 2

 04.04 Listen to the new vocabulary and practise saying it out loud. Then complete the missing English expressions.

FOOD

龍蝦	lùhng-hā	*lobster*
牛肉	ngàuh-yuhk	*beef*
生果	sàang-gwó	*fruit*
沙律	sà-léut	_____
甜品	tìhm-bán	*dessert*
湯	tòng	*soup*

WORD PAIRS

點解？... 因為	dím-gáai? ... yàn-waih	*why? ... because*
因為 ... 所以	yàn-waih ... só-yíh	*because ... therefore*
如果 ... 就	yùh-gwó ... jauh	*if ... _____*

TIME WORDS

今日	gàm-yaht	*today*
朝早	jìu-jóu	*morning; in the morning*
早	jóu	*early*
擒日	kàhm-yaht	*yesterday*

VERBS

當	dong	*to regard as*
介紹	gaai-siuh	*to recommend, introduce*
整	jíng	*to make, prepare*
做生意	jouh-sàang-yi	*to do business, run a business*
識	sīk	*to know how to*
送...俾...	sung X béi Y	*to give X as a present to Y*

BASICS

好味	hóu-meih	*tasty*
再	joi	*in addition, again*
主菜	jyú-choi	*main dish*
垃圾	laahp-saap	*rubbish*
垃圾桶	laahp-saap-túng	*rubbish bin*
唔好	m̀h-hóu	*don't!*
嬲	nàu	*angry*
新鮮	sàn-sìn	*fresh*
少	síu	*few, little*
話	wá	*words, language, speech, saying*

Dialogue 2

 04.05 *Mr Ho tries to order a meal from a waiter.*

1 Look out for juhng yáuh m̀h síu in the dialogue. Can you think of another way of saying that?

Ho	M̀h-gòi, ngóh séung yiu yāt go tòng. Néih-deih ge tòng sàn m̀h sàn-sìn a?	*Excuse me, I'd like to order a soup. Is your soup fresh?*
Waiter	Sìn-sàang, néih yiu go ngàuh-yuhk tòng lā. Hóu sàn-sìn ga.	*Sir, you should order the beef soup. It's very fresh.*
Ho	Hóu, ngóh jauh yiu go ngàuh-yuhk tòng. Jyú-choi yáuh māt-yéh hóu gaai-siuh a?	*Alright, I'll have the beef soup. What have you to recommend as a main course?*
Waiter	Lùhng-hā-faahn lā, hóu hóu-meih ge. Yùh-gwó néih yiu nī go faahn, ngóh-deih sung sàang-gwó sà-léut béi néih.	*The lobster rice, it's very tasty. And if you order it we give you a complimentary fruit salad.*
Ho	Dím-gáai sung sàang-gwó sà-léut a?	*Why are you giving away fruit salad?*
Waiter	Yàn-waih ngóh-deih ge chyùh-fóng kàhm-yaht jíng-jó taai dò, gàm-yaht juhng yáuh m̀h síu, só-yíh jauh sung béi néih sihk lā.	*It's because yesterday our chef made too much, and there's still quite a lot left today, so we give it away to you.*
Ho	Néih-deih kàhm-yaht jíng ge sàang-gwó sà-léut gàm-yaht béi ngóh sihk, néih sīk m̀h sīk jouh-sàang-yi ga?	*You give me yesterday's fruit salad today … do you know how to do business?*
Waiter	Sìn-sàang, néih m̀h-hóu nàu. Ngóh joi sung gàm-jìu-jóu jíng ge tìhm-bán béi néih, hóu ma? Juhng haih hóu hóu-meih ga.	*Don't be cross, sir. I'll give you some dessert that was made this morning as well, OK? It's still very tasty.*
Ho	Māt-yéh wá? Kàhm-yaht ge sàang-gwó sà-léut; gàm-jìu-jóu ge tìhm-bán! Néih dong ngóh haih laahp-saap-túng àh!	*What? Yesterday's fruit salad, this morning's dessert! Do you think I'm a rubbish bin?*

何	唔該，我想要一個湯。你哋嘅湯新唔新鮮呀？
侍應	先生，你要個牛肉湯啦。好新鮮㗎。
何	好，我就要個牛肉湯。主菜有乜嘢好介紹呀？
侍應	龍蝦飯啦，好好味嘅。如果你要呢個飯，我哋送生果沙律俾你。
何	點解送生果沙律呀？
侍應	因為我哋嘅廚房擒日整咗太多，今日重有唔少，所以就送俾你食啦。
何	你哋擒日整嘅生果沙律今日俾我食，你識唔識做生意㗎？
侍應	先生，你唔好嬲。我再送今朝早整嘅甜品俾你，好嗎？重係好好味㗎。
何	乜嘢話？擒日嘅生果沙律；今朝早嘅甜品！你當我係垃圾桶吖！

> **LANGUAGE TIP**
> You have just learned **jyú-choi** for *main dish*. **Choi** really means *vegetables*: **Kéuih séung sihk yuhk, m̀h séung sihk choi** *She wants to eat meat, not vegetables*. But it also means *a type of food*, or *cuisine*: **Gàm-yaht ngóh séung sihk Faat-gwok choi** *I'd like to have French food today.*

2 In this dialogue the waiter is very keen to say how good the food is. Suppose Mr Ho, who is clearly in a bad mood, tries it and doesn't agree. How would he say *All this food tastes very nasty?*

3 Pair Practice: Translate into Cantonese.
   a If you go, I'll go.
   b Because I'm French I can cook French food very well.
   c Why doesn't she want to go to the restaurant: is it because she doesn't want to eat anything?

Language discovery

4.10 M̀H-GÒI AND POLITENESS

You know that **m̀h-gòi** means *thank you*, but you should note that **m̀h-gòi** or **m̀h-gòi néih** can also be used to mean *please*. And quite often **m̀h-gòi** is used to attract someone's attention, rather as we might say *Excuse me …*, and you will see that Mr Ho calls the waiter over at the beginning of the dialogue with a masterful **M̀h-gòi!** So **m̀h-gòi** is a kind of all-purpose expression of politeness.

> **POLITENESS TO WAITERS**
> A word of caution. You will certainly hear waiters addressed and referred to as **fó-gei** 伙記. It is a term which was commonly used for non-management people in the workforce, such as factory hands and police constables, but there is a growing tendency to avoid it nowadays on the grounds that it sounds patronizing. We suggest that you should always use the neutral term **m̀h-gòi** to call a waiter over.

4.11 TO GIVE

Sung means *to present, to make a gift*. It usually appears with **béi** which itself means *to give, to give to*. The word order for giving a present to someone is a comfortable one for an English speaker:

Kéuih sung yāt jì bāt béi ngóh.   *He gives a pen to me (as a gift).*

Béi is sometimes used on its own to mean *to present*, but it is more commonly found meaning just *to give to, to hand over to*:

Kéuih béi yāt jì bāt ngóh.   *He hands a pen to me / hands me a pen.*

4.12 DON'T!

To tell someone not to do something, Cantonese uses **m̀h-hóu** *it's not good to …* or **néih m̀h-hóu** *it's not good that you should …*:

M̀h-hóu heui!   *Don't go!*
Néih m̀h-hóu máaih chē!   *Don't buy a car!*

4.13 SHORTCUTS

Cantonese is a lively, quick-fire language and speakers often find ways of shortening phrases which seem to them to be tediously long. Here are a couple of shortened forms of phrases which you have met so far:

gàm-yaht jìu-jóu → **gàm-jìu-jóu** or even shorter → **gàm-jìu**

m̀h-hóu → **máih** *don't* (**máih** is a little ruder because it is so abrupt sounding)

What do you think the 'tediously long' versions of these shortened phrases might be?

Wòhng Sàang

Wòhng Táai

> **LANGUAGE TIP**
> Chinese soups tend to be very liquid and thin (but not tasteless), so naturally enough they are 'drunk' not 'eaten' – **yám tòng** 飲湯 – and it is not uncommon to see people spooning most of it, then picking up the bowl and drinking the remainder.

Some more things *to eat* (**sihk**) …

豬肉	**jyù-yuhk**	*pork*
麵	**mihn**	*noodles*
粥	**jūk**	*congee, rice gruel*
青菜	**chèng-choi**	*green vegetables*
蕃茄	**fàan-ké**	*tomatoes*
雞	**gāi**	*chicken*
薑	**gèung**	*ginger*

… and *to drink* (**yám**)

牛奶	**ngàuh-náaih**	*milk*
水	**séui**	*water*
汽水	**hei-séui**	*pop, soda*
橙汁	**cháang-jāp**	*orange juice*
咖啡	**ga-fē**	*coffee*
啤酒	**bē-jáu**	*beer*
酒	**jáu**	*any alcoholic drink*

Listen and understand

04.06 **Listen to the audio as many times as you need to and write down the English translation. Don't check the answers at the back until you've finished.**

🔓 Practice

1 **Make meaningful sentences from the jumbled words. You have done exercises like this before, but it gets more difficult now that you know more complicated patterns.**

   a Hòh Taai-táai séung Wòhng Sìn-sàang sihk-faahn dáng yāt-chàih.

   b chyùh-fóng hái jyú-gán faahn Hòh Taai-táai.

   c ma? mahn Wòhng Sìn-sàang Hòh Taai-táai hóu-meih jyú ge sung kéuih.

   d sáu Hòh Taai-táai Hòh Sìn-sàang yáuh a? móuh bòng.

   e jyú ge sung jáu-làuh yāt-yeuhng ge hóu-chíh Hòh Taai-táai.

2 **Try to answer these questions in Cantonese.**

   a Néih sīk m̀h sīk jyú ngàuh-yuhk tòng a? (Answer: *Yes*)

   b Néih ūk-kéi fuh-gahn yáuh móuh jáu-làuh a? (Answer: *No*)

   c Kàhm-yaht néih yáuh móuh bòng néih màh-mā sáu jyú-faahn a? (Answer: *No*)

   d Dím-gáai néih gàm-jìu-jóu gam nàu a? (Answer: *I'm not*)

   e Néih jí-haih sīk jouh sàang-yi m̀h sīk jyú-faahn, haih m̀h haih a? (Answer: *It's not so*)

3 **There's an oddity or error in each of the following. Can you spot it?**

   a Ngàuh-yuhk tòng haih tìhm-bán.

   b Dī sung hóu sàn-sìn, ngóh m̀h séung sihk.

   c Hái Bāk-gìng jyuh ge Jùng-gwok yàhn m̀h dò.

   d Néih yáuh m̀h yáuh Méih-gwok chē a?

   e Wòhng Síu-jé Hòh Síu-jé yih go yàhn dōu haih Jùng-gwok yàhn.

a Hái chyùh-fóng yáuh māt-yéh a?
  See how many answers you can make up along the lines of: **Hái chyùh-fóng yáuh lùhng-hā, dōu yáuh …**
b Hái chyùh-fóng yáuh móuh laahp-saap-túng a?
  If your answer is *yes*, try to explain it. If your answer is *no*, think again but less seriously!

買嘢 *Máaih-yéh*
Shopping

In this unit you will learn about:
- both ... and.
- *colours.*
- *days of the week.*
- Let me ...
- *more classifiers.*
- *more verb endings.*
- *prices.*
- *ways to say* thank you.

CEFR: *(A2) Can ask about things and make simple transactions in shops; can give and receive information about quantities, numbers, prices, etc.*

Colour symbolism in Chinese culture

The dominant colour in Chinese culture is **hùhng** 紅 *red*. It stands for happiness and good luck. Brides traditionally have dressed in red and wept into red handkerchiefs, their grooms wear red sashes, and the house where they set up home is decorated with auspicious sayings written on red paper. **Baahk** 白 *white* is the colour for funerals (although people also wear a flash of something red about them in order to offset the ill luck which surrounds death and burial). **Wòhng** 黃 *yellow* was the Imperial colour, and the roofs of the Forbidden City in Beijing are still covered with yellow tiles: yellow also stands for China, probably because it is the colour of the loess soil which covers the northern homeland of the Chinese.

A geography test! The yellow loess soil of Northern China gets carried along by the _____ River and deposited in the _____ Sea.

Vocabulary builder 1

 05.01 **Listen to the new vocabulary and practise saying it out loud.**

SHOP TALK

大減價	daaih-gáam-ga	*sale*
平	pèhng	*cheap*
舖頭	pou-táu	*shop* (cl: **gàan**)

CLOTHING

次貨	chi-fo	*seconds, discards*
款式	fún-sīk	*style*
件	gihn	cl: *for most items of clothing*
紅色嘅	hùhng-sīk ge	*red*
質地	jāt-déi	*quality*
顏色	ngàahn-sīk	*colour*
衫裙	sāam-kwàhn	*dress* (cl: **gihn**)

VERBS AND VERB ENDINGS

等	dáng	*to let, allow*
……吓	-háh	ve: *to have a little …*
睇	tái	*to look at*
入	yahp	*to enter*

BASICS

丫嗎	ā-ma	fp: *you should realize, don't you know*
噃!	bo!	fp: *let me remind you, I'll have you know*
其他	kèih-tà	*other*
爛	laahn	*broken, damaged*
禮拜日	Láih-baai-yaht	*Sunday*
禮拜一	Láih-baai-yāt	*Monday*
咩?	mē?	fp: *do you mean to say that …?*
呢度	nī-douh	*here*
新	sàn	*new; up to date*
少少	síu-síu	*a little bit, somewhat*
嘩!	wà!	*Wow!*
又 … 又 …	yauh … yauh …	*both … and …*
咦	yí	(surprise): *Hello, what's this?*

> **LANGUAGE TIP**
> Be especially careful with the tones on *Sunday* and *Monday*, they need to be very clearly distinguished.

Dialogue 1

> **THE BAD NEWS IS ...**
> We aren't going to spoon-feed you with translations of the dialogues any more. Stay calm and take your time in working out the meaning. Remember that you can always look words up in the Cantonese–English vocabulary if you can't recall their meanings.

 05.02 *Miss Wong and Miss Cheung are shopping in a fashion store.*

1 Look out for hóu m̀h hóu a? It doesn't mean *Are you well?*, so what is it doing there?

Wong	Gàm-yaht haih Láih-baai-yāt, m̀h haih Láih-baai-yaht, dím-gáai nī gàan pou-táu gam dò yàhn nē?
Cheung	Nī gàan pou-táu daaih-gáam-ga ā-ma. Ngóh-deih yahp-heui tái-háh, hóu m̀h hóu a?
Wong	Hóu a. Wà! Néih tái, gó gihn sāam-kwàhn jàn-haih hóu pèhng bo!
Cheung	Haih bo. Jāt-déi yauh hóu; fún-sīk yauh sàn; ngàahn-sīk yauh leng: jàn-haih hóu lak.
Wong	Gám, ngóh jauh máaih nī gihn lā.
Cheung	Ngóh dōu séung máaih gó gihn hùhng-sīk ge.
Wong	Yí, nī-douh yáuh síu-síu laahn-jó bo!
Cheung	Haih mē? Où! Haih bo! Ngóh nī gihn dōu yáuh síu-síu laahn-jó. Dáng ngóh tái-háh kèih-tà ge yáuh móuh laahn nē.
Wong	M̀h-sái tái la, gihn-gihn dōu yáuh síu-síu laahn ge, yàn-waih kéuih-deih dōu haih chi-fo, só-yíh gam pèhng.

王	今日係禮拜一，唔係禮拜日，點解呢間舖頭咁多人呢？
張	呢間舖頭大減價吖嗎。我哋入去睇吓，好唔好呀？
王	好呀，嘩！你睇，嗰件衫裙真係好平嗬！
張	係嗬。質地又好；款式又新；顏色又靚；真係好嘞。
王	噉，我就買呢件啦。
張	我都想買嗰件紅色嘅。
王	咦，呢度有少少爛咗嗬。
張	係咩？噢！係嗬！我呢件都有少少爛咗。等我睇吓其他嘅有冇爛呢。
王	唔駛睇喇，件件都有少少爛嘅，因為佢哋都係次貨，所以咁平。

2 Answer in Cantonese.

a Wòhng Síu-jé gó gihn sāam-kwàhn pèhng m̀h pèhng a? Leng m̀h leng a?

b Wòhng Síu-jé gó gihn sāam-kwàhn yáuh móuh laahn ga? Jèung Síu-jé gó gihn nē?

> **LANGUAGE TIP**
> Does **nī-douh** ring a bell with you? Remember **bīn-douh?** *where?* in Unit 3? **Bīn-douh** literally means *which place?*, so **nī-douh** means *this place*, *here*, and we won't insult you by asking you to guess what **gó-douh** means.

Language discovery

5.1 NĒ? AGAIN

You have met **nē?** as a final particle which asks a follow-up question (see Unit 1). It is also used after rhetorical questions, that is when you do not expect an answer or perhaps when you are wondering to yourself:

Gó go yàhn haih bīn-go nē?   *I wonder who that can be?*

YOUR TURN There are two examples of nē? in the dialogue. How would you translate those sentences?

5.2 DAYS OF THE WEEK

The good news is that the Cantonese have a very straightforward way of naming the days. There are two words for *week*, **sìng-kèih** ('star-period') and **láih-baai** ('ritual worship'). Both of these are common, so you can please yourself which you use. *One week* is **yāt go láih-baai** or **yāt go sìng-kèih**. *Monday* is the first day, and so it is called 'Star-period one' (**Sìng-kèih-yāt**) or 'Ritual worship one' (**Láih-baai-yāt**), *Wednesday* is the third day and is called **Láih-baai-sàam** or **Sìng-kèih-sàam**, and so on through to Saturday. *Sunday* goes a bit haywire and is called 'Star-period sun' **Sìng-kèih-yaht** 星期日 or **Láih-baai-yaht** (sometimes contracted to just **Láih-baai**).

05.03 Here are the days of the week in order. Repeat them after the voice and watch out for the tones on the numbers – it is all too easy to make the mistake of repeating the same tone as in the previous line.

星期一	Sìng-kèih-yāt	or	禮拜一	Láih-baai-yāt	Monday
星期二	Sìng-kèih-yih	or	禮拜二	Láih-baai-yih	Tuesday
星期三	Sìng-kèih-sàam	or	禮拜三	Láih-baai-sàam	Wednesday
星期四	Sìng-kèih-sei	or	禮拜四	Láih-baai-sei	Thursday
星期五	Sìng-kèih-ńgh	or	禮拜五	Láih-baai-ńgh	Friday
星期六	Sìng-kèih-luhk	or	禮拜六	Láih-baai-luhk	Saturday
星期日	Sìng-kèih-yaht	or	禮拜日	Láih-baai-yaht	Sunday

 You now know how to say *Tuesday* in Cantonese, but what about *two weeks*?

5.3 COMING AND GOING

Làih *to come* and **heui** *to go* are often used with other verbs of movement to show which direction the movement is in. For instance:

fàan	*to return*	**yahp**	*to enter*
fàan-heui	*to go back*	**yahp-heui**	*to go in*

 What do **fàan-làih** and **yahp-làih** mean?

5.4 ANOTHER VERB ENDING: -HÁH

In Unit 4 you met the verb endings **-jó** and **-gán**. Another one is **-háh**, which gives the idea of doing something for a bit:

tái-háh	*to have a glance at (look a bit)*
dáng-háh	*to wait for a moment (wait a bit)*
chóh-háh	*to sit for a while (sit a bit)*

> **REMEMBER**
> ▶ **Dōu** can mean *also* or *all / both*, but in all cases it is necessary to place it after what it refers to and directly in front of the verb. It is one of a number of 'fixed adverbs' which can only ever appear before a verb. English can say *Me too!*, but that would be impossible to translate using **dōu**, because there is no verb for it to come before.
> ▶ Every noun has its classifier. When nouns are singular (*one American*) or plural and counted (*four pens, six people*), the appropriate classifier must be used. When they are plural but uncounted (*those pens, which people?*) they all take **dī** as the classifier.

5.5 YAUH ... YAUH ... *BOTH ... AND ...*

Yauh basically means *furthermore* and it is an adverb. It has to obey the rule for such adverbs and come in front of a verb (see **dōu** in Units 1 and 4), even when it is being repeated to give the meaning *both ... and ...* In the dialogue you can see that it does obey (the three verbs are **hóu** *to be good*, **sàn** *to be new* and **leng** *to be pretty*). If you bear that rule in mind you will easily understand why the translation of *both Mr and Mrs Wong are going* might be **Wòhng Sìn-sàang yauh heui, Wòhng Taai-táai yauh heui**.

5.6 COLOURS

Hùhng means *red*, but it is most easily used in combination with **sīk** *colour* as **hùhng-sīk** *red-coloured*. **Ge** is added to link **hùhng-sīk** with a noun (see Unit 4).

Kéuih ge chē haih māt-yéh ngàahn-sīk ga?	*What colour is his car?*
Haih hùhng-sīk ge.	*It's a red one.*

or

Haih hùhng-sīk ge chē.	*It's a red car.*

The rest of the colours all work with **-sīk** in the same way as **hùhng**:

白色	**baahk-sīk**	*white*	橙色	**cháang-sīk**	*orange*
灰色	**fūi-sīk**	*grey*	咖啡色	**(ga-)fē-sīk**	*brown*
金色	**gām-sīk**	*gold*	黑色	**hāak-sīk** or **hāk-sīk**	*black*
紅色	**hùhng-sīk**	*red*	紫色	**jí-sīk**	*purple*
藍色	**làahm-sīk**	*blue*	綠色	**luhk-sīk**	*green*
銀色	**ngàhn-sīk**	*silver*	黃色	**wòhng-sīk**	*yellow*

You will notice that the word for *brown*, ga-fē 咖啡, is literally *coffee colour*. So, why do you think what English calls a *brown cow* Cantonese calls a **wòhng-ngàuh** and *dark tan shoes* are deemed to be **hùhng-sīk**?

5.7 FINAL PARTICLE MĒ?

If you want to express great incredulity in a question in English (*You can speak 56 languages fluently?!*), you raise your voice almost to a squeak at the end of the question; but, of course, it is less easy to do that in Cantonese because of the need to observe tones. **Mē?** does the job for you. It indicates great surprise, astonishment, near disbelief: *Surely that's not the case, is it?*, *Do you mean to say that …?* The answer given is almost always **haih** or **m̀h haih** (*it is the case* or *it is not the case*).

5.8 DÁNG AGAIN

Dáng means *to wait*, as you saw in Unit 4. **Dáng ngóh** means *wait for me* or *wait for me to*, and so **dáng ngóh sihk-faahn** means *wait for me to eat*. From *wait for me to eat* to *let me eat* is not a big jump and you will find that Cantonese often uses **dáng ngóh** where English would say *let me …*

Generally, if **dáng ngóh** comes at the beginning of a sentence it is likely to be used in the sense *of let me …* ; and if it comes embedded in a sentence then it is likely to mean *wait for*:

Dáng ngóh bòng néih sáu.	*Let me help you.*
M̀h-hóu dáng ngóh sihk-faahn.	*Don't wait for me to eat.*

In restaurants you will often hear Chinese customers vying with each other to pay the bill, the winner gaining in face what he/she loses in pocket. The standard wording used is **Dáng ngóh béi!** *Let me pay!* (lit. 'Let me give!') You too can play that game, but be sure you have the money about you in case you should be (un)lucky enough to win!

5.9 DOUBLE CLASSIFIERS

Doubling-up classifiers and adding **dōu** all before the verb is a useful way of conveying the idea *every one of, each one of*:

Gàan-gàan ūk dōu hóu leng.   *All the houses are very nice.*
Jì-jì Méih-gwok bāt dōu gwai.   *All the American pens are expensive.*
Gihn-gihn sāam-kwàhn dōu m̀h pèhng.   *None of the dresses is cheap.*

Note how the translations of these examples build on the usage of the classifier to show definite reference (*the houses, the pens, the dresses*) that you met in Unit 4.

Vocabulary builder 2

 05.04 **Listen to the new vocabulary and practise saying it out loud.**

HOW MUCH?

錢	chín	*money*
斤	gàn	*catty (approx. 20 ounces avoirdupois)*
幾多？	géi-dō?	*how much? how many?*
蚊	mān	*dollar*
免費	míhn-fai	*free of charge*

VERBS

死	séi	*to die; dead*
會	wúih	*to be able to, know how to*
游水	yàuh-séui	*to swim*

BASICS

得	dāk	*OK, acceptable, 'can do'*
點樣？	dím-yéung?	*how? in what way?*
多謝（你）	dò-jeh (néih)	*thank you*
檔口	dong-háu	*street stall*
嘅喇	ge-la	fp: giving strong emphasis
蝦	hā	*prawn* (cl: **jek**)
隻	jek	cl: for animals
即係	jīk-haih	*that is precisely, that is to say*
嗱	nàh	*there, here you are, here it is, look*
細	sai	*small*

> **LANGUAGE TIP**
> **Wúih** means *to know how to*. In this usage it is interchangeable with **sīk**, which you met in Unit 4. So **sīk yàuh-séui** and **wúih yàuh-séui** both mean *know how to swim*.

Dialogue 2

 05.05 *Miss Cheung gets a bargain (perhaps) from the fish seller in the market.*

1 Why is Miss Cheung not happy with her purchase?

Cheung	Nī dī hā géi-dō chín yāt gàn a?
Seller	Baat-sahp-ńgh mān yāt gàn.
Cheung	Nī dī hā gam sai, baat-sahp-ńgh mān yāt gàn taai gwai lak. Chāt-sahp mān yāt gàn dāk m̀h dāk a?
Seller	M̀h dāk! Síu-jé, néih tái, jek-jek hā dōu hóu sàn-sìn wúih yàuh-séui. Baat-sahp-ńgh mān yāt gàn m̀h gwai ge-la.
Cheung	Gó-douh ge dong-háu jí-haih yiu chāt-sahp-yih mān yāt gàn jē. Dím-gáai néih-deih yiu baat-sahp-ńgh mān yāt gàn a?
Seller	Yàn-waih ngóh-deih haih 'máaih-yāt-sung-yāt' ā-ma.
Cheung	Dím-yéung máaih-yāt-sung-yāt a?
Seller	Jīk-haih máaih yāt gàn hā, mihn-fai sung yāt gàn hā lā.
Cheung	Hóu! Ngóh yiu yāt gàn lā. Nàh, nī-douh baat-sahp-ńgh mān.
Seller	Dò-jeh. Nàh, nī-douh léuhng gàn hā.
Cheung	Dím-gáai gam dò séi hā ga?
Seller	Máaih yāt gàn yàuh-séui hā, sung yāt gàn séi hā ā-ma.

張	呢啲蝦幾多錢一斤呀?
檔主	八十五蚊一斤。
張	呢啲蝦咁細，八十五蚊一斤太貴嘞。七十蚊一斤得唔得呀?
檔主	唔得! 小姐，你睇，隻隻蝦都好新鮮會游水。八十五蚊一斤唔貴嘅喇。
張	嗰度嘅檔口只係要七十二蚊一斤啫。點解你哋要八十五蚊一斤呀?
檔主	因為我哋係 '買一送一' 丫嗎。
張	點樣買一送一呀?
檔主	即係買一斤蝦，免費送一斤蝦啦。
張	好! 我要一斤啦。嗱，呢度八十五蚊。
檔主	多謝。嗱，呢度兩斤蝦。
張	點解咁多死蝦㗎?
檔主	買一斤游水蝦，送一斤死蝦丫嗎。

 2 05.06 **Answer these questions on the dialogue in Cantonese.**

    a Jèung Síu-jé hái dong-háu séung máaih māt-yéh a?

    b Dī hā géi-dō chín yāt gàn a?

    c Kèih-tà dong-háu ge hā, géi-dō chín yāt gàn a?

 3 Here's a hard one. If we tell you that there are 16 Chinese ounces (léung 兩) in one catty, can you think of an English expression which has a similar construction to and the same meaning as Bun-gàn baat-léung 半斤八兩?

Language discovery

5.10 SO MUCH EACH

Note the simple formula for giving prices:

Géi-dō chín yāt gàn a?	*How much per catty?*
Léuhng mān yāt gàn.	*$2 a catty.*

The same kind of formula can be used with other terms:

Sāam-kwàhn luhk-sahp mān yāt gihn.	*Dresses cost $60 each.*
Yāt go yàhn sàam jì bāt.	*Three pens per person.*

5.11 SEAFOOD

You have met the *prawn* (**hā**) and his big brother the *lobster* (**lùhng-hā,** lit. 'dragon-prawn'). Time to meet some of the other salt-water harvest that Cantonese chefs are so brilliant with:

蝦	**hā**	*prawn* (cl: **jek**)	**léuhng jek hā**	兩隻蝦
蟹	**háaih**	*crab* (cl: **jek**)	**yāt jek háaih**	一隻蟹
鱔	**síhn**	*eel* (cl: **tìuh**)	**sàam tìuh síhn**	三條鱔
魚	**yú**	*fish* (cl: **tìuh**)	**sei tìuh yú**	四條魚

The word for *seafood* is **hói-sīn** 海鮮 (lit. 'sea fresh'), and there are plenty of **hói-sīn jáu-làuh** 海鮮酒樓 throughout Hong Kong and wherever there are Cantonese people.

5.12 *HOW ABOUT IT?* AGAIN

In Unit 2 you met **hóu m̀h hóu a?** as a way of asking someone's opinion after making a statement. **Dāk m̀h dāk a?** is perhaps even more commonly used for the same purpose, meaning *will that do?, is that OK by you?, are you happy with that?*

How would you answer Dāk m̀h dāk a? (yes and no)

5.13 THANK YOU

You have now met two words for *thank you*: **m̀h-gòi** and **dò-jeh**. They are used in different ways and it is important to try to sort them out.

M̀h-gòi is used for everyday minor politenesses, such as thanking someone for holding a door open for you, for passing you the soy sauce or for doing the washing-up.

Dò-jeh is used for more heartfelt thanks, for example in gratitude to someone for a present received, for saving your life or for finding you a job. It is always used when receiving money.

So, when you take the goods from a shopkeeper, you may or may not say **m̀h-gòi** (depending on how polite you feel like being), but they will certainly say **dò-jeh** when they take your money. The polite response to someone who thanks you is **m̀h-sái** *there's no need to*. The longer forms **m̀h-sái m̀h-gòi** and **m̀h-sái dò-jeh** can be used too.

Listen and understand

05.07 Listen to the passage as many times as you need to understand it, then answer the questions. At the back of the book you will find the text of the passage, as well as model answers.

1 You will have heard hóu-séung 好想 and hóu-sīk 好識. Hóu of course is the word for *good*, but what does it do to séung and sīk?

2 Answer the questions in Cantonese.
   a Ngóh tùhng bīn-go heui máaih-yéh a?
   b Ngóh-deih séung máaih māt-yéh a?
   c Taai-táai dím-gáai m̀h máaih a?
   d Taai-táai m̀h sīk máaih-yéh, haih m̀h haih a?

Practice

1 Untangle this web. Nothing is in the right place. Translate the verbs into Cantonese and then assign them to their correct tone slots:
   a To buy _____   1 High level
   b To come _____   2 Mid rising
   c To look for _____   3 Mid level
   d To know how to _____   4 Low rising
   e To go _____   5 Low level
   f To use _____   6 Low falling

2 Supply the appropriate Cantonese final particles.
   a You live in a mansion? I'm in a tiny wooden shack _____.
   b Is your salary adequate _____?
   c Go on, be nice and buy me an ice cream, go on _____.
   d I'm right, aren't I? Wasn't it last year that he emigrated _____?
   e You climbed Everest three times in one week _____?

3 Give the opposites for the following. If you don't know the precise word, find a way round it – it's very good practice for not getting stuck when you are talking with people.
   a pèhng   e laahn
   b leng   f dò
   c sai   g heui
   d dāk

4 **Insert the bracketed element to make a sentence which is still meaningful. For example, the answer to the first question would be: Hùhng-sīk ge Méih-gwok chē hóu gwai.**

   a Méih-gwok chē hóu gwai. (hùhng-sīk ge)

   b Ngóh sīk yàuh-séui. (bàh-bā)

   c Wòhng Taai-táai heui máaih-yéh. (pou-táu)

   d Kéuih gàm-yaht m̀h sihk-faahn. (séung)

   e Hòh Sàang m̀h sihk Hòh Táai jyú ge sung. (Taai-)

5 **Here is a test of your understanding of classifiers. See if you can choose the correct classifier to complete each sentence. Beware that there are two trick sentences, so you will need to keep your wits about you!**

   a Gó _____ ūk haih Hòh Sìn-sàang ge.

   b Kéuih ge _____ sāam-kwàhn yáuh síu-síu laahn-jó.

   c Wòhng Síu-jé ge bàh-bā m̀h haih _____ Jùng-gwok-yàhn.

   d Nī _____ Méih-gwok bāt hóu gwai.

   e Gó _____ lùhng-hā dōu hóu daaih.

   f _____ _____ hā dōu séi-jó.

6 **Now try your mathematical skills!**

   a Lùhng-hā sahp-sei mān yāt jek. Wòhng Táai máaih-jó léuhng jek. Kéuih yiu béi géi-dō chín a?

   b Dī hā m̀h gwai: sàam-sahp-yih mān yāt gàn, máaih yāt gàn sung bun gàn. Wòhng Táai yiu sàam gàn – kéuih yiu béi géi-dō chín a?

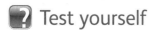 Test yourself

Translate into Cantonese:

a Do you know how to swim?

b Please have a little look at my car. Is it damaged?

c The pen he is buying is a purple one.

d Where in Japan is the house your younger brother lives in?

e Today it's Friday, so I'm going to Kowloon to buy two catties of fish.

交通 *Gàau-tùng*
Getting around

In this unit you will learn about:

▶ *can/may.*
▶ *compass directions.*
▶ *different kinds of time.*

▶ *means of transport.*
▶ *ordinal numbers.*
▶ *yet more verb endings.*

CEFR: *(A2) Can get simple information about travel, use of public transport; can ask for and give directions.*

Finding your way

In many cities in China directions are given in compass terms (*turn north, go three blocks west*), but in Hong Kong this is not so common, perhaps because of the twists and turns of the natural landscape. Still, the compass directions are very handy, and quite a few place names reflect that. The basic words you need are:

東 **dùng** *east*　　南 **nàahm** *south*　　西 **sài** *west*　　北 **bāk** *north*

Cantonese lists the four directions in the order given here, while English speakers normally start with north.

The intermediate directions (*northeast*, etc.) are straightforward provided you remember that they are systematically different from the English versions.

 Looking at the compass, can you spot that difference?

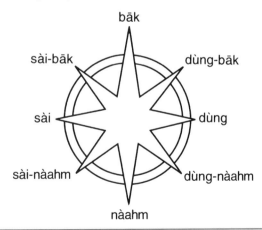

Vocabulary builder 1

 06.01 Listen to the new vocabulary and practise saying it out loud. Then complete the missing English expressions.

PUBLIC TRANSPORT

巴士站	bā-sí-jaahm	_____ *stop*
地下鐵路	deih-hah-tit-louh	*underground railway*
地鐵站	deih-tit-jaahm	*underground* _____
飛機	fèi-gèi	*aircraft* (cl: **ga**)
飛機場	fèi-gèi-chèuhng	*airport*
街口 / 路口	gàai-háu / louh-háu	*road junction*
落	lohk	*to alight from, disembark*
馬路	máh-louh	*main road* (cl: **tìuh**)
上	séuhng	*to board, get onto*
小巴	síu-bā	*minibus* (cl: **ga**)
船	syùhn	*ship, boat* (cl: **jek**)

> **LANGUAGE TIP**
> **Deih-hah-tit-louh** is far too much of a mouthful for most people, so it is usually shortened to **deih-tit**.

POLITENESS

| 請問 | chéng-mahn | *please, may I ask …?* |

VERBS

到	dou	*to arrive, arrive at, reach*
過	gwo	*to go past, go across, go by*
轉	jyun	*to turn; to change to*
話	wah	*to say*

BASICS

但係	daahn-haih	*but*
大會堂	Daaih-wuih-tòhng	*City Hall*
市區	síh-kèui	*urban area*
先	sìn	*first* (adverb or fp)
入口	yahp-háu	*entrance*
一直	yāt-jihk	*straight, directly*
由	yàuh	*from*

Dialogue 1

 06.02 *Mr Wong is a stranger in town and asks a local person the way.*

1 The formula for asking where something or someone is is so useful. Make sure you can find it in the dialogue, and then burn it into your memory – you are bound to need it in a hurry sometime.

Wong	Ngóh yiu daap fèi-gèi fàan Yìng-gwok, chéng-mahn heui fèi-gèi-chèuhng yiu daap géi-dō houh bā-sí a?
Local	Nī-douh móuh bā-sí heui fèi-gèi-chèuhng bo. Néih yiu sìn yàuh nī-douh daap síu-bā yāt-jihk heui, gwo sàam go gàai-háu dou daaih máh-louh, hái bā-sí-jaahm néih yiu lohk síu-bā, joi jyun daap sahp-ńgh houh bā-sí heui fèi-gèi-chèuhng lā.
Wong	Gám, yáuh móuh syùhn heui fèi-gèi-chèuhng nē?
Local	Móuh syùhn heui gèi-chèuhng bo.
Wong	Ngóh hóu séung daap deih-tit. Yáuh móuh deih-tit heui gèi-chèuhng nē?
Local	Dōu móuh bo! Deih-tit jí heui síh-kèui jē.
Wong	Gám, ngóh heui Daaih-wuih-tòhng lā! Yáuh móuh deih-tit heui a? Deih-tit-jaahm hái bīn-douh a?
Local	Yáuh, deih-tit-jaahm ge yahp-háu hái gó-douh, daahn-haih néih wah yiu daap fèi-gèi fàan Yìng-gwok. Hái Daaih-wuih-tòhng móuh chē heui fèi-gèi-chèuhng bo.
王	我要搭飛機返英國，請問去飛機場要搭幾多號巴士呀？
居民	呢度冇巴士去飛機場嘞。你要先由呢度搭小巴一直去，過三個街口到大馬路，喺巴士站你要落小巴，再轉搭十五號巴士去飛機場啦。
王	噉，有冇船去飛機場呢？
居民	冇船去機場嘞。
王	我好想搭地鐵。有冇地鐵去機場呢？
居民	都冇嘞！地鐵只去市區啫。
王	噉，我去大會堂啦！有冇地鐵去呀？地鐵站喺邊度呀？
居民	有，地鐵站嘅入口喺嗰度，但係你話要搭飛機返英國。喺大會堂冇車去飛機場嘞。

2 True or false?

    a Wòhng Sìn-sàang yiu daap fèi-gèi fàan Yìng-gwok.

    b Wòhng Sìn-sàang yiu daap sahp-ńgh houh bā-sí heui fèi-gèi-chèuhng.

    c Yáuh syùhn heui fèi-gèi-chèuhng.

    d Dōu yáuh deih-hah-tit-louh heui fèi-gèi-chèuhng.

    e Daahn-haih móuh deih-tit heui Daaih-wuih-tòhng.

Language discovery

6.1 PLEASE MAY I ASK …?

Chéng-mahn, a combination of *please* and *ask*, is the polite way to begin a question to a stranger and is very useful therefore when asking directions. It is also the respectful way to begin a question to someone of higher status than yourself.

6.2 TO TRAVEL BY

In Unit 3 you were introduced to **daap** *to travel by*, and in the same unit you met **chóh** *to sit*. **Chóh** can actually be used like **daap** to mean *to travel by* as well, probably because when you take transport you sit on it (if you're lucky!). So **daap bā-sí** and **chóh bā-sí** both mean *to travel by bus* and **daap syùhn** and **chóh syùhn** both mean *to take a boat*. Beware, however: you cannot do the opposite and get away with making **daap** mean *to sit*!

6.3 FIRST THIS, THEN THAT

The adverbs *first* and *then* are **sìn** and **joi**. Being adverbs they come before verbs (see Units 1, 4 and 5):

Kéuih sìn heui gèi-chèuhng joi chóh bā-sí fàan ūk-kéi.
First he's going to the airport and then he's taking the bus home.

Sìn can also come at the end of a sentence as a final particle, and it still means *first*:

Dáng ngóh yám dī bē-jáu sìn lā!   *Let me have some beer first!*

6.4 MORE SHORTCUTS

You've seen that the full formal word for an *underground railway*, **deih-hah-tit-louh**, gets reduced to **deih-tit**. Similarly, Hong Kong's Chek Lap Kok airport (赤鱲角 **Chek-laahp-gok fèi-gèi-chèuhng**) is such a common feature of everybody's life that the shortening of the term was almost inevitable. People mostly reduce it to just **gèi-chèuhng**.

> **LANGUAGE TIP**
> To get into an MTR station you find the **yahp-háu** *entrance*. **Yahp-háu** literally means 'enter mouth', and you will not be surprised to learn that the exit, **chēut-háu** 出口, means 'exit mouth'. Both terms are the standard ones on signs in public buildings.

ENTRANCE 入口	EXIT 出口

6.5 WÁ AND WAH

In Unit 4 you met **wá** meaning *speech* or *language*. You can use it with country or regional names very easily to make the names of different languages.

⋮ YOUR TURN What are Gwóng-jàu-wá, Yaht-bún-wá and Yìng-gwok-wá?

Now you meet **wah** with a low level tone meaning *to say*:
Kéuih wah, 'Chéng-mahn, deih-tit-jaahm hái bīn-douh a?'
She said, 'Excuse me, where is the MTR station?'

The word *tell* has various meanings in English, and in the next dialogue you will see that when it means *tell someone something* you can use **wah** with either **tèng** 聽 *to listen to* or **jì** 知 *to know*:
Kéuih wah ngóh tèng kéuih m̀h sīk jà-chē.
He told me he doesn't know how to drive.
Ngóh wah Léih Táai jì gàm-yaht haih Láih-baai-sei.
I tell Mrs Li that today is Thursday.

As you might expect, **wá** and **wah** are closely connected and they both use the same Chinese character, but you should not draw the conclusion that the same kind of tone change from one part of speech to another is common in other words.

Listen and understand

 06.03 Listen to the audio and then translate the conversation into English. The text and translation can be found at the back of the book, but try not to look at them until you have done the exercise.

Vocabulary builder 2

 06.04 Listen to the new vocabulary and practise saying it out loud.

GOING PLACES

參觀	chàam-gwùn	*to visit*
地方	deih-fòng	*place, location, spot*
火車	fó-chè	*railway train*
劍橋大學	Gim-kìuh Daaih-hohk	*Cambridge University*
行	hàhng	*to journey, go towards*
鄉下	hèung-há	*countryside*
揸車	jà chē	*to drive (a vehicle)*
離島	lèih-dóu	*outlying island*
倫敦	Lèuhn-dēun	*London*
世界	sai-gaai	*the world*
漁港	yùh-góng	*fishing port*

VERBS AND VERB ENDINGS

... 過	-gwo	*ve: to have experienced*
好似 ..., 唔似 ...	hóu-chíh X m̀h-chíh Y	*to be more like X than like Y*
可以	hó-yíh	*can, may*
走難	jáu-naahn	*to flee from disaster, be a refugee*
中意	jùng-yi	*to like, be fond of*
送	sung	*to deliver, escort, send*
玩	wáan	*to play, enjoy, amuse oneself*
... 完	-yùhn	*ve: finished*

BASICS

部	bouh	*area, part, portion*
次	chi	*time, occasion*
第 ...	daih-...	*(for ordinal numbers) the first, second, etc.*
向	heung	*towards, facing*
最	jeui	*most*
... 之後	... jì-hauh	*after ...*
... 之內	... jì-noih	*within ...*
... 之一	... jì-yāt	*one of the ...*
主意	jyú-yi	*idea*
老	lóuh	*elderly, aged, old*
晚	máahn	*evening, night*
日	yaht	*day*
有名	yáuh-méng	*famous*

Dialogue 2

1 Can you be an expert? Mr Wong says Ngóh hóu jùng-yi heui hèung-há deih-fòng wáan. How would you translate wáan here? *To play* hardly seems right for an adult; *to play around* doesn't sound like the staid Mr Wong that we know; and *to amuse myself* doesn't really work either. There surely must be a way to translate it …

Wong	Lóuh Chán, ngóh daih-yāt chi làih Lèuhn-dēun, chéng néih wah ngóh tèng <u>heui bīn-douh wáan hóu nē?</u>
Chan	Dáng ngóh daai néih heui wáan lā. Ngóh-deih daap fó-chè sìn heung bāk hàhng, heui chàam-gwùn Gim-kìuh Daaih-hohk.
Wong	Hóu a. Gim-kìuh Daaih-hohk haih <u>sai-gaai jeui yáuh-méng ge daaih-hohk jì yāt</u>.
Chan	Chàam-gwùn-yùhn jì-hauh, ngóh-deih daap bā-sí heui Yìng-gwok dùng bouh tái-háh gó-douh ge hèung-há.
Wong	Hóu jyú-yi. Ngóh hóu jùng-yi heui hèung-há deih-fòng wáan.
Chan	Hái gó-douh ngóh yáuh yāt go hóu pàhng-yáuh, ngóh-deih hó-yíh hái kéuih ūk-kéi jyuh yāt máahn. Daih-yih yaht chéng kéuih jà chē sung ngóh-deih heui <u>Yìng-gwok nàahm bouh ge yùh-góng tái-háh.</u>
Wong	Hèung-góng dōu yáuh yùh-góng, ngóh heui-gwo hóu dò chi lak.
Chan	Ngóh-deih yàuh yùh-góng joi daap syùhn heui lèih-dóu.
Wong	Ngóh m̀h séung heui lèih-dóu lak. Léuhng yaht jì-noih heui <u>gam dò</u> deih-fòng, <u>yauh</u> daap gam noih chē, ngóh wah hóu-chíh jáu-naahn m̀h-chíh heui wáan gám.

王	老陳，我第一次嚟倫敦，請你話我聽去邊度玩好呢？
陳	等我帶你去玩啦。我哋搭火車先向北行，去參觀劍橋大學。
王	好呀。劍橋大學係世界最有名嘅大學之一。
陳	參觀完之後，我哋搭巴士去英國東部睇吓嗰度嘅鄉下。
王	好主意。我好中意去鄉下地方玩。
陳	喺嗰度我有一個好朋友，我哋可以喺佢屋企住一晚。第二日請佢揸車送我哋去英國南部嘅漁港睇吓。
王	香港都有漁港，我去過好多次嘞。
陳	我哋由漁港再搭船去離島。
王	我唔想去離島嘞。兩日之內去咁多地方，又搭咁耐車，我話好似走難唔似去玩嗽。

2 Translate the five underlined words and phrases. You can check in the back to make sure you are right.

3 Answer the questions.

    a Chàhn Sìn-sàang haih m̀h haih daih-yāt chi làih Lèuhn-dēun a?

    b Gim-kìuh Daaih-hohk haih m̀h haih hái Lèuhn-dēun fuh-gahn a?

    c Yìng-gwok dùng bouh yáuh hóu dò yáuh-méng ge yùh-góng, haih m̀h haih a?

    d Chàhn Sìn-sàang hóu jùng-yi heui lèih-dóu wáan, haih m̀h haih a?

Language discovery

6.6 LÓUH

Lóuh means *elderly, aged* and is used only for people and animals (that is, you would not describe a building or a book as **lóuh**). It is often used with the surname as a familiar or affectionate way of addressing or referring to a man (rarely to a woman):

Lóuh Wóng, …   *Wong, old chap, …; Old Wong*

 Did you notice what happens to the surnames when they are combined with lóuh?

6.7 ORDINAL NUMBERS

You met the cardinal numbers (*one, two, three, four*, etc.) in Unit 2. The ordinal numbers (*the first, the second, the third, the fourth*, etc.) are formed by putting **daih-** in front of the cardinal number:

yāt go yàhn   *one person*
daih-yāt go yàhn   *the first person*

You will remember that *two* obeys different rules from other numbers, so that **yih** becomes **léuhng** in front of classifiers. Note that with ordinal numbers there is no such exception:

léuhng go yàhn   *two people*
daih-yih go yàhn   *the second person*

While we are on the subject we might as well look at a couple of other peculiarities of **daih-yih**. It can mean *the next*:

Daih-yih yaht kéuih jáu-jó lak.   *He left the next day (the second day).*

It can also logically extend to mean *the other*:

Ngóh juhng yáuh daih-yih jì bāt.   *I've still got another pen.*

But you need to stretch your mind a little further to take in the notion that **daih-yih** can mean *the others*:

Daih-yih dī bāt dōu haih kéuih ge.   *The other pens are all hers.*

> **REMEMBER**
> ▶ The names of the days of the week are numbered 1–6, **Sìng-kèih-yāt** *Monday* to **Sìng-kèih-luhk** *Saturday*, and then comes **Sìng-kèih-yaht** *Sunday*.
> ▶ To count the weeks you need to use the classifier **go**, so *two weeks* is **léuhng go sìng-kèih** and *12 weeks* is **sahp-yih go sìng-kèih**.
> ▶ Many people say **láih-baai** instead of **sìng-kèih**. The two terms are interchangeable in all the uses you have met here.

6.8 ANOTHER VERB ENDING: -YÙHN *FINISHED*

Yùhn means *the end* or *to finish*. It is used as a verb ending to show that the action of the verb is all over with:

sihk-yùhn	*finished eating*
chàam-gwùn-yùhn	*finished visiting*

6.9 'TIME WHEN'

Time expressions that begin with *after* are translated with **jì-hauh** in Cantonese, but **jì-hauh** is placed at the end of the time expression, not at the beginning:

Néih jáu-jó jì-hauh, kéuih wah ngóh tèng néih m̀h jùng-yi sihk hā.

After you'd gone she told me you don't like prawns.

In the English, *after you'd gone* could come at the end of the sentence (*She told me you don't like prawns after you'd gone*), but with expressions that pinpoint the time when something happens Cantonese likes to have the information before the verb of the main statement is given, so you do not have the option of putting **néih jáu-jó jì-hauh** at the end. Other time-when expressions you have met so far, such as **gàm-yaht** and **Láih-baai-ńgh**, as well as the many you haven't yet met (*at 6 o'clock*; *in May last year*; *when I got there*; *before he had breakfast*; *in 1492*), all obey the same rule:

Láih-baai-luhk néih heui m̀h heui a?	*Are you going on Saturday?*
Ngóh gàm-yaht séung yàuh-séui.	*I'd like to swim today.*

> **LANGUAGE TIP**
> Cantonese word orders can be very strict. The rule for 'time when' is a case in point. You have the option of putting it either before or after the subject, though there may be some difference in emphasis depending on which option you select, but the time-when expression <u>must</u> come somewhere <u>before</u> the verb.

6.10 CAN, ABLE TO

You met **sīk** in Unit 4 and in this unit comes **hó-yíh**: both mean *can, be able*, but they are not usually interchangeable. **Sīk** really means *to have learned how to* and implies that you are able to do something because you have acquired the skill to do it (speak a foreign language, ride a bicycle, eat with chopsticks, etc.). **Hó-yíh** operates in the realm of permission (*may*) and absence of obstacles to doing something:

Néih sīk m̀h sīk jà-chē a?	*Can you drive? (Do you know how to drive?)*
Néih hó-yíh m̀h hó-yíh jà-chē a?	*Can you drive? (Have you a licence? Is the car available?)*

Another way to say *can, be able* is by using the verb ending **-dāk**. This is the same word that you met in Unit 5, but in this use it must go directly onto a verb:

Ngóh m̀h heui-dāk.	*I can't go.*
Kéuih jà-dāk chē.	*He can drive.*

With **-dāk** there is no telling whether he can drive because he knows how to, because his father says he may, because he has his full physical powers or because there is a car available, so it is a good all-purpose way of saying *can*. Do remember though that **-dāk** can only be put onto a verb, not onto any other part of speech. That's why it attaches to **jà**, because even though we translate **jà chē** as *to drive*, in Cantonese it is a verb + noun (*drive + vehicle*) and so **-dāk** cannot attach to **chē**.

> **LANGUAGE TIP**
> And here's a bit of a giggle. The basic meaning of **jà** is *to grasp in the hand*, and *to hold chopsticks* or *to use chopsticks* is **jà faai-jí** 揸筷子 (remember **Héi faai!** from Unit 4?). So **jà chē** conjures up a cartoon-like image of an anxious little man in a Model T Ford hunched over the wheel and clutching it for dear life. Worse, *to fly a plane* is **jà fèi-gèi** – not a reassuring thought for nervous flyers!

6.11 'TIME HOW LONG'

Time expressions which show how long something goes on for (as opposed to the time when something happens) come after the main verb in Cantonese:

daap gam noih chē	*travelling in a car for so long*
Ngóh-deih hái Hèung-góng jyuh léuhng go láih-baai.	*We're staying in Hong Kong for two weeks.*
Kéuih chóh-jó ńgh go jūng-tàuh fèi-gèi.	*He was on the plane for five hours.*

6.12 YET ANOTHER VERB ENDING: -GWO *TO HAVE HAD THE EXPERIENCE*

Gwo literally means *to go past*, as you saw earlier in this unit. As a verb ending **-gwo** shows that the verb has been experienced at some time:

Ngóh sihk-gwo hā.	*I have tried prawns. (I have experienced eating prawns.)*

The following pairs of sentences illustrate the difference between the two verb endings **-jó** and **-gwo**: **-jó**, as we saw in Unit 4, shows that an action has been completed at a particular point in time; **-gwo** shows that an action has occurred at some time or other.

YOUR TURN Translate the -gwo sentences into English.

Kéuih heui-jó Hèung-góng.	*He went to Hong Kong.*
Kéuih heui-gwo Hèung-góng.	_____
Wòhng Taai-táai gàm-yaht tái-jó yī-sāng.	*Mrs Wong went to the doctor's today.*
Néih yáuh móuh tái-gwo yī-sāng a?	_____

Pitch perfect

 06.06 This exercise is designed to contrast the three pitches. Listen to the audio and then repeat the sounds in the pauses which come after each line.

1 私 sì   試 si   事 sih

2 兆 siuh   笑 siu   消 sìu

3 機 gèi   記 gei   技 geih

Just to cleanse the palate as it were, do the same for the following set of six words in each of the major tones:

三 sàam   點 dím   半 bun   嚟 làih   我 ngóh   度 douh

Now comes the tricky bit: go back to line 1 and read it out without first hearing the recorded voice, then listen to the voice, and then repeat again. Do the same for lines 2 and 3. By now you should be able to hear the difference among the three pitches more clearly, and hopefully you'll notice a growing ease and accuracy of pronunciation in your own efforts. This medicine can be taken as often as you feel you want or need it, but read the label carefully – it says 'May induce drowsiness'.

> **PUBLIC TRANSPORT IN HONG KONG**
> Hong Kong has a very comprehensive transport system, including *trams* (**dihn-chè** 電車 cl: **ga**) and even *helicopters* (**jihk-sìng-gèi** 直昇機 cl: **ga**). Hong Kong's *underground railway* (**deih-hah tit-louh**, *the Mass Transit Railway*, usually abbreviated to *MTR*) was opened in 1979, and new extensions are constantly being added. The *Airport Express Line* (**Gèi-chèuhng Faai-sin** 機場快綫) shuttles at up to 135 kph between Chek Lap Kok Airport and the very heart of Hong Kong in *Central District* (**Jùng-wàahn** 中環) near the famous *Star Ferry Pier* (**Tìn-sìng Máh-tàuh** 天星碼頭).

Practice

1 Translate into Cantonese.

  a Today is the first time I've travelled by tram.

  b Crab, prawns, lobster, I don't like any of them. I only like fish.

  c Are there many buses in Beijing? I don't know.

  d That gold dress is very pretty. Whose is it?

  e There are lots of houses in London. I want to buy one, but the big ones are too expensive and the small ones aren't very cheap either.

2 All of the sentences are already complete, but each of them will allow one of the lettered elements to be inserted and still make sense. For example, if you insert element 3 into sentence a you create a new sentence which reads:
Gim-kìuh Daaih-hohk haih sai-gaai jeui yáuh-méng ge daaih-hohk jì-yāt.
Cambridge is one of the most famous universities in the world.

Now try the rest.

a Gim-kìuh Daaih-hohk haih daaih-hohk jì-yāt.

b Yàuh Lèuhn-dēun heui Gim-kìuh Daaih-hohk chàam-gwùn yiu heung bāk hàhng.

c Yàuh nī-douh daap bā-sí heui fèi-gèi-chèuhng yiu géi-dō chín a?

d Nī-douh ge deih-hah-tit-louh jí heui Daaih-wuih-tòhng.

e Néih yiu daap bā-sí heui fèi-gèi-chèuhng.

1 daap chē

2 sahp-ńgh houh

3 sai-gaai jeui yáuh-méng ge

4 m̀h heui fèi-gèi-chèuhng

5 gwo sàam go gàai-háu dou Fà-yùhn Douh

3 How many verbs can you think of that can be sensibly put in front of **chē**? Give yourself three minutes to write out your list (with correct tones), and then check in the back. You may be surprised how many you already know. Tip: You can find one in Exercise 2 to give you a start.

Test yourself

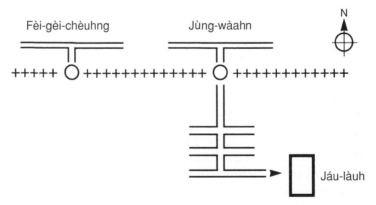

Jèung Sìn-sàang Jèung Taai-táai chéng ngóh sihk-faahn. M̀h-gòi néih wah ngóh tèng yàuh gèi-chèuhng dím-yéung heui jáu-làuh a?

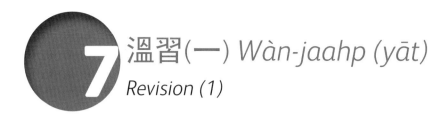

溫習(一) *Wàn-jaahp (yāt)*
Revision (1)

This unit gives you no new vocabulary or grammar rules. Instead it goes back over a lot of the material from the first six units, presenting it in a new way so that you can become more fluent through the extra practice. If you are stuck for any of the words, remember that there are word lists at the end of the course to help you. Units 14, 21 and 26 are also revision units, and just to make sure that you can check on your progress properly you will find translations and answers in the Key to the exercises.

 Passage 1

Read this passage out loud.

Kàhm-yaht màh-mā mahn ngóh-deih séung m̀h séung sihk sà-léut? Ngóh-deih go-go dōu wah hóu séung sihk. Màh-mā wah, 'Hóu hóu, ngóh jauh jíng lùhng-hā sà-léut béi néih-deih sihk lā. Nàh, yìh-gā ngóh heui máaih lùhng-hā, néih-deih heui máaih dī sàn-sìn sàang-gwó fàan-làih lā.' Ngóh-deih máaih-jó hóu dò sàn-sìn sàang-gwó fàan ūk-kéi, yauh yāt-chàih hái chyùh-fóng yuh-beih gó dī sàang-gwó. Bun go jūng-tàuh jì-hauh màh-mā fàan-làih lak. Kéuih wah, 'Gàm-yaht dī lùhng-hā yauh sai yauh m̀h sàn-sìn, só-yíh ngóh móuh máaih, jí-haih máaih-jó dī daaih hā jē. Néih-deih jauh sihk daaih hā sà-léut dong lùhng-hā sà-léut lā!'

 07.01 Now listen to the audio, then read the passage again, and finally just listen to the voice again, trying to translate what you hear into English in your head. Only check the translation when you think you have understood it all or have reached a point where you are completely stuck.

1 True or false?
   a Kàhm-yaht màh-mā wah kéuih hóu séung sihk sà-léut.
   b Màh-mā jeui sīk jíng lùhng-hā sà-léut.
   c Ngóh-deih máaih-jó hóu dò sàn-sìn sàang-gwó fàan ūk-kéi.
   d Màh-mā máaih-jó yāt jek hóu daaih ge lùhng-hā.
   e Màh-mā kàhm-yaht jíng ge lùhng-hā sà-léut hóu hóu-meih.

2 Answer in Cantonese.
   a Màh-mā máaih-jó māt-yéh fàan ūk-kéi a?
   b Ngóh-deih máaih-jó māt-yéh fàan ūk-kéi a?
   c Kàhm-yaht dī lùhng-hā sàn m̀h sàn-sìn a?
   d Néih sīk m̀h sīk jíng sà-léut a?
   e Hái néih ūk-kéi fuh-gahn ge jáu-làuh yáuh móuh sà-léut maaih a?

3 **Translate into Cantonese.**

  a Have you ever tasted beef salad?

  b This American pen is one of the pens I most want to buy.

  c This is the first time I've been to your office.

4 **07.02 Eavesdrop on the phone conversation on the audio. You can only hear one end of them: see if you can guess and say (out loud) what the other end might be.**

X	**a**
Y	M̀h gán-yiu. Néih yìh-gā hái bīn-douh a?
X	**b**
Y	Òu, hái ūk-kéi. Māt-yéh sih a?
X	**c**
Y	Hóu, hóu. Dò-jeh, dò-jeh. Hái bīn-douh sihk a?

07.03 Now you can hear the full conversation. After you have done your best you can confirm how well you did by reading the text in the usual place at the end of the book.

07.04 Easy, isn't it? Now try this one.

X	**d**
Y	Hóu hóu. Néih nē?
X	**e**
Y	Kéuih dōu géi hóu. Yáuh-sàm. Néih taai-táai nē?
X	**f**
Y	Deui-m̀h-jyuh, ngóh gàm-yaht m̀h fàan sé-jih-làuh, m̀h hó-yíh tùhng néih fàan. Sìng-kèih-sei, hóu m̀h hóu a?
X	**g**
Y	Ngóh m̀h séung jà-chē heui, séung chóh bā-sí heui.
X	**h**
Y	Chóh luhk houh lā.
X	**i**
Y	Hóu, Láih-baai-sei joi-gin.

5 **Complete the sentences.**

  a Wòhng Sàang haih kéuih bàh-bā, Wòhng Táai haih _____.

  b Ngóh móuh bàh-bā, màh-mā, hìng-daih, jí-muih, ūk-kéi jí yáuh ngóh _____ go yàhn jē.

  c Chóh fèi-gèi gwai, daahn-haih chóh bā-sí _____.

  d Ngóh-deih Láih-baai-yaht _____ sái fàan sé-jih-làuh.

  e Hòh Sìn-sàang móuh chín, m̀h _____ daap dīk-sí.

6 Insert the appropriate plugs (1–5) to create meaningful new sentences.

   a Ngóh-deih nī go Sìng-kèih-luhk daap fèi-gèi heui   **1** sai-gaai
      Yìng-gwok wáan.

   b Wòhng Taai-táai tùhng Wòhng Sìn-sàang làih ngóh   **2** sàam go yàhn
      ge sé-jih-làuh.

   c Néih ge jyú-yi haih jeui hóu ge.   **3** jì-yāt

   d Nī gàan daaih-hohk haih yáuh-méng ge daaih-hohk.   **4** yāt-dihng

   e Lèuhn-dēun haih Yìng-gwok jeui dò yàhn ge deih-fòng.   **5** yāt-chàih

7 07.05 **Same tune different words. Each of the three (rather silly) sentences has the same tone sequence, but of course the sounds and the meanings are different. You don't know all the words, and so we'll translate them for you – all you have to do is concentrate on getting the sounds right and repeating them after the recorded voice until you sound as natural as the native speaker.**

真好笑牛上樹。 **Jàn hóu siu ngàuh séuhng syuh.**   *Very amusing, a cow climbing a tree.*

三點半嚟我度。 **Sàam dím bun làih ngóh douh.**   *Come to my place at half past three.*

歡喜到流眼淚。 **Fùn-héi dou làuh ngáahn-leuih.**   *Pleased to the point of tears.*

Passage 2

Finally, here is another passage for you to read and understand. When you have understood it, read it out loud several times until it feels natural and easy on the tongue.

Gàm-yaht ngóh fàan sé-jih-làuh. Hòh Sìn-sàang wah ngóh tèng Láih-baai-luhk kéuih yiu daap fèi-gèi fàan-heui Yìng-gwok, só-yíh hái Láih-baai-sàam jì-hauh jauh m̀h fàan sé-jih-làuh lak. Hòh Sìn-sàang haih ngóh jeui hóu ge pàhng-yáuh jì-yāt, kéuih nī chi fàan-heui Yìng-gwok jì-hauh, ngóh gú jauh m̀h fàan-làih ge lak. Gám, ngóh yiu sung māt-yéh béi kéuih hóu nē? Ngóh séung-jó hóu noih dōu móuh jyú-yi, jauh heui mahn Wòhng Síu-jé tùhng Jèung Taai-táai. Wòhng Síu-jé wah, 'Ngóh-deih sàam go yàhn yāt-chàih chéng Hòh Sìn-sàang sihk-faahn lā! Hóu m̀h hóu a?' Jèung Taai-táai wah, 'Yùh-gwó Hòh Taai-táai hó-yíh tùhng Hòh Sìn-sàang yāt-chàih làih, gám jauh jeui hóu lak.'

Ngóh wah síu-jé tùhng taai-táai ge jyú-yi yāt-dihng haih jeui hóu ge. Néih wah haih m̀h haih a?

8 天氣 *Tìn-hei*
Weather

In this unit you will learn about:

▶ *days and years.*
▶ *hot and cold.*
▶ *how?*
▶ *adverbs from adjectives.*

▶ *the seasons.*
▶ *succeeding.*
▶ *time when.*

CEFR: *(A2) Can agree and disagree, can describe plans.*

 ## Hong Kong weather

Everyone knows that Hong Kong has hot summers, but the winters can be cold too. Not that the temperatures get particularly low – maybe 6 or 7°C – but the high humidity which makes the summers feel so hot also makes the winters seem very cold. Hong Kong people do talk about snow, as Mr Wong does in the dialogue, but it is mostly to wonder at what they have never seen, and he has to be joking here. On the other hand **Gàm-yaht hóu chìuh-sāp** 今日好潮濕 *It's very humid today* can be heard at almost any time of year. Useful weather words are

天氣 **tìn-hei** *weather*
冷 **láahng** *cold*
落雨 **lohk-yúh** *to rain*
落雪 **lohk-syut** *to snow*

天文臺 **tìn-màhn-tòih** *observatory*
熱 **yiht** *hot*
遮 **jē** *umbrella* (cl: **bá** 把)
晒太陽 **saai taai-yèuhng** *to sunbathe*

What English weather word almost certainly comes from the Cantonese word **daaih-fùng** *great wind?*

Vocabulary builder 1

 Read through the new vocabulary and practise saying it out loud.

TIME WORDS

舊年	gauh-nín	*last year*
幾時?	géi-sí? *or* géi-sìh?	*when?*
漸漸	jihm-jím	*gradually*
年	nìhn	*year*
時時	sìh-sìh	*always, frequently*
聽日	tìng-yaht	*tomorrow*
已經	yíh-gìng	*already*

VERBS

擠	jài	*to put, place*
知道 / 知	jì-dou *or* jì	*to know a fact, understand*
怕	pa	*to fear; to dislike*
嘥	sàai	*to waste*
同意	tùhng-yi	*to agree*
會	wúih	*it is likely that* (future possibility)

BASICS

吖?	ā?	fp: (scoring a point) *didn't I tell you so!*
牆角	chèuhng-gok	*corner* (of house, room)
電暖爐	dihn-nyúhn-lòuh	*electric heater* (cl: **ga**)
走廊	jáu-lóng	*passage, corridor*
重	juhng	*in addition, furthermore; even more*
滅火筒	miht-fó-túng	*fire extinguisher*
衫	sāam	*clothing* (cl: **gihn**)
實用	saht-yuhng	*practical*
手提	sáu-tàih	*hand held, portable*
添	tìm	fp: *as well, also, what's more*

Dialogue 1

1 Note how Mrs Wong lectures her husband on wasting money. Casting your mind back to Unit 3, how do you think she would tell him not to waste time?

Mr Wong	Yìh-gā tìn-hei jihm-jím láahng lak. Ngóh hóu pa láahng: ngóh jeui jùng-yi saai taai-yèuhng ge. Tìn-màhn-tòih wah gàm-yaht wúih lohk-yúh, nī go Sìng-kèih-luhk juhng wúih lohk-syut tìm.
Mrs Wong	Ngóh yíh-gìng yuh-beih-jó dī láahng-tīn sāam la.
Mr Wong	Ngóh séung tìng-yaht máaih go dihn-nyúhn-lòuh fàan-làih, néih wah hóu m̀h hóu a?
Mrs Wong	M̀h hóu.
Mr Wong	Gám, ngóh yiu géi-sí máaih a?
Mrs Wong	M̀h-hóu máaih dihn-nyúhn-lòuh lā! Néih máaih ge yéh sìh-sìh dōu m̀h saht-yuhng ge.
Mr Wong	Ngóh m̀h tùhng-yi. Ngóh máaih ge yéh jeui saht-yuhng ge lak.
Mrs Wong	Néih yiu jì-dou máaih m̀h saht-yuhng ge yéh jīk-haih sàai-chín.
Mr Wong	Néih wah ngóh tèng, ngóh máaih-jó māt-yéh m̀h saht-yuhng a?
Mrs Wong	Jài hái jáu-lóng chèuhng-gok gó go sáu-tàih miht-fó-túng, néih gauh-nín máaih ge, yāt nìhn jì-noih dōu móuh yuhng-gwo. Néih wah haih m̀h haih m̀h saht-yuhng ā!
王生	而家天氣漸漸冷嘞。我好怕冷，我最中意晒太陽嘅。天文臺話今日會落雨，呢個星期六重會落雪添。
王太	我已經預備咗啲冷天衫啦。
王生	我想聽日買個電暖爐返嚟，你話好唔好呀？
王太	唔好。
王生	噉，我要幾時買呀？
王太	唔好買電暖爐啦！你買嘅嘢時時都唔實用嘅。
王生	我唔同意，我買嘅嘢最實用嘅嘞。
王太	你要知道買唔實用嘅嘢即係嘥錢。
王生	你話我聽，我買咗乜嘢唔實用呀？
王太	擠喺走廊牆角嗰個手提滅火筒，你舊年買嘅，一年之內都冇用過，你話係唔係唔實用丫！

2 **Have you understood? Read the dialogue again and then select the correct phrases from the ones in brackets in the following sentences. You will no doubt feel insulted if we tell you that the answer to the first one is dihn-nyúhn-lòuh … so we won't!**

a Wòhng Sìn-sàang séung máaih (dihn-nyúhn-lòuh / miht-fó-túng).

b Wòhng Taai-táai wah Wòhng Sìn-sàang máaih ge yéh sìh-sìh dōu (yáuh-yuhng / móuh-yuhng / m̀h saht-yuhng).

c Gó go sáu-tàih miht-fó-túng jài hái (jáu-làuh / sé-jih-làuh / chèuhng-gok).

d Gó go sáu-tàih miht-fó-túng (yuhng-gwo yāt chi / móuh yuhng-gwo / sìh-sìh dōu yuhng).

3 **Looking at the underlined part of the dialogue, follow the same pattern to translate the following:**

a These buses which go to Shanghai Street

b The Mrs Chan who is now eating noodles

c The seafood restaurant where I frequently go to eat crab

d That very polite young lady who hates sitting at home

> **LANGUAGE TIP**
> When is afraid not afraid? No, it's not a riddle. Cantonese, like English, uses *I'm afraid* (**pa** or **ngóh pa**) to mean either *I am in a state of fear* or *I'm sorry to say*. In addition, in Cantonese it can mean *I really dislike*, and in the dialogue you will read that Mr Wong **hóu pa láahng** *hates the cold*.

Language discovery

8.1 WHAT'S MORE

Juhng means *furthermore, in addition* (you met the same word in Unit 3, where it meant *still, yet*). It is an adverb and therefore, as you now know, comes before the verb in the sentence. The final particle **tìm** is usually added on at the end to give additional force to **juhng**:

Ngóh juhng yáuh léuhng go tìm.	*I've got two more as well.*
Kéuih juhng séung heui Méih-gwok yāt chi tìm.	*What's more she wants to go to the USA once as well.*

8.2 THE SEASONS

Láahng means *cold*, and **láahng-tīn** 冷天 *cold days* comes to mean *winter*. But the proper word for *winter* is **dùng-tīn**, which forms part of the set of four which you would expect:

春天	**chèun-tīn**	*spring*
夏天	**hah-tīn**	*summer*
秋天	**chàu-tīn**	*autumn*
冬天	**dùng-tīn**	*winter*

8.3 WHEN?

Géi-sí? *when?* is the question word which asks for a time-when answer. Not surprisingly then, you will find **géi-sí?** in the same place in the sentence where the time-when answer comes. If you have forgotten the rule, refresh your memory by re-reading Unit 6.

Néih géi-sí heui a?	*When are you going?*
Ngóh Láih-baai-yaht heui.	*I'm going on Sunday.*

8.4 MORE ON DŌU

You are well aware by now that **dōu** is an adverb which means *all, both, also* and that it is placed like other adverbs immediately in front of the verb. Sometimes it is used where there seems no need for it in English: for instance, in the dialogue Mrs Wong says **Néih máaih ge yéh sìh-sìh dōu m̀h saht-yuhng ge** *The things you buy are always impractical.* What **dōu** is doing is backing up the word **sìh-sìh** *always,* and it does so because **sìh-sìh** feels like a plural idea in Cantonese – it literally means 'time-time'. You first met this in Unit 5 where **dōu** was used to back up doubled classifiers. So whenever there are plural ideas (*the cows all …; Mr and Mrs Wong …; electric heaters …*) or ideas of wholeness (*the entire population …; the whole busload …*), you can expect **dōu** to be thrown in for good measure.

8.5 MORE ABOUT MOST

In Unit 6 you met **jeui** *most* and you will have had no difficulty in using it to make superlatives (*biggest, coldest,* etc.). Quite often you will find that the final particle **lak** is tacked onto the sentence to back up **jeui**, just as **tìm** backs up **juhng**:

jeui daaih lak	*biggest*
jeui hóu-sihk lak	*most delicious*
jeui hóu lak	*best*
Rolls-Royce haih Yìng-gwok jeui gwai ge chē lak.	*The Rolls-Royce is Britain's most expensive car.*

8.6 TONE CHANGES

Did you spot another exception to the rule that a word is always pronounced in the same tone? If not, check back through the Vocabulary builder and Dialogue before you read on.

You will remember that in Unit 6 you met **wá** *speech* and **wah** *to say,* and you learned that they are actually the same word with different meanings according to the different tones. In the last speech of this unit's dialogue you will see that the word for *year* also has two different tones. The usual tone is **nìhn** (low falling), but in *last year* **gauh-nín** it becomes mid rising. There is no obvious reason why this tone change should occur, but take heart that you will only meet **nín** in the following common words, in all other cases year is pronounced **nìhn**:

gauh-nín	*last year*
gàm-nín	*this year*
chēut-nín	*next year*

8.7 *YEARS* AND *DAYS*

While we are talking about **nìhn**, you might note that it is one of a very small number of nouns which do not need a classifier. You have learned that nouns must have a classifier when they are counted or specified with words like *this*, *that* and *which* (see Unit 2), so you know that *two pens* must be **léuhng jì bāt** and *three Americans* must be **sàam go Méih-gwok-yàhn**. **Nìhn** *year* and **yaht** *day,* however, along with just one or two other nouns that you have not met, do not have a classifier; they seem to combine the role of classifier and noun at the same time. So *one day* is **yāt yaht** and *two years* is **léuhng nìhn**.

This is a convenient place to set out in clear form the words for *years* and *days* that you have met so far:

gàm-yaht	*today*	**gàm-nín**	*this year*
kàhm-yaht	*yesterday*	**gauh-nín**	*last year*
tìng-yaht	*tomorrow*	**chēut-nín**	*next year*

Pronouncing trios

08.02 You have now met quite a lot of three-character terms. Listen to the audio carefully and note how each syllable has more or less equal weight, a feature of Cantonese which marks it off from other languages. Repeat after the voice until you can copy it comfortably. Oh, and make sure that you know what each trio actually means as well.

Vocabulary builder 2

 Read through the new vocabulary and practise saying it out loud. Then complete the missing English expressions.

VERBS AND VERB ENDINGS

打風	dá-fùng	*to have a typhoon*
打算	dá-syun	*to intend; intention*
… 倒	-dóu	*ve: successfully*
見	gin	*to see, meet*
改	gói	*to alter, change (for the better)*
慳	hàan	*to save; to be miserly, stingy*
… 成	-sèhng	*ve: become, change into*
算	syun	*to be regarded as, be reckoned*

NOUNS AND CLASSIFIERS

百貨公司	baak-fo-gūng-sī	*department store*
比堅尼	béi-gìn-nèih	_____ (cl: **tou**)
風	fùng	*wind* (cl: **chèuhng**)
公司	gūng-sī	*company* (cl: **go**)
海灘	hói-tàan	*beach*
冷氣機	láahng-hei-gèi	*air-conditioner* (cl: **ga**)
領呔	léhng-tàai	*necktie* (cl: **tìuh**)
時候	sìh-hauh	*time*
雪糕	syut-gōu	*ice cream*
條	tìuh	cl: for long, thin, flexible things
套	tou	cl: a set of, a suit of
游水褲	yàuh-séui-fu	*swimming trunks* (cl: **tìuh**)

BASICS

點樣 … 法？	dím-yéung … -faat?	*in what way …?*
舊	gauh	*old, used*
開心	hòi-sām	*happy*
有用	yáuh-yuhng	_____

Dialogue 2

 08.03 *Mr Chan and Mr Cheung demonstrate how buying an air-conditioner can lead to a conflict of stinginess.*

1 Who does Mr Chan see in the department store?

Chan	Jèung Sìn-sàang, néih hóu. Heui bīn-douh a?
Cheung	Ngóh heui máaih láahng-hei-gèi.
Chan	Haih àh? Tìn-hei jihm-jím yiht, máaih láahng-hei-gèi haih sìh-hauh la.
Cheung	Chàhn Sìn-sàang, néih yáuh māt-yéh dá-syun nē?
Chan	Ngóh móuh chín máaih láahng-hei-gèi. Tìn-hei taai yiht ge sìh-hauh, ngóh wúih heui hói-tàan yàuh-séui, yám bē-jáu, sihk syut-gōu, gám jauh m̀h yiht la.
Cheung	Daahn-haih yùh-gwó dá-fùng jauh m̀h hó-yíh heui hói-tàan, lohk-yúh jauh m̀h hó-yíh heui máaih syut-gōu … gám, jauh dím a? Láahng-hei-gèi m̀h syun hóu gwai, daahn-haih hóu yáuh-yuhng: néih dōu m̀h máaih, jàn-haih hàan lak!
Chan	Ngóh m̀h syun hàan la! Ngóh wah néih taai-táai juhng hàan lā!
Cheung	Kéuih dím-yéung hàan-faat a?
Chan	Nī go Láih-baai-yih ngóh hái baak-fo-gūng-sī máaih yàuh-séui-fu ge sìh-hauh, gin-dóu néih taai-táai, kéuih hóu hòi-sām gám wah ngóh jì, kéuih jí-haih yuhng-jó yāt tìuh néih ge gauh léhng-tàai jauh hó-yíh gói-sèhng yāt tou 'béi-gìn-nèih' lak. Néih wah kéuih hàan m̀h hàan nē?

陳	張先生，你好。去邊度呀？
張	我去買冷氣機。
陳	係吖？天氣漸漸熱，買冷氣機係時候啦。
張	陳先生，你有乜嘢打算呢？
陳	我冇錢買冷氣機。天氣太熱嘅時候，我會去海灘游水，飲啤酒，食雪糕，咁就唔熱喇。
張	但係如果打風就唔可以去海灘，落雨就唔可以去買雪糕……噉，就點呀？冷氣機唔算好貴，但係好有用：你都唔買，真係慳嘞！
陳	我唔算慳啦！我話你太太重慳啦！
張	佢點樣慳法呀！
陳	呢個禮拜二我喺百貨公司買游水褲嘅時候，見倒你太太，佢好開心嘅話我知，佢只係用咗一條你嘅舊領呔就可以改成一套 '比堅尼' 嘞。你話佢慳唔慳呢！

2 Use Cantonese to answer these questions:

  a Jèung Sàang séung máaih māt-yéh a?

  b Chàhn Sàang jùng m̀h jùng-yi yám jáu a?

  c Sihk syut-gōu ne?

  d Kéuih géi-sí yám bē-jáu tùhng-màaih sihk syut-gōu ne?

  e Chàhn Sàang sīk m̀h sīk yàuh-séui a?

3 Picture quiz

  a Néih wah Jèung Táai yuhng nī tìuh léhng-tàai gói-sèhng béi-gìn-nèih dāk m̀h dāk a?

  b Yāt tou béi-gìn-nèih haih géi-dō gihn a?

Language discovery

8.8 IN WHAT WAY?

You first met **dím-yéung** *in what way? how?* in Unit 5. In the dialogue you see that it appears with the verb ending **-faat** *way of …* You do not have to use this new form, but it is good racy-sounding Cantonese to do so. Here are two example sentences each using both forms:

Kéuih dím-yéung heui fèi-gèi-chèuhng a?   *How is he going to the airport?*
→ Fèi-gèi-chèuhng kéuih dím-yéung heui-faat a?
Kéuih dím-yéung hàan chín a?   *How does she save money?*
→ Chín kéuih dím-yéung hàan-faat a?

 Look carefully at the examples using the -faat form. What has happened to the object of the verb in each case?

There is a useful principle to be learned: Cantonese verbs are sensitive creatures (remember how some of them feel lonely?) and they don't feel happy with too many ideas hanging on them. Verb endings must add directly onto the verb, and so if there is an object as well and it makes the verb feel overburdened, it often feels more comfortable to shift that object to the front of the sentence.

8.9 SÌH-HAUH *TIME*

Haih sìh-hauh is a colloquial way to say *it is the right time to …* Here are two ways of using it, both of which mean *it's time to go to the office now*:

Yìh-gā haih sìh-hauh fàan sé-jih-làuh la.

Yìh-gā fàan sé-jih-làuh haih sìh-hauh la.

Perhaps more common is the expression **… ge sìh-hauh**, which means *when … or while …* Study these two sentences carefully:

Ngóh jyú-sung ge sìh-hauh m̀h séung màh-mā bòng ngóh sáu.

I don't want mummy to help me while I'm cooking.

Kéuih hái Yìng-gwok ge sìh-hauh sìh-sìh dōu làih taam ngóh.

She often comes to see me when she's in Britain.

Now think back to Unit 4 and see how **… ge sìh-hauh** is really just like other **ge** phrases:

hóu gwai ge ga-fē	*coffee which is very expensive*
máaih-gán bāt ge yàhn	*the person who is buying a pen*
kéuih hái Yìng-gwok ge sìh-hauh	*the time when she is in Britain*

8.10 MAKING ADVERBS FROM ADJECTIVES

If you bracket an adjective with **hóu … gám**, you turn it into an adverb:

hòi-sām	*happy*	→	**hóu hòi-sām gám**	*happily*
haak-hei	*polite*	→	**hóu haak-hei gám**	*politely*

YOUR TURN Translate these two sentences:

Kéuih hóu nàu.

Kéuih hóu nàu gám wah ngóh jì …

8.11 -DÓU *TO SUCCEED IN*

It is not easy to put a specific meaning on the verb ending **-dóu**. Sometimes you might want to translate it as *to succeed in*, sometimes as *successfully*, sometimes as *actually* and quite often it seems to add nothing much at all to the meaning of the verb to which it is attached. Here are four examples of it with different verbs:

Ngóh tái-dóu Wòhng Síu-jé hái gó-douh.	*I caught sight of Miss Wong there.*
Ngóh gú-dóu néih hái chyùh-fóng.	*I guessed rightly that you were in the kitchen.*
Kéuih daap-dóu bā-sí.	*He actually caught the bus.*
Ngóh gin-dóu néih taai-táai.	*I met your wife.*

> **LANGUAGE TIP**
> You have now met two words for *old*. **Gauh** means *old* in the sense of *used, not new*, and it is applied to inanimate things like cars, shoes, books, etc. **Gauh-nín** *last year* literally means 'the old year'. When it comes to people and animals, the word for *old* is **lóuh** – it would sound very odd to describe an old man or an old dog as **gauh**. There are some idiomatic exceptions to this split: you might, for instance, hear either **lóuh pàhng-yáuh** or **gauh pàhng-yáuh** used to mean *an old friend*.

8.12 -SÈHNG *TO BECOME*

As a verb ending **-sèhng** means *to become* or *to make into*. You will find an example in the dialogue where Mrs Cheung claims to make a tie into a bikini. Here is another one:

Ngóh yuhng ngàuh-yuhk jyú-sèhng yāt go tòng.
I'm making the beef into a soup.

Practice

1 **Here we have to expose our ignorance. Each of these sentences would start with**
   ***We don't know* in English, but what should the Cantonese be?**

   a _____ néih sing māt-yéh.

   b _____ yàuh-séui.

   c _____ jà Yaht-bún faai-jí.

   d _____ bīn ga chē haih néih ge.

2 **Match the correct part (a–d) with (1–4) to make meaningful sentences.**

   a Tìn-hei jihm-jím yiht …   **1** … jīk-haih sàai chín.

   b Láahng-hei-gèi m̀h syun hóu gwai …   **2** … máaih láahng-hei-gèi haih sìh-hauh la.

   c Yùh-gwó máaih m̀h saht-yuhng ge   **3** … ngóh-deih dī láahng-tīn sāam la.
       yéh …

   d Ngóh yíh-gìng yuh-beih-jó …   **4** … daahn-haih hóu yáuh-yuhng.

3 **How can you turn each of these pairs of sentences into one?**

   Example: Gó-douh yáuh chē. Chē hóu gwai. → *Gó-douh yáuh hóu gwai ge chē.*

   a Jèung Síu-jé haih Yaht-bún-yàhn. Kéuih hóu leng.

   b Ngóh m̀h séung máaih bāt. Chàhn Sìn-sàang ge pou-táu maaih Méih-gwok bāt.

   c Ngóh hóu séung sihk lùhng-hā. Hòh Táai jíng lùhng-hā.

4 **Select the right words and phrases from the box to complete sentences a–d.**
   Obviously, that means you will have to reject five of them as unsuitable or less
   suitable.

   > 1 sàn-sìn   2 Méih-gwok ge   3 Yìng-gwok ge
   > 4 sáu-tàih   5 míhn-fai   6 yāt tou leng ge
   > 7 gaai-siuh   8 hùhng-sīk   9 yùh-góng

   a _____ miht-fó-túng hóu yáuh-yuhng.

   b Hái nī-douh yám séui haih _____ ge: néih m̀h sái béi chín.

   c _____ béi-gìn-nèih m̀h pèhng.

   d Yùh-gwó dī ngàuh-yuhk m̀h _____, ngóh jauh m̀h séung sihk.

? Test yourself

Can you supply the cartoon caption in Cantonese? Mr Wong is saying:
Don't be angry. Didn't I tell you this fire extinguisher was a practical object?!

9 娛樂同運動 *Yuh-lohk tùhng wahn-duhng*

Fun and games

In this unit you will learn about:
- *age with a difference.*
- *electricity.*
- *gender.*
- *keeping fit.*

- *leisure activities.*
- *more lonely verbs.*
- *several.*
- *wholeness.*

CEFR: *(A2) Can use a series of phrases and sentences to describe family, other people, daily routines; can describe something in a simple list of points.*

A problem of age

Cantonese people reckon their age in **seui** 歲 *harvests*, rather like the old-fashioned English custom of reckoning age in summers. **Nìhn**, as you know, means *year*, but it cannot be used to mean *year of age*. Well, that's easy enough. What is sometimes a problem is sorting out what **seui** means in real terms, because traditionally Chinese people were born one **seui** old and then added another **seui** to their age at each Lunar New Year. So a Chinese baby born on the last day of the lunar year would already be **léuhng seui** old the next day, while a Western baby born at the same time would not even have got to 'one' yet! If it is ever important to be certain of someone's age, you can always ask whether the Chinese or the **Sài-yàhn** 西人 *Westerner* **seui** is meant.

Given that the lunar years vary in length between 353 and 385 days, if our Chinese baby above was born just before a short lunar year, how many **seui** might he have time to become before the poor little Western baby had opened his score?

We have seen so many harvests that we can't remember where we heard the next silly dialogue, but it has some useful material in it.

Vocabulary builder 1

 Read through the new vocabulary and practise saying it out loud.

VERBS

打波	dá-bō	*to play a ball game*
放假	fong-ga	*to be on holiday, take days off*
記得	gei-dāk	*to remember*
覺得	gok-dāk	*to feel*
離開	lèih-hòi	*to leave, depart from*

BASICS

齣	chēut	cl: for films and stage plays
刺激	chi-gīk	*exciting*
前日	chìhn-yaht	*the day before yesterday*
電影	dihn-yíng	*cinema film, movie*
男	nàahm	*male*
內容	noih-yùhng	*contents*
一啲	yāt-dī	*a little bit*
而且	yìh-ché	*moreover*

Dialogue 1

 09.01 *Mr Chan finds out how his colleague Miss Cheung spends her time off.*

1 Why is nē used in Mr Chan's second speech?

Chan	Jèung Síu-jé, kàhm-yaht tùhng chìhn-yaht dōu fong-ga. Néih yáuh móuh heui dá-bō a?
Cheung	Ngóh m̀h jùng-yi dá-bō ge.
Chan	Yáuh móuh heui kèih-tà deih-fòng wáan nē?
Cheung	Ngóh dōu m̀h jùng-yi lèih-hòi Hèung-góng ge, ngóh jí-haih jùng-yi tái-dihn-yíng jē.
Chan	Ngóh jì-dou kàhm-yaht hái Daaih-wuih-tòhng yáuh <u>yāt chēut hóu yáuh-méng hóu hóu-tái ge dihn-yíng</u>. Néih yáuh móuh heui tái a?
Cheung	Yáuh a! Jàn-haih hóu hóu-tái a. Yìh-ché juhng hóu chi-gīk tìm.
Chan	Chi-gīk! Ngóh m̀h gok-dāk bo. Néih gei m̀h gei-dāk gó chēut dihn-yíng ge noih-yùhng a?
Cheung	Deui-m̀h-jyuh, ngóh yāt-dī dōu m̀h gei-dāk lak, yàn-waih ngóh tùhng nàahm-pàhng-yáuh yāt-chàih heui tái ge.
陳	張小姐，擒日同前日都放假。你有冇去打波呀？
張	我唔中意打波嘅。
陳	有冇去其他地方玩呢？
張	我都唔中意離開香港嘅，我只係中意睇電影啫。
陳	我知道擒日喺大會堂有一齣好有名好好睇嘅電影。你有冇去睇呀？
張	有呀！真係好好睇呀。而且重好刺激添。
陳	刺激！我唔覺得㗎。你記唔記得嗰齣電影嘅內容呀？
張	對唔住，我一啲都唔記得嘞，因為我同男朋友一齊去睇嘅。

> **LANGUAGE TIP**
> You may or may not have realized that in Miss Cheung's third speech in the dialogue, she uses three different ways of saying moreover (**yìh-ché / juhng / tìm**). This may feel like overkill in English, but it is perfectly alright, indeed common, in Cantonese.

2 There seems to be an awful lot of hóu in the underlined section of the dialogue, doesn't there? It's actually fine, but can you understand how it works? Pay particular attention to it and make sure that you can explain every word and what it is doing there. You will find help at the end of the course.

3 In Unit 8 you learned about the use of dōu to back up plurals and ideas of completeness. Did you spot examples of both in the dialogue?

Language discovery

9.1 TO HAVE A HOLIDAY

Fong-ga literally means *to release on leave*:

Hái Yìng-gwok fong-ga yiu gei-dāk daai bá jē lā.

If you're holidaying in Britain you should remember to take your umbrella.

Fong-ga is one of quite a large group of expressions which are made up of a verb and an object, and these expressions can all be split up if the sense allows. Here are a couple of examples:

Ngóh séung fong sàam yaht ga.	*I want to have three days' holiday.*
Kéuih jouh jáu-làuh ge sàang-yi.	*He is in the restaurant business* (lit. 'does … business').

9.2 PLAYING BALL

The original Cantonese word for *ball* was **kàuh** 球, but then along came the English word *ball*, it was 'Cantonesized' into **bō**, and both words have stuck. **Dá** means *to hit* and **dá-bō** is the regular way to say *to play a ball game*. The problem is: which ball game? For a majority of people it means *soccer*, but it can mean any game played with a ball. Here are some of them:

乒乓波	**bìng-bām-bō**	*table tennis, ping-pong*
高爾夫球	**gòu-yíh-fù-kàuh**	*golf*
足球	**jūk-kàuh**	*soccer*
欖球	**láam-kàuh**	*rugby, American football*
籃球	**làahm-kàuh**	*basketball*
網球	**móhng-kàuh**	*tennis*
枱波	**tói-bō**	*billiards, snooker*
羽毛球	**yúh-mòuh-kàuh**	*badminton*

To play soccer **is either dá jūk-kàuh or tek jūk-kàuh. Can you guess what the verb tek** 踢 **means?**

You might note the very logical difference between the following:

Ngóh heui dá-bō.	*I'm going off to play ball.*
Ngóh heui tái dá-bō.	*I'm going off to watch the game.*

9.3 GOING TO THE CINEMA

Tái-dihn-yíng means *to see a film* and **heui tái-dihn-yíng** is *to go to the cinema*. You will notice that **tái-dihn-yíng** is also a verb-plus-object expression, so another example of splitting verb from object would be:

Wòhng Táai séung heui tái Méih-gwok dihn-yíng.

Mrs Wong wants to go to see an American film.

There is another expression, **tái-hei** 睇戲, which means *to see a play*, but far more people go to the cinema than go to the live theatre, and it is now very common to hear someone say **ngóh heui tái-hei** when they mean *I'm going to the cinema*.

9.4 TAKING SHORTCUTS AGAIN

In Unit 3 we explained that the sentence **Néih fàan m̀h fàan-heui a?** was a common shortened form of **Néih fàan-heui m̀h fàan-heui a?** You can do the same thing with any two-syllable verb, and in the dialogue you will have noticed **néih gei m̀h gei-dāk** where Mr Chan might correctly but long-windedly have said **néih gei-dāk m̀h gei-dāk**. Here is another example:

Néih jùng m̀h jùng-yi Lèuhn-dēun a?   *Do you like London?*

YOUR TURN Supply the caption for the market researcher's question. He is asking: Did you feel that this was an exciting film?

9.5 NOT EVEN A LITTLE BIT!

Yāt-dī means *a little bit*, and combined with **dōu** and the negatives **m̀h** or **móuh** it means *not even a little bit, absolutely nothing*. In a later unit you will find that this fits in with a regular grammar pattern, but for the time being you should just accept it as an idiomatic expression.

 Along the same lines you can also say Ngóh-deih yāt-dī chín dōu móuh. If you are like us you probably have to say it quite often – what does it mean?

9.6 MALES AND FEMALES

Nàahm *male* pairs with **néuih** 女 *female*. The two terms can be prefixed to almost any human role, such as driver, lawyer, servant, teacher, etc., but are not generally used with reference to the gender of animals. In the dialogue, Miss Cheung talks about her **nàahm-pàhng-yáuh** *boyfriend*, and he would describe her as his **néuih-pàhng-yáuh** *girlfriend*. The words for an adult man and an adult woman are **nàahm-yán** 男人 *male person* and **néuih-yán** 女人 *female person*.

 Did you just spot another tone change?

The characters for *male* and *female* are well worth memorizing for practical purposes, because they are what appear on the entrances to public conveniences.

| WOMEN 女 | MEN 男 | 女 LADIES 界 | 男 GENTLEMEN 界 |

LANGUAGE TIP

Dihn-yíng *movie, film* literally means 'electric shadows' and was an ingenious way of naming the new concept when it first burst onto the Chinese scene. The word **dihn** *electricity* was itself originally borrowed from the word meaning *lightning*, and it has been put to very good use ever since. You met *electric heater* **dihn-nyúhn-lòuh** in Unit 8. Nowadays everyone is familiar with **dihn-chè** ('electric vehicle') for *tram*, dihn-wá 電話 ('electric speech') for *telephone*, **dihn-sih** 電視 ('electric vision') for *television*, **dihn-nóuh** 電腦 ('electric brain') for *computer*, 電燈 **dihn-dāng** ('electric lamp') for *electric light*, 電飯煲 **dihn-faahn-bōu** ('electric rice pan') for *electric rice cooker*, and many more.

Vocabulary builder 2

 Read through the new vocabulary and practise saying it out loud.

THE BODY

肌肉	gèi-yuhk	*muscle*
健康	gihn-hòng	*health, healthy*
下巴	hah-pàh	*chin*
口部	háu-bouh	*mouth*
脂肪	jì-fōng	*(body) fat*
身體	sàn-tái	*body*

VERBS

減少	gáam-síu	*to reduce, cut down*
講	góng	*to speak, talk, say*
行路	hàahng-louh	*to walk*
爬山	pàh-sàan	*to climb mountains, walk the hills*
運動	wahn-duhng	*to exercise; physical exercise*

BASICS

對	deui	*with regard to, towards*
多餘	dò-yùh	*surplus*
咁上下	gam-seuhng-há	*approximately, thereabouts*
幾	géi	*several*
只要	jí-yiu	*so long as, provided that*
裡便	léuih-bihn	*inside*
山	sàan	*mountain, hill* (cl: **joh**)
成日	sèhng-yaht	*the whole day*
雙	sēung	*double*

Dialogue 2

 09.02 *Mr Wong and Mr Cheung discuss keeping fit, but Mr Wong is not sure that the theories apply to his wife!*

1 It is true that it is always cold at the South Pole, but in English does *always* always mean 'always'? If it did, Mr Cheung's first speech would say that he would never ever sit or lie down. So you should bear in mind that always has another less absolute meaning, and that is reflected in the Cantonese word too. How would you translate sìh-sìh in the dialogue to show this?

Wong	Jèung Sìn-sàang, néih wah sìh-sìh wahn-duhng hó-yíh gáam-síu sàn-tái léuih-bihn dò-yùh ge jì-fōng, deui gihn-hòng hóu hóu, haih m̀h haih a?
Cheung	Haih a! Ngóh sìh-sìh dōu hàahng-louh, pàh-sàan, tùhng dá-bō. Néih tái ngóh yíh-gìng ńgh-sahp-géi seui lak, juhng haih hóu gihn-hòng, hóu-chíh sei-sahp seui gam-seuhng-há.
Wong	Daahn-haih ngóh gok-dāk wahn-duhng deui ngóh taai-táai yāt-dī yuhng dōu móuh.
Cheung	Yāt-dihng yáuh yuhng ge. Jí-yiu néih taai-táai sìh-sìh wahn-duhng, sàn-tái léuih-bihn yāt-dihng móuh dò-yùh jì-fōng ge.
Wong	Ngóh taai-táai sèhng-yaht góng-yéh, háu-bouh ge gèi-yuhk yáuh hóu dò wahn-duhng lā. Dím-gáai kéuih juhng yáuh yāt go hóu dò jì-fōng ge sēung hah-pàh nē?
王	張先生，你話時時運動可以減少身體裡便多餘嘅脂肪，對健康好好，係唔係呀？
張	係呀！我時時都行路，爬山，同打波。你睇我已經五十幾歲嘞，重係好健康，好似四十歲咁上下。
王	但係我覺得運動對我太太一啲用都冇。
張	一定有用嘅。只要你太太時時運動，身體裡便一定冇多餘脂肪嘅。
王	我太太成日講嘢，口部嘅肌肉有好多運動喇。點解佢重有一個好多脂肪嘅雙下巴呢？

> **LANGUAGE TIP**
>
> **Deui** means *to face*, and from this a number of other meanings and expressions derive. You have already met **deui-m̀h-jyuh** ('I face you but can't stand my ground') *I'm sorry*. And, if you face something, you are looking towards it, so **deui** also means *towards* and *regarding*, and from that it means *with regard to, concerning*. Things which face each other and match make a pair, and **deui** means *a pair* too, so it is the classifier for chopsticks. And from there an answer which matches a question is also **deui** *correct* (or at least it is in Guangzhou, but Hong Kong people tend to use another word for correct – **ngāam** 啱).

2 Answer the questions.

   a Wòhng Táai m̀h jùng-yi góng-wá, ngāam m̀h ngāam a?

   b Jèung Sìn-sàang gok-dāk wahn-duhng deui sàn-tái gihn-hòng hóu hóu. Wòhng Sàang tùhng m̀h tùhng-yi nē?

Language discovery

9.7 GÉI *SEVERAL*

You met **géi** in the expression **géi-dō?** *how many?* in Unit 5 and **géi-sí?** *when?* in Unit 8. On its own **géi** can also mean *how many?*, but it has the meaning *several* as well, and that could be quite confusing. Supposing someone were to say to you **géi go yàhn**, you couldn't be sure whether they were saying *how many people?* or *several people*. Obviously the context in which they said it would help a lot, but in practice if it were a question most people would probably add **a?** on the end or use **géi-dō**, and that would of course make it clear.

In its *several* meaning, **géi** gets involved with numbers quite a lot, and it will often be useful to translate it as *and some* or *and a few more*.

 Find the example of géi in Mr Cheung's first speech in the dialogue. How would you translate this?

Here are a few more examples:

yih-sahp-géi go yàhn	*more than 20 people* (i.e. more than 20 but fewer than 30)
sahp-géi seui ge Jùng-gwok-yàhn	*a teenaged Chinese*
géi-sahp go yàhn	*dozens of people* (several tens of people)
géi-sahp nìhn	*several decades*

9.8 SEUI *YEARS OF AGE*

There are two points to be noted about **seui**. First, it is one of those very few words which (like **yaht** and **nìhn**) do not need a classifier. Second, it is often used without a verb. Look again at the dialogue where Mr Cheung says **ngóh yíh-gìng ńgh-sahp-géi seui lak**: there is no verb in this expression at all, yet it is perfectly acceptable Cantonese. If you feel the need to put in a verb, the most commonly used one is **haih** *to be*. Mr Cheung could have said: **ngóh yíh-gìng haih ńgh-sahp-géi seui lak** and it would have meant the same.

9.9 APPROXIMATELY

Gam-seuhng-há literally means 'thus up and down' and from that comes to mean *approximately*. It usually follows whatever it refers to, as it does where you met it in the dialogue: **sei-sahp seui gam-seuhng-há** *about 40 years old*.

9.10 THE BODY

Did you notice in the comprehension question after the dialogue that **sàn-tái** and **gihn-hòng** can combine as **sàn-tái gihn-hòng** to make a longer term for *healthy*? They also can split, as in **Kéuih sàn-tái hóu gihn-hòng** *He's very healthy*. Here are a few more body terms for you:

鼻哥	**beih-gò**	*nose*	眼	**ngáahn**	*eye* (cl: **jek**)
背脊	**bui-jek**	*back*	手	**sáu**	*hand, arm* (cl: **jek**)
頸	**géng**	*neck* (cl: **tìuh**)	手指	**sáu-jí**	*finger* (cl: **jek**)
腳	**geuk**	*foot, leg* (cl: **jek**)	頭	**tàuh**	*head*
腳趾	**geuk-jí**	*toe* (cl: **jek**)	肚	**tóuh**	*stomach, belly*
脷	**leih**	*tongue* (cl: **tìuh**)	耳仔	**yíh-jái**	*ear* (cl: **jek**)

9.11 THE WHOLE

Sèhng- combines with classifiers to make *the whole* … So **sèhng-go láih-baai** is *the whole week*, **sèhng-yaht** is *the whole day* or *all day long* and **sèhng-nìhn** is *the whole year long*.

> **LANGUAGE TIP**
> Remember that **yaht** and **nìhn** as well as **seui** are nouns which act as if they are their own classifiers.

9.12 ANOTHER 'LONELY VERB'

In Mr Wong's last speech, he says: **Ngóh taai-táai sèhng-yaht góng-yéh**. **Yéh** means *things*, as you learned in Unit 8, but here it is merely doing duty as the supplied object for the verb **góng**, which is one of those which gets lonely on its own. **Yéh** is quite handy for this purpose: here are a few more examples of it with lonely verbs:

Néih séung m̀h séung sihk-yéh a?	*Do you want to eat?*
Ngóh taai-táai heui-jó máaih-yéh.	*My wife's gone shopping.*
Kéuih sèhng-yaht dōu yám-yéh.	*He drinks all day long.*

YOUR TURN Now, just for fun, have a shot at translating *I can speak Cantonese*. If you get it right then you are truthful, but if you get it wrong it makes you a **daaih-wah-gwái** 大話鬼 ('big talk devil') *liar*. *To tell lies* is **góng daaih-wah**.

Practice

1 Here are some jumbled elements from which to make meaningful sentences.

   a gam-seuhng-há / Hòh Sìn-sàang / ńgh-sahp seui / hóu-chíh

   b hóu hóu / sìh-sìh / deui / wahn-duhng / gihn-hòng

   c ngóh / dá-bō / jùng-yi / jē / pàh-sàan / jí-haih / tùhng yàuh-séui

2 There is a relationship (strong or in some cases weak) between each of the words on the left and one of the words on the right. Make the connections.

   a sung   **1** yàuh-séui

   b daaih-gáam-ga   **2** sàn-sìn

   c laahn   **3** laahp-saap-túng

   d hói-tāan   **4** dihn-nyúhn-lòuh

   e lohk-syut   **5** baak-fo-gūng-sī

3 Pair off the most likely objects on the right with their verbs on the left. Some of the objects of course won't do at all, but sometimes there may be more than one possible pairing.

   a tái   **1** yéh

   b jyú   **2** dihn-yíng

   c góng   **3** tìhm-bán

   d chàam-gwùn   **4** chyùh-fóng

   e sihk   **5** yī-sāng

                         6 chi-fo

                         7 chèuhng-gok

                         8 Gim-kìuh Daaih-hohk

4 **Answer these questions in Cantonese so that all the answers have one word in common.**

a Wòhng Sàang jouh māt-yéh a?

b Wòhng Táai jouh mī-yéh a?

c Wòhng Síu-jé jouh mī-yéh a?

d Jèung Sìn-sàang jouh mī-yéh a?

e Nī sàam go yàhn jouh māt-yéh a?

Test yourself

09.03 **You've made it to the big time: you are a professional interpreter. The fate of nations hangs in the balance, so make sure you translate the remarks between the British Foreign Secretary (FS) and Mr Wong accurately or there may be a diplomatic incident with the state of Cantonesia! If you are feeling brave you can attempt this using the audio without looking at the text. After you have done your best you can check how well you did against our version in the usual place at the back of the book, and then you can listen to the complete audio version after that.**

FS	*Good morning, Mr Wong.*
You	**a**
Wong	Jóu-sàhn.
You	**b**
FS	*Would you like to have a beer?*
You	**c**
Wong	Ngóh m̀h jùng-yi yám bē-jáu.
You	**d**
FS	*Oh, well how about coffee? Or tea?*
You	**e**
Wong	Ga-fē tùhng chàh dōu deui sàn-tái m̀h hóu. Ngóh jí-haih yám séui jē.
You	**f**
FS	*I'm sorry, we have no water. My wife told me that the water here is not good to drink. Why don't you have some beer?*
You	**g**
Wong	Néih sèhng-yaht wah ngóh yiu yám bē-jáu. Ngóh yíh-gìng wah néih jì ngóh m̀h jùng-yi yám. Néih jàn-haih hóu m̀h haak-hei.
You	**h**
FS	*The beer is very good, it's British beer. Please drink a little.*
You	**i**
Wong	Nī go yàhn jeui m̀h haak-hei lak! Ngóh jáu lak!
You	**j**
FS	*Oh, he's going!*
You	**k**

Oh dear, it doesn't look as though that went too well, and you wasted your breath translating the last remark, didn't you? Still it wasn't your fault, was it? Or was it?

10 健康 *Gihn-hòng*
Health

In this unit you will learn about:

▶ *approximate numbers.*
▶ *before* and *after.*
▶ *duration of time.*

▶ *medical consultation.*
▶ *not until.*
▶ *weeks.*

CEFR: *(A2) Can discuss what to do next, making and responding to suggestions.*

 ## Chinese and Western medicine

Chinese medicine (**Jùng-yì** 中醫) and *Western medicine* (**Sài-yì** 西醫) have very different traditions and practices. Each has begun to acknowledge and learn from the other in recent years, and some practitioners now combine elements of both schools in their treatments. The contrast between *Chinese* (**Jùng**) and *Western* (**Sài**) is echoed in a number of expressions, perhaps most basically in **Jùng-gwok-yàhn** *Chinese* and **Sài-yàhn** *Westerner.* Another pair of terms which are more earthy and less formal are **Tòhng-yàhn** *Chinese* and **gwái-lóu** 'devil chap'. This last term for *Westerner* is in very common use and is hardly to be considered offensive, although the politically correct would avoid it.

Isn't it weird that we say in English *I'm going to see the doctor* when what is required is for the doctor to look at us? Weird too that Cantonese idiom also gets it back to front: **Ngóh heui tái yī-sāng**.

Vocabulary builder 1

Read through the new vocabulary and practise saying it out loud.

MEDICAL

嘔	áu	*to vomit*
病	behng	*illness*
診所	chán-só	*clinic, surgery*
作嘔	jok-áu	*to retch, be about to vomit*
唔舒服	m̀h syù-fuhk	*unwell, uncomfortable*
頭痛	tàuh-tung	*headache*
頭暈	tàuh-wàhn	*dizzy*
痛	tung	*pain, ache*
嚴重	yìhm-juhng	*serious, desperate*
醫院	yì-yún	*hospital* (cl: **gàan**)

TIME WORDS

間中	gaan-jūng	*occasionally, periodically*
嗰陣時	gó-jahn-sìh	*at that time*
先至	sìn-ji	*only then*

BASICS

幫	bòng	*on behalf of, for the benefit of*
取消	chéui-sìu	*to cancel*
打電話	dá-dihn-wá	*to make a phone call*
掛號	gwa-houh	*to register*
忙	mòhng	*busy*
舒服	syù-fuhk	*comfortable*
喂！	wái!	*hello!* (especially on the phone)
有啲、有一啲	yáuh-dī *or* yáuh-yāt-dī	*some, a little bit*

> **LANGUAGE TIP**
> At this point we would like to share a naughty little language trick with you. The *nurse* (**wuh-sih** 護士) in the next dialogue is a 'pain in the neck'. You know the words for both *neck* and *pain*, but unfortunately there is no such Cantonese idiomatic expression, so you could use **màh-fàahn** 麻煩 *trouble, nuisance, irritating, troublesome*. Fine, but not strong enough here, and Cantonese can spice it up with **gwái** 鬼 *ghost, devil*. You could describe the nurse as **màh-gwái-fàahn** (*devilishly troublesome*) or **gwái-gam-màh-fàahn** (*like a devil so troublesome*) or if you want something even stronger **gwái-séi-gam-màh-fàahn** (*devil death so troublesome*). Now we are on the verge of swearing, so we will go no further.

Dialogue 1

10.01 *Mr Wong phones his family doctor to make an appointment. The nurse answers.*

1 See if you can find the Cantonese for *All you have to do is …* in this dialogue. It's a bit tricky.

Wong	Wái! Nī-douh haih m̀h haih Jèung Yī-sāng ge chán-só a?
Nurse	Haih a!
Wong	Ngóh séung tái-yī-sāng, m̀h-gòi néih bòng ngóh gwa-houh lā.
Nurse	Néih gwai-sing a? Yáuh māt-yéh m̀h syù-fuhk a?
Wong	Ngóh haih Wòhng Yāt Góng Sìn-sàang, ngóh gok-dāk yáuh-dī tàuh-tung, gaan-jūng yáuh-dī tàuh-wàhn, juhng yáuh-dī jok-áu tìm.
Nurse	Néih ge behng m̀h syun hóu yìhm-juhng. Ngóh wah néih jì, Jèung Yī-sāng hóu mòhng …
Wong	Gám, ngóh géi-sí hó-yíh tái-yī-sāng a?
Nurse	Ngóh gú néih yiu dáng sàam-sei yaht sìn-ji hó-yíh gin-dóu Jèung Yī-sāng bo!
Wong	Māt-yéh wá? Sàam-sei yaht jì-hauh! Ngóh gú gó-jahn-sìh ngóh yíh-gìng séi-jó la!
Nurse	M̀h gán-yiu. Gó-jahn-sìh chéng néih taai-táai dá go dihn-wá làih, wah ngóh jì chéui-sìu gwa-houh jauh dāk lā!
Wong	M̀h dāk, m̀h dāk! Ngóh m̀h séung dáng lak, ngóh yìh-gā jauh yiu heui yì-yún lak!

王	喂！呢度係唔係張醫生嘅診所呀？
護士	係呀！
王	我想睇醫生，唔該你幫我掛號啦。
護士	你貴姓呀？有乜嘢唔舒服呀？
王	我係王一港先生，我覺得有啲頭痛，間中有啲頭暈，重有啲作嘔添。
護士	你嘅病唔算好嚴重。我話你知，張醫生好忙……
王	噉，我幾時可以睇醫生呀？
護士	我估你要等三四日先至可以見倒張醫生㗎！
王	乜嘢話？三四日之後！我估嗰陣時我已經死咗喇？
護士	唔緊要，嗰陣時請你太太打個電話嚟話我知取消掛號就得啦！
王	唔得，唔得！我唔想等喇，我而家就要去醫院嘞！

2 Pain in the what?

a Yāt go yàhn ge háu léuih-bihn yáuh sàam-sahp-yih go baahk-sīk ge yéh. Nī dī yéh haih ngàh 牙. Gám, 'ngàh-tung' Yìng-gwok-wá jīk-haih māt-yéh nē?

b Wòhng Sìn-sàang chìhn-yaht sihk-jó hóu dò hóu dò sàang-gwó la. Kàhm-yaht kéuih gok-dāk hóu m̀h syù-fuhk, yauh tàuh-tung yauh _____ tung.

c Gàm-yaht Léih Táai _____ tung, m̀h jà-dāk faai-jí lak.

Language discovery

10.1 ON BEHALF OF

You met the verb **bòng** *to help* in Unit 4. It can be used with other verbs to mean *on behalf of, for the benefit of, for*, but note that it always comes before the main verb in the sentence:

Ngóh bòng néih jíng sà-léut.   *I'll make the salad for you.*

Kéuih bòng ngóh gà-jē heui   *She does the shopping for my elder sister.*
   máaih-yéh.

10.2 COMFORTABLE

Syù-fuhk nicely translates the English word *comfortable*, and it follows naturally enough that **m̀h syù-fuhk** should mean *uncomfortable*. Indeed it does, but it is also very commonly used to mean *unwell, poorly, off colour* and, rather as in English, someone may tell you that they are a bit off colour, even if they are quite seriously ill.

10.3 A CERTAIN AMOUNT OF

Yáuh-dī can be put in front of many other words to indicate *a certain quantity of, some*. Here are some useful examples:

yáuh-dī yàhn   *some people*

yáuh-dī m̀h syù-fuhk   *a bit off colour*

yáuh-dī m̀h séung heui   *a bit reluctant to go*

10.4 APPROXIMATE NUMBERS

In the dialogue the nurse tells Mr Wong he will have to wait *three or four days* (**sàam-sei yaht**). You can make up approximate numbers like that whenever you want to. Here are a few chosen at random:

chāt-baat go yàhn   *seven or eight people*

Kéuih sahp-yih-sàam seui.   *She's 12 or 13 years old.*

sei-ńgh-sahp jek ngàuh   *40 or 50 head of cattle*

But beware! There is one combination you cannot use in this way: if you think about it, **gáu-sahp** cannot mean *nine* or *ten* because it already means *ninety*. So some other way of saying it had to be found and Cantonese has come up with a real humdinger: **sahp-*cl*-baat-*cl*** (*ten or eight classifiers*). So *nine or ten days* is **sahp-yaht-baat-yaht** and *nine or ten pens* is **sahp-jì-baat-jì bāt**.

10.5 ONLY THEN

Sìn-ji is an adverb and obeys the usual rule for adverbs: it must come directly in front of a verb. It is best to think of it as meaning *only then*, but you will find it very useful in coping with the English expression *not until*:

Kéuih tìng-yaht sìn-ji heui Yaht-bún.   *She's not going to Japan until tomorrow.* (lit. 'She tomorrow only then is going to Japan.')

10.6 DÁ *TO HIT*

Although **dá** does literally mean 'to hit' (**kéuih dá ngóh** *he hits me*), it is also used in many idiomatic ways as a general purpose verb. Here are a few you have already met:

dá-bō	*to play ball*
dá-dihn-wá	*to make a phone call*
dá-fùng	*to have a typhoon*
dá-léhng-tàai	*to tie a necktie, wear a tie*
dá-syun	*to reckon on, intend to*

Vocabulary builder 2

 Read through the new vocabulary and practise saying it out loud.

MORE MEDICAL

藥	yeuhk	*medicine* (cl: **júng**)
藥水	yeuhk-séui	*(liquid) medicine*

TIME WORDS

之前	jì-chìhn	*before*
未	meih	*not yet*
啱啱	ngāam-ngāam	*a moment before; have just*
上個禮拜	seuhng-go-láih-baai	*last week*
頭先	tàuh-sīn	*just now*
一分鐘	yāt fàn jūng	*a minute*
然後	yìhn-hauh	*afterwards, after that*

VERBS

補返數	bóu-fàan-sou	*to make up for, make amends*
希望	hèi-mohng	*to hope*
起身	héi-sàn	*to get up in the morning*
左搖右擺	jó-yìuh-yauh-báai	*to shake from side to side*
跳高踎低	tiu-gòu-màu-dài	*to jump up and down*
搖匀	yìuh-wàhn	*to shake up*

BASICS

廁所	chi-só	*toilet, lavatory, washroom* (cl: **go**)
點呀？／點樣呀？	dím a? *or* dím-yéung a?	*how is it? how's things?*
樽	jèun	cl: *a bottle of*
威廉	Wài-lìhm	Cantonese version of *William*

Dialogue 2

 10.02 *Mr Wong talks with his sick son, William.*

1 **The first piece of underlined text starts with a classifier. Why?**

2 **The second starts with Chi-chi. You met chi in Unit 6. What does chi-chi mean? (No, it is not the name of a panda!)**

Wong	Wài-lìhm, néih jouh-māt-yéh jó-yìuh-yauh-báai, tiu-gòu-màu-dài a? Néih m̀h syù-fuhk àh?
William	Haih a! Bàh-bā, ngóh héi-sàn gó-jahn-sìh gok-dāk go tóuh m̀h syù-fuhk. Heui-yùhn chi-só jì-hauh, dōu juhng yáuh-dī tung, só-yíh ngóh jauh yám-jó seuhng-go-láih-baai màh-mā máaih-fàan-làih gó jèun yeuhk-séui lak.
Wong	Yìh-gā dím a? <u>Go tóuh juhng tung m̀h tung a?</u>
William	Ngóh ngāam-ngāam yám-jó yeuhk-séui sahp fàn jūng jē, juhng meih jì.
Wong	Gám, jouh māt-yéh néih yiu jó-yìuh-yauh-báai nē?
William	<u>Chi-chi yám yeuhk-séui jì-chìhn</u>, màh-mā dōu yiu ngóh yìuh-wàhn dī yeuhk-séui sìn yìhn-hauh ji yám. Daahn-haih tàuh-sīn yám yeuhk-séui gó-jahn-sìh, ngóh m̀h gei-dāk yìuh-wàhn, só-yíh yìh-gā jó-yìuh-yauh-báai, hèi-mohng hó-yíh bóu-fàan-sou lā.

王	威廉，你做乜嘢左搖右擺，跳高踎低呀？你唔舒服吖？
威廉	係呀！爸爸，我起身嗰陣時覺得個肚唔舒服。去完廁所之後，都重有啲痛，所以我就飲咗上個禮拜媽媽買返嚟嗰樽藥水嘞。
王	而家點呀？個肚重痛唔痛呀？
威廉	我啱啱飲咗藥水十分鐘啫，重未知。
王	噉，做乜嘢你要左搖右擺呢？
威廉	次次飲藥水之前，媽媽都要我搖勻啲藥水先然後至飲。但係頭先飲藥水嗰陣時，我唔記得搖勻，所以而家左搖右擺，希望可以補返數啦。

3 **True or false?**

Respond with haih or m̀h haih to the statements, then spell out a longer answer in Cantonese. So for the first one you could reply: M̀h haih. Dī yeuhk-séui haih màh-mā seuhng-go-láih-baai máaih-fàan-làih ge.

a Gó jèun yeuhk-séui haih màh-mā kàhm-yaht máaih-fàan-làih ge.

b Chi-chi yám yeuhk-séui jì-chìhn, màh-mā dōu yiu Wài-lìhm yìuh-wàhn dī yeuhk-séui sìn.

c Wài-lìhm gok-dāk go tóuh m̀h syù-fuhk.

d Wài-lìhm yám-jó yeuhk-séui léuhng go jūng-tàuh lak.

Language discovery

10.7 FOUR-CHARACTER PHRASES

All the Chinese languages love using combinations of four characters as set phrases. There are two in Mr Wong's first speech in the dialogue. It can often be misleading to translate such phrases literally, but these two contain useful words which you might as well learn now:

tiu-gòu màu-dài	**tiu** means *to jump* and **gòu** means *high, tall*. In athletics **tiu-gòu** is the *high jump*. **màu-dài** means *to squat down, to crouch down*.
jó-yìuh-yauh-báai	**jó** is *left* and **yauh** is *right*, and **yìuh** and **báai** mean *to shake* and *to wave*.

You will be meeting **jó** and **yauh** again later on.

10.8 *LAST WEEK*, *THIS WEEK* AND *NEXT WEEK*

Seuhng-go-láih-baai means *last week*. **Seuhng** means *above*, so it literally means 'the week above'. Logically enough, the word for *next week* is 'the week below' **hah-go-láih-baai**. You now have the full set:

seuhng-go-láih-baai / sìng-kèih	*last week*
nī-go-láih-baai / sìng-kèih	*this week*
hah-go-láih-baai / sìng-kèih	*next week*

See if you can take this further and translate these:

seuhng-go-Láih-baai-sei

nī-go-Sìng-kèih-luhk

hah-go-Sìng-kèih-sàam

As a matter of fact you have met **seuhng** and **hah** as a pair meaning *up* and *down*, *above* and *below* before (see Unit 9: **hah** in that case had changed its tone to **há**), and you will meet them again later.

10.9 'TIME HOW LONG' AGAIN

In Unit 6 you met the idea of time how long, and you will remember that such time expressions are placed after the verb. *An hour* was **yāt go jūng-tàuh** and now you can deal in minutes too: *a minute* is **yāt fàn jūng**. In the dialogue, William says: **Ngóh ngāam-ngāam yám-jó yeuhk-séui sahp fàn jūng jē** *I've only had the medicine down me for ten minutes.*

10.10 *BEFORE* AND *AFTER*

In Unit 6 you met **jì-hau** *after*. Its opposite is **jì-chìhn** *before*. Both words follow the phrases they refer to, although in English they come in front of them:

Ngóh sihk-faahn jì-chìhn, hóu séung heui máaih bē-jáu.
Before I eat, I would very much like to go and buy some beer.
Kéuih fàan ūk-kéi jì-hauh, néih yiu wah kéuih jì!
After he returns home, you must tell him!

 Like seuhng and hah, chìhn and hauh are a regular pair. You learned chìhn-yaht *the day before yesterday* in Unit 9, so you can now make a good guess at what *the day after tomorrow* must be ...

And likewise:

chìhn-nín	*the year before last*
hauh-nín	*the year after next*

10.11 SÌN-JI AGAIN

You met **sìn-ji** earlier in this unit. It is made up of **sìn** *first* and **ji** *only then*, and sometimes they can be separated, as in William's last speech in the dialogue: **Màh-mā dōu yiu ngóh yìuh-wàhn dī yeuhk-séui sìn yìhn-hauh ji yám**. Translated literally this means, *Mummy requires me to shake the medicine first (and) afterwards only then to drink it.* It is a little more long-winded than **Màh-mā dōu yiu ngóh yìuh-wàhn dī yeuhk-séui sìn-ji yám** and sounds as though William is relaying the lesson his mother carefully taught him. Sometimes people use **sìn** on its own or **ji** on its own, in both cases still meaning *only then*.

  # Practice

1 **Read these questions aloud in Cantonese, then give the answer clearly and as quickly as you can. Remember that most of the answer will be the same as the question, but there will of course be no a?!**
   a Yī-sāng hái bīn-douh tái behng-yàhn a?
   b Wòhng Sìn-sàang haih bīn-gwok-yàhn a?
   c Màh-mā hái bīn-douh máaih-yéh a?
   d Hèung-góng-yàhn hái bīn-douh jyuh a?
   e Wòhng Wài-lìhm ge bàh-bā sing māt-yéh a?

2 **Wòhng Sàang, Wòhng Táai dōu yáuh-behng. Dím-gáai yáuh-behng nē? Yàn-waih Wòhng Taai-táai yám ga-fē yám-jó taai dò lak, Wòhng Sìn-sàang yám bē-jáu yám-jó taai dò lak. Léuhng go yàhn dōu heui tái Léih Yī-sāng. Néih gú yī-sāng deui kéuih-deih dím-yéung góng nē?**

   Make up some lines for a very severe Dr Li, who tells them that they are both ruining their health and then tells each of them separately not to indulge in their favourite vice any more.

3 Describe in Cantonese what Mr Chan is doing in each of the five pictures. Begin the first answer with Chàhn Sàang ..., and the others with Kéuih ...

🔲 Test yourself

You are advanced enough now to translate a suitably modified nursery rhyme into Cantonese. *A pig* is jyù and the word for *a son* (jái) can be tacked onto any noun to show that it is *a little one*, so jyù-jái is *a piglet*, *a piggy*, or just *a small pig*; and jyù-yuhk is *pork*. **OK, off you go ... and forgive us for the last line!**

This little piggy went to market (went shopping).

This little piggy stayed at home.

This little piggy had roast beef (well, you can forget the 'roast' bit).

And this little piggy had none.

And this little piggy went 'Oh! Oh! Oh!' to see the doctor.

時裝 *Sìh-jōng*
Fashion

In this unit you will learn about:

▶ *dressing.*

▶ *evenings.*

▶ *expressing likes and dislikes.*

▶ *large numbers.*

▶ *more verb endings.*

▶ *the indicated place.*

▶ *wrong thinking.*

CEFR: *(A2) Can explain what you like or dislike.*

 ## Fashion

Hong Kong has come a long way since the days of sweatshops and low-grade textiles, and there are plenty of prosperous international fashion house outlets there to prove it. It is whispered that if you have enough money you can even get yourself a designer face-mask to wear when everyone else is walking around with the plain pharmacy-bought ones on to prevent the spread of colds. There is a great range of dressiness everywhere now, from *tuxedos* (**láih-fuhk** 禮服) to *jeans* (**ngàuh-jái-fu** 牛仔褲) and *t-shirts* (**T-sēut** T恤), not of course forgetting the middle-class Western *suit* (**sài-jōng** 西裝) for men.

 Fu means *trousers*, but why does **ngàuh-jái-fu** mean *jeans*?

Vocabulary builder 1

 Read through the new vocabulary and practise saying it out loud.

FASHION TALK

設計	chit-gai	*design; to design*
戴	daai	*to wear, put on* (accessories)
大方	daaih-fōng	*tasteful, sophisticated*
帽	móu	*hat, cap* (cl: **déng** 頂)
硬	ngaahng	*hard, unyielding*
新款	sàn-fún	*new style*

COST

百	baak	*hundred*
千	chìn	*thousand*
價錢	ga-chìhn	*price*
價錢牌	ga-chìhn-páai	*price tag* (cl: **jèung**)
萬	maahn	*ten thousand*
億	yīk	*hundred million*

VERBS AND VERB ENDINGS

… 起嚟	-héi-làih	ve: *when it comes to, once you start*
… 住	-jyuh	ve: *ongoing state of*
試	si	*to test, try, try on*
運、運輸	wahn *or* wahn-syù	*to transport*
運到、運輸到	wahn-dou *or* wahn-syù-dou	*to arrive by transport*

BASICS

可惜	hó-sīk	*it is a pity that, unfortunately*
正係	jing-haih	*just happens to be*
唔錯	m̀h-cho	*not bad, pretty good*
唔知	m̀h-jì	*I wonder*

Dialogue 1

 11.01 *Miss Wong shops for a new hat and finally thinks she has found the very thing, but …*

1 **Si-háh dī ngàuh-yuhk!** means *Have a taste of the beef!* Miss Wong is very excited about a particular hat, and says **Dáng ngóh si-háh!** *Is she going to eat it?*

Wong	Nī déng móu ge chit-gai m̀h-cho, ngàahn-sīk yauh hóu – hó-sīk taai gwai lak!
Assistant	Síu-jé, si-háh nī déng lā: haih jeui sàn wahn-dou ga.
Wong	Ngóh m̀h jùng-yi kéuih ge jāt-déi, ngóh gok-dāk taai ngaahng lak, daai-héi-làih hóu m̀h syù-fuhk.
Assistant	Síu-jé, joi si-háh nī léuhng déng lā. Kéuih-deih dōu m̀h-cho ga.
Wong	Haih, kéuih-deih dōu m̀h-cho, daahn-haih nī léuhng déng móu dōu haih gauh-nín ge fún-sīk. Néih-deih juhng yáuh móuh dī sàn-fún ge a? … Yí! Nī déng m̀h-cho bo, yauh sàn-fún yauh daaih-fōng. Dáng ngóh si-háh!
Customer	Jàn-haih hóu leng!
Wong	Néih dōu wah leng àh! M̀h-jì yiu géi-dō chín nē?
Customer	Gáu-baak-ńgh-sahp mān.
Wong	Kéuih dōu móuh ga-chìhn-páai, néih dím jì a?
Customer	Síu-jé, néih daai-jyuh ge móu jing-haih ngóh ge!
王	呢頂帽嘅設計唔錯，顏色又好：可惜太貴嘞！
店員	小姐，試吓呢頂啦：係最新運到㗎。
王	我唔中意佢嘅質地，我覺得太硬嘞，戴起嚟好唔舒服。
店員	小姐，再試吓呢兩頂啦。佢哋都唔錯㗎。
王	係，佢哋都唔錯，但係呢兩頂帽都係舊年嘅款式，你哋重有冇啲新款嘅呀？… 咦！呢頂唔錯嗱，又新款又大方。等我試吓！
顧客	真係好靚！
王	你都話靚吖！唔知要幾多錢呢？
顧客	九百五十蚊。
王	佢都冇價錢牌，你點知呀？
顧客	小姐，你戴住嘅帽正係我嘅！

2 Bearing in mind what you have just learned in the dialogue, translate these four sentences into Cantonese:

a Do you know how much that white car costs?

b I wonder whether it will rain tomorrow?

c How should I know?

d I know how to cook Cantonese food, but Beijing food I can't cook.

3 Complete the sentences.

a Ngóh m̀h _____-dāk kéuih-deih hái _____-douh jyuh.

b Bàh-bā, màh-mā, daaih-lóu, tùhng _____, ngóh-deih sei go yàhn hái yāt-_____ sihk máahn-_____.

c Hái Hèung-góng _____ deih-tit pèhng m̀h pèhng a? Syù m̀h syù-_____ a?

d Kéuih ge Gwóng-jàu-wá _____ _____ gam faai. Ngoh m̀h jì kéuih _____ māt-yéh bo!

Language discovery

11.1 WHEN IT COMES TO IT

-héi-làih is a verb ending which will mean *once you start … or when it comes to …* depending on context. Here are two examples which should give you the feel of its use:

Góng-héi-làih, ngóh dōu sīk Hòh Sìn-sàang.

Now you come to mention it, I know Mr Ho as well.

Yuhng-héi-làih, néih jauh gok-dāk hóu syù-fuhk.

When you start using it, you will find it very comfortable.

11.2 HIGHER NUMBERS

Up to now you have been able to count as far as 99 only. Now for more:

100	**yāt-baak**
200	**yih-baak** or **léuhng-baak** (but usually **yih-baak** for 201–99)
350	**sàam-baak-ńgh-sahp**
714	**chāt-baak-yāt-sahp-sei**
999	**gáu-baak-gáu-sahp-gáu**
1,000	**yāt-chìn**
2,000	**yih-chìn** or **léuhng-chìn**
2,863	**yih-chìn-baat-baak-luhk-sahp-sàam**
9,999	**gáu-chìn-gáu-baak-gáu-sahp-gáu**

But after that there is a difference from English. The Chinese have a special word for *10,000*, which is **maahn**.

10,000	**yāt-maahn**
20,000	**yih-maahn** or **léuhng-maahn**
90,000	**gáu-maahn**
100,000	**sahp-maahn**
1,000,000	**yāt-baak-maahn**
10,000,000	**yāt-chìn-maahn**

In short, while English goes up to 1,000 and starts counting in units of 1,000 until it gets to units of a million, Cantonese goes up to 10,000, then starts counting in units of 10,000 up to 10 million, and finally has another term, **yīk**, for *100 million*:

1	**yāt**
10	**(yāt-) sahp**
100	**(yāt-) baak**
1,000	**(yāt-) chìn**
10,000	**(yāt-) maahn**
100,000	**(yāt-) sahp-maahn** (i.e. 10 x 10,000)
1,000,000	**(yāt-) baak-maahn** (100 x 10,000)
10,000,000	**(yāt-) chìn-maahn** (1,000 x 10,000)
100,000,000	**(yāt-) yīk**

Be warned that some overseas Chinese (notably those in Singapore and Britain) seem to be slipping into Western ways, so that you might hear them saying **sahp-chìn** instead of **yāt-maahn** for 10,000.

The natural progression in Cantonese, then, is from **sahp** to **baak** to **chìn** to **maahn** to **yīk**. If one or more of these categories is missed out, as for instance with the number 103 where there is no number in the **sahp** column, Cantonese indicates this by throwing in the word **lìhng** 零 *zero*. So *103* is **yat-baak-lìhng-sàam**. If more than one category is missed out it is still only necessary to put in one **lìhng**, so *10,003* is **yāt-maahn-lìhng-sàam**.

YOUR TURN **Put these into Cantonese:**

a 322 cars

b 1,802 cows

c 400,000,046 Chinese people

d $283,915

> **LANGUAGE TIP**
> Chinese culture loves round numbers. To wish someone well it was common to say *May you have 100 sons and 1,000 grandsons*. The *Old Hundred Surnames* is a regular way of referring to the Chinese people. *Thousand Mile Eyes* was the name of a protective god who acted as lookout for trouble. The *10,000-Mile Long Wall* is what is known in English as the Great Wall of China. None of these numbers is meant to be taken literally: they all mean something like *lots of*.

11.3 THE VERB ENDINGS -JYUH AND -GÁN COMPARED

In Unit 4 **-gán** was introduced as a verb ending which showed continuing action. At first sight **-jyuh** does not seem so different, but they are not interchangeable. **-gán** tells us that activity is still going on, but **-jyuh** says that the activity has come to a halt and that we are left with a steady ongoing state. The examples should make it clear:

Wòhng Táai daai-gán yāt déng hóu leng ge móu.

Mrs Wong is putting on a beautiful hat.

Wòhng Táai daai-jyuh yāt déng hóu leng ge móu.

Mrs Wong is wearing a beautiful hat.

11.4 DRESSING UP

Here are some clothing words for you, with classifiers in brackets.

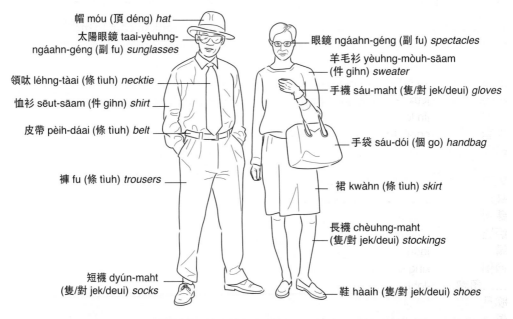

帽 móu (頂 déng) *hat*

太陽眼鏡 taai-yèuhng-ngáahn-géng (副 fu) *sunglasses*

領呔 léhng-tàai (條 tìuh) *necktie*

恤衫 sēut-sāam (件 gihn) *shirt*

皮帶 pèih-dáai (條 tìuh) *belt*

褲 fu (條 tìuh) *trousers*

短襪 dyún-maht (隻/對 jek/deui) *socks*

眼鏡 ngáahn-géng (副 fu) *spectacles*

羊毛衫 yèuhng-mòuh-sāam (件 gihn) *sweater*

手襪 sáu-maht (隻/對 jek/deui) *gloves*

手袋 sáu-dói (個 go) *handbag*

裙 kwàhn (條 tìuh) *skirt*

長襪 chèuhng-maht (隻/對 jek/deui) *stockings*

鞋 hàaih (隻/對 jek/deui) *shoes*

(Oh, of course, we can't tell from the drawing, but those stockings could be tights, in which case we should label them 襪褲 **maht-fu (條 tìuh)** *tights*.)

 A pair of gloves is **yāt deui sáu-maht**. What is the Cantonese for *two pairs of trousers*?

Vocabulary builder 2

 Read through the new vocabulary and practise saying it out loud.

MORE FASHION TALK

布料	bou-líu	*material, fabric* (cl: **júng**)
花樣	fā-yéung	*pattern*
酒會	jáu-wúi	*reception, cocktail party*
着(著)	jeuk	*to wear* (clothes)
展覽	jín-láahm	*show, exhibition*
外套	ngoih-tou	*jacket* (cl: **gihn**)
時裝	sìh-jōng	*fashion*

VERBS AND VERB ENDINGS

被迫	beih-bīk	*to be forced to, compelled to*
參加	chàam-gà	*to take part in*
經過	gìng-gwo	*to pass by*
讚	jaan	*to praise*
傾偈	kìng-gái	*to chat*
......落嚟	-lohk-làih	ve: *downwards*
睇見	tái-gin	*to see* (lit. 'look at and see')
停	tìhng	*to stop*
以為	yíh-wàih	*to assume, regard as*

BASICS

大聲	daaih-sèng	*loud, in a loud voice*
今晚	gàm-máahn	*tonight, this evening*
空	hùng	*empty, vacant*
張	jèung	cl: *for flat things (paper, chairs, tables, sheets, etc.)*
實在	saht-joih	*in fact, really*
相反	sèung-fáan	*on the contrary*
梳化椅	sō-fá-yí	*sofa, easy chair* (cl: **jèung**)
一樣	yāt-yeuhng	*the same*
有人	yáuh-yàhn	*somebody, some people*
椅	yí	*chair* (cl: **jèung**)

Dialogue 2

11.02 *Mrs Wong explains to her husband why she talked so much at a party.*

1 The last word of the dialogue is tìm, which you will remember means *in addition*. That doesn't seem to make sense here, so can you come up with a translation which reflects what tìm does to the meaning of the sentence?

Mr Wong	Taai-táai, gàm-máahn ngóh-deih chàam-gà ge sìh-jōng jín-láahm jáu-wúi néih yāt-dihng gok-dāk hóu hòi-sām lak.
Mrs Wong	M̀h haih bo! Ngāam-ngāam sèung-fáan. Ngóh gok-dāk hóu m̀h hòi-sām.
Mr Wong	M̀h haih a: ngóh tái-gin néih chóh hái sō-fá-yí douh, m̀h tìhng gám tùhng Jèung Taai-táai, Hòh Taai-táai, Wòhng Síu-jé kéuih-deih kìng-gái. Néih juhng daaih-sèng jaan Wòhng Síu-jé gihn sāam-kwàhn hóu leng, yauh jaan Jèung Taai-táai gihn ngoih-tou ge fún-sīk hóu sàn.
Mrs Wong	Ngóh haih beih-bīk yiu m̀h tìhng gám daaih-sèng kìng-gái jē, saht-joih ngóh m̀h séung ga.
Mr Wong	Dím-gáai nē?
Mrs Wong	Yàn-waih ngóh jeuk gó tou sāam-kwàhn ge ngàahn-sīk tùhng fā-yéung, tùhng dī sō-fá-yí ge bou-líu yāt-yeuhng. Ngóh chóh hái sō-fá-yí douh, yùh-gwó m̀h góng-yéh, yáuh-yàhn gìng-gwo yíh-wàih yáuh yāt jèung hùng yí, séung chóh-lohk-làih tìm.
王生	太太，今晚我哋參加嘅時裝展覽酒會你一定覺得好開心嘞。
王太	唔係嗎！啱啱相反，我覺得好唔開心。
王生	唔係丫：我睇見你坐喺梳化椅度，唔停噉同張太太，何太太，王小姐佢哋傾偈。你重大聲讚王小姐件衫裙好靚，又讚張太太件外套嘅款式好新。
王太	我係被迫要唔停噉大聲傾偈啫，實在我唔想㗎。
王生	點解呢？
王太	因為我着嗰套衫裙嘅顏色同花樣，同啲梳化椅嘅布料一樣。我坐喺梳化椅度，如果唔講嘢，有人經過以為有一張空椅，想坐落嚟添。

2 Have you understood? What does the cartoon caption mean?

Kàhm-yaht ngóh yíh-wàih nī jèung yí hóu syù-fuhk, daahn-haih yìh-gā…!

3 Quickly decide which of the alternatives in brackets will leave a correct statement.

   a Wòhng Sìn-sàang tùhng Wòhng Taai-táai chàam-gà ge haih (jouh-sàang-yi / dihn-yíng / sìh-jōng) jáu-wúi.
   b Wòhng Táai wah kéuih (m̀h hòi-sām / hòu hòi-sām).
   c Wòhng Táai jaan Jèung Táai (sàn-tái hóu hóu / hóu sīk jyú-sung / hóu sīk yàuh-séui / gihn ngoih-tou hóu leng).
   d Wòhng Taai-táai tou saam-kwàhn ge ngàahn-sīk, fā-yéung tùhng (sō-fá-yí / laahp-saap-túng / dihn-nyúhn-lòuh) yāt-yeuhng.

Language discovery

11.5 LATE IN THE DAY

Máahn means *evening, late in the day* (not *late for an appointment*). *This evening* or *tonight* is **gàm-máahn**, and from there you can build another little set of terms:

gàm-máahn	*this evening, tonight*
kàhm-máahn	*yesterday evening, last night*
tìng-máahn	*tomorrow evening, tomorrow night*
chìhn-máahn	*the evening of the day before yesterday*
hauh-máahn	*the evening of the day after tomorrow*

11.6 NGĀAM-NGĀAM AGAIN

In Unit 10 we met **ngāam-ngāam** meaning *a moment ago*. It has a second meaning of *exactly, precisely*. In the dialogue Mrs Wong says **ngāam-ngāam sèung-fáan** – *it's exactly to the contrary* – and you might note these other examples:

ngāam-ngāam yāt go jūng-tàuh	*exactly one hour*
ngāam-ngāam hóu	*exactly right*

11.7 HÁI-DOUH *AT THE INDICATED PLACE*

You met **nī-douh** *here*, **gó-douh** *there* and **bīn-douh** *where?* in Units 3 and 5. **Hái-douh** (lit. 'at the place') is used rather loosely to mean either *here* or *there* and really seems to mean *at the place we both have in mind*. So you might say **Néih hái-douh jouh māt-yéh a?** to someone on the phone and it would mean *What are you doing there?* or you might say it to someone who is in the same room as you and it would mean *What are you doing here?*

Hái-douh can be split to surround a noun and then it indicates a rather vague relationship with the noun, like *in / on / at / in the general vicinity of*. For example, in the dialogue Mr Wong says: **Ngóh tái-gin néih chóh hái sō-fá-yí douh** *I saw you sitting there on the sofa*, and *on* seems the most likely place for Mrs Wong to be.

 But if you were to ask someone where they had thoughtlessly left their keys, and they replied hái chē douh, where could the keys potentially be?

It can be quite useful to be able to be so vague, so **hái-douh** is worth remembering.

> **LANGUAGE TIP**
> When a teacher takes the register, school children reply **Hái-douh**, just as they would say *Present* or *Here* in the same situation in Britain. And the answer to the question *Have you got your mobile phone?* might well be **Hái-douh** *It's here. I've got it.*

11.8 THREE VERBS FOR *TO WEAR*

You have now met three verbs which can all be translated as *to wear* in English:

jeuk   to wear clothing, that is shirts, jackets, trousers, underclothes, shoes and socks

daai   to wear accessories, that is hats, spectacles, watches, rings, jewellery, gloves, etc.

dá   (the least common) to wear something which has to be tied on like a necktie or headscarf

11.9 YÍH-WÀIH *TO THINK WRONGLY*

Yíh-wàih means *to assume* or *to think, consider*, but it is probably most often used to show that what was thought was actually wrong. In the dialogue Mrs Wong says that she was talking non-stop so that no one would fail to know she was there and think (wrongly) that there was a vacant chair. Here are some more examples:

Ngóh yíh-wàih kéuih haih Yaht-bún-yàhn.

I thought she was Japanese (but now I know that she is actually Korean).

Kéuih yíh-wàih gàm-yaht haih Láih-baai-yaht.

He thought that today was Sunday (but of course it's actually Saturday).

> **LANGUAGE TIP**
> You might like to learn a very slangy expression: **Néih yíh-wàih lā!** which corresponds to the English *You reckon! That's what you think! Think again, pal!*

11.10 VERB ENDING -LOHK-LÀIH

You met **lohk** in **lohk síu-bā** *to alight from the mini-bus* and in **lohk-syut** *to snow*. The basic meaning of **lohk** is *to come down, fall down, go down*. As a verb ending **-lohk-làih** shows that the action of the verb is happening in a downward direction:

chóh-lohk-làih	*sits down*
yàuh fèi-gèi gó-douh tái-lohk-làih	*looking down from the aircraft*

Listen and understand

EAVESDROPPING

 11.03 **Listen to the audio as you read Miss Wong's side of the phone conversation.**

1 **It's intriguing … but what is going on? And what impression do you get of Miss Wong?**

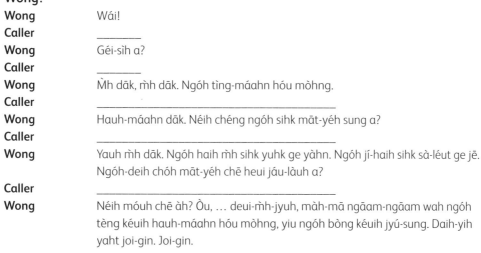

Wong	Wái!
Caller	_____
Wong	Géi-sìh a?
Caller	_____
Wong	M̀h dāk, m̀h dāk. Ngóh tìng-máahn hóu mòhng.
Caller	_____
Wong	Hauh-máahn dāk. Néih chéng ngóh sihk māt-yéh sung a?
Caller	_____
Wong	Yauh m̀h dāk. Ngóh haih m̀h sihk yuhk ge yàhn. Ngóh jí-haih sihk sà-léut ge jē. Ngóh-deih chóh māt-yéh chē heui jáu-làuh a?
Caller	_____
Wong	Néih móuh chē àh? Òu, … deui-m̀h-jyuh, màh-mā ngāam-ngāam wah ngóh tèng kéuih hauh-máahn hóu mòhng, yiu ngóh bòng kéuih jyú-sung. Daih-yih yaht joi-gin. Joi-gin.

 2 **Listen again and try to supply the missing side of the conversation.**

 3 11.04 **Now, listen to what we think must have been the full conversation.**

ⓘ Practice

1 Try your number skills by putting these figures into Cantonese. You probably know that one of the hardest things to do is to count naturally in a second language, so the more practice you do the better.

a 16 young ladies
b 200 sheets of paper
c $5,600
d 1,000,000 Chinese people

e 12,750
f 8,034
g 11 hours
h two lobsters

2 Warning: only do this if you are not the driver! When you are in a car or a bus, watch the vehicles that come towards you and try to read off their number plates in Cantonese before they have gone by. Until you get better at it, you can do it by saying sàam-baat-chāt rather than the full version sàam-baak-baat-sahp-chāt. It's quite an addictive little game, you'll find, but very good for making you slick with numbers.

3 Give the opposites of the words on the left by completing the words on the right.

a sàn-fún   _____ fún
b taai gwai   taai _____
c máaih ūk   _____ ūk
d jì-hauh   jì _____
e láahng   _____
f dùng-bāk   _____

ⓘ Test yourself

Here's a brain-teaser for you. Miss Ho's cryptic answer to my question contains enough information to reveal all the facts, but you will have to work hard to find them out!

Hah-go-sìng-kèih Hòh Sìn-sàang, Hòh Taai-táai, Hòh Síu-jé dōu wúih fong yāt yaht ga. Hó-sìk kéuih-deih m̀h haih yāt-chàih fong: yāt go fong Láih-baai-yāt, yāt go fong Láih-baai-yih, yāt go fong Láih-baai-sàam. Kéuih-deih fong-ga séung jouh māt-yéh nē? Yāt go séung heui tái-hei, yāt go séung heui pàh-sàan, yāt go séung heui jáu-làuh sihk lùhng-hā. Ngóh mahn Hòh Síu-jé bīn-go séung hái bīn yāt yaht heui bīn-douh a? Kéuih wah:

'Bàh-bā séung heui pàh-sàan. Ngóh Láih-baai-yih fong-ga. Yáuh yàhn séung Láih-baai-yāt heui sihk lùhng-hā.'

Nàh! Néih hó m̀h hó-yíh wah ngóh jì nī sàam go yàhn léuih-bihn bīn-go séung heui tái-hei? Bīn-go séung heui sihk lùhng-hā? Sìng-kèih-sàam fong-ga haih bīn-go a?

教育 *Gaau-yuhk*
Education

In this unit you will learn about:

▶ *classifiers as possessives.*

▶ *comparisons.*

▶ *each / every.*

▶ *relative position.*

▶ *studying.*

▶ *the passive.*

CEFR: *(A2) Can use simple descriptive language to make brief statements about and compare objects and possessions.*

A little learning

As a starting bonus you will be pleased to hear that you already know a word for *teacher* (male or female) – it is **sìn-sàang**, which you met in Unit 1 meaning *Mr*. The more formal word is **lóuh-sì** 'old teacher', which in English doesn't sound formal at all. But this book is about learning rather than teaching, so let's look at the other side of the process.

To learn is **hohk** 學, and **hohk-sāang** 學生 is a *pupil* or *student*. **Hohk-haauh** 學校 'learning institute' is a *school*, **síu-hohk** 小學 'small learning' is a *primary school*, **jùng-hohk** 中學 'middle learning' is a *secondary school* and … well, you already know what a university is, don't you? *Books* (**syù** 書) are an important aid to learning. **Duhk-syù** 讀書 'to read books out loud' is *to study* and **gaau-syù** 教書 'to teach books' means *to teach*.

Have a guess what **tái-syù** means.

Vocabulary builder 1

 Read through the new vocabulary and practise saying it out loud.

STUDYING

測驗	chāak-yihm	to test; evaluation
地理學	deih-léih(-hohk)	geography
科	fō	subject, discipline
課本	fo-bún	textbook (cl: **go**)
科學	fō-hohk	science
功課	gùng-fo	homework
中文	Jùng-màhn	Chinese language
歷史學	lihk-sí(-hohk)	history
練習簿	lihn-jaahp-bóu	exercise book (cl: **go**)
數學	sou-hohk	mathematics
溫習	wàn-jaahp	to revise lessons; revision (see Unit 7)
英文	Yìng-màhn	English language

VERBS

被	beih	to endure, suffer; by
過	gwo	to go past; than
管	gwún	to control, be in charge of
明白	mìhng-baahk	to understand, be clear about

BASICS

磅	bohng	pound (weight)
差唔多	chà-m̀h-dō	almost
重	chúhng	heavy
公斤	gūng-gàn	kilogram
後生	hauh-sāang	young
後生仔	hauh-sāang-jái	youngsters
好彩	hóu-chói	lucky; fortunately
之嘛	jī-máh	fp: only
每	múih	each, every
平均	pìhng-gwàn	average, on average
辛苦	sàn-fú	hard, distressing
尤其(係)	yàuh-kèih (haih)	especially
如果唔係(呢)	yùh-gwó-m̀h-haih(-nē)	otherwise, if not so

Dialogue 1

12.01 *Parents chat about the hardships of education.*

1 In Mr Wong's first speech you will see duhk-syù, the verb *to study*, but is it used as a verb here?

Wong	Ngóh gok-dāk Hèung-góng hohk-sāang duhk-syù jàn-haih sàn-fú lak.
Cheung	Haih a! Ngóh dōu tùhng-yi. Kéuih-deih múih yaht dōu yiu duhk Jùng-màhn, Yīng-màhn, Sou-hohk, Deih-léih, Lihk-sí tùhng Fō-hohk. Yìh-ché pìhng-gwàn múih go láih-baai dōu yáuh léuhng-sàam fō yiu chāak-yihm.
Wong	Juhng yáuh a! Kéuih-deih ge fo-bún yauh chúhng yauh dò, múih yaht yiu daai-fàan hohk-haauh ge fo-bún tùhng lihn-jaahp-bóu jauh m̀h wúih síu-gwo sahp bohng chúhng.
Lee	Wà! Jīk-haih ńgh gūng-gàn bo! Ngóh go jái gàm-nín jí-haih sahp seui jī-máh, hái síu-hohk duhk-syù, daahn-haih kéuih máahn-máahn dōu yiu wàn-jaahp chà-m̀h-dō sei go jūng-tàuh sìn-ji hó-yíh jouh-yùhn dī gùng-fo. Ngóh m̀h mìhng-baahk dī sìn-sàang dím-gáai béi gam dò gùng-fo kéuih-deih.
Wong	Ngóh wah hái jùng-hohk gaau-syù juhng màah-fàahn a! Yauh yiu gaau kéuih-deih yauh yiu gwún kéuih-deih, yàuh-kèih haih gwún kéuih-deih, yàn-waih yìh-gā dī hauh-sāang-jái go-go dōu m̀h jùng-yi beih yàhn gwún ge-la.
Cheung	Hóu-chói ngóh-deih go-go dōu m̀h haih gaau-syù sìn-sàang jē. Yùh-gwó-m̀h-haih, ngóh-deih dōu móuh sìh-gaan yāt-chàih hái nī-douh kìng-gái lā.
王	我覺得香港學生讀書真係辛苦嘅。
張	係呀！我都同意。佢哋每日都要讀中文、英文、數學、地理、歷史同科學。而且平均每個禮拜都有兩三科要測驗。
王	重有呀！佢哋嘅課本又重又多，每日要帶返學校嘅課本同練習簿就唔會少過十磅重。
李	嘩！即係五公斤噃！我個仔今年只係十歲之嘛，喺小學讀書，但係佢晚晚都要溫習差唔多四個鐘頭先至可以做完啲功課。我唔明白啲先生點解俾咁多功課佢哋。
王	我話喺中學教書重麻煩呀！又要教佢哋又要管佢哋，尤其係管佢哋，因為而家啲後生仔個個都唔中意被人管嘅喇。
張	好彩我哋個個都唔係教書先生啫。如果唔係，我哋都冇時間一齊喺呢度傾偈啦。

2 Try to choose from the brackets the words which will complete the sentences correctly.

a Wòhng Sìn-sàang wah dī hohk-sāang ge fo-bún (yauh gwai yauh leng / yauh pèhng yauh sàn / yauh chúhng yauh dò).

b Léih Taai-táai go jái máahn-máahn dōu yiu wàn-jaahp (sei go jūng-tàuh / sàam go jūng-tàuh / yāt go jūng-tàuh).

c Wòhng Sìn-sàang wah gaau (síu-hohk / jùng-hohk / daaih-hohk) juhng màah-fàahn.

d Jèung Sàang wah hóu-chói kéuih-deih m̀h haih (gíng-chaat / sī-gēi / gaau-syù sìn-sàang).

Language discovery

12.1 MÚIH *EACH, EVERY*

There are two things to remember about using **múih**. First, it requires the use of a classifier:

múih go yàhn	*each person, everybody*
múih jì bāt	*each pen*
múih yaht	*every day* (refer back to Unit 8 if this one puzzles you)

Second, because **múih** involves wholeness and inclusiveness it is almost always backed up by **dōu** placed before the verb:

Múih gihn sāam-kwàhn dōu yáuh síu-síu laahn-jó.

Each one of the dresses is slightly damaged.

12.2 SIMPLE COMPARISONS WITH **GWO**

The same word **gwo** which you met in Unit 6 (meaning *to go past, to go by*) is used to make simple comparisons (*X is -er than Y*):

Ngóh ge chē daaih-gwo néih ge chē.

My car is bigger than yours.

Yìng-gwok chē gwai m̀h gwai-gwo Yaht-bún chē a?

Are British cars more expensive than Japanese cars?

So the pattern is X adjective **gwo** Y, and you can probably see how logically it works – *X is adjective surpassing Y*:

Ngóh gòu-gwo kéuih.   *I am taller than he is* (lit. 'I am tall surpassing him').

In the dialogue Mr Wong talks about the heavy load of books and exercise books carried by students and he says: **M̀h wúih síu-gwo sahp bohng chúhng** *They cannot be less than ten pounds in weight.*

12.3 CLASSIFIERS AS POSSESSIVES

You learned in Unit 2 that the useful word **ge** shows possession, so that *my pen* is **ngóh ge bāt**. There is a minor snag with this: as you know, nouns can be either singular or plural without changing their form and so **ngóh ge bāt** could mean either *my pen* or *my pens*. In many cases it doesn't matter that this is unclear or else the context makes it obvious whether you mean *pen* or *pens*. If you wish to be more precise, however, you can be, and it is the classifier which gives you the power:

ngóh ge bāt	*my pen* or *my pens*
ngóh jì bāt	*my pen* (singular only)
ngóh dī bāt	*my pens* (plural only)

 Look back at the dialogue. How many sons do you think Mrs Lee has?

12.4 BEIH: THE PASSIVE CONSTRUCTION

Beih literally means 'to suffer, endure', but you will seldom need to worry about that. You will usually only meet it used like the English word *by* in the passive construction. These two examples should suffice to show how it works:

Hòh Sìn-sàang chéng Wòhng Sìn-sàang heui sihk-faahn.

Wòhng Sìn-sàang beih Hòh Sìn-sàang chéng heui sihk-faahn.

The first sentence is <u>active</u> (*Mr Ho invites Mr Wong out for a meal*) and the second is <u>passive</u> (*Mr Wong is invited out for a meal by Mr Ho*). Cantonese does not use this passive construction very often, but you need to be aware that it exists so that you will not be taken by surprise when you do meet it.

12.5 LANGUAGE AND CULTURE

Jùng-màhn easily translates as *Chinese language*, but it carries with it a more complex meaning which includes the Chinese writing system and even Chinese culture. **Jùng-gwok-wá** 中國話 (you met **wá** *speech* in Unit 4) also translates as *Chinese language*, but it is clearly limited to speaking and listening and may not imply the ability to read and write Chinese. The two terms can be applied to most languages, though **màhn** seems to sit most comfortably with single syllable country names:

Dāk-gwok-wá	or	**Dāk-màhn**	*German*
Faat-gwok-wá	or	**Faat-màhn**	*French*
Ngòh-gwok-wá	or	**Ngòh-màhn**	*Russian*
Yaht-bún-wá	or	**Yaht-màhn**	*Japanese*
Yìng-gwok-wá	or	**Yìng-màhn**	*English*

12.6 HOHK

And we're not done with **hohk** *to learn* yet. Did you notice that the names of many study disciplines ('-ologies') also include the word **hohk**? *Geography* is literally 'land principles-ology', *science* 'system-ology', *history* 'past history-ology', and *mathematics* 'numbers-ology'.

Can you guess the proper English terms for these two disciplines?
yúh-yìhn-hohk 語言學 'language-ology'   **séh-wúi-hohk** 社會學 'society-ology'

RECAP ON CLASSIFIERS

You have now met all the major uses of classifiers, so perhaps this little checklist will be helpful to you:

When you specify a noun with **nī, gó, bīn, múih, géi, sèhng-** (*this, that, which?, each, how many? / several, the whole*) you should use the correct classifier between the specifier and the noun:

nī go yàhn	*this person*	**gó tìuh léhng-tàai**	*that tie*
bīn jek lùhng-hā?	*which lobster?*	**múih gihn sāam-kwàhn**	*each dress*
géi jì bāt	*how many pens?*	**sèhng-go láih-baai**	*the whole week*

When you count nouns you should use the correct classifier between the specifier and the noun:

yāt go Yaht-bún-yàhn	*one Japanese*	**léuhng chàan faahn**	*two meals*
sàam gàan ūk	*three houses*	**yih-sahp-sei jì bāt**	*24 pens*

The classifier for uncountable things (like water) is **dī**. **Dī** also is the plural classifier; that is, the classifier used when a noun is plural but uncounted:

gó dī séui	*that water*	**nī dī sung**	*this food*
nī dī Yìng-gwok-yàhn	*these British people*	**bīn dī Jùng-màhn syù?**	*which Chinese books?*

The classifier can be used at the beginning of a sentence where English uses the definite article:

Dī sung hóu hóu-sihk.	*The food is delicious.*
Gihn sāam leng m̀h leng a?	*Is the garment nice?*

Doubling the classifier and adding **dōu** before the verb gives the meaning *every one of, each one of*:

Gihn-gihn sāam-kwàhn dōu hóu leng.	*Each of the dresses is beautiful.*
Gàan-gàan ūk léuih-bihn dōu móuh yàhn.	*There is no-one in any of the houses.*

The correct classifier or the plural classifier **dī** can be used to indicate possession:

kéuih gàan ūk	*her house*	**Wòhng Sìn-sàang dī chē**	*Mr Wong's cars*

Very few words seem to act as noun and classifier combined. Of these you have already met the three most common – **nìhn, yaht** and **seui**:

sàam nìhn	*three years*	**léuhng yaht**	*two days*	**sahp seui**	*ten years old*

Finally, here are two new classifiers which can be used interchangeably for any kind of book:

部 **bouh**   or   本 **bún**   cl: for books

Vocabulary builder 2

 Read through the new vocabulary and practise saying it out loud.

TRAFFIC

衝	chùng	*to rush, dash against*
燈	dāng	*light, lamp* (cl: **jáan 盞**)
交通	gàau-tùng	*traffic, communications*
交通燈	gàau-tùng-dāng	*traffic light*
檢控	gím-hung	*to accuse, book*
警察	gíng-chaat	*policeman*
汽車	hei-chè	*vehicle, car* (cl: **ga**)
司機	sī-gēi	*driver*

> **LANGUAGE TIP**
>
> **Hùhng-dāng** is a *red light*. The other traffic light colours are: **wòhng-dāng** *amber light* and **luhk-dāng** *green light*. In the dialogue, *traffic lights* are called **gàau-tùng-dāng**: they are often known as **hùhng-luhk-dāng** too.

BASICS

呀	ā!	*fp: emphatic*
前邊	chìhn-bihn	*in front; the front side*
秩序	diht-jeuih	*order, orderly*
份子	fahn-jí	*element, member*
方面	fòng-mihn	*aspect*
教育	gaau-yuhk	*to educate; education*
公共	gùng-guhng	*public*
政府	jing-fú	*government*
失敗	sāt-baaih	*loss, failure*
社會	séh-wúi	*society*
市民	síh-màhn	*citizen*
壞	waaih	*bad*
一般	yāt-bùn	*general, common, the general run of*

Dialogue 2

 12.02 *An encounter with a traffic policeman shows that education does not always succeed in getting the main point across.*

1 How would you translate juhng yiu (lit. 'still want to') in the policeman's third speech?

Wong	Hèung-góng jing-fú gaau-yuhk Hèung-góng síh-màhn jàn-haih sāt-baaih lak.
Cheung	Néih góng bīn fòng-mihn ge gaau-yuhk nē?
Wong	Hóu dò fòng-mihn lā, yàuh-kèih haih yāt-bùn ge gùng-guhng diht-jeuih fòng-mihn.
Cheung	Yí! Chìhn-bihn yáuh go gíng-chaat hóu-chíh yiu gím-hung go hei-chè sī-gēi bo! Ngóh-deih heui tái-háh lā.
Policeman	Sìn-sàang, néih tái m̀h tái-dóu gó jáan gàau-tùng-dāng a?
Driver	Tái-dóu ā!
Policeman	Néih tái m̀h tái-dóu haih hùhng-dāng a?
Driver	Tái-dóu ā!
Policeman	Gám, dím-gáai néih juhng yiu chùng hùhng-dāng nē?
Driver	M̀h hóu-chói, yàn-waih ngóh tái-m̀h-dóu néih!
Wong	Jèung Táai, néih tái-háh, nī dī jauh haih Hèung-góng-yàhn deui yāt-bùn gùng-guhng diht-jeuih ge gaau-yuhk lak!
Cheung	Múih go séh-wúi dōu yáuh yāt-dī waaih-fahn-jí, m̀h haih go-go yàhn dōu yāt-yeuhng ge. Hèung-góng ge gaau-yuhk dōu yáuh hóu ge fòng-mihn ge.
王	香港政府教育香港市民真係失敗嘞。
張	你講邊方面嘅教育呢？
王	好多方面啦，尤其係一般嘅公共秩序方面。
張	咦！前邊有個警察好似要檢控個汽車司機嘛！我哋去睇吓啦。
警察	先生，你睇唔睇倒嗰盞交通燈呀？
司機	睇倒呀！
警察	你睇唔睇倒係紅燈呀？
司機	睇倒呀！
警察	噉，點解你重要衝紅燈呢？
司機	唔好彩，因為我睇唔到你！
王	張太，你睇吓，呢啲就係香港人對一般公共秩序嘅教育嘞！
張	每個社會都有一啲壞份子，唔係個個人都一樣嘅，香港嘅教育都有好嘅方面嘅。

2 Complete the following:

a Hùhng-luhk-dāng _____ gàau-tùng-dāng.

b Sī-gēi tái-dóu hùhng-dāng yiu _____ chē.

c Waaih-fahn-jí hóu pa _____.

d Kéuih sahp seui, ngóh baat seui jē: kéuih _____-gwo ngóh.

> **LANGUAGE TIP**
>
> Mrs Cheung uses the formal term **gíng-chaat** for *policeman* in the dialogue. You will probably also hear the colloquial **chàai-yàhn** 差人, or even more colloquially **chàai-lóu** 差佬, both of which hark back to the runners who served the imperial Chinese government.

122

Language discovery

12.7 TELLING YOUR WHEREABOUTS

In the dialogue you met the word **chìhn-bihn** *in front, in front of, the front side*. You had better now meet its friends:

前邊	**chìhn-bihn**	*in front, in front of, the front side*
後邊	**hauh-bihn**	*the back, behind, the rear side*
上邊	**seuhng-bihn**	*the top, on top of, above, the top side*
下邊	**hah-bihn**	*the underneath, under, beneath, the underside*
左(手)邊	**jó-(sáu-)bihn**	*on the left, the left(-hand) side*
右(手)邊	**yauh-(sáu-)bihn**	*on the right, the right(-hand) side*
裏邊/入邊	**léuih-bihn** or **yahp-bihn**	*inside, in, the inside*
外邊/出邊	**ngoih-bihn** or **chēut-bihn**	*outside, out, the outside*
對面	**deui-mihn**	*opposite, the opposite side*
斜對面	**chèh-deui-mihn**	*diagonally opposite*

> **LANGUAGE TIP**
> Note that **deui-mihn** is exceptional in that **-bihn** gives place to **-mihn**.

YOUR TURN And having met the compass points back in Unit 6, you should definitely be able to figure these ones out for yourself:

東邊	**dùng-bihn**	*the _____ side*
南邊	**nàahm-bihn**	*the _____ side*
西邊	**sài-bihn**	*the _____ side*
北邊	**bāk-bihn**	*the _____ side*

All these 'whereabouts words' combine happily with **hái** *at, in, on, to be at, to be in, to be on*:

Kéuih hái léuih-bihn.	*She is inside.*
Gàan ūk hái fèi-gèi-chèuhng nàahm-bihn.	*The house is on the south side of the airport.*
Bouh syù hái sō-fá-yíh seuhng-bihn.	*The book is on the sofa.*
Wòhng Síu-jé hái néih hauh-bihn.	*Miss Wong is behind you.*
Hái ūk jó-bihn yáuh chē-fòhng.	*There is a garage on the left of the house.*

Chóh hái gó gàan jáu-làuh chēut-bihn yáuh léuhng go waaih-fahn-jí.
There are two bad characters sitting outside that restaurant.

The last two examples will remind you of what you learned in Unit 3: the verb **yáuh** *to have* is used to mean *there is* or *there are*.

One 'whereabouts word' that needs special care is **jùng-gāan** *in the middle of, in between*. When it means *in the middle of* it acts just like the other words:

Kéuih chóh hái fà-yún jùng-gāan.   *She is sitting in the middle of the garden.*

But when it means *in between* it has a pattern all to itself: **hái X Y jùng-gāan** or **hái X tùhng Y jùng-gāan**:

Kéuih chóh hái Wòhng Sàang (tùhng) Chàhn Táai jùng-gāan.
She sits between Mr Wong and Mrs Chan.

ⓘ Practice

1 **Whoops! Something is wrong! Each of the sentences contains an error either in the sense or in the grammar. Can you spot the deliberate mistakes?**

   a Gó dī hohk-sāang jek-jek dōu sīk góng Yìng-màhn.

   b Ngóh m̀h sīk góng Jùng-màhn.

   c Wòhng Táai go jái m̀h yáuh lihk-sí fo-bún.

   d Gó léuhng Méih-gwok síu-jé m̀h jùng-yi jeuk hùhng-sīk ge sāam-kwàhn.

   e Wòhng Sìn-sàang ge bàh-bā gàm-nín jí-haih baat seui jī-ma.

2 **Imagine you are a worried parent trying to place your son in a Hong Kong school. You have an interview with the headmaster tomorrow and are preparing some questions to ask him, but you are nervous that your newly acquired language will let you down, so you had better write out the questions in Cantonese on a slip of paper in case you get stuck. Go ahead and translate them now:**

   a Does my son need to study Chinese?

   b How many hours of homework must he do each evening?

   c My son has studied at junior school in London for five years. British pupils do not go to secondary school until they are 11 years old. Is it the same in Hong Kong?

   d How much a year does it cost to study in your school?

   e Does the pupil need to buy textbooks and exercise books?

3 **Here are the answers which we happen to know the headmaster will give to your questions, but he is so bored with hearing the same thing from every parent who sees him that he deliberately gives the answers in the wrong order. You will have to try to match the lettered questions with the numbered answers before you know what is what, but our advice is to try another school for your son!**

   1 Yiu. Hóu gwai tìm!

   2 Yiu. Kéuih yāt go sìng-kèih yiu hohk sàam-sahp go jūng-tàuh.

   3 Hèung-góng ge gaau-yuhk tùhng Yìng-gwok ge chà-m̀h-dō lak.

   4 M̀h-sái hóu dò jē. Ńgh-luhk go jūng-tàuh jē.

   5 M̀h-sái hóu dò jē. Yāt nìhn sei-baak-maahn mān jē.

124

? Test yourself

Describe the scene you see here by answering the questions in Cantonese.

a Hái ūk ngoih-bihn yáuh māt-yéh a?

b Wòhng Sàang hái Wòhng Táai bīn-bihn a?

c Bouh syù hái bīn-douh a?

d Néih gú Wòhng Sàang Wòhng Táai jouh-yùhn māt-yéh fàan-làih a?

e Hái Wòhng Táai chìhn-bihn yáuh māt-yéh a?

f Néih gei m̀h gei-dāk gó go miht-fó-túng haih bīn-go máaih ga?

g Wòhng Sàang Wòhng Táai go jái hái bīn-douh a?

h Néih wah Wòhng Táai hòi m̀h hòi-sām a?

投機 *Tàuh-gèi*
Speculation

In this unit you will learn about:
- *alternative questions.*
- *being busy.*
- *different dollars.*
- *dropping classifiers.*
- *gambling.*

- *good to …*
- *shortcut numbers.*
- *similarity.*
- *telling options.*

CEFR: *(A2) Can give and receive information about quantities, numbers, prices, etc.*

The Cantonese as gamblers

The Cantonese have long been renowned for their love of gambling, and they pursue their love with dedication and not infrequently with recklessness. It would hardly be an exaggeration to say that next to eating, the favourite pastimes of Hong Kong have for many years been gambling on mahjong and horse racing, and since the 1960s the stock exchange has become a fourth passion.

Dóu-chín 賭錢 is *to gamble with money, to bet*, and **dóu** 賭 can be used with appropriate nouns to show what is being bet on: **dóu-gáu** 賭狗 *to bet on the dogs*, **dóu-gú-piu** 賭股票 *to gamble on shares*, **dóu-máh** 賭馬 *to bet on the horses*, **dóu-pē-páai** 賭啤牌 *to gamble at cards*, **dóu-bō** 賭波 *to bet on any ball game*, **dóu-lèuhn-pún** 賭輪盤 *to play roulette*.

If we tell you that a racecourse is **máh-chèuhng** 馬場 – have a go at translating *dog-track*, and then be really brave and try to translate *casino*. The answers are at the back – you can bet on it!

Vocabulary builder 1

 Read through the new vocabulary and practise saying it out loud.

GAMBLING

抽獎	chàu-jéung	*lucky draw*
賽馬 or 跑馬	choi-máh *or* páau-máh	*to race horses; horse racing*
獎品	jéung-bán	*prize*
頭獎	tàuh-jéung	*first prize*
投注	tàuh-jyu	*to stake, bet*

POLITICS AND ECONOMICS

籌款	chàuh-fún	*to raise money; fund raising*
慈善	chìh-sihn	*charity*
電台	dihn-tòih	*radio station*
繁榮	fàahn-wìhng	*prosperous*
豐富	fùng-fu	*rich, abundant*
經濟	gìng-jai	*economy, economic*
廣播	gwóng-bo	*broadcast*
罪案	jeuih-on	*criminal case*
新聞	sàn-màhn	*news*
會	wúi	*meeting; club, association*
人數	yàhn-sou	*number of people*
有錢	yáuh-chín	*rich, wealthy*
元	yùhn	*dollar*

BASICS

全	chyùhn	*the whole*
夠鐘	gau-jūng	*time's up, it's time to*
乖	gwàai	*well behaved, obedient, 'good little boy'*
關係	gwàan-haih	*relationship, connection, relevance*
增加	jàng-gà	*increase; to increase*
樣樣	yeuhng-yeuhng	*all kinds of, all sorts of*

Dialogue 1

13.01 *Mr Cheung reveals he isn't entirely immune from Hong Kong's passion for gambling.*

1 Can you work out what síu-jó lak means in Mr Wong's first speech?

Cheung	Kàhm-yaht dihn-tòih ge sàn-màhn gwóng-bo wah, gauh-nín Hèung-góng síh-màhn tàuh-jyu hái choi-máh ge chín yáuh yāt-baak-sàam-sahp-yih-yīk yùhn, yahp máh-chèuhng ge yàhn-sou haih sàam-baak-yih-sahp-maahn yàhn!
Wong	Wàh! Hèung-góng-yàhn gó-jahn-sìh jàn-haih yáuh-chín lak. Daahn-haih yàuh gauh-nín dou yìh-gā chyùhn sai-gaai ge gìng-jai dōu m̀h hóu, heui máh-chèuhng ge yàhn síu-jó lak. Jèung Sìn-sàang, néih jùng m̀h jùng-yi dóu-máh ga?
Cheung	M̀h jùng-yi. Dóu-máh, dóu-gáu, dóu-pē-páai, dóu-gú-piu … yeuhng-yeuhng ngóh dōu m̀h jùng-yi.
Wong	Néih jàn-haih gwàai lak! Hái Hèung-góng hóu-chíh néih yāt-yeuhng ge yàhn yìh-gā jàn-haih hóu síu lak.
Cheung	Yáuh-yàhn wah, Hèung-góng gam fàahn-wìhng haih tùhng Hèung-góng-yàhn jùng-yi dóu-chín yáuh gwàan-haih ge bo! Néih wah ngāam m̀h ngāam a?
Wong	Ngóh wah móuh gwàan-haih, daahn-haih dóu-chín tùhng jeuih-on ge jàng-gà jauh yáuh gwàan-haih lak.
Cheung	Deui-m̀h-jyuh, Wòhng Sìn-sàang, ngóh yìh-gā gau-jūng yiu heui chàam-gà yāt go chìh-sihn chàuh-fún chàu-jéung-wúi.
Wong	Chàu-jéung-wúi àh! Jéung-bán fùng m̀h fùng-fu ga?
Cheung	Tàuh-jéung haih yāt gàan ūk, yih-jéung haih yāt ga chē.
Wong	Yí! Gám, syun m̀h syun haih dóu-chín nē?
張	擒日電台係新聞廣播話，舊年香港市民投注喺賽馬嘅錢有一百三十二億元，入馬場嘅人數係三百二十萬人！
王	嘩！香港人嗰陣時真係有錢嘞。但係由舊年到而家全世界嘅經濟都唔好，去馬場嘅人少咗嘞。張先生，你中唔中意賭馬㗎？
張	唔中意。賭馬、賭狗、賭啤牌、賭股票……樣樣我都唔中意。
王	你真係乖嘞！喺香港好似你一樣嘅人而家真係好少嘞。
張	有人話，香港咁繁榮係同香港人中意賭錢有關係嘅㗎！你話啱唔啱呀？
王	我話冇關係，但係賭錢同罪案嘅增加就有關係嘞。
張	對唔住，王先生，我而家夠鐘要去參加一個慈善籌款抽獎會。
王	抽獎會吖！獎品豐唔豐富㗎？
張	頭獎係一間屋，二獎係一架車。
王	咦！嗰算唔算係賭錢呢？

2 How would you translate the following?
  a To gamble on snooker
  b There are three prizes: the third prize is only $5.

3 Supply Mr Chang's answer to Mr Wong's last question – he denies that it is gambling and says that it is only giving money to people who have none.

Language discovery

13.1 DIFFERENT DOLLARS

In Unit 5 you learned the word **mān** for *dollar*. Now you have a different word, **yùhn**, which has the same meaning. There are in fact two different systems for talking about money, a colloquial system (**mān**) and a more formal written system (**yùhn**). When people write they always use the formal system and when they speak they usually (but not always) use the colloquial system. It is perhaps closest to the American *dollars* and *bucks* system, where no banknote carries the word *bucks* but where, in speech, either *bucks* or *dollars* is acceptable.

In the dialogue Mr Cheung uses **yùhn** because a figure as large and important as 13 billion seems to command more formality and the radio newscaster he is quoting would certainly not descend into the colloquial **mān** for such an important item. The money system will be explained further in Unit 20.

13.2 DROPPING CLASSIFIERS

In Mr Cheung's first speech did you notice that something was missing? He talks of **sàam-baak-yih-sahp-maahn yàhn** *3,200,000 people*, but he does not use the classifier **go** which you would expect between the number and the noun. The larger numbers get, the less likely it is that a classifier will be used: as a rule of thumb you can assume that the classifier will be used up to 100 and will seldom be used for numbers greater than 100, but if you are in doubt put it in; it is never wrong to do so.

13.3 STRIKING IT RICH

The reason why **yáuh-chín** means *rich* is clear enough – it comes from having money. But notice that although **yáuh-chín** is made up of a verb plus a noun (**yáuh** + **chín**) it acts as if it were any other adjective:

Hòh Sìn-sàang hóu yáuh-chín.	*Mr Ho is very rich.*
Yáuh-chín yàhn chóh hái chē hauh-bihn.	*Rich people ride in the back.*

13.4 *THE SAME, ALMOST THE SAME* AND *RELATED TO*

In the dialogue Mr Cheung says **tùhng Hèung-góng-yàhn jùng-yi dóu-chín yáuh gwàan-haih** *is related to Hong Kong people's loving to gamble*. Notice how **tùhng** introduces the construction. You have met similar constructions before, and you might like to consolidate your understanding of them here:

hóu-chíh jáu-làuh ge yāt-yeuhng (Unit 4)	*seems like restaurant food*
tùhng dī sō-fá-yí ge bou-líu yāt-yeuhng (Unit 11)	*the same as the material of the sofa*
hóu-chíh sei-sahp seui gam-seuhng-há (Unit 9)	*seem like about 40*
tùhng Yìng-gwok ge chà-m̀h-dō (Unit 12)	*almost like the British*

Vocabulary builder 2

Read through the new vocabulary and practise saying it out loud.

MORE GAMBLING

打麻雀	dá màh-jeuk	to play mahjong
大檔	daaih-dong	gambling den
番攤	fāan-tāan	fantan (a Chinese gambling game)
非法	fèi-faat	illegal
輸	syù	to lose
廿一點	yah-yāt-dím	blackjack, pontoon, vingt-et-un
贏	yèhng	to win

> **LANGUAGE TIP**
> While *to play fantan* (a game of pure chance) is called **dóu-fāan-tāan**, the far more active and serious process of *playing mahjong* (where a skilled player has some advantage) is called **dá-màh-jeuk**.

FINANCE

本錢	bún-chìhn	capital
外匯	ngoih-wuih	foreign exchange

VERBS

得閒	dāk-hàahn	to be free, at leisure
吸引	kāp-yáhn	to attract
有 / 冇興趣	yáuh / móuh hing-cheui	to have / not have interest in

BASICS

場	chèuhng	cl: for performances, bouts, matches, games
定係	dihng-haih	or, or rather
當然	dòng-yín	of course
好玩	hóu-wáan	good fun, amusing, enjoyable
老實	lóuh-saht	honest; honestly
適合 or 合適	sīk-hahp or hahp-sīk	suitable to, fitting
有時	yáuh-sìh	sometimes
樣	yeuhng	kind, sort, type

Dialogue 2

 13.02 *Why Mr Chan is welcomed at the mahjong table.*

1 Why do you think Mr Lee is so keen to invite Mr Chan to his home?

Lee	Lóuh Chán, néih gam jùng-yi heui Ou-mún dóu-chín, lóuh-saht wah béi ngóh tèng, néih yèhng chín ge sìh-hauh dò dihng-haih syù chín ge sìh-hauh dò nē?
Chan	Dòng-yín haih yèhng chín ge sìh-hauh dò lā. Daahn-haih múih chi dōu haih yèhng síu-síu jē.
Lee	Néih jùng-yi dóu lèuhn-pún dihng-haih yah-yāt-dím a?
Chan	Léuhng yeuhng dōu m̀h jùng-yi; ngóh jùng-yi dóu fāan-tāan.
Lee	Néih heui dóu-chèuhng dihng-haih hái ūk-kéi dóu-chín a?
Chan	Ngóh yáuh-sìh heui dóu-chèuhng, yáuh-sìh hái ūk-kéi, daahn-haih ngóh yāt-dihng m̀h heui daaih-dong dóu-chín, yàn-waih haih fèi-faat ge.
Lee	Gám, dóu-bō tùhng dóu-ngoih-wuih nē?
Chan	Ngóh gú néih wah 'dóu-bō' jauh haih dóu Yìng-gwok jūk-kàuh lak. Nī yeuhng yéh ngóh móuh hing-cheui. Dóu-ngoih-wuih jauh yāt-dihng yiu yáuh hóu dò bún-chìhn. Só-yíh léuhng yeuhng dōu m̀h sīk-hahp ngóh.
Lee	Hèung-góng-yàhn jeui jùng-yi dá-màh-jeuk ge lak: gám néih nē?
Chan	Ngóh gok-dāk dá-màh-jeuk jeui hóu-wáan, jeui kāp-yáhn ngóh, daahn-haih ngóh hóu síu yèhng chín ge.
Lee	Jàn hóu lak! Hah-go-láih-baai yùh-gwó néih dāk-hàahn chéng làih ngóh ūk-kéi, ngóh-deih yāt-chàih dá chèuhng màh-jeuk lā!
李	老陳，你咁中意去澳門賭錢，老實話俾我聽，你贏錢嘅時候多定係輸錢嘅時候多呢？
陳	當然係贏錢嘅時候多喇。但係每次都係贏少少啫。
李	你中意賭輪盤定係廿一點呀？
陳	兩樣都唔中意；我中意賭番攤。
李	你去賭場定係喺屋企賭錢呀？
陳	我有時去賭場，有時喺屋企，但係我一定唔去大檔賭錢，因為係非法嘅。
李	噉，賭波同賭外匯呢？
陳	我估你話‘賭波’就係賭英國足球嘞。呢樣嘢我冇興趣。賭外匯就一定要有好多本錢。所以兩樣都唔適合我。
李	香港人最中意打麻雀嘅嘞；噉你呢？
陳	我覺得打麻雀最好玩，最吸引我，但係我好少贏錢嘅。
李	真好嘞！下個禮拜如果你得閒請嚟我屋企，我哋一齊打場麻雀啦！

2 Answer in Cantonese.

  a Chàhn Sìn-sàang jùng-yi heui bīn-douh dóu-chín a?

  b Kéuih wúih m̀h wúih hái gó-douh yèhng-chín a?

  c Kéuih yèhng-chín ge sìh-hauh, yèhng hóu dò hóu dò, haih m̀h haih a?

Language discovery

13.5 TELLING OPTIONS

In Unit 6 you met **wah … tèng** meaning *to inform someone, tell someone about something*, and in Unit 8 you were told that **wah … jì** meant the same. Now you can add other variants, because **góng** *to speak*, which you met in Unit 9, can be substituted for **wah** in either of the phrases and you can add in **béi** *to* to any of them. So all the following forms mean the same – *she tells me …*:

Kéuih wah ngóh tèng …   Kéuih wah béi ngóh tèng …
Kéuih wah ngóh jì …   Kéuih wah béi ngóh jì …
Kéuih góng ngóh tèng …   Kéuih góng béi ngóh tèng …
Kéuih góng ngóh jì …   Kéuih góng béi ngóh jì …

13.6 DIHNG-HAIH *OR RATHER*

Dihng-haih nicely translates *or* when a question is being asked, and the final particle **nē?** is usually there to back it up:

Kéuih haih Jùng-gwok-yàhn dihng-haih Yaht-bún-yàhn nē?

Is she Chinese or Japanese?

Néih Láih-baai-yāt dihng-haih Láih-baai-yih heui Ou-mún nē?

Is it Monday or Tuesday that you are going to Macau?

Néih séung sihk ngàuh-yuhk dihng-haih jyù-yuhk nē?

Which do you want to have, beef or pork?

But remember that it is only in questions that **dihng-haih** will translate *or*. If you think back to Unit 10 you will remember that *seven or eight people* was translated by **chāt-baat go yàhn**. The difference can be shown by comparing these two examples:

Gó-douh yáuh chāt-baat go yàhn.

There are (approximately) seven or eight people over there.

Gó-douh yáuh chāt dihng-haih baat go yàhn nē?

Are there seven people over there or eight? (which is it?)

13.7 BLACKJACK TEACHES YOU NUMBERS!

The card game Blackjack, sometimes known as Pontoon or Vingt-et-un, is popular among the Cantonese, who call it **yah-yāt-dím**. **Dím** means *dot*, *spot* and **yah-yāt** is an alternative way of saying **yih-sahp-yāt** *21*.

Here is a list of the alternative forms of numbers, all of which really consist of nothing more than slurring over the word **sahp** in numbers above 20:

yih-sahp-yāt = **yih-ah-yāt** = **yah-yāt** = **yeh-yāt** (but this last is less common)

sàam-sahp-yāt = **sàam-ah-yāt** = **sà-ah-yāt**

sei-sahp-yāt = **sei-ah-yāt**

ńgh-sahp-yāt = **ńgh-ah-yāt**

luhk-sahp-yāt = **luhk-ah-yāt**

chāt-sahp-yāt = **chāt-ah-yāt**

baat-sahp-yāt = **baat-ah-yāt**

gáu-sahp-yāt = **gáu-ah-yāt**

We have only shown 21, 31, 41, etc., but the same shortcuts work for 22, 36, 49 … and any other such number up to 99. You can use these alternatives quite freely provided you observe one rule – you should not use the shortcuts for the round numbers 20, 30, 40, … 90, which are nearly always said in their full **yih-sahp**, **sàam-sahp**, **sei-sahp** … **gáu-sahp** form.

13.8 MAKING ADJECTIVES WITH HÓU

In the dialogue you met the word **hóu-wáan** *good fun*, *enjoyable*. You may have realized that this was a new word made up of two that you already knew: **hóu** *good* and **wáan** *to play, enjoy, amuse oneself* and hence *good to enjoy*, *good to play*.

YOUR TURN If you are brave enough, you can make up such words for yourself, but here are a few common ones which you can hardly avoid. Can you translate them?

hóu-sihk	'good to eat'	*delicious*
hóu-yám	'good to drink'	_____
hóu-tái	'good to look at'	_____
hóu-tèng	'good to listen to'	_____

Actually you met **hóu-sihk** and **hóu-yám** in Unit 4, but we did not explain them there.

13.9 AT LEISURE

Dāk-hàahn literally means 'attaining leisure' and so *not busy*. In Unit 10 you learned the word **mòhng** *busy*. Cantonese speakers like to take shortcuts with their language, but, unusually, many people prefer to say **m̀h dāk-hàahn** and **hóu m̀h dāk-hàahn** rather than **mòhng** and **hóu mòhng** despite the extra syllables involved.

13.10 ANOTHER SHORTCUT: DROPPING YĀT

In the dialogue Mr Lee delightedly invites Mr Chan to **dá chèuhng màh-jeuk lā!** *have a round of mahjong.* You might have expected the Cantonese to read **dá yāt chèuhng màh-jeuk lā!** and, of course, that would be grammatically correct, but quite often **yāt** is missed out when it comes between a verb and a classifier with its noun:

sihk chàan faahn   *have a meal*
máaih ga chē   *buy a car*

Sharpen your ears

 13.03 Time for some more listening practice. You will hear some pairs of rather similar sounding expressions – can you hear and write down the sounds and tones?

Practice

1 **In the sentences interchange mòhng and dāk-hàahn without altering the sense.**
   a Chàhn Táai gàm-máahn hóu mòhng.
   b Ngóh bàh-bā sèhng-nìhn dōu mòhng.
   c Ṁh-gòi néih wah béi ngóh tèng néih go jái tìng-yaht dāk ṁh dāk-hàahn a?
   d Kéuih Láih-baai-yih hóu ṁh dāk-hàahn.
   e Ngóh jeui mòhng ge sìh-hauh haih jìu-jóu.

2 **Complete the sentences by using the correct classifiers.**
   a _____ Jùng-màhn syù dōu haih Hòh Sàang ge.
   b Hái gó _____ ūk chìhn-bihn yáuh ńgh _____ jyù-jái.
   c Kàhm-yaht gó _____ jūk-kàuh hóu hóu-tái àh?
   d Bīn léuhng _____ chē haih Chàhn Sàang máaih ga?

3 **Find the words in A which are the opposites of the words in B.**
   A gwàai, síu-síu, tàuh-jyù, dāk-hàahn, syù, sàn-fú, sìn-sàang, jàng-gà, síh-màhn, gwóng-bo, sìh-sìh, fèi-gèi, dihn-wá,
   B mòhng, syù-fuhk, gaan-jūng, yèhng, hohk-saang, jing-fú, fùng-fu, gáam-síu

'Gáu houh! Gáu houh!'

a Néih gú haih Wòhng Sàang yèhng chín dihng-haih Wòhng Táai yèhng chín nē?

b Wòhng Sìn-sàang hóu hòi-sām, haih m̀h haih a?

c Daih-luhk jek máh haih géi-dō houh a?

d Bīn jek máh yèhng a?

e Néih wah haih Wòhng Taai-táai hóu sīk dóu-máh dihng-haih Wòhng Sìn-sàang hóu sīk dóu-máh né?

f Sei houh máh hóu-gwo gáu houh máh, ngāam m̀h ngāam a?

g Sàam houh máh nē? Hóu m̀h hóu-gwo gáu houh a?

h Jeui hóu gó jek máh haih m̀h haih luhk houh máh a?

i Nī yāt chèuhng choi-máh yáuh géi-dō jek máh a?

j Wòhng Sìn-sàang dóu-máh múih chèuhng dōu jùng-yi dóu hóu daaih, yùh-gwó yèhng jauh yèhng hóu dò, syù jauh syù hóu dò. Wòhng Táai m̀h haih gám ge, kéuih chèuhng-chèuhng dōu dóu hóu sai jē. Gám, néih gú, nī chèuhng kéuih-deih haih syù dò-gwo yèhng dihng-haih yèhng dò-gwo syù nē?

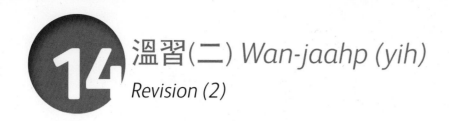

溫習(二) *Wan-jaahp (yih)*
Revision (2)

Another six units under your belt. It all gets more interesting now; you can say so many more things and begin to have some flexibility in your language. Remember that what you are learning is a living colourful language spoken by a very dynamic people, not a bookish sober exercise in style and complex grammar. Try to speak what you learn so that you can hear the cadences and become familiar with the zest of it. Cantonese people enjoy life, they talk loudly and laugh a lot – a Cantonese whisper is almost a contradiction in terms. Start by reading this first passage through, then read it out loud several times until it begins to feel part of you. Even better, learn it off by heart so that you can recite it.

Passage 1

Wòhng Sìn-sàang chāt seui ge jái kàhm-yaht fàan hohk-haauh gó-jahn-sìh hóu hòi-sām gám wah ngóh jì, kéuih bàh-bā seuhng-go-láih-baai máaih-jó yāt gàan sàn ūk. Gó gàan ūk yauh daaih yauh leng, yáuh sàam gàan fan-fóng, gàan ūk chìhn-bihn juhng yáuh go fà-yún tùhng-màaih yāt gàan chē-fòhng tìm. Kéuih wah: 'Yìh-gā ngóh yāt-go-yàhn yuhng yāt gàan fan-fóng, jàn-haih syù-fuhk lak. Daahn-haih màh-mā jauh yiu tùhng bàh-bā yāt-chàih yuhng yāt gàan. Ngóh gú màh-mā yāt-dihng m̀h hòi-sām lak. Ngóh m̀h jì dím-gáai bàh-bā m̀h béi màh-mā yuhng daih-sàam gàan fan-fóng nē? Gó gàan fan-fóng yìh-gā móuh yàhn yuhng, jí-haih bàh-bā jài-jó hóu dò syù hái gó-douh jē.'

>
> **LANGUAGE TIP**
> **fan-fóng** 瞓房 = *bedroom*

1 **Try to answer these questions now without referring back to the passage.**
   a Wòhng Sìn-sàang ge jái géi-dō seui a?
   b Wòhng Sàang seuhng-go-sìng-kèih máaih-jó māt-yéh a?
   c Ūk chìhn-bihn yáuh dī māt-yéh a?
   d Bīn-go yàhn yiu tùhng bàh-bā yāt-chàih yuhng yāt gàan fan-fóng a?
   e Daih-sàam gàan fan-fóng léuih-bihn yáuh dī māt-yéh a?
   f Yáuh móuh yàhn yuhng daih-sàam gàan fan-fóng a?

2 Just a little reminder that you should be paying attention to your tones: if you don't you will never sound like a Cantonese! Put the correct tone marks on the words. You will have to look up those you have forgotten, but that at least will help to cement them in your mind.

   a hei-mohng   **e** dihn-ying   **i** gihn-hong

   b tin-hei   **f** wahn-duhng   **j** noih-yuhng

   c laahng-tin   **g** gei-yuhk   **k** huhng-dang

   d da-syun   **h** do-yuh   **l** pihng-gwan

3 Hunt the yaht. All the words here use yaht *sun* or *day*. What are they?

   a tomorrow   **d** the whole day   **g** today

   b Sunday   **e** yesterday   **h** every day

   c the day before yesterday   **f** Japan   **i** the day after tomorrow

4 The sentence pairs differ by only one word, but the sense changes a great deal. Try to put them into English which will bring out the meanings clearly.

   a 1 Daih-yāt jek máh jīk-haih gáu houh máh.

   2 Daih-yāt jek máh m̀h haih gáu houh máh.

   b 1 Jùng-sàan Síu-jé jing-haih Yaht-bún-yàhn.

   2 Jùng-sàan Síu-jé jàn-haih Yaht-bún-yàhn.

   c 1 Kéuih tìng-yaht jauh heui Gwóng-jàu.

   2 Kéuih tìng-yaht sìn-ji heui Gwóng-jàu.

   d 1 Chàhn Taai-táai heui-gwo Méih-gwok sahp-géi chi lak.

   2 Chàhn Taai-táai heui-gwo Méih-gwok géi-sahp chi lak.

5 Choose the right element from the brackets to complete the sense of the sentences.

   a Yāt go yàhn yuhng yāt gàan fan-fóng hóu (sàn-fú, yáuh-méng, yáuh-yuhng, syù-fuhk).

   b Chē-fòhng yuhng làih (jài syù ge, jyú-faahn ge, wahn-duhng ge, tìhng-chē ge).

   c Hái gó gàan gūng-sī jouh-yéh hóu hóu yàn-waih wúih yáuh (hóu dò chín, m̀h sīk jyú-sung, hóu síu chín, hóu màh-fàahn).

6 Make one sentence out of each of the pairs using the words in brackets to make the link and making whatever other slight adjustments are necessary. For instance, the first pair would give the sentence: Kéuih fàan ūk-kéi jì-chìhn, sìh-sìh dōu heui taam kéuih nàahm pàhng-yáuh.

   a Kéuih fàan ūk-kéi. Kéuih sìh-sìh dōu heui taam kéuih nàahm-pàhng-yáuh. (jì-chìhn)

   b Wòhng Táai séung máaih gó ga chē. Ga chē hóu leng. (yàn-waih)

   c Ngóh m̀h mìhng-baahk. Gó go yàhn láahng-tīn séung máaih láahng-hei-gèi. (jouh-māt-yéh?)

   d Gó dī hā m̀h sàn-sìn. Chàhn Táai m̀h séung máaih. (só-yíh)

   e Kéuih sihk-gán yéh. Kéuih m̀h góng-wah. (ge sìh-hauh)

7 Here are the answers. What were the questions?

   a Máaih gó ga chē yiu sahp-ńgh-maahn mān jē.

   b Wòhng Sàang Sìng-kèih-luhk lèih-hòi Yaht-bún.

   c Hái Léih Táai jó-sáu-bihn gó jek gáu-jái haih Léih Sìn-sàang sung béi kéuih ge.

   d Gó dī yàhn jí-haih Hòh Síu-jé haih gaau-syù jē.

Passage 2

This anecdote finishes with a pun – Cantonese people love them! The pun here is known to all gamblers and it is safe to say that only the naive Mr Ho would take the bad advice which his wife gives him here!

HÒH SÌN-SÀANG MÁAIH-MÁH

Yùh-gwó yāt go yáuh-chín yàhn séung máaih máh, kéuih jauh heui máaih máh, daahn-haih gám-yéung máaih máh hóu gwai bo! Hái Hèung-góng néih sìh-sìh dōu wúih tèng-dóu móuh chín ge yàhn dōu wah 'Gàm-yaht ngóh séung máaih-máh.' Dím-gáai nē? Néih gú-háh, móuh chín ge yàhn wah 'máaih-máh' haih māt-yéh nē? Ngāam lak, 'máaih-máh' jīk-haih 'dóu-máh', só-yíh móuh chín ge yàhn wah kéuih séung heui máaih-máh jīk-haih wah kéuih séung heui dóu-máh.

Hòh Sìn-sàang m̀h haih hóu yáuh-chín. Yáuh yāt yaht kéuih ge hóu pàhng-yáuh Jèung Sìn-sàang dá-dihn-wá làih mahn kéuih: 'Gàm-máahn choi-máh. Ngóh séung chéng néih tùhng ngóh yāt-chàih heui máh-chèuhng wáan-háh, néih wah hóu m̀h hóu nē?' Hòh Sàang hóu hòi-sām gám wah: 'Hóu! Hóu! Hóu jyú-yi!'

Tèng-yùhn dihn-wá jì-hauh kéuih wah béi Hòh Táai tèng. Hòh Táai wah: 'Néih móuh heui-gwo tái choi-máh, nī chi haih néih daih-yāt chi jē. M̀h jì-dou néih wúih m̀h wúih jùng-yi tái nē?' Hòh Sàang wah: 'Òu! Haih bo! Haih ngóh daih-yāt chi heui tái choi-máh bo! Yùh-gwó m̀h hóu tái, gám ngóh yiu chóh hái-douh, móuh yéh jouh bo! Dím-syun-hóu-nē?' Hòh Táai wah: 'Néih jeui hóu máaih bún syù sìn-ji heui máh-chèuhng lak. Néih yùh-gwó gok-dāk tái choi-máh hóu-wáan, jauh hó-yíh m̀h-sái tái-syù. Yùh-gwó-m̀h-haih-nē, gám néih jauh hó-yíh chóh hái-douh tái-syù lā. Néih wah hóu m̀h hóu nē?' Hòh Sàang hóu gwàai: taai-táai wah māt-yéh, kéuih jauh jouh māt-yéh. Dòng-yín kéuih gó máahn heui máh-chèuhng jì-chìhn máaih-jó bún syù sìn.

Hóu-chói Hòh Sìn-sàang gok-dāk choi-máh dōu géi hóu-wáan, m̀h-sái tái-syù. Daahn-haih kéuih yāt-dī chín dōu móuh yèhng, sèung-fáan juhng syù-jó hó dò chín tìm! Kéuih fàan ūk-kéi, hóu nàu gám wah béi taai-táai tèng: 'Ngóh daih-yih chi heui dóu-máh m̀h wúih tèng néih góng lak! Máaih-máh yiu máaih yèhng, m̀h-hóu máaih syù ā-ma!'

> **LANGUAGE TIP**
> **Dím-syun-hóu-nē?**
> = *What's to be done about it? What can I do?*

8 14.01 **That second passage was to get you used to puns and wordplay. When you are sure you understand that last pun, try this one. This time the only clue you have is 'a hyphen'! You can also listen to the conversation, but whether that will help you, we're not sure.**

Jèung Sìn-sàang yàuh gáu-chèuhng dóu-yùhn gáu fàan ūk-kéi. Kéuih go jái mahn kéuih:

'Bàh-bā, néih gàm-yaht dóu-gáu dím a? Yèhng m̀h yèhng chín a?'

'Sahp chèuhng gáu chèuhng yèhng!'

'Wàh! Bàh-bā, néih jàn-haih hóu sīk dóu-gáu bo! Dóu sahp chèuhng jí-haih syù yāt chèuhng.'

'Lóuh-saht góng, ngóh yāt-dī chín dōu móuh yèhng. Ngóh dóu sahp chèuhng dōu haih gáu-chèuhng yèhng bo!'

旅遊 Léuih-yàuh
Travelling

In this unit you will learn about:
- ▶ *adverbs of manner.*
- ▶ *airport check-in.*
- ▶ *anticipating plurality.*
- ▶ *clock time.*

- ▶ *hotel rooms.*
- ▶ *verb ending* totally.
- ▶ *walking around.*

CEFR: *(A2) Can handle numbers, quantities, cost and time; can exchange relevant information and give your opinion on practical problems.*

Five-star travel

A *hotel* is **jáu-dim** 酒店, and both Hong Kong and Macau have plenty of luxury ones, as well as a few cheaper establishments. If you are lucky you will find a special rate promotion, as Mrs Lee has done in the first dialogue. But whatever you pay, you will need the basic essentials, and whether you count a *heated swimming pool* **wihng-chìh** 泳池 amongst them, or three telephones (one by the bed, one on the desk and one in the bathroom) which some boast, we get you started in this unit.

A *hotel room* **fòhng-gàan** 房間 (cl: **go**) should have:

- ▶ a *(double) bed* **(sèung-yàhn-)chòhng** (雙人)床,
- ▶ an *alarm clock* **naauh-jūng** 鬧鐘,
- ▶ a *television set* **dihn-sih-gèi** 電視機 (cl: **ga**),
- ▶ a *bathroom* **sái-sàn-fóng** 洗身房 (cl: **gàan** or **go**),
- ▶ a *towel* **mòuh-gān** 毛巾 (cl: **jèung** 張 or **tìuh** 條),
- ▶ a *wardrobe* **yì-gwaih** 衣櫃,
- ▶ a *refrigerator* **syut-gwaih** 雪櫃 (cl: **ga**),
- ▶ a *desk* **sé-jih-tói** 寫字枱.

Of course a desk isn't much use without a chair, but you learned that word in Unit 11 – you remember, it's **yí**. Well, chairs, desks and tables have something in common as well as four legs: they share a classifier. What is it and why?

Vocabulary builder 1

 Read through the new vocabulary and practise saying it out loud.

HOTELS

設備	chit-beih	*facilities, appointments, equipment*
費用	fai-yuhng	*cost, fee*
服務	fuhk-mouh	*service; to give service*
經理	gìng-léih	*manager*
公關	gùng-gwàan	*public relations*
五星級	ńgh-sīng-kāp	*five-star grade, top class*
遊	yàuh	*tour; to tour*

VERBS AND VERB ENDINGS

抵	dái	*to be worth it*
… 得	-dāk	ve: *in such a way that*
舉辦	géui-baahn	*to conduct, run, hold*
行（路）	hàahng(-louh)	*to walk*
享受	héung-sauh	*to enjoy; enjoyment, entertainment, treat*
旅遊	léuih-yàuh	*to travel; tourism*
洗	sái	*to wash*
洗身	sái-sàn	*to bathe* (lit. 'wash body')

BASICS

等等	dáng-dáng	*et cetera, etc., and so on*
快	faai	*quick, quickly, fast*
飛	fēi	*ticket, fare*
乾淨	gòn-jehng	*clean*
趕住	gón-jyuh	*hurrying to*
囉	lō	fp: *agreement with previous speaker; strong emotion*
唔少得	m̀h-síu-dāk	*not less than, must be at least*
内行人 or 行内人	noih-hóng-yàhn *or* hòhng-noih-yàhn	*insider, expert*
暖	nyúhn	*warm*
熟識	suhk-sīk	*familiar with, well acquainted with*
日頭	yaht-táu	*daytime; by day*
夜晚	yeh-máan	*night-time; at night*

> **LANGUAGE TIP**
> **Gòn-jehng** literally means 'dry and pure', but it is the standard term for *clean*. *Dirty* is either **wù-jòu** 污糟 or **laaht-taat** 辣撻, and quite often both are used together for extra stress – **wù-jòu laaht-taat** 污糟辣撻 *filthy*.

Dialogue 1

 15.01 *Mrs Lee is excited about an inclusive hotel deal.*

1 In Mr Chan's second speech, is he calling Mrs Lee a liar?

Chan	Léih Táai, néih hàahng-dāk gam faai, gón-jyuh heui bīn-douh a?
Lee	Ngóh gón-jyuh heui máaih léuih-yàuh fēi jē. Léuih-yàuh gūng-sī yìh-gā géui-baahn yāt go 'Ou-mún léuhng yaht yàuh', hái Ou-mún wáan léuhng yaht yāt máahn, fai-yuhng jí-haih yāt-chìn mān jì-máh.
Chan	Gam pèhng, ngóh m̀h seun. Nī go léuih-yàuh yáuh dī māt-yéh fuhk-mouh tùhng héung-sauh nē?
Lee	Yaht-táu yáuh dī māt-yéh fuhk-mouh tùhng héung-sauh ngóh m̀h jì, daahn-haih yeh-máan hái ńgh-sīng-kāp jáu-dim jyuh yāt máahn jauh yíh-gìng hóu dái lak. Nī dī jáu-dim fòhng-gàan dòng-yín m̀h-síu-dāk yáuh dihn-sih-gèi lā, syut-gwaih lā, sèung-yàhn-chòhng lā, sái-sàn-fóng lā; jáu-dim juhng yáuh nyúhn-séui wihng-chìh, dáng-dáng. Yauh gòn-jehng yauh syù-fuhk, jàn-haih hóu lak.
Chan	Léih Táai, néih deui Ou-mún ge jáu-dim fuhk-mouh tùhng chit-beih dōu hóu suhk-sīk bo!
Lee	Dòng-yín lā, ngóh haih Ou-mún yāt gàan daaih jáu-dim ge gùng-gwàan gìng-léih bo.
Chan	Néih haih noih-hóng-yàhn dōu wah nī go léuih-yàuh dái wáan, gám ngóh dōu heui máaih fēi chàam-gà lō.
陳	李太，你行得咁快，趕住去邊度呀？
李	我趕住去買旅遊飛啫。旅遊公司而家舉辦一個"澳門兩日遊"，喺澳門玩兩日一晚，費用只係一千蚊之嘛。
陳	咁平，我唔信。呢個旅遊有啲乜嘢服務同享受呢？
李	日頭有啲乜嘢服務同享受我唔知，但係夜晚喺五星級酒店住一晚就已經好抵嘞。呢啲酒店房間當然唔少得有電視機喇、雪櫃喇、雙人床喇、洗身房喇，酒店重有暖水泳池等等。又乾淨又舒服，真係好嘞。
陳	李太，你對澳門嘅酒店服務同設備都好熟識嘞！
李	當然喇，我係澳門一間大酒店嘅公關經理嘛。
陳	你係內行人都話呢個旅遊抵玩，噉我都去買飛參加囉。

2 Answer the questions.

    a Jáu-dim fòhng-gàan léuih-bihn yáuh móuh láahng-hei-gèi a? Miht-fó-túng nē?

    b Māt-yéh haih 'ńgh-sīng-kāp' jáu-dim a?

    c Ńgh-sīng-kāp jáu-dim léuih-bihn yáuh móuh chán-só a? Wahn-duhng-fóng nē?

> **LANGUAGE TIP**
>
> You now know two similar words, **pèhng** *cheap* and **dái** *worth it*, but be careful not to confuse them. A Rolls Royce bought at a bargain price might still be several years' salary for most of us, so it would not really be appropriate to say that it was cheap, and Cantonese would be unlikely to use **pèhng** to describe it either. If you are treated to a meal in a restaurant by a friend and you see the bill and think it small, it would give offence to say it was **hóu pèhng** – that would sound as though your friend should have spent more money on you. You could happily comment **hóu dái**, though, because that sounds as if it was a very good meal and your friend was clever to choose it and not to get cheated into paying over the top. Interestingly, your friend could say **hóu pèhng jē**, because it is quite good manners to belittle one's own efforts as a host.

Language discovery

15.1 TO WALK

Hàahng means *to walk* but it is a lonely verb and the normal object supplied for it is **louh** *road*, so **hàahng-louh** also means *to walk*. **Louh** is used for any grade of road or path, while **máh-louh** literally means 'horse road' and generally is used for a *main road*, often with **daaih** *big* in front (**daaih-máh-louh**). You might note two other common uses of **hàahng**:

hàahng-sàan	'walk hills'	*to go for a country walk; hiking*
hàahng-gāai	'walk street'	*to go out into the streets*

15.2 MAKING ADVERBS WITH THE VERB ENDING -DĀK

Adding **-dāk** to a verb enables you to describe in what way that verb is performed, that is, it gives you a way of forming adverbs. It is helpful to think of **-dāk** as meaning something like *in such a way that, to the extent that*:

Kéuih hàahng-dāk faai.	*He walks quickly.* (He walks in such a way that it is quick.)
Néih góng-dāk ngāam.	*You spoke correctly.*
Wòhng Síu-jé jeuk-dāk leng.	*Miss Wong is dressed beautifully.*

Each of these three examples converts a simple adjective into an adverb, but what comes after **-dāk** does not have to be so simple. In fact this is a very flexible pattern, as the following show:

Kéuih hàahng-dāk hóu faai.	*He walks very quickly.*
Kéuih hàahng-dāk m̀h-haih-géi-faai.	*He walks not very quickly.*
Kéuih hàahng-dāk taai faai la.	*He walks too quickly.*
Kéuih hàahng-dāk faai-gwo ngóh.	*He walks faster than I do.*

Remember that **-dāk** must be added direct to a verb, nothing can come between them. If the verb has an object that you want to put in, you should give the verb and its object first and then give the verb again so that **-dāk** can be added to it. Compare these two sentences:

Kéuih góng-dāk hóu faai.	*He speaks very fast.*
Kéuih góng Jùng-màhn góng-dāk hóu faai.	*He speaks Chinese very fast.*

15.3 QUESTIONS EXPECTING A PLURAL ANSWER

In the dialogue Mr Chan says, **Nī go léuih-yàuh yáuh dī māt-yéh fuhk-mouh tùhng héung-sauh nē?** *What services and entertainments does this tour offer?* Note how the use of the plural classifier **dī** presupposes that the answer is going to list more than one item. You can do this whenever you ask a question if you are expecting a plural answer and, of course, you can show that you expect a singular answer by using the appropriate classifier for whatever you are talking about:

Néih séung máaih māt-yéh syù a?	*What kind of book / books do you want to buy?*
Néih séung máaih bún māt-yéh syù a?	*What kind of book do you want to buy?*
Néih séung máaih dī māt-yéh syù a?	*What kind of books do you want to buy?*

15.4 DOUBLE AND SINGLE

In **sèung-yàhn-chòhng** *double (person) bed*, **sèung** means *double*; it can also mean *a pair of*. The opposite word, *single*, is **dāan** and a *single bed* is **dāan-yàhn-chòhng**.

Vocabulary builder 2

 Read through the new vocabulary and practise saying it out loud.

CHECKING IN

班機	bāan-gèi	*scheduled flight*
保險	bóu-hím	*insurance*
簽証	chìm-jing	*visa*
重量	chúhng-leuhng	*weight*
(飛)機票	(fèi-)gèi-piu	*air ticket* (cl: **jeung**)
服務員	fuhk-mouh-yùhn	*waiter, attendant, clerk, steward, one who serves*
櫃枱	gwaih-tói	*counter*
過重	gwo-chúhng	*overweight*
行李	hàhng-léih	*luggage* (cl: **gihn**)
輕	hèng	*light* (in weight)
閘口	jaahp-háu	*gate, gateway*
免稅	míhn-seui	*tax free, duty-free*
護照	wuh-jiu	*passport*
遊客	yàuh-haak	*tourist, traveller*

VERBS AND VERB ENDINGS

報到	bou-dou	*to check in, register, report for duty*
交	gàau	*to hand over*
過磅	gwo-bóng	*to weigh*
起飛	héi-fèi	*to take off* (of aircraft) (lit. 'rise and fly')
注意	jyu-yi	*to pay attention to*
攞	ló	*to collect, take*
… 晒	-saai	ve: *completely*
通融	tùng-yùhng	*to stretch a point, get round the rules*
… 一吓	-yāt-háh	ve: *a little bit, one time*

BASICS

多啲	dò-dī	*a little more*
下晝	hah-jau	*afternoon, p.m.*
問題	mahn-tàih	*problem, question*
四點半鐘	sei-dím-bun-jūng	*half past four o'clock*
洋酒	yèuhng-jáu	*liquor, (non-Chinese) alcoholic drinks*

Dialogue 2

15.02 *A tourist checks in at the airport.*

1 **There are some underlined words which you should make sure you understand the function of. As you read through, write down what they mean and what they are doing there, then check at the back to confirm that you are right.**

Yàuh-haak	Síu-jé, ngóh yiu daap yāt-ńgh-lìhng houh bāan-gèi heui Lèuhn-dēun. Chéng mahn ngóh hái nī-douh bou-dou, ngāam m̀h ngāam a?
Fuhk-mouh-yùhn	Yāt-ńgh-lìhng houh bāan-gèi hái hah-jau sei-dím-bun-jūng héi-fèi heui Lèuhn-dēun. Néih hái nī-douh bou-dou <u>jauh</u> ngāam lak. Chéng néih gàau néih ge wuh-jiu, chìm-jing tùhng fèi-gèi-piu béi ngóh lā.
Yàuh-haak	Nī léuhng gihn haih ngóh ge hàhng-léih, chéng néih <u>bòng</u> ngóh gwo-bóng lā.
Fuhk-mouh-yùhn	Sìn-sàang, néih ge hàhng-léih gwo-chúhng bo! Juhng yáuh móuh <u>kèih-tà</u> hàhng-léih a?
Yàuh-haak	Juhng yáuh léuhng gihn sáu-tàih hàhng-léih <u>dōu</u> haih hóu hèng ge. Ngóh ge hàhng-léih gwo-chúhng-jó géi-dō gūng-gàn a?
Fuhk-mouh-yùhn	M̀h syun hóu dò, jí-haih léuhng gūng-gàn jē.
Yàuh-haak	Deui-m̀h-jyuh, chéng néih tùng-yùhng yāt-háh lā, dāk m̀h dāk a?
Fuhk-mouh-yùhn	Mahn-tàih m̀h daaih, daahn-haih hah chi néih jauh yiu dò-dī jyu-yi hàhng-léih ge chúhng-leuhng lā. Hóu lak, néih <u>ló-fàan</u> néih ge wuh-jiu tùhng gèi-piu lā.
Yàuh-haak	M̀h-gòi néih wah ngóh jì léuih-yàuh bóu-hím ge gwaih-tói hái bīn-douh a? Míhn-seui yèuhng-jáu yauh hái bīn-douh máaih nē?
Fuhk-mouh-yùhn	Gó léuhng go gwaih-tói dōu hái sei houh jaahp-háu fuh-gahn, néih m̀h wúih wán-m̀h-dóu ge.
Yàuh-haak	M̀h-gòi-saai.

遊客	小姐，我要搭一五零號班機去倫敦。請問我喺呢度報到，啱唔啱呀?
服務員	一五零號班機喺下晝四點半鐘起飛去倫敦。你喺呢度報到就啱嘞。請你交你嘅護照，簽証同飛機票俾我啦。
遊客	呢兩件係我嘅行李，請你幫我過磅啦。
服務員	先生，你嘅行李過重嘞! 重有冇其他行李呀?
遊客	重有兩件手提行李都係好輕嘅。我嘅行李過重咗幾多公斤呀?
服務員	唔算好多，只係兩公斤啫。
遊客	對唔住，請你通融一吓啦，得唔得呀?
服務員	問題唔大，但係下次你就要多啲注意行李嘅重量啦。好嘞，你攞返你嘅護照同機票啦。
遊客	唔該你話我知旅遊保險嘅櫃枱喺邊度呀? 免稅洋酒又喺邊度買呢?
服務員	嗰兩個櫃枱都喺四號閘口附近，你唔會搵唔倒嘅。
遊客	唔該晒。

2 Answer the questions.

a A **fuhk-mouh-yùhn** can be of either gender. How do you know that this one is female? Or isn't he?

b Is the tourist female?

c How much overweight is the luggage?

d How many pieces of luggage has the tourist got altogether?

e Is the tourist likely to be able to locate the duty-free shop?

Language discovery

15.5 SEUHNG AND HAH AGAIN

In Unit 10 you met **seuhng-go-láih-baai** *last week* and **hah-go-láih-baai** *next week*. In the dialogue there are two more cases where **hah** appears. **Hah chi** (or **hah yāt chi**) means *next time*, *on the next occasion*, and **hah-jau** means *afternoon*, *p.m.* As you would expect, **seuhng chi** (or **seuhng yāt chi**) means *last time*, *on the previous occasion*.

 So, what do you think *a.m.* is?

15.6 CLOCK TIME

Telling the time by the clock is very simple; the hours are called **dím** *dots* (you met that in Unit 13) and, of course, there are 12 of them on the clock (**jūng**). *One o'clock* is 'one dot of the clock', that is, **yāt-dím-jūng**, *two o'clock* is **léuhng-dím-jūng** and so on up to *12 o'clock* **sahp-yih-dím-jūng**. *What time is it?* is 'How many dots of the clock?' **Géi-dō dím jūng a?**

Half past uses the word **bun** *half*, which you met in Unit 4. So *half past one* is **yāt-dím-bun(-jūng)**, *half past two* is **léuhng-dím-bun(-jūng)** and *half past 12* is **sahp-yih-dím-bun(-jūng)**. The brackets around **jūng** are to show that people do not usually bother to say it unless for some reason they want to speak particularly clearly.

You met the word for *minutes* (**fān**) in Unit 10 and you can give precise times to the minute as follows:

1.01	**yāt-dím-lìhng-yāt-fān-jūng** (for **lìhng**, see Unit 11)
1.09	**yāt-dím-lìhng-gáu-fān-jūng**
1.10	**yāt-dím-sahp-fān-jūng**
1.59	**yāt-dím-ńgh-sahp-gáu-fān-jūng**

In practice, rather than bothering to give such precise times, people normally deal in five minute periods only, just as you might say 'Oh, it's 20 past two' even if your watch showed that it was 2.19 or 2.22. The five-minute periods are called *characters* (**jih**) after the figures which appear on clock faces:

1.05	**yāt-dím-yāt-go-jih**
1.10	**yāt-dím-léuhng-go-jih**
1.25	**yāt-dím-ńgh-go-jih**
1.50	**yāt-dím-sahp-go-jih**

Some people like to use the word **gwāt** (from the English word *quarter*) in the following way:

yāt-dím-yāt-go-gwāt	*quarter past one*
yāt-dím-sàam-go-gwāt	*quarter to two*

But if you prefer, you can always say:

yāt-dím-sàam-go-jih	*quarter past one*
yāt-dím-gáu-go-jih	*quarter to two*

Finally, remember that Cantonese likes to put the large before the small, and that applies to time as well.

⋮ **YOUR TURN** **So how would you translate *4.35 p.m. on Tuesday*?**

15.7 FĒI AND PIU *TICKETS*

The formal word for *ticket* is **piu**, but generally Cantonese people prefer to use the colloquial word **fēi**. (**Fēi** is probably a corruption of the English word *fare*.) In the case of the word for *air ticket* most people now simply say **gèi-piu** or if there could be any doubt what that means they would use its fuller form **fèi-gèi-piu**. **Fèi-gèi-fēi** sounds rather odd and is not common.

15.8 SÁU-TÀIH *PORTABLE*

In Unit 8 you met **sáu-tàih miht-fó-túng** *portable fire extinguisher* and in the dialogue you met **sáu-tàih hàhng-léih** *hand baggage*. **Sáu-tàih** can be used freely with many other nouns, but probably the most common nowadays is the **sáu-tàih dihn-wá** *portable phone, mobile, cell-phone*.

15.9 MAHN-TÀIH *A PROBLEM*

Mahn-tàih m̀h daaih means *the problem is not a big one, no great problem*. You will frequently hear people respond to a request by saying **móuh mahn-tàih**, a phrase echoed almost precisely in the English *no problem!*

15.10 VERB ENDING -SAAI *COMPLETELY*

The verb ending **-saai** is a very useful one. In the dialogue it has attached itself to **m̀h-gòi** *thank you*. **M̀h-gòi-saai** really means *thank you totally*, but has been devalued so that many people say it rather than just **m̀h-gòi**, much as many English speakers say *thank you very much* rather than just *thank you* without meaning to show any great degree of gratitude. In the same way **dò-jeh-saai** is very common. Otherwise, **-saai** means what it says, as the following illustrate:

Dī yàhn dōu jáu-saai.	*All the people left.*
Ngóh móuh-saai chín.	*I've got no money at all.*
Kéuih ge sáu hāak-saai.	*His hands were completely black.*

1 **Change the pairs of sentences into single sentence questions using dihng-haih …
nē? The first one would become: Néih haih Yìng-gwok-yàhn dihng-haih Méih-
gwok-yàhn nē?**

  a Néih haih Yìng-gwok-yàhn. Néih haih Méih-gwok-yàhn.

  b Fó-chē faai. Fèi-gèi faai.

  c Kéuih Láih-baai-sàam làih. Kéuih Láih-baai-sei làih.

  d Hòh Sìn-sàang séung heui Hèung-góng. Hòh Sìn-sàang séung heui Gwóng-jàu.

  e Léih Táai móuh chín. Chàhn Táai móuh chín.

2 **Give the opposites of these words.**

  a yeh-máan

  b m̀h-síu-dāk

  c nyúhn-séui

  d chúhng

3 **Make adverbial sentences from the following using -dāk and your translations
of the phrases in brackets. The answer to the first one is Kéuih góng-dāk faai.
Careful now!**

  a Kéuih góng. (quickly)

  b Wòhng Sàang máaih hā. (very cheaply)

  c Néih hàahng-louh. (faster than Miss Cheung)

  d Néih yám yèuhng-jáu. (more than I do)

  e Léih Sìn-sàang jà-chē. (not very well)

4 **What are the correct classifiers for the following? Some of them you have not
been specifically told, but by now you should be able to make a guess with a very
good chance of being right.**

  a dāan-yàhn-chòhng   d wahn-duhng-fóng   g jáu-dim

  b gáu-jái   e máh-louh   h fèi-gèi-piu

  c dihn-sih-gèi   f fèi-gèi   i hàhng-léih

5 **These questions are quite difficult. Answer them in Cantonese.**

  a Yāt gàn tùhng yāt bohng bīn yeuhng chúhng a?

  b Hái Yìng-gwok máaih gihn-hòng bóu-hím gwai m̀h gwai a?

  c Hái fèi-gèi-chèuhng léuih-bihn tùhng-màaih hái bīn-douh yáuh míhn-seui yèuhng-jáu
     maaih a?

  d Daap fèi-gèi ge sìh-hauh, sáu-tàih hàhng-léih yiu m̀h yiu gwo-bóng a?

  e Hái Lèuhn-dēun yáuh géi-dō go fèi-gèi-chèuhng a?

6 Here are some clock times. How do you say them in Cantonese? See if you can come up with three different ways of saying the last one!

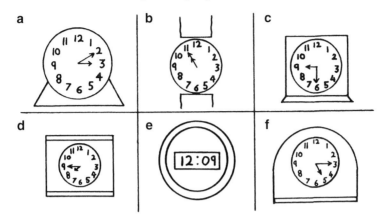

 Test yourself

A question of time. Can you give the answer (in Cantonese) to this puzzle?

Gàm-yaht haih Sìng-kèih-yih.

Ngóh sàam yaht jì-chìhn heui-jó máh-chèuhng.

Ngóh hái máh-chèuhng wáan-jó sàam go bun jūng-tàuh.

Ngóh luhk-dím-jūng lèih-hòi-jó máh-chèuhng.

Gám, ngóh séung mahn néih: Ngóh Láih-baai-géi géi-dō-dím-jūng dou-jó máh-chèuhng nē?

16 駕駛 Ga-sái
Driving

In this unit you will learn about:

▶ *classifiers for pairs.*
▶ *damage and malfunction.*
▶ *different meanings of or.*
▶ *enough.*

▶ *negative comparisons.*
▶ *saying No firmly.*
▶ *the language of cars.*

CEFR: *(B1) Can make your opinions and reactions understood.*

Smile even if …

The word **siu** 笑 *to smile, laugh, laugh at* is heavily used in Cantonese. **Góng-siu** 講笑 means *to joke*, **hóu hóu-siu** 好好笑 is *very funny*, and **láahng-siu** 冷笑 means *to laugh coldly*, but Chinese people also **siu** in tragic and horrific circumstances where Westerners would think it inappropriate. Their so-called 'inscrutability' may be largely owing to this cultural difference, while for their part they often find Western faces hard to read too. **'Kéuih dím-gáai m̀h siu?'** they wonder. *'Have I said something wrong?'*

Driving tests and road accidents are traumatic for all, and not a bit **hóu-siu**. We'll start with a few general motoring terms cunningly paired, but don't worry, there's nothing complicated, we are not trying to cater for the mechanically minded:

開車 **hòi-chē** *to start a car; drive a car*
停車 **tìhng-chē** *to stop a car*
泊位 **paak-wái** *to park a car*
車呔 **chē-tàai** *car tyre*
撞車 **johng-chē** *to have a car crash*

車匙 **chē-sìh** *car key*
腳掣 **geuk-jai** *foot brake*
手掣 **sáu-jai** *hand brake*
爆呔 **baau-tàai** *to have a puncture*
整車 **jíng-chē** *to repair a car*

Jà-chē is *to drive a car or any kind of wheeled vehicle*. Can you remember what **jà faai-jí** means? OK, now have a guess what **jà-sáu** is.

Vocabulary builder 1

 Read the new vocabulary and practise saying it out loud.

DRIVING TEST

斜路	che-lóu	*steep road* (cl: **tiuh**)
局	guhk	*bureau, department, office*
官	gwùn	*official, officer*
考試	háau-si	*to sit an examination; examination, test*
路面	louh-mín	*road surface*
駛、駕駛	sái *or* ga-sái	*to drive; driving*
成績	sìhng-jīk	*result, score, report*

VERBS

掉頭	diuh-tàuh	*to turn to face the other way*
瞓、瞓覺	fan *or* fan-gaau	*to sleep, go to bed, lie down*
考	háau	*to examine, test*
醒	séng	*to wake up, recover consciousness*
抬	tòih	*to carry, lift*

> **LANGUAGE TIP**
> Cantonese uses a number of different verbs meaning *to carry*. *To carry* slung over the shoulder is one, *to carry* in the arms is another, *to carry* on the back is another, *to carry* on a pole over one shoulder is another and so on. **Tòih** is used for *to carry* between two people either holding the load or having it suspended from a pole between them.

BASICS

斜	che	*steep*
情況	chìhng-fong	*situation, circumstances*
反應	fáan-ying	*reaction, response; to respond, react*
夠	gau	*enough*
結果	git-gwó	*end result, in the end*
可能	hó-nàhng	*it is possible that, possibly; possibility*
窄	jaak	*narrow*
重未	juhng-meih	*still, not yet*
慢	maahn	*slow; slowly*
譬如	pei-yùh	*for example, for instance*
同事	tùhng-sih	*colleague*

Dialogue 1

16.01 *Mr Lee has just come back from his driving test.*

1 Is there one thing in particular that Mrs Lee wants to know from her husband?

Mrs Lee	Néih gam hòi-sām, ngóh gú néih gàm-jìu-jóu chàam-gà ge hei-chè ga-sái háau-si sìhng-jīk yāt-dihng hóu hóu lak.
Mr Lee	Ngóh dōu gú ngóh ge sìhng-jīk géi hóu.
Mrs Lee	Háau-si-gwùn háau-jó néih dī māt-yéh a?
Mr Lee	Kéuih háau-jó ngóh hóu dò yéh, pei-yùh paak-wái lā, che-lóu hòi-chē lā, maahn sái lā, tìhng-chē lā, jaak-louh diuh-tàuh lā, sáu-jai tùhng geuk-jai yuhng-dāk hóu m̀h hóu lā, deui louh-mín ge chìhng-fong fáan-ying gau m̀h gau faai lā, dáng-dáng.
Mrs Lee	Git-gwó haih dím-yéung, néih jì m̀h jì a?
Mr Lee	Kéuih móuh góng-yéh bo! Ngóh jà-chē fàan Ga-sái Háau-si-guhk ge sé-jih-làuh gó-jahn-sìh, kéuih hó-nàhng gok-dāk hóu syù-fuhk, fan-jó hái chē léuih-bihn juhng-meih séng, yiu ngóh tùhng kéuih ge tùhng-sìh léuhng go yàhn yāt-chàih tòih kéuih lohk chē.
李太	你咁開心，我估你今朝早參加嘅汽車駕駛考試成績一定好好嘞。
李生	我都估我嘅成績幾好。
李太	考試官考咗你啲乜嘢呀？
李生	佢考咗我好多嘢，譬如泊位啦，斜路開車啦，慢駛啦，停車啦，窄路掉頭啦，手掣同腳掣用得好唔好啦，對路面嘅情況反應夠唔夠快啦，等等。
李太	結果係點樣，你知唔知呀？
李生	佢冇講嘢嗎！我揸車返駕駛考試局嘅寫字樓嗰陣時，佢可能覺得好舒服，瞓咗喺車裡便重未醒，要我同佢嘅同事兩個人一齊抬佢落車。

2 Ngóh-deih séung mahn néih: néih gú gó go háau-si-gwùn jàn-haih fan-jó gaau dihng-haih yàn-waih Léih Sàang jà-chē jà-dāk m̀h hóu só-yíh kéuih pa-dou tàuh-wàhn fan-jó hái chē léuih-bihn nē?

Language discovery

16.1 REACTIONS TO …

You first met **deui** (*with regard to, towards*) in Unit 9, and further examples of its use are to be found in Units 10, 12 and 15. In the dialogue here it teams up with **fáan-ying** to mean *reactions to*: when you have understood that, you will find it easier to make sense of the long section: **deui louh-mín ge chìhng-fong fáan-ying gau m̀h gau faai lā.**

YOUR TURN Now have a go at translating it.

16.2 GAU *ENOUGH*

Gau means *enough*. It works very consistently because it always goes in front of the word it refers to, whether that word is a noun or an adjective, but as you will see from the translations of the examples, English is not so consistent:

Néih gau m̀h gau chín máaih fēi a?	*Do you have enough money to buy the tickets?*
Gó déng móu gau m̀h gau daaih a?	*Is that hat big enough?*

Vocabulary builder 2

 Read the new vocabulary and practise saying it out loud.

MORE WHEELS

賽車	choi-chē	*motor racing*
賽車手	choi-chē-sáu	*racing driver*
單車	dāan-chē	*bicycle* (cl: **ga**)
電單車	dihn-dāan-chē	*motorbike* (cl: **ga**)

MEDICAL

血	hyut	*blood*
傷	sèung	*wound; to wound*

VERBS

撞	johng	*to run into, crash into*
流	làuh	*to flow*
誤會	ngh-wuih	*to misunderstand, get it wrong*
擰	nìng	*to bring, take*
修理	sàu-léih	*to repair, mend*
壞	waaih	*to go wrong, break down; gone wrong*
有事	yáuh sih	*to have something wrong with you, be hurt, be in trouble*

BASICS

千祈	chìn-kèih	*whatever you do don't, don't ever*
黐線	chì-sin	*crazy, mixed up, off the rails*
豈有此理	héi-yáuh-chí-léih	*that's ridiculous, how could that be?*
輪到	lèuhn-dou	*the turn of, it has come to the turn of*
小心	síu-sàm	*careful*
或者	waahk-jé	*or, perhaps*
一時	yāt-sìh	*momentarily, briefly*
認真	yihng-jān	*serious, sincere*

> **CONFLICTING VIEWS**
>
> The next dialogue demonstrates the ability of people to see things in different ways. The Cantonese have a word for it (of course): it is **léuhng-tái** 兩睇 *two ways of looking at it*. But that doesn't mean that both ways are correct, and we agree with the injured **hàahng-yàhn** 行人 *pedestrian* that Mr Chan must indeed 'have a screw loose', which is perhaps the closest English translation for **chì-sin**. We'll see how you feel after reading it.

Dialogue 2

 16.02 *A lucky escape?*

1 Give a nice colloquial English translation for the pedestrian's remark Néih tái, juhng làuh-gán hyut tìm, bringing out the force of Néih tái, juhng, -gán, and tìm.

Chan	Deui-m̀h-jyuh, sìn-sàang, ngóh yāt-sìh m̀h síu-sàm yuhng ga dāan-chē johng-dóu néih. Néih yáuh móuh sih a?
Pedestrian	Daaih mahn-tàih jauh móuh, daahn-haih ngóh jek geuk yìh-gā hóu tung, yáuh-dī sèung. Néih tái, juhng làuh-gán hyut tìm.
Chan	Néih jàn hóu-chói lā, jí-haih beih ga dāan-chē johng-dóu jē.
Pedestrian	Héi-yáuh-chí-léih, néih chì-sin ge. Néih m̀h síu-sàm johng-dóu ngóh, juhng wah ngóh hóu-chói?!
Chan	Haih a, sìn-sàang! Ngóh haih yihng-jàn ga, m̀h haih góng-siu ga. Chìn-kèih m̀h-hóu ngh-wuih a!
Pedestrian	Ngóh dím-yéung ngh-wuih a? Néih góng lā!
Chan	Ngóh haih dīk-sí sī-gēi, yauh haih dihn-dāan-chē choi-chē-sáu. Gàm-yaht hái dīk-sí gūng-sī lèuhn-dou ngóh fong-ga, só-yíh m̀h-sái jà dīk-sí, ngāam-ngāam ngóh ga dihn-dāan-chē yauh waaih-jó, nìng-jó heui sàu-léih, só-yíh ngóh sìn-ji yuhng ngóh go jái ge dāan-chē a. Yùh-gwó haih ngóh ge dīk-sí waahk-jé dihn-dāan-chē johng-dóu néih, gám néih jauh móuh gam hóu-chói la.

陳	對唔住，先生，我一時唔小心用架單車撞倒你，你有冇事呀？
行人	大問題就冇，但係我隻腳而家好痛，有啲傷。你睇，重流緊血添。
陳	你真好彩啦，只係被架單車撞倒啫。
行人	豈有此理，你黐線嘅，你唔小心撞倒我，重話我好彩？！
陳	係呀，先生！我係認真㗎，唔係講笑㗎，千祈唔好誤會呀！
行人	我點樣誤會呀，你講啦！
陳	我係的士司機，又係電單車賽車手，今日喺的士公司輪到我放假，所以唔駛揸的士，啱啱我架電單車又壞咗，擰咗去修理，所以我先至用我個仔嘅單車呀。如果係我嘅的士或者電單車撞倒你，嗽你就冇咁好彩喇。

2 Tell us your views.

    a Néih wah Chàhn Sìn-sàang chì m̀h chì-sin a?

    b Yùh-gwó gó go hàahng-yàhn ge geuk móuh sèung, wúih m̀h wúih làuh hyut nē?

    c Chàhn Sìn-sàang gàm-yaht dím-gáai m̀h yuhng dihn-dāan-chē a?

    d M̀h-gòi néih góng béi ngóh-deih tèng haih hòi-sàm ge yàhn siu dihng-haih m̀h hòi-sàm ge yàhn siu nē?

Language discovery

16.3 JEK *ONE OF A PAIR*

Things that come in pairs are classified with **sèung** 雙 or with **deui** 對:

yāt deui sáu	*a pair of hands, pair of arms*
yāt sèung faai-jí	*a pair of chopsticks*

One of a pair is usually **jek** 隻 regardless of the shape:

yāt jek sáu	*a hand, an arm*
yāt jek faai-jí	*a chopstick*
yāt jek ngáahn	*an eye*
yāt jek dyún-maht	*a sock*

An exception is the case of human beings (such as *husband and wife*), who as a couple are **sèung** but one of the pair is still referred to as **go**. Other exceptions are trousers, spectacles and scissors, which the Cantonese do not consider to be pairs at all – logically enough, since each is a single object – and so do not use **deui** or **sèung** for them.

16.4 ACCENTUATING THE NEGATIVE

Chìn-kèih is a useful word when you want to make a negative command particularly strong:

Chìn-kèih m̀h-hóu góng-siu lā!	*Whatever you do, don't joke!*
Chìn-kèih m̀h-hóu m̀h gei-dāk a!	*You really must not forget!*

16.5 WHEN ELECTRIC IS NOT ELECTRIC

In Unit 9 you met a number of useful words which were made up using **dihn** *electricity, electric*. Cantonese seems to have got rather carried away with the idea, though, and has applied **dihn** to things which have very little to do with electricity. So when *motorbikes* came along they dubbed them 'electric bicycles' **dihn-dāan-chē**. Here is another example:

dihn-yàuh	*petrol, gasoline* (lit. 'electric oil')
yahp dihn-yàuh	*to refuel, put petrol in*

16.6 *BROKEN* AND *BROKEN DOWN*

You met **waaih** *bad* in Unit 12. **Waaih-jó** means *gone bad* or *broken down* and can be applied to fruit, meat, machinery, watches, radios and so on. But if the object is clearly physically damaged, then the word to use is **laahn-jó**, which you met in Unit 5:

Ngóh ge dihn-dāan-chē waaih-jó.	*Something's gone wrong with my motorbike.*
Ngóh ge dihn-daan-chē laahn-jó.	*My motorbike is smashed.*

16.7 MORE ON *OR*

Remember **dihng-haih**? Now you have also met **waahk-jé** and they both mean *or*. The difference is that **dihng-haih** means *or is it the case that?* and always appears in questions, while **waahk-jé** means *or maybe it is, or perhaps* and appears in statements:

Kéuih géi-sí làih a? Haih gàm-yaht dihng-haih tìng-yaht làih nē?

When is she coming? Is it today or tomorrow that she is coming? (Which is it? It must be one or the other.)

Kéuih (waahk-jé) gàm-yaht waahk-jé tìng-yaht làih.

She's coming today or maybe tomorrow. (It could be either.)

Kéuih yiu ga-fē dihng-haih chàh nē?

Does he want coffee or tea?

Kéuih waahk-jé yiu ga-fē waahk-jé yiu chàh.

He may want coffee or he may want tea. (I'm not sure.)

> **LANGUAGE TIP**
> You are quite right, there is yet a third kind of *or* that you have met. Remember **luhk-chāt go** for *6 or 7*? But this neat little formula only works with numbers, you cannot use it with other words.

16.8 NEGATIVE COMPARISONS

In the last line of the dialogue Mr Chan says: **Néih jauh móuh gam hóu-chói la** *You wouldn't be as lucky then*, and this gives you the clue to how to make negative comparisons. The pattern is:

X móuh Y gam ...   *X isn't as ... as Y*

YOUR TURN **Translate these examples:**

Kéuih móuh ngóh gam gòu.

Hei-chè móuh fèi-gèi gam faai.

Ngóh hàahng-dāk móuh néih gam maahn.

156

16.9 A RECAP ON COMPARISONS

Now we can set out the full range of comparisons so that you can bring real subtlety into your speech:

Ngóh hóu gòu.	*I am tall.*
Kéuih gòu dī.	*He's taller.*
Kéuih gòu hóu-dò.	*He's a lot taller.*
Néih juhng gòu.	*You are even taller.*
Kéuih móuh gam gòu.	*He's not so tall.*
Kéuih gòu gwo ngóh.	*He's taller than I am.*
Kéuih gòu gwo ngóh síu-síu or	*He's a bit taller than I am.*
Kéuih gòu gwo ngóh yāt-dī.	
Kéuih gòu gwo ngóh hóu-dò.	*He's a lot taller than I am.*
Kéuih móuh ngóh gam gòu.	*He's not as tall as I am.*

And, of course, there is also the equivalent and the superlative:

Kéuih tùhng ngóh yāt-yeuhng gam gòu.	*He's just as tall as I am.*
Kéuih móuh ngóh yāt-yeuhng gam gòu.	*He's not just as tall as I am.*
Kéuih jeui gòu lak.	*He's tallest.*

 Practice

1 **Here are five English sentences. Which of the two possibilities given is the correct translation?**

  a I think he is also Japanese.
    1 Ngóh gú kéuih dōu haih Yaht-bún-yàhn.
    2 Ngóh dōu gú kéuih haih Yaht-bún-yàhn.

  b Mrs Lee is going to Japan by air.
    1 Léih Taai-táai daap fèi-gèi heui Yaht-bún.
    2 Léih Taai-táai heui Yaht-bún daap fèi-gèi.

  c Mr Wong and I are going to dine at City Hall.
    1 Ngóh tùhng Wòhng Sìn-sàang heui Daaih-wuih-tòhng sihk-faahn.
    2 Wòhng Sìn-sàang tùhng ngóh heui Daaih-wuih-tòhng sihk-faahn.

  d Which lady is ill?
    1 Bīn-go taai-táai yáuh behng a?
    2 Bīn-go ge taai-táai yáuh behng a?

2 **Now give the translations of the sentences in Exercise 1 which you think are incorrect.**

3 **Can you match each of the six verbs a–f with a suitable noun from the box?**
  a dá
  b dóu
  c chàu
  d tèng
  e chùng
  f tái

> jéung-bán   tìn-hei   gwóng-bo
> pē-páai   dihn-yíng   màh-jeuk
> hói-tāan   noih-yùhng   hùhng-dāng
> sou-hohk   yàuh-haak   bē-jáu

4 Use Cantonese to describe Mr Wong's height in comparison with each of the other five people. How would you describe Mr Lee in comparison with Mrs Wong? How would you describe Mr Lee without reference to anyone else?

Mr Wong   Mr Chan   Mr Lee   Mrs Chan   Mrs Lee   Mrs Wong

5 Here are definitions of four words which you have learned in this unit. Can you work out what they are?

a Jīk-haih yāt go yàhn góng ge yéh, jouh ge yéh, séung ge yéh yāt-dī dōu m̀h ngāam.

b Jīk-haih néih góng nī yeuhng yéh, kéuih m̀h mìhng-baahk, yíh-wàih néih góng gó yeuhng yéh.

c Jīk-haih dī yéh laahn-jó, waaih-jó jì-hauh, joi yāt chi jíng-fàan hóu.

d Jīk-haih 'sìh-sìh' ge sèung-fáan.

❓ Test yourself

A really tough one. Can you say who is sitting in each of the six seats?

Gàm-máahn Lùhng Sàang, Lùhng Táai chéng Léih Sàang, Léih Táai tùhng-màaih Chàhn Sàang, Chàhn Táai sihk-faahn. Léih Sàang chóh hái bāk-bihn; Chàhn Sàang hái Lùhng Táai yauh-bihn; Chàhn Táai hái Lùhng Sàang deui-mihn; Léih Táai hái Lùhng Sàang jó-sáu-bihn.

17 紀律部隊 Géi-leuht bouh-déui

The uniformed services

In this unit you will learn about:

▶ *a polite classifier.*
▶ *active / passive verbs.*
▶ *closing a gap.*
▶ *complicated descriptive phrases.*
▶ *even.*

▶ *gender again.*
▶ *hard to …*
▶ *months.*
▶ *more on telling.*
▶ *pull and push.*

CEFR: *(B1) Can give detailed instructions; can obtain more detailed information.*

Uniforms

This unit is not about the *military* **gwàn-déui** 軍隊. Hong Kong does not maintain any of its own, its defence is in the hands of the Chinese People's Liberation Army (PLA), **Gáai-fong-gwān** 解放軍, which generally keeps a low profile; but other *uniforms* **jai-fuhk** 制服 (cl: **tou**) abound and police, *firemen* **sìu-fòhng-yùhn** 消防員, *immigration officers* **yìh-màhn-yùhn** 移民員, bell-hops, doormen, street-market inspectors, waiters, all have their distinctive dress. For the majority of the population, clothing styles tend to be casual and to blur social identities rather than draw attention to them.

 If we tell you that **hói** 海 means *sea*, **luhk** 陸 means *land*, and **hùng** 空 means *air*, have a go at translating *navy, army* and *airforce*.

Vocabulary builder 1

 Read the new vocabulary and practise saying it out loud.

UNIFORMED SERVICES

便服	bihn-fuhk	*plain clothes*
軍服	gwàn-fuhk	*military uniform*
軍人	gwàn-yàhn	*soldier, military personnel*
女警	néuih-gíng	*policewoman*
消防局	sìu-fòhng-guhk	*fire brigade*

VERBS

加入	gà-yahp	*to join, recruit into*
合規格	hahp-kwài-gaak	*to qualify, meet requirements*
准	jéun	*to allow, permit*
規定	kwài-dihng	*to regulate, lay down a rule*
申請	sàn-chíng	*to apply*
移民	yìh-màhn	*to migrate; immigration, emigration*

PHOTOGRAPHY

相機	séung-gèi	*camera* (cl: **go** or **ga**)
相片	seung-pín	*photograph* (cl: **fūk** 幅)
數碼	sou-máh	*digital*
影(相)	yíng(-séung)	*to take a photograph, have a photograph taken*

BASICS

嘞!	baih!	*oh dear! oh heck! alas!*
不過	bāt-gwo	*but, however*
叫	giu	*to tell someone to, order someone to*
裸體	ló-tái	*naked, nude*
尾	méih	*tail, end* (cl: **tìuh**)
任何	yahm-hòh	*any*
意思	yi-sì	*meaning, intention*
月	yuht	*moon, month*

Dialogue 1

 17.01 Problems with a photograph on an immigration application.

1 When you get to the official's third speech in the dialogue you will see -gán. It's a while since you've met this useful little verb ending. What is it doing there?

Official	Síu-jé, néih nī jèung yuhng làih sàn-chíng yìh-màhn ge seung-pín m̀h hahp-kwài-gaak bo!
Applicant	Dím-yéung m̀h hahp-kwài-gaak a? Néih tái nī jèung seung-pín yíng-dāk géi hóu ā! Ngóh yuhng sou-máh séung-gèi yíng ga.
Official	Yìh-màhn-guhk kwài-dihng sàn-chíng-yàhn ge seung-pín m̀h jéun jeuk gwàn-fuhk.
Applicant	Hóu-chói ngóh m̀h haih gwàn-yàhn, ngóh yíh-gìng lèih-hòi-jó gwàn-déui léuhng nìhn lak.
Official	Gám, néih yìh-gā jouh-gán māt-yéh a?
Applicant	Ngóh yìh-gā haih néuih-gíng, bāt-gwo hah-go-yuht-méih ngóh wúih gà-yahp Sìu-fòhng-guhk jouh néuih-sìu-fòhng-yùhn … Baih! Gíng-chaat tùhng sìu-fòhng-yùhn dōu yiu jeuk jai-fuhk ge bo! Ngóh dím-syun-hóu-nē?
Official	Síu-jé, Yìh-màhn-guhk kwài-dihng sàn-chíng yìh-màhn ge yàhn m̀h jéun jeuk yahm-hòh jai-fuhk yíng-séung. Néih hó-yíh m̀h jeuk ga.
Applicant	Māt-yéh wá?! Néih giu ngóh m̀h jeuk sāam ló-tái yíng-séung àh?
Official	M̀h … m̀h … haih … Néih … néih m̀h-hóu ngh-wuih. Ngóh ge yi-sì haih giu néih m̀h jeuk jai-fuhk, jeuk bihn-fuhk jē!

官	小姐，你呢張用嚟申請移民嘅相片唔合規格嘞！
申請人	點樣唔合規格呀？你睇呢張相片影得幾好丫。 我用數碼相機影㗎.
官	移民局規定申請人嘅相片唔准著軍服。
申請人	好彩我唔係軍人，我已經離開咗軍隊兩年嘞。
官	噉，你而家做緊乜嘢呀？
申請人	我而家係女警，不過下個月尾我會加入消防局做女消防員 … 嘞！警察同消防員都要著制服嘅嘞！我點算好呢？
官	小姐，移民局規定申請移民嘅人唔准著任何制服影相，你可以唔著㗎。
申請人	乜嘢話?! 你叫我唔著衫裸體影相吖？
官	唔 … 唔 … 係。你 … 你唔好誤會。我嘅意思係叫你唔著制服著便服啫！

2 In the official's first speech you will see làih. Did you wonder what it means and what it is doing there? We can tell you that it is the word which you know means *come*, but can you get your head round the second part of the question?

3 What is the opposite of méih?

4 How many photos did the applicant submit to the immigration official?

Language discovery

17.1 ADJECTIVES

In Unit 4 you first met **ge** used to link descriptive phrases or clauses to a noun (**hóu gwai ge ga-fē** *very expensive coffee*, **máaih-gán bāt ge yàhn** *the person who is buying a pen*). The first line of the dialogue in this unit has a more complicated version of that **ge** pattern: **nī jèung yuhng làih sàn-chíng yìh-màhn ge seung-pín**. At first sight this is rather frightening, but keep cool, you can quite easily break it down to see how it works.

The basic unit is **nī jèung seung-pín** *this photograph* (remember **jèung** is the classifier for flat sheet-like things). Splitting **nī jèung** and the noun **seung-pín** is the adjective **yuhng làih sàn-chíng yìh-màhn** *used for applying for immigration*, and **ge** does the same job that it was doing when you met it in Unit 4, that is, it is linking the complex adjective to the noun.

⋮ **YOUR TURN So what does the whole thing mean?**

In fact, although it looks complicated, when you break it down it is really only the same basic pattern as **nī go Méih-gwok-yàhn**: specifier–classifier–adjective–noun.

Here are some more examples:

nī chēut nàahm-yán hóu jùng-yi tái ge dihn-yíng *this film that men love watching*
gó ga Wòhng Sàang séung máaih ge Yaht-bún chē *the Japanese car which Mr Wong wants to buy*

17.2 POSSESSIVES WITH ADJECTIVES

Look again at the same speech by the immigration official and you will see that **néih** *you* is positioned in front of that complex adjectival pattern, and it all means *this photograph of yours which is being used for applying for immigration*. This is the regular position for the possessive in such cases and the normal possessive indicator (**ge**) is not necessary:

néih gó ga Wòhng Sàang séung máaih ge Yaht-bún chē
that Japanese car of yours which Mr Wong wants to buy

17.3 JÉUN: A TWO-WAY VERB

Jéun can mean either *to allow* or *to be allowed*, so it can work two ways, both actively and passively:

Kéuih m̀h jéun yám-jáu. *He's not allowed to drink alcohol.*
Kéuih m̀h jéun (ngóh) yám-jáu. *He doesn't allow (me) the drinking of alcohol.*

As you become more familiar with Cantonese you will find other two-way verbs like **jéun**; and already in this unit you will find **yíng-séung**, which can mean either *to photograph* or *to be photographed*.

17.4 VIVE LA DIFFÉRENCE!

You met **nàahm** *male* and his mate **néuih** *female* in Unit 9. As you can see from the dialogue, **néuih** can be attached fairly freely to nouns – **néuih-gíng** *policewoman*, **néuih-sìu-fòhng-yùhn** *firewoman*. In these cases the people are generally assumed to be males, so that you would only meet the terms **nàahm-gíng** and **nàahm-sìu-fòhng-yùhn** if someone were specifically making a contrast between the two genders. In other cases there is no assumption that a noun is male – **yàhn** *person*, for example, is completely non-committal and so you will meet **nàahm-yán** *man* just as often as you will meet **néuih-yán** *woman* (you will remember from Unit 9 that the tone changes from **yàhn** to **yán**). Here are some more:

nàahm-pàhng-yáuh / néuih-pàhng-yáuh	*boyfriend / girlfriend*
nàahm-chi(-só) / néuih-chi(-só)	*gentlemen's / ladies' toilet*
nàahm-hohk-sāang / néuih-hohk-sāang	*boy / girl pupils*

While on the subject, you might note that **néuih** changes its tone when it is used as **néui** *daughter*, the pair to **jái** *son*.

> **LANGUAGE TIP**
>
> **Néuih-pàhng-yáuh** and **nàahm-pàhng-yáuh** are usually applied to a couple who are 'courting', and friends who are of the opposite gender but not courting sometimes refer to each other as **néuih-sing pàhng-yáuh** and **nàahm-sing pàhng-yáuh**, rather laborious terms which might equally laboriously be translated as *a friend who is of the female gender* and *a friend who is of the male gender*.

17.5 YUHT *MONTH*

Yuht means *the moon* and by extension has also come to mean *a month*. The classifier for it is **go**, so *one month* is **yāt go yuht**, *two months* is **léuhng go yuht** and so on. As with **láih-baai** and **sìng-kèih**, *last*, *this* and *next* are **seuhng**, **nī** and **hah**, so *last month* is **seuhng-go-yuht**, *this month* is **nī go yuht** and *next month* is **hah-go-yuht**.

The months of the year do not have fancy names as in English, they are just numbered without classifiers. The two sets that follow should make the system clear to you:

Yāt-yuht	*January*	**yāt go yuht**	*one month*
Yih-yuht	*February*	**léuhng go yuht**	*two months*
Sàam-yuht	*March*	**sàam go yuht**	*three months*
…			
Chāt-yuht	*July*	**chāt go yuht**	*seven months*
…			
Sahp-yih-yuht	*December*	**sahp-yih go yuht**	*12 months*

> **THE LUNAR CALENDAR**
>
> China traditionally used both a solar and a lunar calendar, and the latter is still important for determining the dates of some festivals as well as being the one by which most people reckon their birthdays. The word for *month* (**yuht**) is the same in both, and the months are numbered in the same way, so *February* and the *Second Lunar Month* are both **Yih-yuht**, but there are three exceptions:
>
> 1 the first solar month (*January*) is **Yāt-yuht**, but the first lunar month is known as **Jìng-yuht** 正月 'the principal month'.
> 2 the twelfth lunar month is **Sahp-yih yuht** of course, but it is also known as **Laahp-yuht** 臘月, 'the preserving month', when meats were wind-dried and in ancient times there was a major sacrifice to mark the end of the year.
> 3 seven lunar years in 19 have an extra month, called a **yeuhn-yuht** 閏月 *intercalary month*. It may be added in almost anywhere during the year, so in 2014 there was a *Yeuhn Ninth Month* **Yeuhn-gáu-yuht** that came between the *Ninth Month* **Gáu-yuht** and the *Tenth Month* **Sahp-yuht** making a 13-month year of 384 days.

17.6 TO TELL

To tell has different meanings in English and different words are used for them in Cantonese. When *to tell* means *to inform, tell a fact*, you have learned that it is translated by **wah / góng … jì / tèng** (see Unit 13). When *to tell* means *to tell someone to do something, order someone to do something*, then **giu** is used:

Sìn-sàang giu hohk-sāang tái Yìng-màhn syù.

The teacher told the pupils to read their English books.

Ngóh giu kéuih m̀h-hóu làih.

I told him not to come.

Sometimes English uses *to tell* when it would be more fitting to use *ask* or *invite* (**chéng** in Cantonese). Note the following sentence:

Bàh-bā giu kéuih go jái chéng Wòhng Yī-sāng yahp-làih.

The father told his son to tell Dr Wong to come in.

A child is unlikely to feel able to order a doctor around, although the father feels quite happy with ordering his own son around, so in this example *told* and *tell* become **giu** and **chéng** respectively.

Vocabulary builder 2

 Read the new vocabulary and practise saying it out loud.

POLICE WORDS

便衣	bihn-yì	*plain clothes, civilian clothes*
幫辦	bòng-báan	*inspector*
巡邏車	chèuhn-lòh-chē	*patrol car* (cl: **ga**)
警員証	gíng-yùhn-jing	*warrant card*
權	kyùhn	*right, authority, powers*
沙展	sà-jín	*sergeant*
身份証	sàn-fán-jing	*identity card*
手槍	sáu-chēung	*handgun, pistol* (cl: **jì**)
手足	sáu-jūk	*brothers* (triad slang, lit. 'hands and feet')
死仔	séi-jái	*deadbeats, bastards, rats* (strong abuse)
上司	seuhng-sī	*superior officer, direct boss*

VERBS AND VERB ENDINGS

瞪	dàng	*to stare, open the eyes*
瞪大對眼	dàng-daaih-deui-ngáahn	*to take a good look* (lit. 'open big pair eyes')
販毒	fáahn-duhk	*to peddle drugs*
企	kéih	*to stand*
拉	làai	*to pull; to arrest*
… 埋	-màaih	ve: *close up to*
散水	saan-séui	*to scatter away*
搜身	sáu-sàn	*to conduct a body search*
懷疑	wàaih-yìh	*to suspect*
郁	yūk	*to move, make a movement*

BASICS

班	bàan	cl: *a group of, gang of*
出	chēut	*out*
方便	fòng-bihn	*convenient*
假	gá	*false*
連 … 都 …	lìhn … dōu …	*even …*
路邊	louh-bīn	*roadside*
難	nàahn	*difficult, hard*
喂!	wai!	*hoy! hey!*
位	wái	cl: *(polite) for people*

Dialogue 2

17.02 *Plain-clothes police have a tough time with some suspects.*

1 **Tease out how the underlined passage works, and then try to produce an idiomatic English translation of it.**

Sergeant	Wai, néih-deih géi go, m̀h-hóu yūk a! Faai-dī màu-dài, nìng néih-deih ge sàn-fán-jing chēut-làih.
Youth	Néih-deih haih māt-yéh yàhn a? Néih-deih móuh kyùhn tái ngóh-deih ge sàn-fán-jing bo!
Sergeant	Ngóh haih Wòhng Sà-jín, nī wái haih ngóh seuhng-sī Chàhn Bòng-báan. Ngóh-deih wàaih-yìh néih-deih fáahn-duhk. Néih-deih kéih-màaih louh-bīn, béi ngóh sáu-sàn.
Youth	Néih-deih dōu móuh jeuk jai-fuhk, yauh m̀h haih chóh gíng-chaat chèuhn-lòh-chē. Néih-deih wah haih gíng-chaat, yiu làai-yàhn, yiu sáu-sàn, bīn-go seun néih a?
Sergeant	Ngóh-deih móuh jeuk gíng-chaat jai-fuhk, haih yàn-waih fòng-bihn ngóh-deih jouh-yéh. Ngóh-deih léuhng go dōu haih bihn-yī gíng-chaat. Néih-deih dàng-daaih-deui-ngáahn tái-háh ngóh-deih ge gíng-yùhn-jing lā!
Youth	Néih-deih lìhn sáu-chēung dōu móuh, gíng-yùhn-jing dōu hó-nàhng haih gá ge, <u>yiu ngóh-deih seun néih-deih haih gíng-chaat jauh nàahn la</u>. Wai, sáu-jūk! Ngóh-deih saan-séui lō!
Sergeant	Máih jáu a! Néih bàan séi-jái, dáng ngóh làai-saai néih-deih séuhng gíng-chaat-guhk sìn!

沙展	喂！你哋幾個，唔好郁呀！快啲踎低，擰你哋嘅身份証出嚟。
青年	你哋係乜嘢人呀？你哋冇權睇我哋嘅身份証㗎！
沙展	我係王沙展，呢位係我上司陳幫辦。我哋懷疑你哋販毒，你哋企埋路邊，俾我搜身。
青年	你哋都冇著制服，又唔係坐警察巡邏車。你哋話係警察，要拉人，要搜身，邊個信你呀？
沙展	我哋冇著警察制服，係因為方便我哋做嘢。我哋兩個都係便衣警察。你哋瞪大對眼睇吓我哋嘅警員証啦！
青年	你哋連手槍都冇，警員証都可能係假嘅，要我哋信你哋係警察就難喇。喂，手足！我哋散水囉！
沙展	咪走呀！你班死仔，等我拉晒你哋上警察局先！

2 **You are a Hong Kong immigration official. A foreign national in army uniform, wearing a handgun, comes up to your desk. Ask him for his passport and visa, ask him when he will be leaving Hong Kong and tell him that he is not allowed to bring a handgun into the territory and will he please hand it to that police sergeant at Counter No. 41.**

3 These are hard! You will have to work out which word goes in the blank spaces before you can understand. It is the same word in each sentence: that's your only clue. Then translate them into English.

a Taai-táai wah Chàhn Sìn-sàang chìhn-yaht jà-chē jà-dāk taai faai, johng-jó bā-sí, yáuh sèung, waahk-jé wúih _____ tìm.

b Néih daaih-lóu góng ge Yaht-màhn ngóh gok-dāk hóu hóu-siu. Kàhm-yaht ngóh tèng kéuih góng jauh siu-_____-yàhn lak.

c Màh-mā wah ngóh yùh-gwó m̀h gwàai kéuih jauh wúih dá-_____ ngóh. Ngóh yauh m̀h seun, yauh m̀h pa kéuih.

> **LANGUAGE TIP**
> In its history China has suffered more than most from the import and effects of addictive drugs, and it is hardly surprising that they are referred to as *poison* (**duhk 毒**), just as the police sergeant does in the second dialogue. **Duhk** is both a noun and a verb, and the composite verb **duhk-séi 毒死** is *to die of poison* or *to kill by poisoning*, that is, it is another of the two-way active-passive verbs you met earlier in this unit.

Language discovery

17.7 HURRY UP!

Faai-dī means *quicker*, *faster*, as you will remember from your work on comparatives in Unit 16, but it has become the most common way of saying *get a move on!*, *hurry up!* Harassed mothers say it to their children constantly.

17.8 WÁI: THE POLITE CLASSIFIER

The normal classifier for people is of course **go**, but if you wish to be polite to someone or about someone, you should use **wái** instead. So you might say **nī go yàhn** *this person*, but you would almost certainly say **nī wái sìn-sàang** *this gentleman* and **gó wái síu-jé** *that young lady*. In the dialogue the sergeant uses **wái** when he refers to his superior officer, Inspector Chan. If you are introducing someone, you say **Nī wái haih Wòhng Taai-táai, gó wái haih Léih Síu-jé … ,** etc.

17.9 -MÀAIH *CLOSE UP TO*

The verb ending **-màaih** can be used to indicate movement towards something or location close up to something. Its opposite, showing movement away from something, or location away from something is **-hòi**. You can use these two words quite freely where you feel them to be appropriate.

Chóh-màaih-dī.	*Sit a bit closer. (Cuddle up to me!)*
Chóh-hòi-dī.	*Sit further away. (Stop crowding me!)*
Tek-màaih ngóh nī-douh lā!	*Kick it over here to me!*
Kéuih hàahng-hòi-jó.	*He's walked away.*

> **LANGUAGE TIP**
> **Kéuih hàahng-hòi-jó** is often said by secretaries over the telephone when you want to talk to their boss. It implies that the boss has just walked out of the room for a minute, and is a standard euphemism for *He's gone to the toilet*, but cynics know it really means *He's not here, he's on the golf course.*

17.10 LÀAI *TO PULL*

Làai is the normal verb *to pull* and it is the character which you see marked on doors: the opposite is **tèui** *to push*. **Làai** also means *to pull someone in, to arrest.*

> **LANGUAGE TIP**
> Doors are often marked **tèui** 推 *push* or **làai** 拉 *pull*, and it is probably worth learning these two characters now. On the other hand, we have noticed that, with a refreshing frailty shared by the rest of the world, Chinese people nearly always pull on the one marked push and vice versa, so maybe you needn't bother. Just do it by trial and error like everyone else.

17.11 LÌHN ... DŌU ... *EVEN* ...

Lìhn is a very useful word provided you remember how to position it. The golden rules are:

▶ **lìhn** is placed before the word which it refers to, and
▶ they both must come before **dōu**.

You will also remember from as far back as Unit 1 that **dōu** must itself always come before a verb, so there is a certain rigidity about this pattern. A couple of examples will show you how to use it:

Lìhn Wòhng Sìn-sàang dōu m̀h jùng-yi Wòhng Síu-jé.	*Even Mr Wong doesn't like Miss Wong.*
Ngóh lìhn yāt mān dōu móuh.	*I haven't got even one dollar.*

YOUR TURN Now see if you can translate this one:
Kéuih lìhn faahn dōu m̀h séung sihk.

17.12 SÉUHNG *TO GO UP*

The real meaning of **séuhng** is *to go up*, *ascend*. **Séuhng-sàan** means *to go up the hill* and **séuhng-chē** is *to get (up) onto the vehicle*. In some cases, though, **séuhng** is used meaning *to go to*. In the dialogue there is an example, **séuhng gíng-chaat-guhk** *to go to the police station*. You are advised not to make up your own phrases using **séuhng** in the sense of *to go to*. Only use the ones you meet in this book.

> **LANGUAGE TIP**
> One of the biggest influences on contemporary Cantonese language has been the great popularity of gangster films and programmes on television and in the cinema. The racy slang which gives authenticity to the shows passes rapidly into ordinary people's speech, but equally quickly is discarded again. At the end of the dialogue we have included just a couple of terms which seem to be likely to stay around, but there is little point in your learning any more – by the time that you are able to use it, it may well not be current any longer!

17.13 **NÀAHN** VERSUS **HÓU**

The opposite of **hóu** is normally **m̀h hóu**, but now that you have met **nàahn** *hard*, *difficult* it is worth pointing out that it can act as the opposite of **hóu** in **hóu** + verb expressions like **hóu-sihk** *delicious*.

hóu-sihk	*delicious*		**nàahn-sihk**	*unpalatable*
hóu-tèng	*melodious*		**nàahn-tèng**	*unpleasant to hear*
hóu-tái	*good to look at*		**nàahn-tái**	*ugly*

 Practice

1 Try to describe in Cantonese what Mr Wong is doing in each of these pictures.

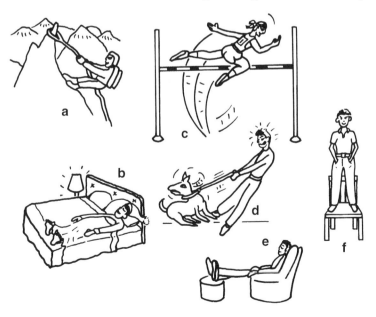

2 Complete the sentences to show the people's occupations.

    a Chàhn Sìn-sàang làai fáahn-duhk ge yàhn: kéuih haih _____.

    b Wòhng Síu-jé hái jùng-hohk gaau-syù: kéuih haih _____.

    c Léih Sàang sèhng-yaht jà dīk-sí: kéuih haih _____.

    d Jèung Sàang hái jáu-làuh nìng yéh béi yàhn sihk: kéuih haih _____.

    e Ngóh bàh-ba hái chán-só jouh-yéh: kéuih haih _____.

3 Answer briefly in Cantonese.

    a Yāt nìhn yauh géi-dò yaht a?

    b Chìhn-yaht haih Láih-baai-sei: tìng-yaht nē?

    c Sei-yuht yáuh géi-dò yaht a?

    d Sàam go sìng-kèih dò m̀h dò yaht gwo yāt go yuht a?

    e Yāt-chìn yaht noih dihng-haih sàam nìhn noih nē?

4 Three complicated sentences laden with adjectives for you to put into Cantonese. Remember, keep cool – they aren't so bad if you work out what the basic patterns must be.

    a That young lady who is standing on the left of Mrs Chan is Mr Wong's 17-year-old daughter.

    b Which is the Japanese car you bought when you were touring in the States?

    c This old fire extinguisher of yours is not big enough. How about buying a bigger one?

Test yourself

Into each of the sentences put one of the randomly listed inserts from the box, then translate the sentences into English.

dōu	lìhn	jeuk sāam-kwàhn	sìn-ji	jì-hauh

a Kéuih wah kéuih Sìng-kèih-yāt wúih fàan-làih, daahn-haih kéuih Sìng-kèih-sàam _____ fàan.

b Néih jáu-jó _____, ngóh jauh dá dihn-wá béi néih taai-táai lak.

c Seuhng-go-yuht Wòhng Táai _____ yāt ga chē dōu maaih-m̀h-dóu: kéuih ge gìng-léih hóu m̀h hòi-sām.

d Kéuih yaht-yaht _____ dá-màh-jeuk, só-yíh m̀h dāk-hàahn tùhng ngóh heui máaih-sung.

e Yàuh-séui ge sìh-hauh _____ m̀h haih géi fòng-bihn.

18 治安 *Jih-òn*
Law and order

In this unit you will learn about:

- as much as that.
- *common.*
- *comparative age.*
- *crimes and punishment.*

- ▶ *foreigners.*
- ▶ *meih v móuh.*
- ▶ *more on lonely verbs.*
- ▶ *succeeding with verbs.*

CEFR: *(B1) Can give an opinion about factual information on familiar matters; can make suggestions.*

Crime

Hong Kong is not a dangerous territory to live in or visit, but of course it has its darker side, and this unit looks at that and its consequences. Here is some dark vocabulary to start with:

打交 **dá-gāau** *brawling; to fight*

打劫 **dá-gip** *robbery; to rob*

打荷包 **dá-hòh-bāau** *purse-snatching*

罪 **jeuih** *crime* (cl: **tìuh**)

治安 **jih-òn** *public order*

吸毒 **kāp-duhk** *to smoke drugs*

強姦 **kèuhng-gàan** *rape; to rape*

謀殺 **màuh-saat** *murder; to murder*

貪污 **tàam-wù** *corruption*

偷嘢 **tàu-yéh** *theft; to steal*

And two very important words which you really MUST learn, though we hope you never need to use them. When you want to warn someone of danger or something that they should avoid, you say (or shout, depending on the urgency) **Tái-jyuh**! 睇住! *Look out! Mind your step!*, and if you find yourself in dire danger and your life is at stake, you shout **Gau-mehng a!** 救命呀! *Help! Save me!*

What is the difference between **Tái-háh, bā-sí làih!** and **Tái-jyuh, bā-sí làih!**?

Vocabulary builder 1

 Read the new vocabulary and practise saying it out loud.

VERBS

報導	bou-douh	*to report; report*
出街	chēut-gāai	*to go out into the street*
發生	faat-sàng	*to occur, happen, transpire*
敢	gám	*to dare, dare to*
吸	kāp	*to inhale, smoke*
令	lihng	*to cause*
想像	séung-jeuhng	*to imagine*

BASICS

報紙	bou-jí	*newspaper* (cl: **fahn** 份)
本地	bún-deih	*local, indigenous*
親眼	chàn-ngáahn	*with one's own eyes*
前幾年	chìhn-géi-nìhn	*a few years ago*
到而家為止	dou-yìh-gā-wàih-jí	*up to now*
幾乎	gèi-fùh	*almost but not quite*
幾咁 … 嘞!	géi-gam- … lak!	*how very … !*
最少	jeui-síu	*at least*
唔只	m̀h-jí	*not only*
紐約	Náu-yeuk	*New York*
外國	ngoih-gwok	*foreign country; foreign*
普遍	póu-pin	*common (widespread)*
普通	póu-tùng	*common (ordinary)*
十分	sahp-fàn	*totally, 100 per cent*
雖然 … 但係	sèui-yìhn … daahn-haih	*although … yet …*
城市	sìhng-síh	*city, town*
一個人	yāt-go-yàhn	*alone*

Dialogue 1

18.01 *Three friends discuss the crime rate.*

1 Do you think Mrs Wong has ever been to a foreign country?

Lee	Ngóh múih yaht tái bou-jí dōu yāt-dihng tái-dou dī lihng ngóh hóu m̀h hòi-sām ge sàn-mán ge, pei-yùh haih màuh-saat lā, kèuhng-gàan lā, kāp-duhk lā, dá-gāau lā, dá-gip lā, dá-hòh-bāau lā, dáng-dáng.
Wong	Léih Táai, nī dī gám ge chìhng-fong m̀h-jí hái Hèung-góng hóu póu-pin, hái ngoih-gwok hóu dò daaih sìhng-síh dōu yāt-yeuhng póu-pin ga.
Cheung	Chìhn-géi-nìhn ngóh jyuh hái Náu-yeuk, hái ngóh jyuh ge fuh-gahn, gèi-fùh múih yaht dōu yáuh jeuih-on faat-sàng, yìh-ché dōu haih ngóh chàn-ngáahn tái-gin ge, daahn-haih dōu m̀h gin bún-deih bou-jí yáuh bou-douh. Néih hó-yíh séung-jeuhng jeuih-on dò dou géi-gam yìhm-juhng lak!
Wong	Jèung Táai, tèng néih gám-yéung góng, Hèung-góng ge jih-òn sèui-yìhn m̀h haih sahp-fàn hóu daahn-haih dōu m̀h syun taai waaih bo!
Cheung	Haih a, jàn-haih m̀h syun taai waaih. Jeui-síu dou-yìh-gā-wàih-jí ngóh-deih póu-tùng-yàhn juhng gám yāt-go-yàhn hái yeh-máan chēut-gāai máaih-yéh.
李	我每日睇報紙都一定睇到啲令我好唔開心嘅新聞嘅，譬如係謀殺啦，強姦啦，吸毒啦，打交啦，打劫啦，打荷包啦，等等。
王	李太，呢啲噉嘅情況唔只喺香港好普遍，喺外國好多大城市都一樣普遍㗎。
張	前幾年我住喺紐約，喺我住嘅附近，幾乎每日都有罪案發生，而且都係我親眼睇見嘅，但係都唔見本地報紙有報導，你可以想像罪案多到幾咁嚴重嘞！
王	張太，聽你咁樣講，香港嘅治安雖然唔係十分好，但係都唔算太壞嗎！
張	係呀，真係唔算太壞，最少到而家為止，我哋普通人重敢一個人喺夜晚出街買嘢。

2 Answers in Cantonese, please.

  a Néih gú-háh, Jèung-táai haih m̀h haih yaht-táu fàan-sé-jih-làuh a?

  b 'M̀h gin bún-deih bou-jí yáuh bou-douh': 'bún-deih' ge yi-sì haih bīn-douh a?

> **LANGUAGE TIP**
>
> **Ngoih** means *outside*, as you will remember from **ngoih-bihn**. **Ngoih-gwok** 'outside country' is the standard word for *foreign country* and, as you might expect, **ngoih-gwok-yàhn** means a *foreigner* and **ngoih-gwok-wá** means a *foreign language*. **Ngoih-gwok** is contrasted with **Jùng-gwok** 'central country', the country around which all others revolve, *China*. The Chinese have always considered themselves to be at the centre of the world, just as the Romans did with their tellingly named 'Mediterranean' sea and this means that it is something of a contradiction in terms for Chinese in another country to describe themselves as **ngoih-gwok-yàhn** – wherever they go they remain Chinese and so the indigenous peoples tend to be called foreigners in their own lands.

Language discovery

18.1 PÓU-TÙNG AND PÓU-PIN: *COMMON*

Both **póu-pin** and **póu-tùng** mean *common*, but there is a difference between them. **Póu-pin** means *common* in the sense of widespread, universal, two-a-penny; and **póu-tùng** means *common* in the sense of ordinary, normal. A **póu-tùng-yàhn** is an ordinary chap, the man on the Clapham / Shanghai omnibus.

> **LANGUAGE TIP**
> One quirky use of **póu-tùng** is as a way of responding to a compliment. So, on being congratulated on his calligraphy (*How beautiful your handwriting is, Mr Wong!*), the response might be **'Póu-tùng jē'**. (*It's just run of the mill*). But sometimes this very modest disclaimer is said with a cock of the head which belies its apparent humility, and Mr Wong can be understood in a boastful way to be saying something like *I'm just an ordinary genius, you know!*

18.2 PÓU-TÙNG-WÁ AND OTHER LANGUAGES

Wah means *to say*, as you learned in Unit 6, but when its tone is changed to **wá** it means *speech*, *language* and often appears as the object of the lonely verb **góng** *to speak*. **Póu-tùng-wá** is 'common language', that is, the language which is to be used throughout China, what in English is usually called *Mandarin* and in China is known officially as *Putonghua*. **Góng Póu-tùng-wá** is *to speak Mandarin*; *to speak a foreign language* is **góng ngoih-gwok-wá**, and you know that you can add **wá** to the name of any country to give the language spoken there (**Faat-gwok-wá** for *French*, **Taai-gwok-wá** for *Thai*, etc.). In Unit 12 you learned about adding **màhn** to the root of country names, but it is a risky thing to do if you have not met the word before – could you have predicted that the **màhn** word for **Yaht-bún** is **Yaht-màhn**, for instance? – so as a rule you are safer to stick to the **wá** words.

18.3 UP TO NOW

Dou-yìh-gā-wàih-jí seems an awful mouthful to translate *up to now*: it may help you to remember it if you analyse it. **Dou** means *to arrive at*, **yìh-gā** means *now*, **wàih-jí** means *as a stop*, so *arriving at now as a stop – up to now*.

 You can adapt this expression to some extent. How do you think you would say *up until this year*? And *up until yesterday*?

> **LANGUAGE TIP**
> Hong Kong has had a long fight against corruption (**tàam-wù**), which was rife in the years of expanding population growth after the Pacific War. In 1974 the *Independent Commission Against Corruption* (ICAC) was set up and has produced a major improvement in the situation, though its continuing existence demonstrates that there is still a need for vigilance. The Cantonese name for the *ICAC* is the **Lìhm-jing Gùng-chyúh** (廉政公署 'office for honest government'), but you will often hear it called 'ICAC' even when Cantonese is being spoken.

Vocabulary builder 2

 Read the new vocabulary and practise saying it out loud.

LAW COURT WORDS

犯	faahn	to offend, commit a crime
罪名	jeuih-mìhng	charge, accusation
判	pun	to sentence
囚犯	chàuh-fáan	prisoner
坐監	chóh-gāam	to be in prison
上訴	seuhng-sou	to appeal to a higher court
法官	faat-gwùn	judge
大人	Daaih-yàhn	Your Honour, Your Excellency, Your Worship
罰錢	faht-chín	to fine, be fined

BASICS

辦法	baahn-faat	method, way, means
清楚	chìng-chó	clear, clearly
救濟金	gau-jai-gām	relief money
自願	jih-yuhn	voluntarily; willing
再次	joi-chi	another time, a second time
老人	lóuh-yàhn	the elderly, the aged
生活	sàng-wuht	to live; livelihood
成立	sìhng-laahp	established; to establish

> **LANGUAGE TIP**
>
> In a fair world, crime leads inexorably to punishment, and the next dialogue is set in a law court, but it is a rather unusual case. The *prisoner* **chàuh-fáan** 囚犯 seems to be **chì-saai sin** *totally barmy*, but it turns out that he has his reasons.

Dialogue 2

 18.02 *A thoughtful prisoner makes a special pleading.*

1 What would the prisoner say to a $10,000 fine? And a $2,000 fine?

Judge	Néih faahn-jó tàu-yéh jeuih, yìh-ché jeuih-mìhng sìhng-laahp. Ngóh pun néih chóh léuhng nìhn gāam. Néih yùh-gwó m̀h tùhng-yi hó-yíh seuhng-sou. Néih tèng m̀h tèng dāk chìng-chó a?
Prisoner	Faat-gwùn Daaih-yàhn, ngóh mìhng-baahk, bāt-gwo yùh-gwó ngóh chóh-yùhn léuhng nìhn gāam jì-hauh chēut-làih, yāt-dihng wán-m̀h-dóu yéh jouh, yàn-waih ngóh chóh-gwo gāam, móuh yàhn wúih chéng ngóh jouh-yéh. Só-yíh ngóh wán-m̀h-dóu chín, móuh baahn-faat sàng-wuht, wúih joi-chi tàu-yéh … gám, yauh wúih joi-chi chóh-gāam ge bo!
Judge	Gám, néih séung dím-yéung nē? Haih m̀h haih m̀h séung chóh-gāam, séung faht-chín nē?
Prisoner	M̀h haih a, Daaih-yàhn. Ngóh saht-joih <u>móuh chín béi néih faht</u>. Ngāam-ngāam sèung-fáan, ngóh hèi-mohng néih yìh-gā jauh pun ngóh chóh yih-sahp-ńgh nìhn gāam lak.
Judge	Dím-gáai néih jih-yuhn yiu chóh yih-sahp-ńgh nìhn gāam gam noih nē?
Prisoner	Yàn-waih chóh-yùhn yih-sahp-ńgh nìhn gāam jì-hauh, gó-jahn-sìh ngóh wúih haih yāt go luhk-sahp seui ge lóuh-yàhn, hó-yíh heui ló lóuh-yàhn gau-jai-gām, m̀h sái joi jouh-yéh lak.
法官	你犯咗偷嘢罪，而且罪名成立。我判你坐兩年監。你如果唔同意可以上訴。你聽唔聽得清楚呀？
囚犯	法官大人，我明白，不過如果我坐完兩年監之後出嚟，一定搵唔倒嘢做，因為我坐過監，冇人會請我做嘢。所以我搵唔倒錢，冇辦法生活，會再次偷嘢 … 嗽，又會再次坐監嘅噃！
法官	嗽，你想點樣呢？係唔係唔想坐監，想罰錢呢？
囚犯	唔係呀，大人。我實在冇錢俾你罰，啱啱相反，我希望你而家就判我坐二十五年監嘞。
法官	點解你自願要坐二十五年監咁耐呢？
囚犯	因為坐完二十五年監之後，嗰陣時我會係一個六十歲嘅老人，可以去攞老人救濟金，唔駛再做嘢嘞。

2 What is béi doing in the underlined phrase of the dialogue?

176

Language discovery

18.4 MORE ON LONELY VERBS

You have met plenty of verbs which normally require objects and you will recognize more as your Cantonese improves. **Tàu** *to steal* is another one and you will notice that **yéh** *things* is the supplied object. But you should not feel that because a verb has a fall-back object assigned to it you cannot embellish it – you could, for instance, say **kéuih tàu-jó hóu dò yéh** *he stole a lot of things*. The same applies to other verb–object pairings: **chóh-gāam** 'to sit in prison' means *to be imprisoned*, but you can see from the dialogue that the verb and its object can be split: **kéuih chóh léuhng nìhn gāam** *he's doing two years*.

18.5 MEIH AND MÓUH

Both **meih** *not yet* and **móuh** *have not* are used to form questions with the verb ending **-gwo**:

Néih yáuh móuh sihk-gwo lùhng-hā α?
Néih sihk-gwo lùhng-hā meih α?

These two examples can both be translated by *Have you ever had lobster?*, but note that the second one implies that at some time you probably will try it, so that you might prefer to translate the first one as *Have you ever had lobster?* and the second as *Have you had lobster yet?* or *Have you tried the lobster yet?*

Meih (but not **móuh**) can happily be used also with the verb ending **-jó** when you want to know whether something has taken place yet. As you saw in Unit 1, it is very common to greet someone with:

Sihk-jó faahn meih α?   Have you eaten yet?

18.6 CAN DO / NO CAN DO?

In Unit 12 you met **tái-m̀h-dóu** *could not see* and in Unit 15 came **wán-m̀h-dóu** *cannot find*. In both cases you were left to guess what they meant, but you were owed an explanation and it is time you had one. In the dialogue the prisoner says **yāt-dihng wán-m̀h-dóu yéh jouh** *I'll certainly not be able to find work to do*. **Wán**, of course, means *to look for* and **dóu** you met in Unit 8 meaning *to succeed in*, so **wán-m̀h-dóu** means *to look for but not succeed in it – to be unable to find*. Here are a few more examples:

tái-m̀h-dóu   *unable to see*
daap-m̀h-dóu bā-sí   *unable to catch the bus*
gú-m̀h-dóu kéuih haih bīn-go   *can't guess who she is*

The positive form of this pattern uses **dāk** instead of **m̀h**.

⋮ **YOUR TURN** So how would you say *able to see, able to catch* and *able to guess*?

To ask a question you can, of course, as always, put positive and negative together:

Néih daap-dāk-dóu daap-m̀h-dóu bā-sí a? *Can you catch the bus?*

But it would save breath to say:

Néih daap-m̀h-daap-dāk-dóu bā-sí a?

18.7 AS MUCH AS THAT

To stress the size of numbers it is quite common to add a **gam** *so* expression, just as in the dialogue the judge says **chóh yih-sahp-ńgh nìhn gāam gam noih**. **Gam noih** means *so long a time* and the effect is to say *as long as 25 years in prison*. Here are some other examples:

Kéuih yáuh sàam-maahn mān gam dò.	*He's got as much as $30,000.*
Néih yáuh yih-baak bohng gam chúhng.	*You weigh as much as 200 lbs.*
Ngóh gáu-sahp-yāt seui gam lóuh.	*I'm all of 91 years old.*

18.8 OLDER AND YOUNGER

You will need to be careful with *old*. **Lóuh** means *really old, elderly, aged* and is therefore the appropriate word in the term for *old age relief*. But when you are comparing ages (Jack is older than Jill) it would be absurd to use **lóuh** if both of them are children or middle-aged. Cantonese prefers to use **daaih** *big* for *old* in such a case:

Wòhng Síu-jé daaih-gwo Jèung Síu-jé.	*Miss Wong is older than Miss Cheung.*
Ngóh móuh néih gam daaih.	*I am not as old as you.*

Of course neither of these sentences has anything to do with size.

It is not impossible to say **Kéuih lóuh-gwo ngóh**, but only if I am already very elderly and he is even more so.

Practice

1 Mr Wong is insatiably curious. Unfortunately, although he writes down the answers, his memory is so bad he can't remember what his questions were afterwards. Can you help him by supplying them (in Cantonese of course)? Here is his list of answers:

a Gàm-yaht haih Sìng-kèih-yih.

b Lèuhn-dēun Fèi-gèi-chèuhng hái sìhng-síh sài-bihn.

c Ngóh sing Jèung.

d Dī hā sei-sahp-luhk mān yāt gàn.

e Yauh m̀h haih chāt-dím-jūng heui, yauh m̀h haih baat-dím-jūng heui, yàn-waih kéuih saht-joih móuh chéng ngóh heui.

2 Nī sàam go yàhn léuih-bihn, bīn-go jeui daaih a?

3 Tone practice time again. Put in the tone marks on the following where necessary.

a faai-di! (*hurry up!*)   **e** yihng-jan (*sincere*)

b fong-ga (*be on holiday*)   **f** yi-sang (*doctor*)

c seuhng-bihn (*on top of*)   **g** ngoih-tou (*jacket*)

d suhk-sik (*familiar with*)   **h** ngaam-ngaam (*a moment ago*)

4 Complete the unfinished words, remembering to get the tones right.

a _____-wìhng (*prosperous*)

b fòng-_____ (*aspect*)

c _____-léih (*to repair*)

d yahm-_____ (*any*)

e _____-seui (*duty-free*)

f _____-bihn (*convenient*)

5 A quick and simple test. What are the opposites of the following?

a nàahm-bihn   **d** chēut-bihn   **g** jàn

b nàahm-yán   **e** chēut-nín   **h** jái

c nī-douh   **f** chìhn-yaht   **i** jìu-jóu

6 Positive word power: dig into your vocabulary memory and find a word you know which is similar in meaning for each of the following.

  a bihn-yì   **d** bāt-gwo

  b gíng-chaat-chē   **e** m̀h hó-yíh

  c m̀h haih jàn ge

 # Test yourself

 18.03 One-way phone-call. You can overhear what Mr Wong is saying at your end, but you can't hear the person at the other end of the line, so you will have to use your imagination and perhaps go through it all more than once to be sure you have extracted what clues you can. If you can do it just by listening to the audio, so much the better. Now try to supply the missing dialogue:

Wong	Wái!
X	**a**
Wong	M̀h-gòi daaih-sèng-dī. Néih haih bīn wái wán bīn-go a? Wái! Wái!
X	**b**
Wong	Óh, ngóh jauh haih. Daahn-haih néih wah néih haih Wòhng Taai-táai m̀h ngāam bo! Ngóh taai-táai chēut-jó gāai máaih-sung, móuh sáu-tàih-dihn-wá, m̀h hó-yíh dá dihn-wá làih, só-yíh ngóh jì-dou néih m̀h haih ngóh taai-táai. Néih …
X	**c**
Wong	Taai-táai, m̀h-hóu wah ngóh chì-sin lā. Ngóh góng-siu jī-máh, dòng-yín jì-dou haih néih làih-ge. Daahn-haih ngóh jàn-haih m̀h mìhng-baahk néih dím-yéung hó-yí dá dihn-wá làih.
X	**d**
Wong	Māt-yéh wá?! Hái bīn-douh ló-jó gam dò chín máaih dihn-wá-gèi nē?
X	**e**
Wong	Baih-lak! Gàm-máahn ngóh-deih sihk māt-yéh a? Dihn-wá-gèi haih m̀h sihk-dak ge bo!

19 經濟 *Gìng-jai*
Economics

In this unit you will learn about:

▶ *banking.*
▶ *commands.*
▶ *continents and oceans.*
▶ *currencies.*
▶ *errors.*

▶ *fractions.*
▶ *identifying things.*
▶ look one look.
▶ the more … the more.
▶ *undesirable difference.*

CEFR: *(B1) Can cope with less routine situations in banks; can make a complaint.*

 ## Money

Money is the root of … this unit. Hong Kong is said to be besotted with money and highly materialistic, but if it is so it is not alone, and it has more reason to be so than many places have, because it has few resources other than its people and their ingenuity, hard work and command of material rewards. Almost any currency is freely and legally traded in Hong Kong, and there are no restrictions on its flow either way across the borders. The principal currencies are:

Hong Kong dollar ($)	**Góng-yùhn** 港元 or **Góng-baih** 港幣 or **Góng-jí** 港紙
Renminbi (RMB) (¥)	**Yàhn-màhn-baih** 人民幣 or **Yàhn-jái** 人仔
American dollar ($)	**Méih-yùhn** 美元 or **Méih-gām** 美金
Euro (€)	**Aù-yùhn** 歐元 or **Aù–lòh** 歐羅

 Can you guess what currency the **Yìng-bóng** 英鎊 is?

Vocabulary builder 1

 Read the new vocabulary and practise saying it out loud.

BANKING

部門	bouh-mùhn	*department of an organization*
赤字	chek-jih	*in the red, deficit* (lit. 'red characters')
儲蓄	chyúh-chūk	*savings; to save*
兌	deui	*to cash a cheque, exchange currency*
兌換率	deui-wuhn-léut	*exchange rate*
支票	jì-piu	*cheque* (cl: **jèung**)
職員	jīk-yùhn	*staff, employee, clerk*
來往	lòih-wóhng	*coming and going; current (account)*
銀行	ngàhn-hòhng	*bank*
透支	tau-jì	*overdraft; to overdraw*
戶口	wuh-háu	*bank account*
現金	yihn-gām	*cash, ready money*
月結單	yuht-git-dāan	*monthly statement* (cl: **jèung**)

VERBS AND VERB ENDINGS

查	chàh	*to check, investigate*
… 錯	-cho	ve: *in error; wrong, incorrect*
開	hòi	*to open*
收倒	sàu-dóu	*to receive*
寫	sé	*to write*
相信	sèung-seun	*to believe, trust*

BASICS

呃	ak	fp: *that will be quite alright; certainly, sir*
嘅嘞	ge-lak	fp: *anticipated result; this will happen*
儘(量)	jeuhn(-leuhng)	*so far as possible, to the best of one's ability*
寫明	sé-mìhng	*written clearly*
信	seun	*letter* (cl: **fùng**)
有關	yáuh-gwàan	*relevant, concerned*

Dialogue 1

A customer has problems with his bank account.

1 What does the clerk's third speech mean, and how does it come to mean it?

Customer	Síu-jé, nī jèung yihn-gām jì-piu m̀h-gòi néih bòng ngóh deui-jó kéuih, yìhn-hauh yuhng gó dī chín máaih ńgh-chìn mān Méih-yùhn.
Clerk	Hóu ak. Sìn-sàang, juhng yáuh māt-yéh sih nē?
Customer	Nàh, nī jèung haih ngóh seuhng-go-yuht ge ngàhn-hòhng yuht-git-dāan, haih gàm-jìu-jóu sàu-dóu ge. Jèung dāan seuhng-bihn sé-mìhng ngóh go lòih-wóhng wuh-háu seuhng-go-yuht yáuh chek-jih, yìh-ché juhng heung ngàhn-hòhng tau-jì-jó yāt-maahn-sàam-chìn mān tìm. Ngóh saht-joih móuh heung ngáhn-hòhng tau-jì-gwo yahm-hòh chín. Ngóh sèung-seun ngóh ge wuh-háu yāt-dihng m̀h wúih yáuh chek-jih. M̀h-gòi néih bòng ngóh chàh-yāt-chàh, tái-háh hái bīn-douh cho-jó.
Clerk	Hóu, chéng néih gàau jèung yuht-git-dāan béi ngóh lā, ngóh wúih gàau béi yáuh-gwàan ge bouh-mùhn. Yáuh git-gwó jì-hauh, ngàhn-hòhng jauh wúih sé-seun béi néih ge-lak.
Customer	M̀h-gòi-saai. Ngóh hèi-mohng néih jeuhn faai wah ngóh tèng go git-gwó haih dím-yéung.
Clerk	Hóu ak. Ngóh jì-dou lak.
Customer	M̀h-gòi-saai. Ngóh juhng séung néih bòng ngóh hòi yāt go ngoih-wuih chyúh-chūk wuh-háu, hóu m̀h hóu a?
Clerk	Hóu, móuh mahn-tàih.
Customer	A, juhng yáuh. Gàm-yaht Aù-yùhn deui Yìng-bóng tùhng-màaih Góng-jí deui Yàhn-màhn-baih ge deui-wuhn-léut haih géi-dō a?
Clerk	Deui-m̀h-jyuh, ngóh m̀h jì bo! Chéng néih heui daih-sàam-houh gwaih-tói mahn gó-douh ge jīk-yùhn lā!
人客	小姐，呢張現金支票唔該你幫我兌咗佢，然後用嗰啲錢買五千蚊美元。
職員	好呢。先生，重有乜嘢事呢？
人客	嗱，呢張係我上個月嘅銀行月結單，係今朝早收倒嘅。張單上便寫明我個來往戶口上個月有赤字，而且重向銀行透支咗一萬三千蚊添。我實在冇向銀行透支過任何錢。我相信我嘅戶口一定唔會有赤字。唔該你幫我查一查，睇吓喺邊度錯咗。
職員	好，請你交張月結單俾我啦，我會交俾有關嘅部門，有結果之後，銀行就會寫信俾你嘅嘞。
人客	唔該晒。我希望你儘快話我聽個結果係點樣。
職員	好呢。我知道嘞。
人客	唔該晒。我重想你幫我開一個外匯儲蓄戶口，好唔好呀？
職員	好，冇問題。
人客	呀，重有。今日歐元兌英鎊同埋港紙兌人民幣嘅兌換率係幾多呀？
職員	對唔住，我唔知喎！請你去第二號櫃檯問嗰度嘅職員啦！

2 Answer the questions.

a Tòhng-yàhn jùng-yi hùhng-sīk ge yéh. Gám, nī wái sìn-sàang jì-dou yuht-git-dāan yáuh chek-jih jauh hóu hòi-sām, haih-m̀h-haih a?

b Chàhn Sìn-sàang go jái gàm-jìu-jóu hóu m̀h séung fàan-hohk. Kéuih wúih m̀h wúih jeuhn-faai hàang-louh heui hohk-haauh a?

> **LANGUAGE TIP**
> Money is tricky stuff, and Chinese words for *money* are legion. A favourite slang word for it is **séui** *water*, and **Ngóh móuh séui** means *I'm broke*. But even at a more formal level there are different terms in regular usage. As you have seen, the American dollar, the Hong Kong dollar and the Euro all can use the word **yùhn**, but each of them has at least one common alternative form, and all the alternatives are different from each other. Sorry about this, it's not our fault, honest!

Language discovery

19.1 POSITIVE COMMANDS WITH -JÓ

You first met the verb ending **-jó** in Unit 4. It indicates that an action has been completed. The same verb ending also gives the idea *go ahead and do it!*, a polite and gentle exhortation. You will see an example in the dialogue where the customer says **m̀h-gòi néih bòng ngóh deui-jó kéuih** *please cash it for me*. Often the final particle **lā** gives additional force to the exhortation:

Sihk-jó kéuih lā! *Eat it up!*

You should note that this use of **-jó** is always accompanied by an object, either **kéuih** or a more specific noun:

Jyú-jó tìuh yú lā! *Cook the fish!*

19.2 LÒIH-WÓHNG

Lòih-wóhng means *coming and going*, so a *current account* is literally 'a coming and going account'. You will sometimes hear people saying **lòih-lòih-wóhng-wóhng**, meaning *great to-ings and fro-ings*.

> **LANGUAGE TIP**
> It is hard to find red-coloured things which are not considered lucky by the Chinese, but to be in the red at the bank is no more desirable in a Chinese context than in a Western one. It is perhaps significant that the usual word for *red* (**hùhng**) is not used, but instead the word **chek** (which also means *red*) appears in the expression **chek-jih**. **Chek** has another meaning (*naked*) and appears in the term **chek-geuk-yī-sāng** *barefoot doctors*, the practitioners who were trained to an elementary level in an effort to bring medical benefits down to the most deprived areas of China as it strove to develop after the Communist Revolution of 1949. There is a link of poverty between these two uses of **chek**, it seems.

19.3 LOOK ONE LOOK!

As you will remember from Unit 15, **yāt-háh** conveys the idea of *doing something for a little while*. You can also show this same idea by doubling a verb with **yāt** in the middle:

chàh-yāt-chàh	*to run a little check*
tái-yāt-tái	*to have a peep*

19.4 CHO *MISTAKE*

Cho is a very useful little word. Its basic meaning is *incorrect, mistaken* and this is the meaning which you will find in the dialogue (**tái-háh hái bīn-douh cho-jó** *and see where the error has occurred*). It can also be attached to other verbs as a verb ending:

Ngóh tèng-cho lak.	*I misheard.*
Nī go jih néih sé-cho lak.	*You've written this character wrongly.*

In Unit 11 you met the same word **cho** in **m̀h-cho** *not bad, pretty good*; and it appears yet again in another useful expression **móuh-cho** *there's no mistake, quite right*.

Vocabulary builder 2

 Read the new vocabulary and practise saying it out loud.

DOING BUSINESS

百分之三	baak-fahn-jì-sàam	*3 per cent*
幫趁	bòng-chan	*to patronize, give custom to*
伙伴	fó-buhn	*partner*
減薪	gáam-sàn	*to reduce wages; salary cut*
衰退	sèui-teui	*to go into decline, recession*
貿易	mauh-yihk	*trade*
人客	yàhn-haak	*customer*
員工	yùhn-gūng	*staff, employees, workforce*

VERBS AND VERB ENDINGS

超過	chìu-gwo	*to exceed*
裁減	chòih-gáam	*to cut, reduce*
跌	dit	*to fall, fall down*
結束	git-chūk	*to come to an end, resolve*
掛鈎	gwa-ngāu	*to peg up, peg*
… 落去	-lohk-heui	ve: *carry on, continue*
受到	sauh-dou	*to suffer, receive*
升	sìng	*to rise, go up*
影響	yíng-héung	*to affect, influence*

TIME WORDS

最近	jeui-gahn	recent, recently
一向	yāt-heung	all along, up to now

BASICS

唉	àai!	alas!
歐洲	Aù-jàu	Europe
不如	bāt-yùh	it would be better if
比較	béi-gaau	comparatively; to compare
差	chà	poor, not up to scratch, lacking
火車頭	fó-chè-tàuh	(railway) engine
跟住	gàn-jyuh	following, accordingly
嘅	gé	fp: puzzlement, surprise
國家	gwok-gà	country, state
其實	kèih-saht	in fact, in reality
嚟嘅 / 㗎?	làih-ge /-ga?	fp: for identification
唔掂	m̀h-dihm	unable to cope, incompetent, can't do it
外行人	ngoih-hóng-yàhn	layman, outsider
枱	tói	table (cl: **jèung**)
胃口	waih-háu	appetite
一成	yāt-sìhng	one tenth
越 … 越 …	yuht … yuht …	the more … the more …

 When you saw ngoih-hóng-yàhn in the list above, did it ring a bell? Fear not, you were not imagining things and there is no mistake in the text. What you are remembering looks and sounds very similar but has a directly opposite meaning. No doubt you can guess what the sound-alike word means?

Dialogue 2

19.02 *Two worried friends discuss the financial situation.*

1 Where are Mr Wong and Mr Chan chatting?

Wong Lóuh Chán, nī gàan jáu-làuh dím-gáai gam síu yàhn làih bòng-chan gé? Néih tái-háh, chà-mh-dō yāt-bun ge tói dōu haih hùng ge, dím-gáai wúih gám-yéung nē?

Chan Haih a! Jeui-gahn Hèung-góng ge jáu-làuh gàan-gàan dōu haih gám-yéung ge la. Nī gàan ge sàang-yi syun béi-gaau hóu ge la. Gàm-máahn chà-mh-dō yáuh yāt-bun ge tói dōu yáuh yàhn-haak, yíh-gìng syun géi hóu ge la.

Wong Hèung-góng ge gìng-jai jàn-haih gam chà mē? Ngóh yíh-wàih jí-haih Méih-gwok ge gìng-jai mh dihm jē.

Chan Aài, Góng-yùhn tùhng Méih-yùhn gwa-ngāu …

Wong Lóuh Chán, 'gwa-ngāu' kèih-saht haih māt-yéh làih ga?

Chan Óh, gwa-ngāu jīk-haih wah: Méih-gām sìng, Góng-yùhn yāt-dihng yiu gàn-jyuh sìng, Méih-gām dit, Góng-yùhn yauh yiu gàn-jyuh dit gám-yéung lā. Juhng yáuh, Méih-gwok ge gìng-jai yāt-heung dōu haih sai-gaai gìng-jai ge fó-chè-tàuh, Méih-gwok yauh haih Hèung-góng jeui daaih ge mauh-yihk fó-buhn, gám Hèung-góng gìng-jai dím wúih mh sauh-dou yíng-héung nē?

Wong Gám, néih-deih gàan gūng-sī sauh-dou ge yíng-héung, syun mh syun daaih a?

Chan Hóu-chói ngóh-deih gàan gūng-sī yāt-heung jí jouh Aù-jàu sàang-yi, yíng-héung mh syun taai daaih. Bāt-gwo jeui-gahn gūng-sī chòih-gáam-jó chìu-gwo yih-sahp go yùhn-gūng la, chà-mh-dō haih sèhng gàan gūng-sī yùhn-gūng ge yāt sìhng. Kèih-tà yùhn-gūng go-go dōu yiu gáam-sàn baak-fahn-jì-sàam.

Wong Nī chi Hèung-góng tùhng kèih-tà gwok-gà ge gìng-jai sèui-teui, néih gú géi-sìh sìn-ji wúih git-chūk nē?

Chan Hái nī fòng-mihn ngóh haih ngoih-hóng-yàhn, ngóh jàn-haih mh jì. Ngóh dòng-yín hèi-mohng yuht faai yuht hóu lā … Ngóh-deih bāt-yùh mh hóu joi gòng la, néih gai-juhk góng, ngóh wúih móuh waih-háu sihk-faahn ge lak.

王　老陳，呢間酒樓點解咁少人嚟幫趁嘅？你睇吓，差唔多一半嘅枱都係空嘅，點解會咁樣呢？

陳　係呀。最近香港嘅酒樓間間都係咁樣嘅喇。呢間嘅生意算比較好嘅喇。今晚，差唔多有一半嘅枱都有人客己經算幾好嘅喇。

王　香港嘅經濟真係咁差咩？我以為只係美國嘅經濟唔掂啫。

陳　唉，港元同美元掛鈎 …

王　老陳，《掛鈎》其實係乜嘢嚟㗎？

陳　哦，掛鈎即係話美金升，港元一定跟住升，美金跌，港元又跟住跌咁樣啦。重有，美國嘅經濟一向都係世界經濟嘅火車頭，美國又係香港最大嘅貿易伙伴，噉香港經濟點會唔受到影响呢？

王　噉，你哋間公司受到嘅影响算唔算大呀？

陳　好彩我哋間公司一向只做歐洲生意，影响唔算太大。不過最近公司裁減咗超過二十個員工喇，差唔多係成間公司員工嘅一成。其他員工個個都要減薪百分之三。

王　呢次香港同其他國家嘅經濟衰退你估幾時先至會結束呢？

陳　喺呢方面我係外行人，我真係唔知。我當然希望越快越好啦。我哋不如唔好再講喇，你繼續講我會冇胃口食飯嘅嘞。

2 Answer in Cantonese.

  a Chàhn Sàang haih m̀h haih wah Méih-gwok maaih hóu dò fó-chè-tàuh béi kèih-tà gwok-gà a?

  b Chàhn Sàang ge gūng-sī hái Bà-sài jouh ge sàang-yi dò m̀h dò a?

  c Chàhn Sàang dím-gáai giu kéuih pàhng-yáuh m̀h-hóu gong-wá nē?

Language discovery

19.5 CHÀ *TO DIFFER*

You met **chà** in **chà-m̀h-dō** (Unit 12), which literally means 'differs not much', and hence *almost*. On its own, **chà** is not a neutral word – it implies not just that something differs but that it is less than desirable that it is so. *Short of the mark, not up to scratch, not as good as it ought to be, could have done better, lacking in oomph, unremarkable, underperforming* all could be translated by **chà**, and you can quantify the idea too:

chà-dī	*not quite up to standard*
hóu chà	*awful, very bad*

19.6 M̀H-DIHM *NOT MAKING IT*

From the dialogue you can see that **chà** and **m̀h-dihm** both indicate unsatisfactory performance. **M̀h-dihm** is most commonly met with in the slang phrase **gáau-m̀h-dihm** *can't be done, I can't manage that, he can't cope with it*. The positive form is **gáau-dihm** *I can do that no problem*, or **gáau-dihm lak** *that's fixed*. Woe betide anyone whom an underworld boss decides to **gáau-dihm** – they get terminally 'fixed' – but don't be put off using the word with less extreme meaning, it is very common in both positive and negative forms.

19.7 FINAL PARTICLE FOR IDENTIFICATION

When something is defined or described for recognition by the listener, the speaker uses the final particle **làih-ge** *that's what it is*. The question form is **làih-ga?** *what is it?* and is most often heard in **haih māt-yéh làih-ga?** *what is it?*

Haih māt-yéh làih-ga?	*What is it?*
Haih séung-gèi làih ge.	*It's a camera.*

19.8 CONTINENTS AND OCEANS

You have now met **Aù-jàu** *Europe*. The other continents are:

亞洲	**A-jàu**	*Asia*
非洲	**Fèi-jàu**	*Africa*
美洲	**Méih-jàu**	*America*
澳洲	**Ou-jàu**	*Australia*

And while we are thinking big, here are the major seas:

北冰洋	**Bāk-bìng-yèuhng**	*Arctic Ocean*
大西洋	**Daaih-sài-yèuhng**	*Atlantic Ocean*
地中海	**Deih-jùng-hói**	*Mediterranean Sea*
太平洋	**Taai-pìhng-yèuhng**	*Pacific Ocean*
印度洋	**Yan-douh-yèuhng**	*Indian Ocean*

19.9 SÌHNG *TENTHS*

Yāt-sìhng is *one tenth*, **gáu-sìhng** is *nine tenths*, and the numbers in between are just as you would expect. Beware that *two tenths* is **léuhng-sìhng** … but you would expect that, wouldn't you? If you order a steak in a Western restaurant in Hong Kong you will be asked **Yiu géi-dō-sìhng suhk a?** *How many tenths cooked do you want it?* (**suhk** means *cooked*). You can be as fussy as you want, and ask for **sàam-sìhng suhk** or **chāt-sìhng suhk**, or whatever. **Chyùhn-suhk** is *very well done* and **chyùhn-sàang** would be *very rare*, though few Chinese would order the latter. If you like it *medium*, you say **bun-sàang-suhk** 'half raw cooked'.

What do you think these same words sàang (生) and suhk (熟) mean with regards to fruit?

19.10 MAKING FRACTIONS

Baak-fahn-jì-sahp literally means 'ten of 100 parts' and therefore *ten parts in 100* or more normally *10 per cent*. All percentages are done the same way, so *12 per cent* is **baak-fahn-jì-sahp-yih**, and *75 per cent* is **baak-fahn-jì-chāt-sahp-ńgh**. In fact, all fractions are made in this way too:

sàam-fahn-jì-yāt	*one third*
sei-fahn-jì-sàam	*three quarters*
sahp-ńgh-fahn-jì-sahp-sei	*fourteen fifteenths*

19.11 THE MORE … THE MORE …

Yuht … yuht … appears in two similar patterns. There is an example of the first one in the dialogue: **yuht-làih-yuht-nàahn** (lit. 'the more comes the more difficult') *it gets more and more difficult*. You can add any adjective to the **yuht-làih-yuht-** formula:

Chóh fó-chē yuht-làih-yuht-gwai. *It gets more and more expensive to travel by train.*

Kéuih go jái yuht-làih-yuht-gòu. *Her son gets taller and taller.*

The second pattern does not use **làih** but instead uses two different adjectives or verbs to give the sense *the more it is this then the more it is that*:

Tái-bō, yàhn yuht dò yuht hóu-wáan. *When watching football, the more people there are the more fun it is.*

Wòhng Táai yuht góng yuht hòi-sām. *The more Mrs Wong talks the happier she is.*

 Practice

1 **Brush up your maths.**
   a Yāt go jūng-tàu yáuh géi-dō fàn-jùng a?
   b Yāt-baak ge sei-fahn-jì-yāt haih géi-dō a?
   c Bun-sàang-suhk haih baak-fahn-jì-géi suhk a?
   d Bun-yeh haih géi-dō-dím jūng a?
   e Chāt Sahp-yāt haih māt-yéh làih-ga?

2 **Give simple answers to these simple alternative questions. You have a 50–50 chance of being right even if you do not understand the question!**
   a Daaih-wuih-tòhng haih hái hèung-há dihng-haih hái sìhng-síh nē?
   b Néih yáuh-behng ge sìh-hauh gok-dāk syù-fuhk dihng-haih sàn-fú nē?
   c Geuk-jai yuhng-làih tìhng-chē dihng-haih hòi-chē nē?
   d Néih gú jóu-chāan haih māt-yéh a? Haih yeh-máahn sihk ge dihng-haih yaht-táu sihk ge nē?

3 Which is the correct translation of each English sentence?

   a I can't go there with you.
      1 Ngóh m̀h hó-yíh tùhng néih heui gó-douh.
      2 Ngóh tùhng néih m̀h hó-yíh heui gó-douh.

   b I can't drive to the outlying islands.
      1 Ngóh m̀h hó-yíh hái lèih-dóu jà-chē.
      2 Ngóh m̀h hó-yíh jà-chē heui lèih-dóu.

   c I won't be able to come until this afternoon.
      1 Ngóh hah-jau jauh làih-dāk lak.
      2 Ngóh hah-jau sìn-ji làih-dāk.

   d I like eating fruit salad.
      1 Ngóh jùng-yi sihk sàang-gwó tùhng sà-léut.
      2 Ngóh jùng-yi sihk sàang-gwó sà-léut.

   e What do you intend to do when you go to Japan?
      1 Néih géi-sí heui Yaht-bún, séung jouh māt-yéh a?
      2 Néih heui Yaht-bún ge sìh-hauh, séung jouh māt-yéh a?

4 Write out the English translations of the five sentences in Exercise 3 that you decided were incorrect.

 Test yourself

Look at the picture and answer the questions in Cantonese. (NB: The baby is a girl!)

   a Chàhn Sàang ūk-kéi, bīn-go jeui daaih a?
   b Nī dī yàhn léuih-bihn néuih-ge haih baak-fahn-jì-géi a?
   c Nàahm-ge nē?
   d Haih Chàhn Sàang gòu nē dihng-haih Chàhn Táai gòu nē?
   e Chàhn Sàang, Chàhn Táai yáuh géi-dō go jái a?

郵政 *Yàuh-jing*

The postal system

In this unit you will learn about:

- *dates.*
- *hahm-bah-laahng.*
- *how long a time?*
- *in fact.*
- *money.*
- *stamps.*
- *subtle classifiers.*
- *temporarily.*
- *yet more verb endings.*

CEFR: *(B1) Can cope with less routine situations in post offices; can obtain more detailed information.*

 ## Money again

We keep coming back to it. This time we want to introduce you to Hong Kong's coinage and banknote system.

Principal coins in circulation are: 50 cents, $1, $2, $5 and $10.

Banknotes are: $10, $20, $50, $100, $500 and $1,000.

The word for *cent* has dropped out of everyday language because as a result of inflation over the years the lowest coin in regular use is no smaller than the *50¢ piece*, which is called **yāt go ńgh-hòuh-jí** 一個五毫子. (**Yāt go hòuh-jí** and **yāt go léuhng-hòuh-jí** were the names for a *10¢* and a *20¢ coin*, accepted by only a few shops now and scheduled to be withdrawn altogether.) The higher values, as you might expect, are called **yāt-mān** *$1*, **léuhng-mān** *$2*, **ńgh-mān** *$5* and **sahp-mān** *$10*.

The banknotes are simply **sahp-mān** *$10*, **yih-sahp-mān** *$20*, **ńgh-sahp-mān** *$50*, **yat-baak-mān** *$100*, **ńgh-baak-mān** *$500* and **yat-chin-mān** *$1,000*.

Have a guess what the classifier for banknotes is.

Vocabulary builder 1

Read the new vocabulary and practise saying it out loud.

THE POST

特快	dahk-faai	*express*
特快郵遞	dahk-faai yàuh-daih	*express mail*
寄	gei	*to post*
空郵	hùng-yàuh	*airmail*
平郵	pìhng-yàuh	*surface mail*
手續費	sáu-juhk-fai	*procedure fee, handling charge*
首日	sáu-yaht	*first day*
信封	seun-fūng	*envelope* (cl: **go**)
郵費	yàuh-fai	*postage*
郵柬	yàuh-gáan	*airletter form* (cl: **jèung**)
郵局	yàuh-gúk	*post office*
郵政總局	yàuh-jing-júng-gúk	*general post office*
郵票	yàuh-piu	*postage stamp* (cl: **jèung**)

TIME WORDS

幾耐?	géi-noih? *or* géi-nói?	*how long?*
號	houh	*day of the month* (in dates)
暫時	jaahm-sìh	*temporary; temporarily*

BASICS

紀念	géi-nihm	*memorial; to commemorate*
冚吧(唪)呤	hahm-bah(baang)-laahng	*all told, altogether, all*
找(返)錢	jáau(-fàan)-chín	*to give change*
一共	yāt-guhng	*altogether, in total*

Dialogue 1

 20.01 *A post office clerk patiently explains something to an anxious customer.*

1 Here's an old friend: gwa-houh: you met it in Unit 10, but can you remember what it means?

Customer	M̀h-gòi béi sahp go yàuh-gáan, yah-ńgh go yāt mān ge yàuh-piu, tùhng yah-ńgh go go-bun ge yàuh-piu ngóh. Chéng-mahn géi-sìh yáuh sàn géi-nihm yàuh-piu maaih a?
Clerk	Sahp-yuht sahp-baat-houh.
Customer	Hóu ak! Gám, hah-go-yuht géi-sìh yáuh sàn sáu-yaht-(seun)-fūng maaih a?
Clerk	Hah-go-yuht sahp-yih-houh.
Customer	Nī fùng seun ngóh gei hùng-yàuh heui Yìng-gwok, chéng néih bòng ngóh bohng-háh, yiu géi-dō yàuh-fai?
Clerk	Sahp-sàam mān lā.
Customer	Yùh-gwó haih pìhng-yàuh yiu géi-dō chín a? Yiu gei géi-noih a?
Clerk	Yiu sàam-go-bun ngàhn-chín. Yiu sàam go géi láih-baai.
Customer	Nī fùng seun yùh-gwó gei gwa-houh yiu géi-dō chín a?
Clerk	Gwa-houh-seun ge sáu-juhk-fai haih sàam mān.
Customer	Gám, nī fùng seun ngóh yāt-guhng yiu béi géi-dō chín a?
Clerk	Hahm-bah-laahng sahp-luhk mān.
Customer	Nī-douh haih yih-sahp mān.
Clerk	Jáau-fàan sei mān béi néih, dò-jeh.
Customer	Néih-deih yáuh móuh dahk-faai yàuh-daih fuhk-mouh a?
Clerk	Ngóh-deih nī gàan yàuh-gúk taai sai lak, jaahm-sìh meih yáuh, chéng néih heui yàuh-jing-júng-gúk lā.
人客	唔該俾十個郵柬，廿五個一蚊嘅郵票，同廿五個個半嘅郵票我。請問幾時有新紀念郵票賣呀？
職員	十月十八號。
人客	好呃！噉，下個月幾時有新首日(信)封賣呀？
職員	下個月十二號。
人客	呢封信我寄空郵去英國，請你幫我磅吓，要幾多郵費？
職員	十三蚊啦。
人客	如果係平郵要幾多錢呀？要寄幾耐呀？
職員	要三個半銀錢。要三個幾禮拜。
人客	呢封信如果寄掛號要幾多錢呀？
職員	掛號信嘅手續費係三蚊。
人客	噉，呢封信我一共要俾幾多錢呀？
職員	冚吧呤十六蚊。
人客	呢度係二十蚊。
職員	找返四蚊俾你，多謝。
人客	你哋有冇特快郵遞服務呀？
職員	我哋呢間郵局太細嘞，暫時未有，請你去郵政總局啦。

2 Answer the questions.

   a Haih hùng-yàuh gwai, dihng-haih pìhng-yàuh gwai nē?

   b Yàuh-jing-júng-gúk wúih m̀h wúih daaih-gwo póu-tùng yàuh-gúk a?

   c Bā-sí fēi yiu luhk mān yāt go yàn. Sei go yàn chóh bā-sí hahm-baah-laahng chìu m̀h chìu-gwo yih-sahp mān nē?

Language discovery

20.1 SUBTLETIES OF CLASSIFIERS

You are now happily at home with the idea of classifiers and the way in which they help to describe or categorize the nouns which follow them. Sometimes their ability to categorize makes them of use in conveying shades of meaning. In the first line of the dialogue the customer asks for **yah-ńgh go go-bun ge yàuh-piu** *25 x $1.50¢ stamps*. Now if you think about it, the 'correct' classifier for stamps should be **jèung** because of their flat sheet-like nature, but in this case the customer is not thinking of them as physical shapes but rather as abstract items, so he uses **go** instead of **jèung**. Don't be alarmed if you occasionally hear people doing such things – mostly it is clear enough what is meant.

20.2 MORE ON MONEY

If you want to refer to coins as physical coins you classify them with **go**:

M̀h-gòi béi ńgh mān gwo ngóh.	*Please give me $5.*
M̀h-gòi béi yāt go ńgh-mān gwo ngóh.	*Please give me a $5 coin.* (for the slot machine perhaps)

Most of the coins are silver, and you will sometimes hear the noun *silver* added in:

M̀h-gòi béi yāt go ńgh-mān-ngàhn gwo ngóh.   *Please give me $5.*

When whole dollars are involved, the word for *dollar* is **mān**, as you know; but when the amount consists of dollars plus cents, the word for *dollar* becomes the classifier **go** with or without the noun **ngàhn-chín**. So:

léuhng mān *$2*   **sahp-sei mān** *$14*   **baat-sahp-sàam mān** *$83*

but:

léuhng-go-bun (ngàhn-chín) *$2.50¢*   **sahp-ńgh-go-bun (ngàhn-chín)** *$15.50¢*

and you might (only very occasionally now) be in a situation where other amounts in cents are needed, such as **baat-go-yih (ngàhn-chín)** *$8.20¢* or **sahp-sei-go-gáu (ngàhn-chín)** *$14.90¢*.

20.3 DATES

The months are simply expressed with numbers (see Unit 17). Days of the month use the same number word (**-houh**) that you met for addresses (**Fà-yùhn Douh yih-sahp-baat-houh**) and bus numbers (**sahp-ńgh-houh bā-sí**).

⋮ YOUR TURN How would you say *1 January*? *23 May*? (Remember that the general always comes before the particular.)

The years are given in 'spelled out' number form followed by **nìhn**:

Yāt-gáu-gáu-chāt-nìhn Luhk-yuht sàam-sahp-houh
30 June 1997

> **LANGUAGE TIP**
> Don't forget always to add **nìhn** on the end when giving the year!

> **1997**
> The date 30 June 1997 was an important one for Hong Kong. At midnight, Britain's rule of more than 150 years came to end, and under the **yāt-gwok léuhng-jai** 一國兩制 *one country, two systems* policy Hong Kong became a *Special Administrative Region* (**Dahk-biht hàhng-jing kèui** 特別行政區 or **Dahk-kèui** 特區 for short) of the People's Republic of China. The government of the SAR is headed by the *Chief Executive* (**Hàhng-jing jéung-gwùn** 行政長官) or **Dahk-sáu** 特首 ('Special Head', as he is more informally known). An impressive midnight handover ceremony was televized all over the world, and **Wùih-gwài** 回歸 *Reversion, Handover* has become a date marker for Hong Kong people, who now talk of **Wùih-gwài-chìhn** 回歸前 *before the Handover* and **Wùih-gwài-hauh** 回歸後 *after the Handover*.

20.4 HOW LONG A TIME?

In Unit 8 you met **géi-sí?** *when?*, the question word asking for a time-when answer. The question word asking for a time-how long answer is **géi-noih?**:

Néih géi-sí heui Yaht-bún a?	*When are you going to Japan?*
Ngóh Sahp-yuht sei-houh heui.	*I'm going on 4 October.*
Néih hái Yaht-bún séung jyuh géi-noih a?	*How long do you intend to stay in Japan?*
Ngóh hái gó-douh séung jyuh léuhng go yuht.	*For two months.*

And of course the question word and its answer come in the same place in each case – before the verb with 'time when' and after the verb with 'time how long'.

20.5 A WORD YOU CANNOT FORGET

Hahm-bah-laahng or its variant **hahm-baahng-laahng** just has to be the strangest word in the Cantonese language. It is peculiar because each of the three syllables is completely meaningless on its own and because it doesn't even sound much like a Cantonese word. Once heard it is very hard to forget, so we don't think you will have any difficulty with it. One of its meanings is *altogether*, as you will have seen from the dialogue.

Lùhng-hā, gáu-sahp-sei mān; hā, sàam-sahp-yih-go-bun; hahm-bah-laahng yāt-baak-yih-sahp-luhk-go-bun ngàhn-chín.

$94 for the lobster; $32.50 for the prawns: $126.50 altogether.

Its other meaning is *the whole lot* or *all*, and in this it is usually accompanied by **dōu** (the adverb meaning *all* with which you are now very familiar).

Kéuih-deih sèhng-gà yàhn hahm-baahng-laahng dōu jáu-saai lak.

The whole family went away, every last one of them.

20.6 NOT FOR THE TIME BEING

The last line of the dialogue contains the expression **jaahm-sìh meih yáuh** (lit. 'temporarily not yet have') *for the time being it hasn't got it*. The expression is much used as a polite way of saying *not in stock* or *nothing yet*, and it appears to offer hope that soon everything will be alright, but it would be best not to put too much faith in that hope; sometimes it seems to be merely a kindly way of saying *no*.

Vocabulary builder 2

 Read the new vocabulary and practise saying it out loud.

MORE POST

白紙	baahk-jí	*blank paper* (cl: **jèung**)
包	bàau	*to wrap up*
包裹	bàau-gwó	*parcel*
表格	bíu-gaak	*form*
地址	deih-jí	*address*
明信片	mìhng-seun-pín	*postcard* (cl: **jèung**)
信紙	seun-jí	*letter paper* (cl: **jèung**)
填寫	tìhn-sé	*to fill in a form*
貼上	tip-séuhng	*to stick on*
郵筒	yàuh-túng	*pillar box*

VERBS

保證	bóu-jing	*to guarantee*
諗	nám	*to think, ponder, think over*

BASICS

大門口	daaih-mùhn-háu	*main doorway*
大約	daaih-yeuk	*approximately*
簡單	gáan-dàan	*simple*
紙	jí	*paper* (cl: **jèung**)
近	káhn	*near, close*
門	mùhn	*door, gate* (cl: **douh** 度)
門口	mùhn-háu	*doorway, gateway*
首先	sáu-sìn	*first of all*
容易	yùhng-yih	*easy*
原來	yùhn-lòih	*originally, actually, in fact*

> **LANGUAGE TIP**
> Keep an eye open for the tourist's third speech in this next dialogue. He uses a pattern which you met way back in Unit 8, which you should re-read if you have forgotten it.

Dialogue 2

20.02 *A tourist plagues his hotel clerk with questions about mail.*

1 Why is Dò-jeh used in the Clerk's first speech?

Tourist	Ngóh gàan fóng ge seun-jí yuhng-saai lak, néih-deih juhng yáuh móuh a? Yí! Nī dī mìhng-seun-pín chit-gai-dāk géi leng bo! Ngóh séung máaih ńgh jèung yiu géi-dō chín a?
Clerk	Dò-jeh sahp-yih-go-bun la, sìn-sàang.
Tourist	Hái jáu-dim fuh-gahn yáuh móuh yàuh-gúk a?
Clerk	Gei mìhng-seun-pín m̀h-sái heui yàuh-gúk, hái nī-douh waahk-jé hái jáu-dim daaih-mùhn-háu yauh-bihn dōu yáuh yàuh-túng.
Tourist	Ngóh m̀h haih gei mìhng-seun-pín, ngóh séung gei yāt go bàau-gwó fàan Yìng-gwok, dím-yéung gei-faat a?
Clerk	Óh, yùhn-lòih néih séung gei bàau-gwó. Gám, hóu yùhng-yih jē. Néih sáu-sìn yuhng baahk-jí bàau-hóu gó go bàau-gwó, yìhn-hauh sé-seuhng deih-jí …
Tourist	Jeui káhn jáu-dim ge yàuh-gúk hái bīn-douh a?
Clerk	Hái jáu-dim mùhn-háu heung jó-bihn hàahng daaih-yeuk sahp fàn-jūng jauh dou lak. Dou-jó yàuh-gúk jì-hauh, néih yiu tìhn-sé yāt jèung hóu gáan-dàan ge gei bàau-gwó bíu-gaak. Bàau-gwó gwo-bóng jì-hauh, tái-háh yiu géi-dō chín, yìhn-hauh máaih yàuh-piu, tip-séuhng yàuh-piu, gám jauh dāk lak!
Tourist	Ngóh ge bàau-gwó m̀h-haih-hóu-daaih, daahn-haih hóu yùhng-yih laahn ge bo!
Clerk	Gám jauh màh-fàahn lak, yàn-waih yàuh-gúk m̀h bóu-jing bàau-gwó léuih-bihn ge yéh móuh laahn ge bo!
Tourist	Gám àh? Dáng ngóh nám yāt-háh sìn. M̀h-gòi-saai.
遊客	我間房嘅信紙用晒嘞，你哋重有冇呀？咦！呢啲明信片設計得幾靚噃！我想買五張要幾多錢呀？
職員	多謝十二個半喇，先生。
遊客	喺酒店附近有冇郵局呀？
職員	寄明信片唔駛去郵局，喺呢度或者喺酒店大門口右便都有郵筒。
遊客	我唔係寄明信片，我想寄一個包裹返英國，點樣寄法呀？
職員	哦，原來你想寄包裹。噉，好容易啫。你首先用白紙包好嗰個包裹，然後寫上地址 ⋯
遊客	最近酒店嘅郵局喺邊度呀？
職員	喺酒店門口向左便行大約十分鐘就到嘞。到咗郵局之後，你要填寫一張好簡單嘅寄包裹表格。包裹過磅之後，睇吓要幾多錢，然後買郵票，貼上郵票，噉就得嘞！
遊客	我嘅包裹唔係好大，但係好容易爛嘅噃！
職員	噉就麻煩嘞，因為郵局唔保證包裹裡便嘅嘢冇爛嘅噃！
遊客	噉吖？等我諗一吓先。唔該晒。

2 Translate into Cantonese.

   a After eating two kilos of prawns he felt very unwell.

   b When I was in London last year it rained all day.

   c I don't like chatting while I am driving.

   d Before the handover there were more British people in Hong Kong than there are now.

   e Mr Cheung went to Taiwan last year and won't be coming back until May.

Language discovery

20.7 YÙHN-LÒIH

The basic meaning of **yùhn-lòih** is *originally*, but you will probably most often meet it meaning *in fact, so now I understand how it is*. When people use the phrase they usually are acknowledging that they had been under the wrong impression about something, so it is a natural partner of the verb **yíh-wàih** *to assume* which you met in Unit 11:

Ngóh yíh-wàih kéuih haih Yaht-bún-yàhn, daahn-haih yùhn-lòih kéuih haih Jùng-gwok-yàhn.

I thought she was Japanese, but actually she is Chinese.

20.8 THE VERB ENDING -HÓU

Hóu of course means *good* and *very*, but as a verb ending it gives the idea that the action of the verb has been completed satisfactorily:

Néih dī mìhng-seun-pín sé-hóu meih a?   *Have you written your postcards yet?*
Dī seun ngóh dá-hóu lak.   *I've typed the letters.*

There is only a slight difference between **-hóu** and **-yùhn** as verb endings: they both show that an action has come to an end, but **-hóu** adds the nuance that the result of the action is a satisfactory one.

> **REMEMBER**
> When giving a year date you must always add **nìhn** to the figures. Probably you would do best to commit your own year of birth to memory and practise saying it frequently – **yāt-gáu-gáu-lìhng-nìhn**, **yāt-gáu-gáu-lìhng-nìhn**, **yāt-gáu-gáu-** ….

20.9 SÉUHNG AS A VERB ENDING

Séuhng means *onto; to go up*. As a verb ending it also means *on* or *onto*, and you will find that it often matches English usage quite closely:

sé-séuhng deih-jí   *to write the address on*
tip-séuhng yàuh-piu   *to stick on stamps*
M̀h-gòi néih daai-séuhng gó déng móu.   *Please put on that hat.*

 Practice

1 How many?

Yāt ga dihn-dāan-chē ge chē-tāai, yāt jek geuk ge geuk-jí, yāt nìn ge sìng-kèih, yāt mān ge houh-jí, luhk jek wòhng-ngàuh ge geuk, tùhng-màaih yāt go láih-baai ge yaht, hahm-bah-laang géi-dō yéh a?

2 Some of the words in this exercise you have not met for quite a while. Try writing out your translations of the sentences and if you have to look up some of the words make a list of them for special study later.

a Wòhng Sàang jeui m̀h jùng-yi yám yeuhk-séui.

b M̀h-hóu dàng-daaih-deui-ngáahn tái-jyuh ngóh.

c M̀h hahp-kwài-gaak ge bou-líu dōu dong haih chi-fo.

d Hái daaih-dong dóu-chín dòng-yín haih fèi-faat lā.

e Ngóh-deih yiu dò-dī jyu-yi ngóh-deih dī jái tùhng néui ge duhk-syù chìhng-fong.

3 Give the Cantonese for these dates and times.

a 4 June

b 1 July 1997

c 15 May 2004

d 6.15 p.m. Sunday 11 December

e 31 August next year

4 Choose which of the items in brackets best fits the sentence.

a Jeui sìn yáuh yàuh-piu ge gwok-gà haih (Jùng-gwok / Yìng-gwok / Yaht-bún).

b Sai-gaai daih-yāt gàan yàuh-gúk haih hái (Lèuhn-dēun / Náu-yeuk / Gwóng-jàu).

c Yìh-gā sai-gaai seuhng jeui gwai ge yāt go yàuh-piu haih (chìu-gwo yāt-maahn Yìng-bóng / yāt-maahn Yìng-bóng / m̀h gau yāt-maahn Yìng-bóng).

d Yáuh-dī deih-fòng, yàuh-piu dong haih (yihn-gām / sàn-fán-jing / fo-bún).

5 Find suitable two-syllable Cantonese expressions using the clues supplied. The answer to the first one would be chēut-gāai or perhaps hàahng-gāai.

a Lèih-hòi ūk-kéi.　　　　　　　(_____ _____)

b Chà-m̀h-dō, jīk-haih …　　　　(_____ _____)

c Yuhng fèi-gèi wahn ge seun.　　(_____ _____)

d Hái sé-jih-làuh gwún-jyuh néih ge yàhn.　(_____ _____)

e Yāt go yàhn m̀h jeuk sāam.　　(_____ _____)

❓ Test yourself

Dóu-chèuhng ge gìng-léih hóu m̀h hòi-sàm lak! Nī n̄gh go pàhng-yáuh dóu Lèuhn-pún, hahm-baahng-laahng dōu yèhng-gán chín. Dou-yìh-gā-wàih-jí kéuih-deih yāt-guhng yèhng-jó n̄gh-maahn-sei-chìn-luhk-baak mān Méih-gām. Yèhng jeui dò ge haih Jèung Taai-táai, kéuih yèhng-jó n̄gh-maahn-sei-chìn-luhk-baak mān ge sàam-fahn-jì-yāt. Daih-yih haih Hòh Sìn-sàang, kéuih yèhng-jó sei-fahn-jì-yāt. Daih-sàam haih Wòhng Sìn-sàang, yèhng-jó n̄gh-fahn-jì-yāt. Daih-sei haih Léih Taai-táai, yèhng-jó luhk-fahn-jì-yāt. Yèhng jeui síu ge haih Chàhn Sìn-sàang, kéuih bāt-gwo yèhng-jó yih-sahp-fahn-jì-yāt jē. (Chàhn Sàang wah m̀h-gán-yiu, yèhng ge chín m̀h dò daahn-haih dōu haih hóu-gwo syù!)

> **LANGUAGE TIP**
> **bāt-gwo** means *but, however*, but it also can mean *only* and is most often used in this way with numbers.

a M̀h-gòi néih nám-yāt-nám, tái-háh múih yāt go pàhng-yáuh yèhng-jó géi-dō chín nē?

b Juhng yáuh nē … Jèung Táai yèhng-jó gam dò chín séung chéng dī pàhng-yáuh yám-jáu. Dī jáu m̀h pèhng, máaih n̄gh go yàhn ge jáu yāt-guhng yiu béi sei-ah-chāt-go-bun gam dò. Jèung Táai gàau-jó yāt jèung yāt-baak mān jí béi fuhk-mouh-yùhn, yìh-gā dáng kéuih jáau-fàan géi-dō a?

21 温習(三) Wàn-jaahp (sàam)
Revision (3)

Two short anecdotes about horses. The first is an old story about faith and unflappability. The second is a typical Chinese joke about someone who gets things wrong through being literal-minded.

📖 Passage 1

Géi baak nìhn jì-chìhn, hái Jùng-gwok bāk-bouh deih-fòng, yáuh yāt go sing Wòhng ge yáuh-chín-yàhn. Kéuih yáuh hóu dò yauh gòu yauh daaih yauh leng ge máh, kéuih dōu hóu jùng-yi nī dī máh tìm. Yáuh yāt yaht, yāt jek hóu leng daahn-haih géi lóuh ge máh m̀h-gin-jó. Wòhng Sìn-sàang dī pàhng-yáuh go-go dōu gok-dāk hóu hó-sīk, kéuih-deih dōu gú Wòhng Sàang wúih hóu nàu, hóu m̀h hòi-sām, daahn-haih ngāam-ngāam sèung-fáan, kéuih m̀h-jí m̀h nàu, yìh-ché juhng sèung-seun jek máh hóu faai jauh wúih fàan-làih tìm. Géi yaht jì-hauh, jek lóuh máh jàn-haih fàan-jó-làih lak. Dī pàhng-yáuh dōu wah Wòhng Sàang hóu-chói, kéuih jí-haih siu-háh-gám wah: 'Gó jek lóuh máh sīk louh, kéuih wúih wán louh fàan-làih jē.'

> **LANGUAGE TIP**
> m̀h-gin-jó 'no longer could be seen' = lost, go missing

📖 Passage 2

Hóu noih jì-chìhn hái Gwóng-jàu yáuh yāt go yī-sāng. Yáuh yāt yaht kéuih sé-jó yāt fùng hóu gán-yiu ge seun béi jyuh hái daih-yih go sìhng-síh ge yī-sāng. Gó-jahn-sìh Jùng-gwok juhng-meih yáuh yàuh-gúk, yìh-ché kéuih hóu mòhng m̀h dāk-hàahn nìng seun heui gó-douh, só-yíh kéuih giu kéuih go jái bòng kéuih nìng-heui. Kéuih deui go jái wah 'Nī fùng seun hóu gán-yiu, yiu jeuhn faai sung-dou bo! Nàh, geuk yuht dò yuht faai: néih jí-yáuh léuhng jek geuk m̀h gau sei jek geuk faai ge. Néih bāt-yùh chóh ngóh jek máh heui lā! Faai-dī a!'

Go hauh-sāang-jái jáu-jó laak, bàh-bā dáng kéuih fàan-làih. Kéuih jì-dou yāt jek máh lòih-wóhng gó go deih-fòng dōu yiu baat go jūng-tàuh gam-seuhng-há. Gú-m̀h-dóu kéuih go jái gwo-jó léuhng yaht sìn-ji fàan-làih, deui bàh-bā hóu hòi-sām gám wah: 'Bàh-bā, ngóh fàan-làih lak. Néih wah faai m̀h faai nē? Ngóh séung-làih-séung-heui git-gwó séung-dóu yāt go hóu faai ge baahn-faat. Néih wah geuk yuht dò yuht faai, léuhng jek geuk m̀h gau sei jek geuk faai ā … gám, ngóh làai-jyuh jek máh tùhng kéuih yāt-chàih hàahng … léuhng jek geuk m̀h gau sei jek geuk faai, luhk jek geuk yāt-dihng faai gwo sei jek geuk, haih m̀h haih a?'

> **LANGUAGE TIP**
> gán-yiu means important. You met it in Unit 2 in m̀h gán-yiu never mind, it doesn't matter or literally 'it is not important'.

1 Did you manage to work out what séung-làih-séung-heui means? If you skipped over it, go back and try again. And then make an intelligent guess at the English equivalents of the following.
   a hàahng-làih-hàahng-heui
   b jáu-làih-jáu-heui
   c Ngóh-deih góng-ga góng-làih-góng-heui dōu góng-m̀h-màaih lak

2 Perhaps you know something about horses? Choose which of the alternatives offered are correct, and then translate the full sentences.
   a Yāt jek póu-tùng ge máh daaih-yeuk yáuh (ńgh-baak bohng / chāt-baak bohng / yāt-chìn bohng) chúhng.
   b Yāt jek máh daaih-yeuk dou (sahp-ńgh seui / yih-sahp seui / yih-sahp-ńgh seui) jauh wúih séi ge lak.
   c Yāt jek máh múih yaht jeui-síu yiu wahn-duhng (bun go jūng-tàuh / yāt go jūng-tàuh / sei go jūng-tàuh) sìn-ji wúih gihn-hòng ge.
   d Yāt jek máh múih yaht jeui-síu yiu sihk (sahp bohng / yih-sahp bohng / sàam-sahp bohng) yéh.

3 Oh dear, it's my memory again! I have to keep a diary or I will forget what I have to do, but it seems that when I was filling it in for 23 May I put in the times but forgot to enter what they referred to! I'm sure that lunch was involved, because my stomach keeps rumbling **aan-jau**, **aan-jau** 晏晝, 晏晝 *lunch, lunch* at me, but … I think this scrap of paper I found in my pocket has all the information on it, but it's not in chronological order and I don't want to miss any of the appointments. Can you fill in the diary entries correctly for me in English, please?

Thursday 23rd May

10.00am

10.30am

12.15pm

3.30pm

6.45pm

7.30pm

Friday 24th May

Hái Daaih-wuih-tòhng tùhng Jèung Síu-jé sihk aan-jau.

Tùhng Hòh Síu-jé hái Hèung-góng Jáu-dim yám-jó baat go jih jáu, yìhn-hauh jauh yāt-chàih hàahng ńgh fān jūng louh heui tái-hei.

Dou léuih-yàuh gūng-sī ló gèi-piu.

Heui Wòhng gìng-léih sé-jih-làuh bun go jūng-tàuh jì-chìhn jauh yiu dá-dihn-wá giu dīk-sí làih lak.

4 You have learned a lot of vocabulary now, so much that you know more than one way of saying some things. Try finding another word with the same or almost the same meaning as the following.

a daaih-yeuk

b yāt-guhng

c bāt-gwo

d tàuh-sīn

e gaan-jūng

f dím-gáai

5 A few more Chinese children's puzzles to make you groan. What are the (fiendishly difficult) answers – in Cantonese please?

   a Kàhm-yaht tìn-hei hóu yiht. Jèung Sìn-sàang hái ūk ngoih-bihn jouh wahn-duhng, jouh-jó yāt go jūng-tàuh gam noih. Kéuih dōu wah m̀h-haih-hóu-sàn-fú, m̀h taai yiht. Dím-gáai nē?

   b Jèung Sìn-sàang haih yāt go laahp-saap-chē sī-gēi, múih yaht kéuih jà laahp-saap-chē chēut-gāai ge sìh-hauh dōu yáuh hóu dò yàhn nìng dī laahp-saap làih kéuih ga chē douh. Jí-haih gàm-yaht kéuih jà-chē chēut-gāai, móuh yàhn nìng laahp-saap làih. Dím-gáai nē?

   c Wòhng Sìn-sàang m̀h jouh-yéh. Kéuih yaht-yaht dōu yuhng hóu dò chín, nìhn-nìhn dōu heui léuih-yàuh, sìh-sìh dōu máaih jeui gwai ge sàn chē. Yih-sahp nìhn jì-hauh kéuih sìhng-wàih yāt go yáuh yāt-baak-maahn mān ge yáuh-chín yàhn lak. Dím-gáai nē?

6 No two people seem to agree exactly on anything. Here are some comments by different people about Mr Wong's new car. Can you put their different views accurately into Cantonese?

   a It's a very handsome car.

   b It's handsome, it's true, but not as handsome as Mr Cheung's new car.

   c It's not very handsome.

   d It's not big enough.

   e It's too expensive.

   f It's the most handsome car in the world.

   g It's much more handsome than my car is.

   h It's just as large and just as expensive as Mr Cheung's new car.

7 Supply the missing words in the sentences. Be careful: there may be more than one possibility and you should try to get the best one.

   a Nī _____ sìn-sàang haih Wòhng gìng-léih.

   b Kéuih_____ yāt mān dōu m̀h háng béi gó go móuh chín ge yàhn.

   c Ngóh màh-mā haih baat-sahp-ńgh seui gam _____.

   d Kéuih làih-jó _____-noih a? Ngóh m̀h jì, daaih-yeuk léuhng-sàam go sìng-kèih, waahk-jé yáuh sei go sìng-kèih gam _____ lak.

   e Ngóh ńgh-sahp-chāt seui, néih bāt-gwo haih sei-sahp-gáu seui jē. Ngóh _____-gwo néih baat seui.

8 Usually one person picks up the bill when Cantonese people dine out, and 'going Dutch' is rare. Still, sometimes it is felt that for one person to pay for everyone would be too much, so different shares are agreed. Someone draws a *ghost's leg* waahk-gwái-geuk 畫鬼腳 (gwái *ghost*), a ladder diagram with one vertical line for each person and a share written at the bottom of each. With the shares covered up, each person can add a horizontal line anywhere in the diagram or indeed can choose not to add a line at all. Then one by one they trace out their fate, going down their vertical until the first horizontal, which they must follow to the next vertical, down that to the next horizontal, follow that ... and so on down to the bottom. Six friends have recently had two meals each costing $2,000. On each occasion they agreed to make one share of $800, one of $500, one of $400, one of $300 and two zero-sum shares. Diagram A shows the ghost's leg as drawn at the first meal. Diagram B shows four additional lines, which four of the participants decided to put in at the second meal. You should have no difficulty in working out who had to pay how much each time and how the situation was changed by the extra lines.

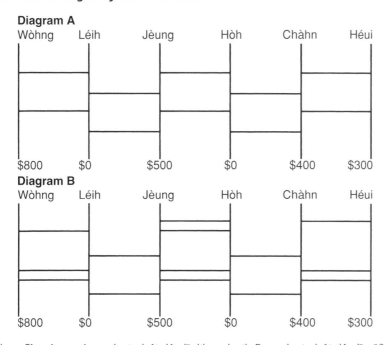

a Wòhng Sìn-sàang A-geuk yiu béi dò-dī dihng-haih B-geuk yiu béi dò-dī nē?

b B-geuk haih bīn wái yiu béi baat-baak mān a?

c Jèung Sìn-sàang A-geuk yiu béi, B-geuk dōu yiu béi. B-geuk kéuih yiu béi dò géi-dō chín a?

d Kéuih-deih yāt-chàih wáan A-geuk tùhng B-geuk, gám, bīn wái yiu béi jeui síu chín nē? bīn wái yiu béi jeui dò chín nē?

9 Each of the sentences in this exercise uses one of the new grammar patterns from the last six units. If you can put them all into good Cantonese you can congratulate yourself on having really mastered some difficult material.

   a When my mother speaks on the telephone she speaks quite slowly.

   b This coffee is not hot enough.

   c Would you like beer or water?

   d That pen of yours which you bought last month is not as expensive as this one of mine.

   e She told me to tell you what time you should come.

   f Mr Wong doesn't even like eating lobster.

   g Two-thirds of these books are in Chinese.

   h He gets richer and richer.

10 **Translate into English.**

   Hèung-góng ge tìn-hei hái Chāt-yuht, Baat-yuht, Gáu-yuht hóu yiht. Tìn-hei yiht ge sìh-hauh dī yàhn hóu jùng-yi chóh dīk-sí, yàn-waih dīk-sí yauh dò yauh syù-fuhk. Dím-gáai syù-fuhk nē? Yàn-waih ga-ga dōu yauh láahng-hei. Yāt ga dīk-sí hó-yíh chóh-dāk sei waahk-jé ńgh go yàhn, m̀h-sái hóu dò chín, hóu pèhng jē. Póu-tùng hei-chē yáuh làahm-sīk ge, yáuh luhk-sīk ge, baahk-sīk, hùhng-sīk, hāk-sīk, wòhng-sīk, māt-yéh sīk dōu yáuh, daahn-haih dīk-sí m̀h tùhng, ga-ga dōu haih hùhng-sīk tùhng-màaih ngàhn-sīk ge.

22 寫字樓 Sé-jih-làuh
The office

In this unit you will learn about:

- *children.*
- *familiar address.*
- *meals.*
- *opposites.*
- *reluctant agreement.*

- *sàm-gèi.*
- simply must.
- *the tail.*
- *water.*
- *working conditions.*

CEFR: *(B1) Can invite others to give their views; can explain why something is a problem.*

 Water

The word for *salary* (**sàn-séui**) includes the word for *water* (**séui**), which you learned in Unit 19 could mean *money*. The other half (**sàn**) means *firewood*: so in Cantonese it seems you can have 'money to burn' and 'spend it like water'!

Séui flows into lots of different places in Cantonese. First of course it is water, then it is money, then it combines with *air* (**hei** 氣) to make *fizzy drink* (**hei-séui**). With *wind* (**fùng** 風) it makes *geomancy* (**fùng-séui**), usually called *Feng Shui* after the Mandarin pronunciation. With *mountains* (**sàan** 山) it makes **sàan-séui** *scenery*. **Séui-gwó** (水果) is another word for *fresh fruit*, and so on. Perhaps the strangest manifestation is in 'skin on water' (**séui-pèih** 水皮) which is old slang for *useless*.

 What do you think **séui-ngàuh** 水牛 means?

Vocabulary builder 1

 Read the new vocabulary and practise saying it out loud.

WORK

返工	fàan-gùng	*to go to work*
放工	fong-gùng	*to finish work*
假期	ga-kèih	*holiday*
工作	gùng-jok	*work, job; to work*
過時	gwo-sìh	*overtime*
薪水	sàn-séui	*salary*
上班	séuhng-bāan	*to go to work, go on shift*
雙粮	sèung-lèuhng	*double salary*
退休	teui-yàu	*to retire*
退休金	teui-yàu-gām	*pension*

VERBS

補	bóu	*to compensate*
分娩	fàn-míhn	*to give birth*
歡迎	fùn-yìhng	*to welcome; welcome*
醫療	yì-lìuh	*to heal; medical*

BASICS

呀 …	A-	*familiar prefix for names and relationships*
晏晝	aan-jau	*midday, early afternoon, lunchtime; lunch*
長	chèuhng	*long*
彈性	daahn-sing	*flexible*
短	dyún	*short*
非常(之)	fèi-sèuhng (jì)	*extraordinarily*
福利	fūk-leih	*benefits, welfare*
制度	jai-douh	*system*
仔女	jái-néui	*sons and daughters, children*
津貼	jèun-tip	*allowance, grant*

Dialogue 1

 22.01 *Two friends discuss office working conditions.*

1 **When listening to the dialogue make a special effort to understand the phrase yáuh gáu go jih sihk aan-jau. Only continue when you think you have fully understood it. It isn't that it is particularly difficult, but you haven't met the vocabulary for some time and it may take a moment or two to register. When you go on you should quickly have your understanding confirmed (or not, as the case may be) by Mr Wong's next speech. And of course you can find help at the back of the book as usual.**

Wong	A-Chán, yìh-gā chà-m̀h-dō gáu-dím la, dím-gáai néih juhng hái nī-douh sihk jóu-chàan nē? M̀h-sái fàan-gùng mē?
Chan	M̀h haih, ngóh yiu fàan-gùng, bāt-gwo ngóh fàan gáu-dím-bun a.
Wong	Néih-deih gūng-sī yáuh daahn-sing séuhng-bāan jai-douh mē?
Chan	Haih a. Yáuh gáu-dím tùhng gáu-dím-bun léuhng bāan.
Wong	Gám, géi-dím fong-gùng a?
Chan	Luhk-dím fong-gùng. Hái hah-jau yáuh gáu go jih sihk aan-jau.
Wong	Gùng-jok sìh-gaan dōu-géi chèuhng bo! Sihk aan-jau ge sìh-gaan jauh taai dýún lak. Gwo-sìh gùng-jok yáuh móuh chín bóu ga?
Chan	Yáuh. Múih go jūng-tàuh bóu-fàan sàam-baak-ńgh-sahp mān.
Wong	Où, fèi-sèuhng jì hóu. Juhng yáuh dī māt-yéh fūk-leih a?
Chan	Múih nìhn yáuh yih-sahp yaht haih yáuh sàn-séui ge ga-kèih. Nìhn-méih yáuh sèung-lèuhng, yáuh yì-lìuh jèun-tip, yáuh jái-néui gaau-yuhk jèun-tip, néuih-jīk-yùhn juhng yáuh sahp go láih-baai fàn-míhn ga-kèih. Teui-yàu ge sìh-hauh juhng hó-yíh dāk-dóu teui-yàu-gām tìm. Wòhng Sìn-sàang, fùn-yìhng néih gà-yahp ngóh-deih gūng-sī fuhk-mouh.
Wong	Néih-deih gūng-sī ge fūk-leih hóu-haih-hóu, daahn-haih ngóh taai lóuh lak, móuh yuhng la. Néih wah juhng fùn-yìhng ngóh gà-yahp, néih góng-siu mē!?

王	呀陳，而家差唔多九點喇，點解你重喺呢度食早餐呢？唔駛返工咩？
陳	唔係，我要返工，不過我返九點半呀。
王	你哋公司有彈性上班制度咩？
陳	係呀。有九點同九點半兩班。
王	噉，幾點放工呀？
陳	六點放工，喺下晝有九個字食晏晝。
王	工作時間都幾長嘛！食晏晝嘅時間就太短嘞。過時工作有冇錢補㗎？
陳	有。每個鐘頭補返三百五十蚊。
王	噢，非常之好。重有啲乜嘢福利呀？
陳	每年有二十日係有薪水嘅假期。年尾有雙粮，有醫療津貼，有仔女教育津貼，女職員重有十個禮拜分娩假期。退休嘅時候重可以得倒退休金添。王先生，歡迎你加入我哋公司服務。
王	你哋公司嘅福利好係好，但係我太老嘞，冇用喇。你話重歡迎我加入，你講笑咩!?

2 Answer the questions.

a Chàhn Sàang múih yaht yāt-guhng fàan géi-dō go jūng-tàuh gùng a?

b Sìng-kèih-yih Chàhn Sàang gùng-jok dahk-biht mòhng, yiu gwo-sìh gùng-jok sàam go jūng-tàuh. Gám kéuih bóu-fàan géi-dō chín a?

Language discovery

22.1 FAMILIAR TERMS OF ADDRESS

In Unit 6 you learned that **lóuh** *old* is used with surnames as a familiar way of addressing someone. You can refer to a younger person or a child by putting **Síu-** *little* in front of their name. In both cases a surname which has a low level or low falling tone usually changes to a mid rising tone. Another way is to put **A-** in front of the surname (again with the same tone changes). In fact the sound **A-** seems to be intimately connected with referring to or addressing people. It can be used with personal names as well (someone with the name **Chàhn Jī Bāk**, for instance, might be addressed as **A-Bāk** by his family and / or **A-Chán** by his friends) and it can be used with kinship terms (you could address your father as **A-bà** instead of **bàh-bā**). It is almost as though when you say **A-** you are warning your listener that you are about to talk to them or to talk about a person.

22.2 FÀAN-GÙNG AND FONG-GÙNG

In Unit 3 you met **fàan** meaning *to return* or *to go where you usually go*: one of the examples was **fàan sé-jih-làuh** *to go to the office*. **Gùng** means *work* and **jouh-gùng** means *to do work, to work*. **Fàan-gùng** means *to go to work* in the same way that **fàan sé-jih-làuh** means *to go to the office*, but *to finish work* and *to leave the office at the end of the day* are both expressed the same way – **fong-gùng**.

It is worth noting for your own use the colloquial way in which Mr Chan says in the dialogue that he goes in to work at 9.30: **ngóh fàan gáu-dím-bun**.

> **FUN WITH CHARACTERS**
> The Chinese character used for **mē?** 咩 is an interesting one: it is made up of pictures of a mouth and a sheep and so indicates the animal's bleating, which is rather what **mē?** sounds like. The character for **ma?** 嗎 shows a mouth and a horse, but you may find that a less convincing sound guide – every English-speaking person knows that horses go 'neigh' not 'ma', don't they?

22.3 OPPOSITES

Another pair of opposites: **chèuhng** *long* and **dyún** *short*. Both of them can be used for periods of time, as they are in the dialogue, but they are equally good for distances (*a long piece of string, a short pencil*) and even for more abstract things like *a long novel* and *a shortcoming*.

And here are a few more useful pairs of adjectives for you:

肥	**fèih**	*fat, obese*	瘦	**sau**	*thin, skinny*
乾	**gòn**	*dry*	濕	**sāp**	*wet*
高	**gòu**	*tall, high*	矮	**ái** or **ngái**	*short, squat, low*
靜	**jihng**	*quiet*	嘈	**chòuh**	*noisy*
勤力	**kàhn-lihk**	*hard-working*	懶惰	**láahn-doh**	*lazy*
叻	**lēk**	*smart, clever*	蠢	**chéun**	*stupid*
肚餓	**tóuh-ngoh**	*hungry*	頸渴	**géng-hot**	*thirsty*

22.4 THE TAIL AGAIN

In Unit 17 you met **yuht-méih** *the end of the month*, and in this unit there is **nìhn-méih** *the end of the year*. **Méih** literally means 'the tail', but since tails are found at the end, it is logical enough that it should also mean *the end* and you will probably meet it quite often. One common expression is **daih-mēi** *the last* (note the tone change), which of course contrasts with **daih-yāt** or **tàuh-yāt** *the first*.

22.5 MEALS

If you are a 'three meals a day' person, they will usually be:

jóu-chāan *breakfast*   **aan-jau** *lunch*   **máahn-chāan** *dinner, supper*

The use of **chāan** gives a hint that they may be thought of as Western meals, though the words are used quite loosely nowadays. You can substitute **faahn** *rice* for **chāan**, and that sounds more as though you are talking about Chinese food, though again the terms are not totally clear-cut.

Cantonese people in big cities like Hong Kong developed the habit of **yám-chàh** *drinking tea*, accompanied by dím-sām, and that tends to be available in tea-houses from early morning to late afternoon, but the other fine old Cantonese custom of going out for **sìu-yé** 宵夜 *midnight snacks* has almost died out, brought to grief by competition from television largely.

22.6 SONS AND DAUGHTERS

Jái-néui means *sons and daughters* and you need to bear that in mind when translating the word *children*. Only use **jái-néui** where *sons and daughters* would be appropriate. In English it would sound odd to say 'Oh look, there are several hundred sons and daughters over there in the school playground' – you would say 'children'. Similarly in Cantonese you would not use **jái-néui** in this case, you would use **sai-màn-jái** *children*.

22.7 RELUCTANT AGREEMENT

In the dialogue, Mr Wong is pressed to join Mr Chan's firm, and he has to admit that the benefits are good but that he is too old and useless for the job. Note the neat little pattern which allows reluctant agreement to be shown but with the inevitable *but* to come: it is verb-**haih**-verb, **daahn-haih ...** :

Ngóh jùng-yi-haih-jùng-yi kéuih, daahn-haih ngóh dōu m̀h séung tùhng kéuih heui tái-hei.

Yes, I like him all right, but I still don't want to go to the pictures with him.

Wòhng Síu-jé leng-haih-leng, daahn-haih móuh Jèung Síu-jé gam leng.

Indeed, Miss Wong is pretty, but she's not as pretty as Miss Cheung.

> **DOUBLE SALARY**
>
> As you know, the Chinese have traditionally used both a lunar and a solar calendar. To keep them roughly in step it has been necessary to add an extra month into seven lunar years in every 19. So lunar years consist of either 12 or 13 months. Chinese monthly salaries are nowadays usually paid according to the Western solar calendar in which, of course, the years always have only 12 months, but it has become a custom among some employers to pay an additional month's salary every solar year as if it were a 13-month lunar year: it is the equivalent perhaps of a Western 'Christmas bonus'. That is what is referred to in the dialogue as **sèung-lèuhng** *double salary*.

Vocabulary builder 2

 Read the new vocabulary and practise saying it out loud.

THE OFFICE

秘書	bei-syù	secretary
傳真	chyùhn-jàn	fax; to fax
傳真機	chyùhn-jàn-gèi	fax machine (cl: **ga**)
打字	dá-jih	to type (lit. 'to hit characters')
打字機	dá-jih-gèi	typewriter (cl: **ga**)
打印	dá-yan	to print
打印機	dá-yan-gèi	printer (cl: **ga**)
電郵	dihn-yàuh	e-mail
文件	màhn-gín	document (cl: **jèung**)
破產	po-cháan	to go bankrupt
收發	sàu-faat	to receive and send
試用期	si-yuhng-kèih	probationary period, trial period
條件	tìuh-gín	condition, terms

VERBS

表現	bíu-yihn	to perform; performance
處理	chyú-léih	to handle, manage, deal with
負責	fuh-jaak	to be responsible
肯	háng	to be willing to

BASICS

詳細	chèuhng-sai	detailed, minute, fine
傳統	chyùhn-túng	traditional
獨立	duhk-laahp	independent; independently
今時今日	gàm-sìh-gàm-yaht	nowadays
機會	gèi-wuih	chance, opportunity
直接	jihk-jip	direct; directly
落後	lohk-hauh	backward, old-fashioned
心機	sàm-gèi	mind, thoughts
先進	sìn-jeun	advanced
一切	yāt-chai	every single one of, the whole run of, all

> **LANGUAGE TIP**
> **Jihk-jip** literally means 'directly in contact' and so *directly*. Its opposite is **gaan-jip** 間接 'touching at an interval', that is, *indirectly*.

Dialogue 2

 22.02 *Interviewing a secretary for a job.*

1 Miss Lee could be described in Cantonese as a húng-lùhng 恐龍 (lit. 'fearsome dragon'), but there is nothing frightening about her, so can you guess what húng-lùhng means?

Manager	Léih Síu-jé, néih sàn-chíng jouh ngóh-deih gūng-sī ge bei-syù, ngóh ngāam-ngāam gin-gwo néih dá-jih lak, bíu-yihn dōu-géi hóu. Daahn-haih ngóh m̀h mìhng-baahk néih dím-gáai yuhng dá-jih-gèi dá, m̀h yuhng dihn-nóuh dá nē. Haih m̀h haih néih m̀h sīk yuhng nē?
Lee	Gìng-léih sìn-sàang, deui-m̀h-jyuh, ngóh m̀h sīk.
Manager	M̀h sīk mē? Hái gàm-sìh-gàm-yaht ge séh-wúi m̀h sīk yuhng dihn-nóuh m̀h dāk bo! Gám, yuhng dihn-nóuh làih sàu-faat dihn-yàuh, sàu-faat chyùhn-jàn, yuhng dá-yan-gèi làih dá-yan màhn-gín, nī dī gam sìn-jeun ge yéh, néih yāt-dihng dōu m̀h sīk lā.
Lee	Haih, ngóh dōu m̀h sīk. Ngóh hái Seuhng-hói jouh bei-syù gó gàan gūng-sī yauh chyùhn-túng yauh lohk-hauh, gauh-nín juhng po-jó cháan tìm. Chyùhn-jàn-gèi ngóh gin dōu meih gin gwo, bāt-gwo ngóh gú m̀h nàahn hohk, yùh-gwó gìng-léih néih háng béi gèi-wuih ngóh, ngóh wúih hóu béi sàm-gèi hohk ge, sèung-seun hóu faai ngóh jauh hó-yíh sīk yuhng ge la.
Manager	Néih hái Seuhng-hói jouh-gwo géi-dō nìhn bei-syù a?
Lee	Chà-m̀h-dō yáuh sahp-chāt nìhn lak.
Manager	Hái Seuhng-hói ge sé-jih-làuh yáuh géi-dō wái bei-syù a?
Lee	Jí yáuh ngóh yāt go haih bei-syù, ngóh yiu duhk-laahp chyú-léih yāt-chai gūng-sī ge màhn-gín, yìh-ché yiu jihk-jip heung gìng-léih fuh-jaak.
Manager	Hóu lā! Ngóh jauh chéng néih lā! Bāt-gwo daih-yāt go yuht haih si-yuhng-kèih, ngóh séung tái-háh néih ge gùng-jok bíu-yihn sìn. Kèih-tà chèuhng-sai ge fūk-leih tùhng gùng-jok tìuh-gín, dáng gwo-jó si-yuhng-kèih joi góng lā. Néih tìng-yaht hó-yíh làih séuhng-bàan lak.
Lee	Dò-jeh gìng-léih. Tìng-yaht gin.
經理	李小姐，你申請做我哋公司嘅秘書，我啱啱見過你打字嘞，表現都幾好。但係我唔明白你點解用打字機打，唔用電腦打呢。係唔係你唔識用呢？
李	經理先生，對唔住，我唔識。
經理	唔識咩？喺今時今日嘅社會唔識用電腦唔得嘑！嗷，用電腦嚟收發電郵，收發傳真，用打印機嚟打印文件，呢啲咁先進嘅嘢，你一定都唔識啦。
李	係，我都唔識。我喺上海做秘書嗰間公司又傳統又落後，舊年重破咗產添。傳真機我見都未見過，不過我估唔難學，如果經理你肯俾機會我，我會好俾心機學嘅，相信好快我就可以識用嘅嘑。
經理	你喺上海做過幾多年秘書呀？
李	差唔多有十七年嘞。
經理	喺上海嘅寫字樓有幾多位秘書呀？
李	只有我一個係秘書，我要獨立處理一切公司嘅文件，而且要直接向經理負責。
經理	好啦！我就請你啦，不過第一個月係試用期，我想睇吓你嘅工作表現先。其他詳細嘅福利同工作條件，等過咗試用期再講啦。你聽日可以嚟上班嘞。
李	多謝經理。聽日見。

2 Translate into Cantonese.

    a He's been living in that city for more than 25 years.

    b I have never drunk French wine.

    c If you want to apply to work in that company you must first write a letter to the manager.

    d Before we invite you to teach Cantonese we want to hear you speak a few words first.

Language discovery

22.8 SIMPLY MUST

You probably found no difficulty with the phrase **m̀h sīk yuhng dihn-nóuh m̀h dāk bo!** *you simply must know how to use a computer!* Note how the pattern works: **m̀h** + verb + **m̀h dāk**, that is, *if you don't* + verb + *it won't do!* or *you simply must* + verb!

YOUR TURN Translate these other examples:

Gó dī hā néih m̀h sihk m̀h dāk.

Wòhng Táai wah néih m̀h heui taam kéuih m̀h dāk.

22.9 NEVER EVEN …

In the dialogue Miss Lee says **Chyùhn-jàn-gèi ngóh gin dōu meih gin gwo** *I haven't even seen a fax machine*. The pattern **gin dōu meih gin-gwo** may have struck a chord with you – do you remember the **lìhn … dōu …** pattern which you met in Unit 17? Here instead of **lìhn** + **dōu** the same verb appears twice + **dōu**, but the meaning is still *not even …*

22.10 SÀM-GÈI

Sàm-gèi is quite a difficult word to grasp. Its closest equivalent in English is *mind*, but perhaps these examples of its most common usages will be the easiest way to come to terms with it:

Ngóh wúih hóu béi sàm-gèi hohk.	*I will do my best to give my mind to learning it.*
Ngóh móuh sàm-gèi heui.	*I have no enthusiasm for going.*
Kéuih hóu móuh sàm-gèi.	*She's very out of sorts / listless / without enthusiasm.*

> **LANGUAGE TIP**
> Poor Miss Lee, the secretary in the dialogue, somehow missed out on recent progress. If she doesn't know how to use a computer, she certainly will not know what **wuh-lyùhn-móhng** 互聯網 *the internet* is or how to **séuhng-móhng** 上網 *get on the internet*, and maybe not even how to **dá go dyún-seun** 打個 短訊 *send a text message*.

22.11 FUH-JAAK *TO BE RESPONSIBLE TO*

Note the way in which **fuh-jaak** is used with **heung**. Miss Lee says in the dialogue that she **jihk-jip heung gìng-léih fuh-jaak** *was directly answerable to the manager.* You met **heung** first in Unit 6 where it meant *towards,* but here it may be better to think of it as meaning something like *vis-à-vis* or *as regards.* There was a similar example in the first dialogue of Unit 19: **heung ngàhn-hòhng tau-jì** *to be overdrawn at (vis-à-vis) the bank.*

Practice

1 **The following questions all use mē? The short answer (either Haih or M̀h haih) has been supplied. In each case supply the long full answer after the short one. For instance, the first answer would be M̀h haih, ngóh m̀h haih Méih-gwok-yàhn. Easy? Well, you may need to watch your step …**

   a Néih haih Méih-gwok-yàhn mē? M̀h haih, …

   b Wòhng Sìn-sàang dī jái-néui yuht-làih-yuht-waaih mē? Haih, …

   c Néih meih sihk-gwo jóu-chāan mē? Haih, …

   d Kéuih m̀h-haih-géi-jùng-yi fàan-gùng mē? M̀h haih, …

   e Yìng-gwok-yàhn tùhng Jùng-gwok-yàhn yat-yeuhng gam jùng-yi tái-bō mē? Haih, …

2 **Complete the sentences.**

   a Gáu go yàhn yāt-go-yāt-go-gám hàahng-louh, daih-yāt go hó-yíh wah haih 'tàuh-yāt go': daih-gáu go nē? Hó-yíh wah haih 'daih-_____ go'.

   b Wòhng Síu-jé sèhng-yaht dá-dihn-wá _____ ngóh, sàai ngóh hóu dò sìh-gaan!

   c Chàhn Táai baat-dím-gáu-go-jih sìn-ji fàan sé-jih-làuh. Ngóh _____ baat-dím.

   d 'Kéuih bàh-ba jí-haih jouh-gwo yih-sahp nìhn yī-sāng jauh teui-yàu lak.' 'Wàh, gam _____ sìh-gaan! Kéuih dī behng-yàhn tái yī-sāng yāt-dihng yiu béi hóu dò chín la!'

3 **Supply an appropriate verb ending to complete the sentences.**

   a Wài-lìhm yìh-gā sihk-_____ faahn, chìh-dī hó-yíh chēut-gāai wáan.

   b Láahng àh? Dòng-yín m̀h gok-dāk láahng. Ngóh jeuk-_____ hóu nyúhn ge sāam a.

   c Ngóh meih si-_____ lùhng-hā. Hóu m̀h hóu sihk a?

   d Dī hā sihk-_____ lak; yìh-gā lìhn yāt jek dōu móuh lak.

   e Wai! Néih wán bīn wái a? Hòh Síu-jé nē? Òu, Hòh Síu-jé ngāam-ngāam hàahng-_____-jó lak. Kéuih fàan-làih ngóh wúih wah kéuih jì néih dá-gwo dihn-wá làih lak.

Test yourself

Some higher mathematical problems for you to solve (in Cantonese, of course).

a Wòhng Síu-jé ge sàn-séui m̀h gòu, bāt-gwo haih ńgh-chìn-sei-baak mān yāt go yuht. Hóu-chói kéuih nìhn-méih yáuh sèung-sàn. Gám, kéuih yāt nìhn yāt-guhng ló géi-dō chín a?

b Chàhn Sàang Sei-yuht ge sàn-séui haih yih-maahn-ńgh-chìn mān. Hòh Sàang Sei-yuht fàan-jó baat yaht gùng, múih yaht ló ge chín yáuh sàam-chìn mān gam dò. Gó go yuht Chàhn Sàang dihng-haih Hòh Sàang ló ge chín dò nē?

c Wòhng Táai hóu hàan. Yàn-waih chóh deih-tit gwai-gwo chóh bā-sí, kéuih juhng-meih chóh-gwo deih-tit. Chóh síu-bā dōu móuh chóh bā-sí gam pèhng, só-yíh kéuih hóu síu daap síu-bā. Gàm-yaht kéuih hàahng-louh heui síh-chèuhng, máaih-jó jeui pèhng jeui pèhng daahn-haih m̀h sàn-sìn ge hā tùhng-màaih bun-gàn ngàuh-yuhk, yauh máaih-jó yāt-dī kèih-tà sung. Ngàuh-yuhk maaih sahp-ńgh mān yāt gàn, dī hā bāt-gwo yiu chāt-go-bun, kèih-tà sung jí-haih luhk mān jē. Kéuih máaih-jó ge yéh hóu chúhng, m̀h chóh bā-sí fàan ūk-kéi m̀h dāk. Daap bā-sí yiu sàam-go-bun ngàhn-chín. Nàh, Wòhng Táai gàm-yaht yāt-guhng yuhng-jó géi-dō chín a?

d Ngóh bàh-bā séi-jó hóu noih lak, màh-mā juhng hái-douh; yáuh sei go hīng-daih, sàam go jí-muih; yáuh ngóh taai-táai tùhng-màaih ńgh go jái-néui. Ngóh-deih hahm-baahng-laahng dōu jyuh hái yāt chàhng m̀h daaih m̀h sai ge láu. Chéng-mahn yāt-guhng yáuh géi-dō go yàhn a?

23 香港酒樓 *Hèung-góng jáu-làuh*

Eating out

In this unit you will learn about:

- *birthdays.*
- *Canton.*
- *chāan v faahn.*
- *cuisines and food.*

- *humility and praise.*
- *not only … but also.*
- *starting from …*
- *the animal cycle.*

CEFR: *(B1) Can describe experiences and impressions.*

 Different restaurants, different food

Entertaining at home in Hong Kong can be a problem, because few families have much room to spare in their crowded flats. This forces people to invite guests to restaurants, but while that sounds expensive it is not necessarily so – restaurants of all types and at many levels of sophistication and cost can be found – and the upside is that the keen competition has resulted in high standards of service and food.

Most, but not all, restaurants that call themselves **chāan-tēng** 餐廳 serve styles of cuisine other than Chinese, but large establishments serving Chinese food are usually known as **jáu-làuh** (see Unit 4) or **jáu-gā** 酒家, the use of **jáu** in the names probably reflecting the fact that Chinese people have generally only drunk alcohol when eating on special occasions. Smaller restaurants offering a limited but delicious menu of noodle dishes and congee are excellent value and are known as **jūk-mihn-pou** 粥麵舖. **Chàh-chāan-tēng** 茶餐廳 are more like cafés, and often serve both Chinese and Western food.

As you learned in Unit 22, **sihk-faahn** would normally imply *eating a proper meal of Chinese food*, whereas **sihk-chāan** means *to have a meal of Western food or some other non-Chinese variety*. English-style breakfast is quite popular and the word for *breakfast* used nowadays is usually **jóu-chāan**, but the *evening meal* is **máahn-faahn** or **máahn-chāan** depending on the style of food eaten. Oddly there is no such distinction in the normal pair of words which contrast Western and Chinese cuisines: *Western food* is **sài-chāan** 西餐, as you might expect, but *Chinese food* is **Tòhng-chāan** 唐餐.

 Have you wondered why we use a capital **T** for **Tòhng-yàhn** and **Tòhng-chāan**?

Vocabulary builder 1

 Read the new vocabulary and practise saying it out loud.

FOOD

顧客	gu-haak	customer, client
香	hèung	fragrant, nice smelling
埋單	Màaih-dāan	May I have the bill? (in restaurants)
食物	sihk-maht	food
色香味	sīk-hèung-meih	presentation, aroma and flavour

VERBS

變暖	bin-nyúhn	to become warm, warm up
開	hòi	to run a business, start a business
認識	yihng-sīk	to recognize, be knowledgeable about, understand

BASICS

齊全	chàih-chyùhn	complete, all embracing
全球	chyùhn-kàuh	the whole world, global
點	dím	point, spot, dot
公里	gūng-léih	kilometre
貴國	gwai-gwok	your country
廣東	Gwóng-dùng	Guangdong (province)
合理	hahp-léih	reasonable
氣候	hei-hauh	climate
好感	hóu-gám	favourable impression, good opinion
集中	jaahp-jùng	concentrated, centralized
種類	júng-leuih	type, kind, species, variety
唔怪得	m̀h-gwaai-dāk	no wonder
損失	syún-sāt	loss
環境	wàahn-gíng	environment
污染	wù-yíhm	pollution; to pollute
一流	yāt-làuh	first rate
原因	yùhn-yàn	reason

Dialogue 1

23.01 *A food-loving visitor talks with a Hong Kong gourmet.*

1 In the dialogue Tòhng-chāan is not used, but another term for it is. Can you identify it?

Visitor	Ngóh làih-jó Hèung-góng chà-m̀h-dō yáuh léuhng go láih-baai lak, deui Hèung-góng ge jáu-gā tùhng chāan-tēng dōu yáuh hóu-gám. Ngóh gok-dāk yāt go làih Hèung-góng wáan ge yàuh-haak yùh-gwó m̀h heui jáu-gā si-háh Jùng-gwok-choi, gám, jàn-haih yāt go daaih syún-sāt lak.
Local	Néih hóu jùng-yi sihk Jùng-gwok-choi mē?
Visitor	Hái Hèung-góng Jùng-gwok-choi m̀h-jí júng-leuih dò, fún-sīk chàih-chyùhn, ga-chìhn hahp-léih, yìh-ché sīk-hèung-meih dōu haih yāt-làuh ge.
Local	Chéng-mahn néih hái gwai-gwok jouh māt-yéh sàang-yi ga?
Visitor	Ngóh haih Faat-gwok-yàhn, ngóh hòi chāan-tēng ge.
Local	M̀h-gwaai-dāk néih deui sihk-maht gam yáuh yihng-sīk lā. Néih jeui jùng-yi sihk māt-yéh Jùng-gwok-choi a?
Visitor	Gwóng-dùng dím-sām tùhng hói-sīn lā.
Local	Hó-sīk jeui-gahn-géi-nìhn Hèung-góng ge hói-sīn yuht-làih-yuht-gwai. Hái jáu-gā sihk-jó hói-sīn jì-hauh ngóh yáuh-sìh m̀h gám giu 'Màaih-dāan', m̀h jì daai-làih ge chín gau m̀h gau. Néih jì-m̀h-jì dím-gáai Hèung-góng ge hói-sīn ga-chìhn yuht-làih-yuht-gwai nē?
Visitor	Wàahn-gíng wù-yíhm tùhng chyùhn-kàuh hei-hauh bin nyúhn. Ngóh gú jauh haih jihk-jip yíng-héung hói-sīn ga-chìhn ge yùhn-yàn lak. Juhng yáuh yāt dím, jauh haih Hèung-góng ge jáu-làuh tùhng chāan-tēng haih sai-gaai seuhng jeui dò, jeui jaahp-jùng ge.
Local	Ngóh jì Hèung-góng yáuh yāt tìuh gāai bāt-gwo léuhng gūng-léih gam chèuhng jī-máh, jáu-làuh tùhng chāan-tēng jauh yáuh chìu-gwo sàam-baak gàan lak.
Visitor	Bīn-douh yáuh gam dò gu-haak yaht-yaht dōu làih bòng-chan nē?
Local	Néih hái Hèung-góng jyuh noih-dī, néih jauh jì dím-gáai ge lak.
遊客	我嚟咗香港差唔多有兩個禮拜嘅，對香港嘅酒家同餐廳都有好感。我覺得一個嚟香港玩嘅遊客如果唔去酒家試吓中國菜，噉，真係一個大損失嘞。
本地人	你好中意食中國菜咩？
遊客	喺香港中國菜唔只種類多，款式齊全，價錢合理，而且色香味都係一流嘅。
本地人	請問你喺貴國做乜嘢生意㗎？
遊客	我係法國人，我開餐廳嘅。
本地人	唔怪得你對食物咁有認識啦。你最中意食乜嘢中國菜呀？
遊客	廣東點心同海鮮啦。
本地人	可惜最近幾年香港嘅海鮮越嚟越貴。喺酒家食咗海鮮之後我有時唔敢叫"埋單"，唔知帶嚟嘅錢夠唔夠。你知唔知點解香港嘅海鮮價錢越嚟越貴呢？
遊客	環境污染同全球氣候變暖。我估就係直接影響海鮮價錢嘅原因嘞。重有一點，就係香港嘅酒樓同餐廳係世界上最多，最集中嘅。
本地人	我知香港有一條街不過兩公里咁長之嘛，酒樓同餐廳就有超過三百間嘞。
遊客	邊度有咁多顧客日日都嚟幫趁呢？
本地人	你喺香港住耐啲，你就知點解嘅嘞。

2 Answer in Cantonese.

a Hái Hèung-góng sihk hói-sīn gàm-nín pèhng-gwo gauh-nín, haih m̀h haih?

b Gó wái Faat-gwok yàhn dím-gáai hóu sīk sihk a?

c Ńgh-sīng-kāp jáu-dim haih _____ (yāt-làuh/ńgh-làuh) ge.

Language discovery

23.1 CHOI AND SUNG

Here are a few common terms using **choi** *food* or *cuisine*:

Jùng-gwok-choi	*Chinese food*
Gwóng-dùng-choi	*Cantonese food*
(Bāk-)gìng-choi	*Peking food*
(Sei-)chyùn-choi	*Sichuan food*

> **LANGUAGE TIP**
> **Sei-chyùn** 四川 =
> *Sichuan / Szechwan*

Remember that **choi** also means *vegetables*:

Ngóh-deih yáuh yuhk, dím-gáai móuh choi a? *We have meat, why no vegetables?*

Both meat and vegetables are included in the word **sung** (see Unit 4), but **máaih-choi** and **máaih-sung** mean the same thing – *shopping for food*. Confusing isn't it?

> **WHERE DOES *CANTONESE* COME FROM?**
> The word *Canton* probably comes from a Portuguese romanization of the Cantonese word **Gwóng-dùng**. **Gwóng-dùng** is the name of the province of which the capital city is **Gwóng-jàu**. It is somewhat confusing that Canton became the name by which the city rather than the province was known to the West. It is even more confusing that in the province there are a number of Chinese languages spoken, of which what we call Cantonese is only one. Casting the history aside, the situation now is clear: the province is called **Gwóng-dùng**, the capital city is called **Gwóng-jàu** and the language which you are learning, which is the language of **Gwóng-jàu** and other major urban centres, is known as **Gwóng-jàu-wá**. By the way, the official name of the city is actually **Guangzhou**, which is the **Putonghua** (*Mandarin*) version of **Gwóng-jàu**.

23.2 NOT ONLY … BUT ALSO …

The pattern which translates *not only … but also …* is quite straightforward: **m̀h-jí … yìh-ché … (dōu) … Dōu** is not essential to the pattern, but as so often when plural ideas are mentioned it is likely to be used:

Wòhng Sìn-sàang m̀h-jí sīk góng Yìng-màhn yìh-ché Yaht-màhn dōu góng-dak hóu hóu.

Mr Wong cannot only speak English, his Japanese is very good too.

23.3 SĪK-HÈUNG-MEIH

You met **meih** in Unit 4 in the term **hóu-meih** *delicious*. Its basic meaning is *flavour*. **Sīk** means *colour* or *appearance*, and **hèung** means *nice smelling, fragrant* (as in **Hèung-góng** 'Fragrant Harbour' = *Hong Kong*). The three together make up the three qualities which ideally all Chinese food is supposed to have – good appearance, good aroma, good flavour. As with other set phrases, do not be tempted to use the individual words outside this phrase. Of the three, only **hèung** is a 'free' word which you can use in normal speech like any other adjective / verb:

Chàhn Táai, nī dī sung hóu hèung. Néih jàn-haih hóu sīk jyú-sung bo!

Mrs Chan, this food smells wonderful. You really know how to cook!

23.4 FLAVOURS

苦	**fú**	*bitter*		鹹	**hàahm**	*salty*
辣	**laaht**	*spicy hot*		酸	**syùn**	*sour*
淡	**táahm**	*bland, tasteless*		甜	**tìhm**	*sweet*

All the flavours are regular adjectival verbs:

Nī dī sàang-gwó m̀h suhk, hóu syùn!

This fruit is not ripe, it's very sour!

Wòhng Táai m̀h séung sihk tìhm yéh, kéuih hóu pa fèih.

Mrs Wong doesn't want to eat anything sweet, she's scared of getting fat.

23.5 TOOLS FOR THE JOB

Here are some essential kitchen tools.

菜刀 **choi-dōu** (cl: **bá**) *kitchen chopper*

鑊 **wohk** (cl: **jek**) *wok*

碗 **wún** (cl: **jek**) *bowl*

茶壺 **chàh-wú** (cl: **go**) *teapot*

砧板 **jàm-báan** (cl: **faai**) *chopping board*

鑊鏟 **wohk-cháan** (cl: **jek**) *wok slice*

碟 **díp** (cl: **jek**) *plate*

匙羹 **chìh-gāng** (cl: **jek**) *spoon*

23.6 HONORIFIC WORDS

Way back in Unit 1 you met **gwai-sing a?** *what is your surname?* and it was explained that this actually meant *what is your distinguished name?* (Later you met the same word **gwai** meaning *expensive*.) Chinese politeness traditionally demanded that other people's attributes and belongings were always spoken of as precious, honourable, distinguished and so on, while one's own were always mentioned as despicable, humble, miserable, etc. In the dialogue the Hong Kong man is properly polite when he asks the visitor what his occupation is in his *honourable country* (**gwai-gwok**). Much of the very fancy honorific terminology is no longer used, you will perhaps be relieved to hear, but it is still polite to 'cry up' other people and to 'play down' yourself. You will find that when you try out your halting Cantonese on people, they will inevitably come back at you by saying what wonderful Cantonese you speak – that is the polite thing for them to say. Do not be fooled into believing them and, above all, even if you happen arrogantly to think them to be correct, do not reply *I know I do* or *Thank you very much, I am a genius at languages*. Always deny a compliment.

YOUR TURN So how do you say:

I speak Cantonese very badly.

I'm sorry, I can only speak a very little.

My Cantonese is not as good as your English.

Vocabulary builder 2

 Read the new vocabulary and practise saying it out loud.

CELEBRATIONS

特別	dahk-biht	*special; especially*
快樂	faai-lohk	*happy*
恭喜！	gùng-héi!	*congratulations!; to congratulate*
生日	sàang-yaht	*birthday*
消息	sìu-sīk	*news, item of news, information*
意義	yi-yih	*meaning, significance*
邀請	yìu-chíng	*to invite*

> **LANGUAGE TIP**
>
> **Gùng-héi!** Even before you began to learn this language, you were probably aware of the Cantonese New Year greeting **Gùng-héi faat-chòi!** 恭喜發財 *Congratulations and get rich!* You really need to have this phrase off by heart and say it 'from the heart' too – *Chinese New Year* (**gwo-nìhn** 過年) is the most important and happiest festival in the calendar.

VERBS AND VERB ENDINGS

拆	chaak	*to demolish, tear down*
加價	gà-ga	*to increase price*
開始	hòi-chí	*to begin, start*
… 剩	-jihng	ve: *left over, surplus*

BASICS

餐牌	chāan-páai	*menu*
全部	chyùhn-bouh	*all, the whole lot*
哈！	hà!	(the sound of laughter) *ha! ha!*
就快	jauh-faai	*soon*
懷舊	wàaih-gauh	*nostalgic; nostalgia*

> **LANGUAGE TIP**
>
> **Yìu-chíng** means *to invite* and so does **chéng** (which is actually a colloquial variant of the second element in **yìu-chíng**). There is no real difference in meaning, but **yìu-chíng** is slightly more formal than **chéng**.

Dialogue 2

William has his own way of beating inflation.

1 What effect does yùhn-lòih have on Mr Ho's last sentence?

Ho	Wài-lìhm, dím-gáai néih gam haak-hei chéng ngóh làih nī gàan chāan-tēng sihk-faahn a? Haih m̀h haih néih gàm-yaht sàang-yaht a? Gùng-héi! Gùng-héi! néih sàang-yaht faai-lohk!
William	Ngóh m̀h haih gàm-yaht sàang-yaht. Móuh dahk-biht yi-yih ge, jí-haih ngóh tèng-dóu yāt go sìu-sīk wah nī gàan chāan-tēng jauh-faai yiu chaak la, ngóh yauh hóu jùng-yi hái nī gàan chāan-tēng sihk-yéh, só-yíh ngóh jauh yìu-chíng néih tùhng ngóh yāt-chàih làih sihk-faahn jē.
Ho	Ngóh m̀h jì-dou néih gam jùng-yi nī gàan gauh chāan-tēng ge bo.
William	Haih a, ngóh juhng hóu jùng-yi wàaih-gauh tìm. Yí! … dím-gáai gàm-yaht chāan-páai dī sung gwai-gwo kàhm-yaht ge gam dò gé? Ngóh kàhm-yaht ngāam-ngāam sìn-ji hái nī-douh sihk-gwo faahn jē!
Waitress	Deui-m̀h-jyuh la, sìn-sàang, néih-deih jàn-haih m̀h hóu-chói lak. Ngóh-deih gàan chāan-tēng ngāam-ngāam yàuh gàm-yaht hòi-chí gà-ga. Yùh-gwó néih-deih kàhm-yaht làih sihk-faahn, ngóh-deih ge chāan-tēng juhng-meih gà-ga.
William	Néih-deih kàhm-yaht ge sihk-maht chyùhn-bouh dōu haih maaih gauh ga àh?
Waitress	Haih a.
William	Gám hóu ak. Ngóh yiu yāt tìuh kàhm-yaht néih-deih maaih-jihng ge yàuh-séui yú, yāt gàn kàhm-yaht maaih-jihng ge yàuh-séui hā, tùhng-màaih yāt dī kàhm-yaht maaih-jihng ge sàang-gwó tìm.
Ho	Hà! Yùhn-lòih néih deui sihk-maht dōu wàaih-gauh ge.

何	威廉，點解你咁客氣請我嚟呢間餐廳食飯呀？係唔係你今日生日呀？恭喜！恭喜你生日快樂！
威廉	我唔係今日生日。冇特別意義嘅，只係我聽倒一個消息話呢間餐廳就快要拆喇，我又好中意喺呢間餐廳食嘢，所以我就邀請你同我一齊嚟食飯啫。
何	我唔知道你咁中意呢間舊餐廳嘅嘜。
威廉	係呀，我重好中意懷舊添，咦！… 點解今日餐牌啲餸貴過擒日嘅咁多嘅？我擒日啱啱先至喺呢度食過飯啫！
服務員	對唔住喇，先生，你哋真係唔好彩嘞。我哋間餐廳啱啱由今日開始加價。如果你哋擒日嚟食飯，我哋嘅餐廳重未加價。
威廉	你哋擒日嘅食物全部都係賣舊價吖？
服務員	係呀。
威廉	噉好呃。我要一條擒日你哋賣剩嘅游水魚，一斤擒日賣剩嘅游水蝦，同埋一啲擒日賣剩嘅生果添。
何	哈！原來你對食物都懷舊嘅。

2 Answer in Cantonese.

a Gó gàan chāan-tēng haih m̀h haih sàn ga?

b Chāan-tēng haih géi-sí gà-ga ga?

c Wài-lìhm jùng m̀h jùng-yi sihk hói-sīn a?

Language discovery

23.7 BIRTHDAYS

Sàang means either *to be born* or *to give birth to*. **Sàang-yaht** is the *day of birth*, *birthday*. **Sàang-yaht** is unusual in that, although it doesn't appear to be a verb, it doesn't seem to need any other verb either. Note the first speech of Mr Ho in the dialogue: **Haih m̀h haih néih gàm-yaht sàang-yaht a?** *Is it your birthday today?* What he actually seems to be saying is *Is it the case that you are birthdaying today?* Don't worry about it, just accept that this is how **sàang-yaht** is usually used.

23.8 THE 12-YEAR CYCLE

There are 12 animals that give their names to the lunar years, and all Chinese people know under which animal sign they were born. The order is of course fixed, starting with the Rat and ending with the Pig, and on the 13th year the cycle starts back with Rat again. Don't be surprised to be asked:

Néih suhk māt-yé ga?   *What were you born under?*

> **LANGUAGE TIP**
> **suhk** 屬 means *belong to.*

To which you reply:

Ngóh suhk ngàuh ge. Néih nē?   *I was born under the Ox. What about you?*

Here are the 12 animals:

1	鼠	**Syú**	*Rat*	7	馬	**Máh**	*Horse*
2	牛	**Ngàuh**	*Ox*	8	羊	**Yèuhng**	*Sheep*
3	虎	**Fú**	*Tiger*	9	猴	**Hàuh**	*Monkey*
4	兔	**Tou**	*Hare*	10	雞	**Gāi**	*Cock*
5	龍	**Lùhng**	*Dragon*	11	狗	**Gáu**	*Dog*
6	蛇	**Sèh**	*Snake*	12	豬	**Jyù**	*Pig*

Remember that these are lunar years and they are never quite in step with the solar calendar, so a child born on 18 February 2015 belonged to the *Year of the Horse* (**Máh-nìhn**) but would have come under the *Year of the Sheep* (**Yèuhng-nìhn**) if born the day after.

 Nī sahp-yih jek néih haih m̀h haih júng-júng dōu gin-gwo a?

23.9 STARTING FROM …

Yàuh means *from* (see Unit 6) and it pairs with **hòi-chí** *to begin* to make a pattern for *starting from …* In the dialogue the waitress says **yàuh gàm-yaht hòi-chí** meaning *starting from today*. You can use the pattern quite freely:

Yàuh luhk-dím-jūng hòi-chí …

From six o'clock onwards …

Yàuh sahp-baat seui hòi-chí kéuih jauh meih sihk-gwo yuhk la.

She hasn't had meat since she was 18.

Cantonese cuisine excels in its treatment of seafood, but the food is only considered properly fresh if it is alive until the last possible moment before cooking. The best *seafood restaurants* (**hói-sīn jáu-gā**) have large saltwater tanks in which the fish, prawns and shellfish are kept alive and customers can select what they wish to eat from this 'swimming seafood' (**yàuh-séui hói-sīn**).

 Practice

1 Select the words which will make sense of the sentences.

  a Hèung-góng yáuh hóu dò (yāt-guhng / yāt-chai / yāt-làuh / yāt-sìh) ge jáu-dim.

  b Jeui-gahn-géi-nìhn Hèung-góng ge (gìng-léih / gìng-gwo / gìng-jai) yuht-làih-yuht-hóu.

  c Hái Hèung-góng, gíng-chaat (gwàn-yàhn / daaih-yàhn / làai-yàhn / lóuh-yàhn) yāt-dihng yiu yáuh léih-yàuh.

  d Hèung-góng ge bā-sí sī-gēi hòi-gùng ge sìh-hauh yiu jeuk (gwàn-fuhk / bihn-fuhk / syù-fuhk / jai-fuhk).

  e Ngóh-deih géi-sìh yáuh (sàn-séui / yàuh-séui / saan-séui / yeuhk-séui) ló a?

2 When you have read this passage carefully, answer the two questions in Cantonese.

Hái Hòh Sìn-sàang ūk-kéi bāk-bihn léuhng gūng-léih gó-douh yáuh yāt gàan hohk-haauh. Hái hohk-haauh dùng-bihn ńgh gūng-léih haih yāt gàan yì-yún. Hái yì-yún nàahm-bihn léuhng gūng-léih jauh haih gíng-chaat-guhk lak. Méih-gwok ngàhn-hòhng hái gíng-chaat-guhk sài-bihn sàam gūng-léih gó-douh. Chéng-mahn:

  a Yàuh ngàhn-hòhng heui Hòh Sàang ūk-kéi yáuh géi-dō gūng-léih a?

  b Ngàhn-hòhng hái Hòh Sàang ūk-kéi bīn-bihn a?

3 Can you remember your colours? Give the answers to the following in Cantonese.

  a Néih jà-chē gin-dóu hùhng-dāng yiu jouh māt-yéh nē?

  b Làahm-sīk gà māt-yéh sīk haih luhk-sīk a?

  c Làahm-sīk gà hùhng-sīk haih māt-yéh sīk a?

  d Hóu dò hóu dò nìhn jì-chìhn hóu gauh ge dihn-yíng haih māt-yéh sīk a?

4 Supply the bubble caption in Cantonese: This is a beautiful fish, sure to be very tasty. Who will give $10,000?

 5 23.03 You need to interpret for your friend who is about to foot the bill for a meal in a restaurant. Unlike you, he has not taken the trouble to learn Cantonese. Try to do the exercise first without looking at the text, though of course you can press the pause button between speeches.

Friend	*Wow! The seafood here is really delicious, very fresh and beautifully cooked. All three of the ideal qualities were superbly realized.*
You	a
Waiter	Ngóh-deih nī-douh dī yú dōu haih yàuh-séui ge, dòng-yín sàn-sìn lā!
You	b
Friend	*May I have the bill, please?*
You	c
Waiter	Dò-jeh. Yih-chìn-baat-baak-gáu-sahp mān.
You	d
Friend	*What?! So much? That's really not cheap!*
You	e
Waiter	Néih yiu jì-dou, yìh-gā yàuh-séui yú dahk-biht nàahn-máaih. Juhng yáuh nē, ngóh-deih jáu-gā sung faai-jí, múih go gu-haak sung yāt deui.
You	f
Friend	*I have never bought such expensive chopsticks before. OK. It wasn't cheap but it was worth it. Here's $3,000.*
You	g
Waiter	Dò-jeh.
You	h

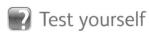 Test yourself

Here are some Chinese brainteaser 'old chestnuts' for you to solve:

a Síu-Jēung wah: 'Ngóh sàn-tái chúhng-leuhng ge yāt bun joi gà yih-sahp bohng jauh haih ngóh sàn-tái ge chyùhn-bouh chúhng-leuhng lak. Chéng mahn ngóh haih géi-dō bohng a?'

b Yáuh yāt yeuhng yéh, néih jí hó-yíh yuhng jó-sáu nìng, m̀h hó-yíh yuhng yauh-sáu nìng. Néih gú haih māt-yéh nē?

c Síu-Wóng wah: 'Ngóh yìh-gā géi-dō seui ngóh m̀h wah néih jì, daahn-haih sàam nìhn jì-chìhn gó-jahn-sìh ngāam-ngāam jauh haih ngóh sàam nìhn jì-hauh ge baak-fahn-jì-sàam-sahp-sàam. Gám, néih jì m̀h jì ngóh yìh-gā géi-dō seui a?'

d Wòhng Sìn-sàang daai-jó yāt-baak mān chēut-gāai. Hái pou-táu máaih-jó sàam bún syù, múih bún dōu haih yih-sahp-ńgh mān. Daahn-haih pou-táu ge fuhk-mouh-yùhn jí-haih jáau-fàan ńgh mān kéuih. Dím-gáai nē?

24

嗜好 Sih-hou
Leisure activities

In this unit you will learn about:

- ▶ as soon as.
- ▶ -ever *words*.
- ▶ *hobbies and pastimes*.
- ▶ *in your opinion*.
- ▶ *losing things*.

- ▶ *machinery*.
- ▶ *more on dōu*.
- ▶ recent *and* recently.
- ▶ self.

CEFR: *(B1) Have sufficient vocabulary to express yourself on most topics pertinent to everyday life such as hobbies and interests.*

Hobbies

The hobbies mentioned in the first dialogue are much as you might find anywhere in the world: Cantonese people like sport and games and collecting things. Mind you, the chess may well be Chinese chess, which is played on a different board with different pieces and operates with different rules from Western chess, or it might be **wàih-kéi** 圍棋 *Surrounding chess*, which is played with black and white stones on the intersections of the lines on a multi-squared board: it tends to be known in the West under its Japanese name *Go*. One hobby which is much more common with the Chinese than with Westerners is *calligraphy* (**syù-faat** 書法). Writing Chinese characters with a brush is a high art form in China and Japan and many people spend hours painstakingly cultivating their skill.

Syù, as you know, means a *book*, but in ancient China it meant *to write*, and that's why **syù-faat** 'way of writing' or 'laws of writing' came to mean *calligraphy*. Can you work out what **syù-fóng** and **syù-póu** mean?

Vocabulary builder 1

 Read the new vocabulary and practise saying it out loud.

PASTIMES

歌劇	gò-kehk	*opera*
鋼琴	gong-kàhm	*piano*
捉棋	jūk-kéi	*to play chess*
散步	saan-bouh	*to stroll, go for a walk*
嗜好	sih-hou	*hobby, pastime*
跳舞	tiu-móuh	*to dance*
畫畫	waahk-wá	*to paint, draw*

TRAINING

初級	chò-kāp	*elementary, beginner grade*
訓練	fan-lihn	*training; to train*
訓練班	fan-lihn-bāan	*training class*
練習	lihn-jaahp	*to practise*
目的	muhk-dīk	*purpose, aim, goal, target*

VERBS

憎	jàng	*to hate, detest*
留	làuh	*to stay, remain; leave behind*
唔見咗	m̀h-gin-jó	*to lose, mislay; lost*

BASICS

秘密	bei-maht	*secret*
奇怪	kèih-gwaai	*strange, weird, odd*
一陣(間)	yāt-jahn(-gāan)	*a moment, in a moment, for a moment*

Dialogue 1

24.01 *Mr Cheung has changed his habits and Mr Wong wonders why.*

1 Let's get back to syù. Bei-maht you now know is *secret* or *a secret*. What do you think bei-syù means?

Wong	Lóuh-Jēung, ngóh jì-dou néih ge sih-hou haih jūk-kéi, yáuh-sìh dōu gin néih yíng-séung tùhng waahk-wá, daahn-haih móuh māt gin néih tiu-móuh waahk-jé saan-bouh ge bo!
Cheung	Haih a! Yàuh-kèih haih nī-géi-go-yuht ngóh waahk-jó hóu dò fūk wá. Daahn-haih wahn-duhng nē, lìhn yāt chi dōu móuh jouh-gwo. Ngóh jeui <u>jàng</u> wahn-duhng ge lak.
Wong	Dím-gáai jeui-gahn ngóh gin néih máahn-máahn sihk-yùhn faahn jì-hauh jauh yāt-go-yàhn <u>lèih-hòi</u> ūk-kéi heui fà-yún saan-bouh nē? Daih-yāt chi gin-dóu néih, ngóh juhng yíh-wàih néih m̀h-gin-jó yéh, <u>chēut-làih wán</u>, daahn-haih néih m̀h wúih máahn-máahn dōu m̀h-gin-jó yéh ga.
Cheung	Àai! Ngóh làih saan-bouh haih yáuh go muhk-dīk ge.
Wong	Gó go muhk-dīk haih m̀h haih bei-maht ga? Hó m̀h hó-yíh góng béi ngóh tèng a?
Cheung	M̀h haih bei-maht, ngóh jí-haih séung lèih-hòi ūk-kéi yāt-jahn jē.
Wong	Jàn kèih-gwaai lak! Néih yāt-heung dōu jùng-yi làuh hái ūk-kéi, hóu síu chēut-gāai ge bo!
Cheung	Lóuh-saht góng néih tèng lā, jeui-gahn ngóh go néui chàam-gà-jó chò-kāp gong-kàhm fan-lihn-bāan; ngóh taai-táai yauh chàam-gà-jó gò-kehk fan-lihn-bāan. Máahn-faahn jì-hauh jauh haih kéuih-deih lihn-jaahp sìh-gaan lak. Néih wah ngóh dím hó-yíh juhng làuh hái ūk-kéi nē?
王	老張，我知道你嘅嗜好係捉棋，有時都見你影相同畫畫，但係冇乜見你跳舞或者散步嘅嘞！
張	係呀！尤其係呢幾個月我畫咗好多幅畫。但係運動呢，連一次都冇做過。我最憎運動嘅嘞。
王	點解最近我見你晚晚食完飯之後就一個人離開屋企去花園散步呢？第一次見倒你，我重以為你唔見咗嘢出嚟搵，但係你唔會晚晚都唔見咗嘢㗎。
張	唉！我嚟散步係有個目的嘅。
王	嗰個目的係唔係秘密㗎？可唔可以講俾我聽呀？
張	唔係秘密，我只係想離開屋企一陣啫。
王	真奇怪嘞！你一向都中意留喺屋企，好少出街嘅嘞！
張	老實講你聽喇，最近我個女參加咗初級鋼琴訓練班；我太太又參加咗歌劇訓練班。晚飯之後就係佢哋練習時間嘞。你話我點可以重留喺屋企呢？

234

2 Silly questions. In the dialogue there are three underlined words and phrases. Can you answer these questions about them?

    a jàng: Can you find a substitute wording which will give the same idea?

    b lèih-hòi: This means *leave*. So does **ga-kèih**, but can you substitute it here and still make sense?

    c chēut-làih wán and **chēut-làih wáan** sound almost the same but what do they each mean?

Language discovery

24.1 WHEN A QUESTION WORD IS NOT A QUESTION WORD

Móuh māt or **móuh māt-yéh** is an idiomatic way of saying *not much*. Clearly **māt-yéh** in this case no longer acts as a question word, as you can tell from Mr Wong's first speech in the dialogue (**móuh māt gin néih tiu-móuh** *I don't see you dancing much*). Similarly you could say:

Ngóh móuh māt(-yéh) chín.	*I haven't got much money.*
Kéuih-deih móuh māt heui tái-hei.	*They don't go to the cinema much.*

Another non-questioning use of question words teams them up with our old friend the adverb **dōu** to make '*-ever*' words like *whatever* and *whoever*. All the question words can perform the same trick, so **māt-yéh** is *whatever*, **bīn-go** is *whoever*, **bīn-douh** is *wherever*, **géi-dō** is *however much*, **géi-sí** is *whenever*, and **dím-yéung** is *however* – and they are all accompanied by **dōu**:

Néih heui bīn-douh a?	*Where are you going?*
Ngóh bīn-douh dōu m̀h heui.	*I'm not going anywhere.* ('I'm not going to any wherevers')
Néih géi-sí heui Yìng-gwok a?	*When are you going to Britain?*
Ngóh géi-sí dōu m̀h heui.	*I'm not going anytime.*

YOUR TURN Compose appropriate replies in Cantonese, using *-ever* words.

    a Which one of those books do you want to read? (none of them)

    b What kind of work do you like doing? (none)

    c How many guests are you inviting to dinner this evening? (none whatsoever)

24.2 THESE LAST FEW ...

In Unit 19 you met **jeui-gahn** *recently, recent*. **Jeui-gahn-géi-nìhn** means *in the last few years*, and another way of saying the same thing is **nī-géi-nìhn**. You can extend either of the patterns to days, weeks and months too:

jeui-gahn-géi-yaht	= **nī-géi-yaht**	*these last few days*
jeui-gahn-géi-go-láih-baai	= **nī-géi-go-láih-baai**	*these last few weeks*
jeui-gahn-géi-go-yuht	= **nī-géi-go-yuht**	*these last few months*

And **géi** is not essential to these patterns: you can be more specific if you wish, although normally only small numbers are involved:

jeui-gahn léuhng-sàam yaht	= **nī léuhng-sàam yaht**	*these last two or three days*
jeui-gahn sei-ńgh nìhn	= **nī sei-ńgh nìhn**	*these last four or five years*

Going back to *recently*, there is another word, **nī-páai** 呢排, which is perhaps a little more colloquial than **jeui-gahn**, but **nī-páai** is only used as an adverb (*recently*) and won't translate *recent* or fit into the other patterns we have just met in this section. There is no problem, though, with saying:

Nī-páai kéuih hóu móuh sàm-gèi la.   *He's been in very low spirits recently.*

24.3 M̀H-GIN-JÓ *LOST*

M̀h-gin-jó literally means 'became unseen, not seen any more' and it is a useful way of saying that you have *lost* or *mislaid* something:

Ngóh m̀h-gin-jó ngóh dī chín; m̀h-jì haih m̀h haih béi yàhn tàu-jó nē?
I can't find my money; I wonder if it's been stolen?

Kéuih m̀h-gin-jó yàhn lak.
She went missing.

24.4 FOR A MOMENT

Yāt-jahn (or its longer form **yāt-jahn-gāan**) means *a moment of time*. It can be used as either a specific time or a duration of time and its position can therefore be either in front of or after the verb in a sentence:

Ngóh yāt-jahn lohk-làih lā!   *I'll be down in a moment!*

Hóu lā! Daahn-haih ngóh jí hó-yíh   *OK, but I can only come down for a moment!*
lohk-làih yāt-jahn jē!

24.5 IN YOUR OPINION

Just in case you have not picked it up without being told, **néih-wah** or **néih-tái** (*you say* or *you see*) are both used in the sense *in your opinion*.

 How would you say *in my opinion*?

Vocabulary builder 2

Read the new vocabulary and practise saying it out loud.

MORE PASTIMES

的士高	dīk-sih-gōu	*discotheque*
種花	jung-fā	*to grow flowers*
卡啦OK	kā-lāai-ōu-kēi	*karaoke*
遊戲	yàuh-hei	*games*
養	yéuhng	*to rear, to keep* (pets)

TECHNOLOGY

科技	fō-geih	*science and technology*
進步	jeun-bouh	*progress*
智能電話	ji-nàhng dihn-wá	*smartphone* (cl: **ga**)
專家	jyūn-gā	*expert, specialist*
手提電腦	sáu-tàih dihn-nóuh	*laptop / notebook computer* (cl: **ga**)

VERBS

改變	gói-bin	*to change, alter*
勸	hyun	*to advise, urge, plead with*
習慣	jaahp-gwaan	*to be accustomed to, get used to; habit*
溝通	kàu-tùng	*to communicate*
缺乏	kyut-faht	*to lack, be short of*
受	sauh	*to suffer*
提醒	tàih-séng	*to remind, alert*
養成	yéuhng-sìhng	*to inculcate, form, breed*
依賴	yí-laaih	*to rely on*
預知	yuh-jì	*to predict*

BASICS

別人	biht-yàhn	*other people*
孤獨	gù-duhk	*solitary, lone*
劫	guih	*tired, weary*
空氣	hùng-hei	*air, fresh air*
雀	jeuk	*bird* (cl: **jek 隻**)
將來	jèung-lòih	*future, in future*
自己	jih-géi	*self, oneself*
貓	māau	*cat* (cl: **jek 隻**)
唔係 … 就係 …	m̀h haih … jauh haih …	*it's either this or that, if it's not this it's that*
悶	muhn	*bored*
危險	ngàih-hím	*dangerous; danger*
生活方式	sàng-wuht fòng-sīk	*lifestyle*
性格	sing-gaak	*temperament, disposition*
同	tùhng	*same, alike*
一 … 就 …	yāt … jauh …	*as soon as … then …*

Dialogue 2

 24.02 *Two parents discuss the changing leisure pursuits of the young.*

1 Can you find an example of an 'indirect command' in this dialogue?

Wong	Ngóh gok-dāk yìh-gā dī hauh-sāang-jái tùhng ngóh-deih hauh-sāang ge sìh-hauh hóu m̀h tùhng.
Lee	Néih góng bīn fòng-mihn m̀h tùhng nē?
Wong	Ngóh góng ge haih sih-hou fòng-mihn. Ngóh-deih hauh-sāang ge sìh-hauh hóu jùng-yi jung-fā, yéuhng-jeuk, yéuhng-māau, hàahng-sàan kāp hùng-hei, dáng-dáng. Daahn-haih yìh-gā dī hauh-sāang-jái jauh jùng-yi heui dīk-sih-gōu, kā-lāai-ōu-kēi, wáan dihn-nóuh yàuh-hei, tùhng-màaih séuhng-móhng, nī dī gám-yéung ge yéh.
Lee	Haih a, ngóh go jái hó-yíh yāt-go-yàhn deui-jyuh ga dihn-nóuh yàuh-hei-gèi wáan yāt máahn dōu m̀h gok-dāk guih, m̀h gok-dāk muhn. Juhng yáuh, kéuih sèhng-yaht sàu-faat dyún-seun tìm. M̀h haih gáau ji-nàhng dihn-wá jauh haih wáan sáu-tàih dihn-nóuh. Néih-wah, kéuih deui nī fòng-mihn géi yáuh hing-cheui nē.
Wong	Léih Táai, néih yiu hyun néih go jái m̀h-hóu wáan gam dò dihn-nóuh yàuh-hei lak. Jyūn-gā wah yùh-gwó yāt-go-yàhn jaahp-gwaan jih-géi tùhng jih-géi wáan yàuh-hei, jauh wúih kyut-faht tùhng biht-yàhn kàu-tùng, jihm-jím jauh wúih yéuhng-sìhng gù-duhk ge sing-gaak, gám-yéung haih hóu ngàih-hím ge bo!
Lee	Ngóh dōu gok-dāk fō-hohk yuht jeun-bouh, ngóh-deih jauh yuht yí-laaih fō-geih. Yìh-gā lìhn ngóh-deih ge sih-hou tùhng sàng-wuht fòng-sīk dōu sauh-dóu fō-geih ge yíng-héung maahn-máan gói-bin, yìh-ché yuht bin yuht faai, yuht gói yuht dò, jèung-lòih haih dím-yéung móuh yàhn hó-yíh yuh-jì. Tùhng néih kìng-gái jàn-haih hóu lak, dò-jeh néih tàih-séng ngóh, ngóh yāt fàan-dou ūk-kéi jauh yiu giu ngóh go jái m̀h-hóu joi wáan dihn-nóuh yàuh-hei lak. Ngóh yìh-gā yiu jáu la, joi-gin.
王	我覺得而家啲後生仔同我哋後生嘅時候好唔同。
李	你講邊方面唔同呢?
王	我講嘅係嗜好方面。我哋後生嘅時候好中意種花,養雀,養貓,行山吸空氣,等等。但係而家啲後生仔就中意去的士高,卡啦OK,玩電腦遊戲,同埋上網,呢啲噉樣嘅嘢。
李	係呀,我個仔可以一個人對住喫電腦遊戲機玩一晚都唔覺得瘤,唔覺得悶。重有,佢成日收發短訊添。唔係搞智能電話就係玩手提電腦。 你話,佢對呢方面幾有興趣呢。
王	李太,你要勸你個仔唔好玩咁多電腦遊戲嘞。專家話如果一個人習慣自已同自已玩遊戲就會缺乏同別人溝通,漸漸就會養成孤獨嘅性格,噉樣係好危險嘅㗎!
李	我都覺得科學越進步,我哋就越依賴科技。而家連我哋嘅嗜好同生活方式都受倒科技嘅影響慢慢改變,而且越變越快,越改越多。將來係點樣冇人可以預知。同你傾偈真係好嘞,多謝你提醒我,我一返到屋企就要叫我個仔唔好再玩電腦遊戲嘞。我而家要走喇,再見。

2 *Either one or the other. If it isn't this then it must be that*: you can hardly have missed the new pattern in the dialogue, it's so neat and intuitive. You could perhaps have made it up for yourself from what you know already. Use the pattern to translate:

a I saw one of your sons last week: it was either William or his younger brother.

b My father's busy all day, if he's not playing football he's reading a book.

c I'm not clear: she's either going to Beijing on Monday or to Brazil on Wednesday.

Language discovery

24.6 GÈI *MACHINE*

The full word for a *machine* or *machinery* is **gèi-hei** 機器, but there are plenty of instances where **gèi** 機 on its own also means *machine*, usually when it is tacked onto other words:

傳真機	**chyùhn-jàn-gèi**	*fax machine*	**chyùhn-jàn**	*fax*
打火機	**dá-fó-gèi**	*cigarette lighter*	**dá-fó**	*to strike fire*
打字機	**dá-jih-gèi**	*typewriter*	**dá-jih**	*to type*
電視機	**dihn-sih-gèi**	*television set*	**dihn-sih**	*television*
飛機	**fèi-gèi**	*aircraft*	**fèi**	*to fly*
收音機	**sàu-yàm-gèi**	*radio*	**sàu-yàm**	*to receive sound*
遊戲機	**yàuh-hei-gèi**	*games console*	**yàuh-hei**	*games*

24.7 DŌU DOES IT AGAIN!

In Unit 22 you saw how **dōu** could still convey the idea of *even* without the assistance of **lìhn**. In the dialogue there is another rather trickier example: **Ngóh go jái … wáan yāt máahn dōu m̀h gok-dāk guih** *My son can play the whole evening and still not feel tired.* You may find it easier to see how **dōu** achieves its effect if you twist the English slightly – 'my son even though he plays the whole evening does not feel tired'.

24.8 SELF

Jih-géi means *self* and is a very useful word for giving stress to individuality, usually coming after a person's name or a personal pronoun:

Wòhng Sìn-sàang jih-géi m̀h sīk góng Yìng-màhn.	*Mr Wong himself cannot speak English.*
Néih jih-géi séung m̀h séung heui a?	*Do you yourself want to go?*

Jih-géi yāt-go-yàhn means *all by oneself, alone*:

Kéuih jih-géi yāt-go-yàhn chóh hái-douh.	*He sat there all alone.*

> **LANGUAGE TIP**
>
> When you are eating a Chinese meal with chopsticks from communal bowls in the middle of the table, you will find that the host or other people will often select tasty morsels and put them in your personal bowl. Don't find this odd; it is meant as a great politeness. Restaurants provide extra pairs of chopsticks (known as **gùng-faai** 公筷 *communal chopsticks*) so that the guest's food is not touched by ones which have been near the host's mouth. However, it can be embarrassing to be constantly waited on in this way and it is polite to try to stop people doing it. Try saying **m̀h-sái gam haak-hei** *no need to be so polite* and following it with **ngóh jih-géi làih** *I'll come at it myself*.

24.9 AS SOON AS

One of the beauties of Cantonese grammar is that patterns of some complexity are often made up from very simple words. **Yāt** means *one* and **jauh** means *then*: you met them both long ago, but put them together in a grammar pattern and they produce *as soon as …* *then …*:

Kéuih yāt chóh chē jauh tàuh-wàhn.	*He gets dizzy as soon as he gets in a car.*
Ngóh yāt gin-dóu kéuih, kéuih jauh jáu-jó lak.	*As soon as I saw him he ran away.*

Wòhng Taai-táai yāt chēut-jó gaai, jauh m̀h gei-dāk-jó yiu máaih māt-yéh sung.
No sooner had Mrs Wong got outside than she forgot what food she had to buy.

> **LANGUAGE TIP**
> Note that in this pattern both **yāt** and **jauh** act as adverbs and each comes before a different verb.

24.10 THE INTERNET

In Unit 22 you met **séuhng-móhng** *to surf the net, go online*. Reverse the two syllables to **móhng-seuhng** 網上 (note the tone change) and you have *online*. *Online shopping* is **móhng-seuhng kau-maht** 網上購物, usually abbreviated to **móhng-kau**. You can *book a table online* **séuhng-móhng dehng-tói** 上網定枱 for a restaurant or *book a room online* **séuhng-móhng dehng-fóng** 上網定房 at a hotel. And then of course there are the *social media* **séh-gàau móhng-jaahm** 社交網站 (lit. 'social interaction websites'), perhaps the best known of which is *Facebook* **Líhm-syù** 臉書.

Practice

1 **Let's start with a couple of Chinese riddles.**

   a Can you guess (in English) what this represents?

   Yáuh yāt yeuhng yéh móuh chúhng-leuhng ge, daahn-haih sahp go yàhn dōu m̀h hó-yíh tòih-héi kéuih. Yùh-gwó yeh-máahn yāt làih-dou, kéuih jauh m̀h-gin-jó. Néih gú haih māt-yéh nē?

   b And what is the answer to this one (in Cantonese)?

   Síu-Léih deui Síu-Wóng wah: 'Ngóh ge sàang-yaht hái kàhm-yaht ge kàhm-yaht ge tìng-yaht.' Síu-Wóng wah: 'Móuh cho, néih ge sàang-yaht haih tìng-yaht ge chìhn-yaht. Gùng-héi! Gùng-héi!' Síu-Léih haih géi-sí sàang-yaht a?

2 **Make the pairs of sentences into one by incorporating the bracketed idea. The first answer would be: Wòhng Síu-jé sihk jóu-chāan jì-chìhn, jaahp-gwaan heui saan-bouh sìn.**

   a Wòhng Síu-jé sihk jóu-chāan. Kéuih jaahp-gwaan saan-bouh. (*before*)
   b Ngóh hái ūk-kéi. Ngóh m̀h daai móu. (*when*)
   c Nàahm-yán luhk-sahp-ńgh seui. Kéuih-deih hó-yíh ló teui-yàu-gām. (*not until*)
   d Ngóh gàm-jiu-jóu tái bou-jí. Ngóh jì-dou ngóh-deih gūng-sī ge chìhng-fong hóu ngàih-hím. (*as soon as*)
   e Chàhn Sìn-sàang yám bē-jáu. Kéuih jùng-yi yám. (*the more … the more*)

3 Chéng néih yuhng Gwóng-dùng-wá góng nī sei fūk wá léuih-bihn faat-sàng dī māt-yéh sih a.

4 **A quick test of your place words. Supply the missing words as rapidly as you can.**
   a Ngóh hái néih hauh-bihn, gám néih hái ngóh _____.
   b Seuhng-hói hái Bāk-gìng nàahm-bihn, gám Bāk-gìng hái Seuhng-hói _____.
   c Néih hái gó-douh, gám ngóh hái _____.
   d Wòhng Sàang hái Wòhng Táai jó-sáu-bihn, gám Wòhng Táai hái Wòhng Sàang
   _____.
   e Bouh syù hái baahk-jí léuih-bihn, gám baahk-jí hái syù _____.

❓ Test yourself

You are on Hong Kong Island and you want to get to the airport. You have managed to get through on the phone to the airport enquiry office, but the person answering can only speak Cantonese. You have a plane to catch, so you had better produce your best accent and keenest understanding to ask the following.
a Is there a bus which goes to the airport?
b How much is the fare from City Hall?
c How long will it take to get to the airport?
d Is there a toilet on the bus?
e What time does flight 251 take off?
f When does flight 251 get in to London?

房屋 Fòhng-ūk
Housing

In this unit you will learn about:

▸ *containers.*
▸ *deep and shallow.*
▸ *distance from.*
▸ *final words on dōu.*
▸ *influence of English.*

▸ *not any more.*
▸ *rooms.*
▸ *tea.*
▸ *verb + object.*
▸ *workers.*

CEFR: *(B2) Can explain a viewpoint on a topical issue giving the advantages and disadvantages of various options.*

 ## Housing in Hong Kong

In crowded Hong Kong, space is at a premium and housing is mostly cramped and always very expensive. It is a major topic of conversation, and you will soon get used to hearing about the size of people's flats and what rooms they have. The words you need are:

沖涼房	**chùng-lèuhng-fóng**	*bathroom*	厨房	**chyùh-fóng**	*kitchen*
飯廳	**faahn-tēng**	*dining room*	睡房	**seuih-fóng**	*bedroom*
客廳	**haak-tēng**	*living room, lounge*	露台	**louh-tòih**	*balcony*

The balcony of course is a luxury which few can enjoy, and by no means all flats have both a dining and a living room, but a considerable number still come with a *servant's room* **gùng-yàhn-fóng** 工人房. For *bedroom* **seuih-fóng** is an alternative to **fan-fóng**, which you met in Unit 14.

Hong Kong is made up of three parts: Hong Kong Island, Kowloon, and the largest in size – *the New Territories* (**Sàn-gaai** 新界). Housing is cheapest in the New Territories, and most expensive on Hong Kong Island's famous *Peak* (**Sàan-déng** 山頂).

How would you say *Flats on the Peak are much more expensive than in the New Territories*?

Vocabulary builder 1

 Read the new vocabulary and practise saying it out loud.

FITTINGS

窗簾(布)	chēung-lím(-bou)	*curtains* (cl: **fūk** 幅)
地氈	deih-jīn	*carpet, rug* (cl: **faai** 塊)

KITCHEN

煮食爐	jyú-sihk-lòuh	*cooking stove* (cl: **ga**)
微波爐	mèih-bō-lòuh	*microwave oven* (cl: **ga**)
洗碗機	sái-wún-gèi	*dishwasher* (cl: **ga**)
洗衣機	sái-yì-gèi	*washing machine* (cl: **ga**)
碗	wún	*bowl* (cl: **jek** 隻)
碗櫃	wún-gwaih	*cupboard, dresser*

VERBS

堅持	gìn-chìh	*to insist, insist on*
斟	jàm	*to pour into a cup, glass or bowl*
逛	kwaang	*to cruise*
逛公司	kwaang gūng-sī	*to go window shopping*
決定	kyut-dihng	*to decide*
留返	làuh-fàan	*to leave behind*
陪	pùih	*to accompany, keep company with*
提	tàih	*to mention, bring up*

BASICS

後來	hauh-lòih	*later, afterwards*
理由	léih-yàuh	*reason*
深	sàm	*deep*
運費	wahn-fai	*transportation costs*

Dialogue 1

25.01 *Mr Wong's friend Mr Cheung lives alone in a large flat.*

1 Look out for a nice example of a 'change of state' neatly expressed.

Cheung	Lóuh-Wóng, fùn-yìhng néih làih taam ngóh. Chéng yahp-làih chóh lā!
Wong	Yí! Dím-gáai m̀h gin Jèung Táai tùhng néih-deih dī jái-néui ga?
Cheung	Óh, kéuih-deih bun nìhn jī-chìhn yíh-gìng yìh-jó màhn heui Yìng-gwok la! Yìh-gā jí-yáuh ngóh yāt-go-yàhn jyuh hái Hèung-góng jī-máh.
Wong	Wà, néih gàan ūk jàn-haih daaih lak. Ngóh jeui jùng-yi néih ge louh-tòih. Nī gàan ūk yáuh géi-dō gàan fóng a?
Cheung	Yáuh sàam gàan seuih-fóng, léuhng go chi-só tùhng sái-sàn-fóng, yāt gàan haak-tēng, yāt gàan faahn-tēng, tùhng-māaih yāt go chyùh-fóng.
Wong	Néih-deih ge chyùh-fóng chit-beih dōu hóu chàih-chyùhn bo ... yáuh sái-yì-gèi, sái-wún-gèi, jyú-sihk-lòuh, wún-gwaih, juhng yáuh mèih-bō-lòuh tìm.
Cheung	Nī dī yéh ngóh tùhng taai-táai dōu dá-syun wahn-heui Yìng-gwok ge, daahn-haih hauh-lòih jì-dou wahn-fai taai gwai lak, yìh-ché, yùh-gwó hái Yìng-gwok máaih sàn ge, ga-chìhn dōu m̀h syun taai gwai, só-yíh ngóh-deih jauh kyut-dihng m̀h wahn lak, làuh hái Hèung-góng jih-géi yuhng.
Wong	Dī chēung-lím-bou tùhng deih-jīn dōu juhng haih hóu sàn bo! Dím-gáai m̀h wahn-heui Yìng-gwok nē?
Cheung	Aài! M̀h-hóu tàih deih-jīn tùhng chēung-lím-bou lak. Ngóh gó-jahn-sìh dōu tùhng néih yāt-yeuhng, wah yiu wahn-heui Yìng-gwok, daahn-haih ngóh taai-táai gìn-chìh yiu làuh-fàan nī dī yéh hái Hèung-góng. Kéuih ge léih-yàuh jauh haih dī chēung-lím-bou ge ngàahn-sīk taai sàm lak, m̀h hóu-tái, dī deih-jīn ge fā-yéung kéuih yauh m̀h jùng-yi.
Wong	Ngóh làih-jó gam noih, néih dōu móuh jàm chàh béi ngóh yám. Ngóh gú hái nī bun nìhn néih yāt-go-yàhn jyuh yāt-dihng hóu gù-duhk lak. Lóuh-Jèung, dáng ngóh gàm-yaht pùih néih yāt-chàih chēut-gāai heui yám-chàh kwaang-gūng-sī lā.

張	老王，歡迎你嚟探我。請入嚟坐啦！
王	咦！點解唔見張太同你哋啲仔女㗎？
張	哦！佢哋半年之前已經移咗民去英國喇！而家只有我一個人住喺香港之嘛。
王	嘩，你間屋真係大嘞。我最中意你嘅露台。呢間屋有幾多間房呀？
張	有三間睡房，兩個廁所同洗身房，一間客廳一間飯廳，同埋一個廚房。
王	你哋嘅廚房設備都好齊全嘛 ⋯ 有洗衣機，洗碗機，煮食爐，碗櫃，重有微波爐添。
張	呢啲嘢我同太太都打算運去英國嘅，但係後來知道運費太貴嘞，而且，如果喺英國買新嘅，價錢都唔算太貴，所以我哋就決定唔運嘞，留喺香港自己用。
王	啲窗簾布同地氈都重係好新嘛！點解唔運去英國呢？
張	唉！唔好提地氈同窗簾布嘞。我嗰陣時都同你一樣，話要運去英國，但係我太太堅持要留返呢啲嘢喺香港。佢嘅理由就係啲窗簾布嘅顏色太深嘞，唔好睇，啲地氈嘅花樣佢又唔中意。
王	我嚟咗咁耐，你都冇斟茶俾我飲。我估喺呢半年你一個人住一定好孤獨嘞，老張，等我今日陪你一齊出街去飲茶逛公司啦。

2 Answer in Cantonese.

   a Jèung Sàang yìh-gā tùhng bīn-go jyuh a?

   b Wòhng Sàang wah chyùh-fóng chit-beih hóu chàih-chyùhn. Gám, syut-gwaih nē?

   c Jèung Táai géi-dō go yuht chìhn yìh-jó màhn heui Yìng-gwok a?

Language discovery

25.1 VERB + OBJECT VERBS

You may have found Mr Cheung's remark **yíh-gìng yìh-jó màhn heui Yìng-gwok la** grammatically strange because **-jó** has split **yìh** and **màhn**. The reason is quite simple: the verb **yìh-màhn** *to migrate* is composed of **yìh** *to move* and **màhn** *people*, so that it is actually a verb + object verb and, of course, **-jó** is an ending which must be attached to a verb, not to an object.

25.2 ANOTHER CLASSIFIER ODDITY

Mr Cheung uses the classifier **gàan** for **seuih-fóng**, **haak-tēng** and **faahn-tēng**, but uses **go** for **chi-só** and **chyùh-fóng**. Somehow toilets and kitchens do not seem to qualify as proper rooms (rooms in which people socialize, perhaps), so they are often not given **gàan** status.

> **BEDROOMS**
> For *bedroom* you may hear either **fan-fóng** or the slightly more formal **seuih-fóng**, both terms meaning 'sleep room', but it has become a convention in Hong Kong that people talk of a flat as having so many **fóng**, when they actually mean *bedrooms*. So a flat with **léuhng gàan fóng** usually means a *two-bedroom flat*, not one with only two rooms. Leaving off the **fan-** or the **seuih-** sounds rather coy, as though it were slightly improper to mention such a thing as sleep in polite society. So be prepared to be asked **Néih chàhng láu yáuh géi-dō gàan fóng a?**

25.3 BOWLS AND OTHER CONTAINERS

Wún *bowl* is a very handy word, because bowls are used so much at the Chinese table.

 Can you guess what faahn-wún, tòng-wún and chàh-wún are? And how about daaih-wún and sai-wún?

But **wún** is even more useful because it is also a classifier, as in **yāt wún tòng** *a bowl of soup* and **léuhng wún baahk-faahn** *two bowls of boiled rice* (**baahk-faahn** 白飯 literally means 'white rice', hence *steamed* or *boiled rice* as opposed to **cháau-faahn** 炒飯 *fried rice*). You can see how the two functions of **wún** operate in the following comparison:

sàam wún faahn	*three bowls of rice*
sàam jek faahn-wún	*three rice bowls* (the classifier for a bowl can be either **jek** or **go**)

Other container words or measure words work the same way. Most common perhaps is **bùi** *cup, glass, mug*:

léuhng jek chàh-būi	*two teacups* (note the tone change on **bùi**)
léuhng bùi chàh	*two cups of tea*

25.4 NOT ANY MORE

In Unit 3 you were given an example of the use of **lak** with **m̀h**. In the previous dialogue Mr Cheung says **ngóh-deih kyut-dihng m̀h wahn lak** *we decided not to transport them after all*, that is, they had at first decided otherwise but not any more. **M̀h** + **lak** is a very convenient way of conveying the notion *not any more*.

YOUR TURN Complete the sentences using the *not any more* pattern:

a Kàhm-yaht kéuih wah wúih làih taam ngóh, daahn-haih (*now she's not coming*).

b Tàuh-sìn néih hóu jihng gám chóh hái-douh tái bou-jí, (*why have you stopped*)?

c Gàm-yaht lohk daaih yúh a. Tìn-màhn-tòih ge jīk-yùhn yíh-wàih (*it won't rain any more after Thursday*).

25.5 *DEEP* AND *SHALLOW*: *DARK* AND *LIGHT*

Sàm literally means *deep* (**Néih yiu síu-sàm bo! Gó-douh di séui hóu sàm!** *You should be careful, the water is very deep there!*) and the opposite word *shallow* is **chín** 淺. Both words are capable of being extended in use, so that you can describe someone's thought as **sàm**, for example. With colours, **sàm** means *dark* or *deep* and **chín** means *light*, so **sàm-hùhng-sīk** is *crimson* or *dark red* and **chín-làahm-sīk** is the colour sported by **Gim-kìuh Daaih-hohk** on boat-race day.

25.6 MORE THAN A CUP OF TEA

As you know, Cantonese people never say 'let's go and have some **dím-sām**', they always say 'let's go and drink tea' (**yám-chàh**). In the teahouse or restaurant you order your preferred tea and you then sit back and wait till a tray or trolley of steaming hot **dím-sām** comes round. Some favourite teas are:

香片茶	**hèung-pín-chàh**	*jasmine tea*
龍井茶	**lùhng-jéng-chàh**	*dragon well tea*
普洱茶	**póu-néi-chàh**	*pu-er tea*
水仙茶	**séui-sīn-chàh**	*narcissus tea*
鐵觀音茶	**tit-Gwùn-yàm-chàh**	*iron Guan-Yin tea*

Vocabulary builder 2

 Read the new vocabulary and practise saying it out loud.

MORE FITTINGS

車位	chē-wái	*parking space*
地面	deih-mín	*floor*
主人房	jyú-yàhn-fóng	*master bedroom* (cl: **gàan**)
樓底	làuh-dái	*ceiling*
樓梯	làuh-tài	*staircase* (cl: **douh**)
軨	līp	*lift, elevator* (cl: **ga**)
煤氣	mùih-hei	*town gas*
鎖	só	*lock; to lock*
套房	tou-fóng	*en suite*
熱水爐	yiht-séui-lòuh	*boiler, water heater* (cl: **ga**)

HOUSEKEEPING

保安	bóu-ōn	*security; to keep secure*
清潔	chìng-git	*cleanliness; cleaning*
打掃	dá-sou	*to sweep*
檢查	gím-chàh	*to check, inspect*
工人	gùng-yàhn	*worker, servant*
管理	gwún-léih	*management; to manage*
安全	òn-chyùhn	*safe; safety*
屋價	ūk-ga	*house price*
人員	yàhn-yùhn	*personnel, staff*

VERBS

包括	bàau-kwut	*to include*
發夢	faat-muhng	*to dream*
發噩夢	faat-ok-muhng	*to have a nightmare*
瞓唔著(覺)	fan-m̀h-jeuhk(-gaau)	*unable to get to sleep*
離	lèih	*to be distant from*
換	wuhn	*to change, exchange*

BASICS

呎	chek	*foot* (length)
電子	dihn-jí	*electronic*
度	douh	cl: *for doors, stairways*
光(猛)	gwòng(-máahng)	*bright*
座	joh	cl: *for massive things (large buildings, mountains, etc.)*
小時	síu-sìh	*hour*
一係 … 一係	yāt-haih … yāt-haih	*either … or …*

DIALOGUE 2

 25.02 *Mr Wong looks at a house purchase.*

1 The salesman in his second speech says Sìn-sàang, dou la. What does he mean?

Salesman	Sìn-sàang, néih tái nī joh láu ge gwún-léih m̀h cho bo! Yah-sei síu-sìh dōu yáuh bóu-ōn fuhk-mouh, múih-yaht bóu-ōn yàhn-yùhn wúih làih léuhng chi, yáuh chìhng-git gùng-yàhn dá-sou jáu-lóng tùhng làuh-tài, múih go yuht dōu yáuh yàhn gím-chàh nī sàam ga līp … hóu òn-chyùhn ga!
Mr Wong	Haih, dōu m̀h-cho. Yáuh móuh chē-wái a?
Salesman	Yáuh yāt go chē-wái bàau-kwut hái ūk-ga léuih-bihn. Sìn-sàang, dou la, chéng chēut līp lā. Néih tái nī douh daaih-mùhn yáuh Faat-gwok dihn-jí-só, waaih-yàhn hóu nàahn hòi ga.
Mr Wong	M̀h-cho, m̀h-cho. Ngóh-deih yahp ūk tái-háh lō.
Salesman	Nàh, néih tái, haak-tēng tùhng faahn-tēng yauh daaih yauh gwòng-máahng, go louh-tòih deui-jyuh go hói, jàn syù-fuhk lak.
Mr Wong	M̀h-cho. Hó-sīk làuh-dái taai ngái jēk.
Salesman	Sìn-sàang, m̀h syun taai ngái la, lèih deih-mín dōu yáuh gáu chek ge la. Chéng gwo-làih nī-douh tái-háh dī fòhng-gāan lā.
Mr Wong	Yí, dím-gáai móuh tou-fóng chi-só tùhng chùng-lèuhng-fóng gé?
Salesman	Yáuh ak, jyú-yàhn-fóng jauh yáuh lā. Nàh, chéng tái-háh nī gàan lā.
Mr Wong	Wàh, juhng haih yuhng mùih-hei yiht-séui-lòuh gam lohk-hauh gé.
Salesman	Sìn-sàang, yùh-gwó néih m̀h jùng-yi, ngóh hó-yíh wuhn yāt go dihn-jí yiht-séui-lòuh béi néih. Néih tái, jyú-yàhn-fóng gam syù-fuhk, deih-fòng gam jihng, yāt-dī dōu m̀h chòuh. Hái nī-douh fan-gaau yāt-dihng wúih faat hóu muhng ge.
Mr Wong	Ngóh wah m̀h haih lak. Ūk-ga gam gwai, yùh-gwó ngóh máaih-jó, yāt-haih ngóh wúih máahn-máahn dōu fan-m̀h-jeuhk, yāt-haih jauh wúih sèhng-máahn faat ok-muhng jauh-jàn.

推銷員	先生，你睇呢座樓嘅管理唔錯嗱！廿四小時都有保安服務，每日保安人員會嚟兩次，有清潔工人打掃走廊同樓梯，每個月都有人檢查呢三架軚 … 好安全㗎！
王生	係，都唔錯。有冇車位呀？
推銷員	有一個車位包括喺屋價裡便。先生，到喇，請出軚喇。你睇呢度大門有法國電子鎖，壞人好難開㗎。
王生	唔錯，唔錯。我哋入屋睇吓囉。
推銷員	噇，你睇，客廳同飯廳又大又光猛，個露台對住個海，真舒服嘞。
王生	唔錯。可惜樓底太矮啫。
推銷員	先生，唔算太矮喇，離地面都有九呎嘅喇。請過嚟呢度睇吓啲房間啦。
王生	咦，點解冇套房廁所同沖涼房嘅？
推銷員	有呢，主人房就有啦，噇，請睇吓呢間啦。
王生	嘩，重係用煤氣熱水爐咁落後嘅。
推銷員	先生，如果你唔中意，我可以換一個電子熱水爐俾你。你睇，主人房咁舒服，地方咁靜，一啲都唔嘈，喺呢度瞓覺一定會發好夢嘅。
王生	我話唔係嘅。屋價咁貴，如果我買咗，一係我會晚晚都瞓唔著，一係就會成晚發噩夢就真。

2 Ūk means *house*, but we have just met **ūk-ga** and **yahp ūk** with reference to a block of flats, so what does **ūk** mean here?

3 What does **waaih-yàhn** mean?

4 How does **fan-m̀h-jeuhk** work?

Language discovery

25.7 YAH-SEI SÍU-SÌH

Síu-sìh is an alternative word for **jūng-tàuh** *hour*, which you have met, and **yah-sei síu-sìh** is the regular way to say *24 hour* (as in *24-hour service*).

25.8 WORKERS

Gùng-yàhn means quite simply 'work person', but just like *worker* in English it implies that the person works for someone else, that he or she is not in charge. In Hong Kong it is the common word for a *house servant* and there is a general assumption that house servants are female, so that if you have a male house servant you would refer to him as a **nàahm-gùng-yàhn** (compare this with the police situation described in Unit 17).

25.9 THE ENGLISH INVASION

Līp is the Cantonese attempt at the English word *lift*, the proper Cantonese word being tediously long (**sìng-gong-gèi** 升降機 'rising and falling machine'). You have met **bō** *ball*, **bā-sí** *bus*, **dīk-sí** *taxi*, **sà-léut** *salad* and **fēi** *fare*.

 Have a guess what these are: fēi-lám, sih-dō, bō-sí, baht-lāan-déi.

There are many many more, but it is possible that the trend is away from using such words and towards a more pure Cantonese vocabulary. Incidentally, *to ride in a lift* is **daap-līp** 搭軩.

25.10 DISTANT FROM

Lèih means *to be distant from, be separated from* and it is very handy for showing distance relationships. In the dialogue the salesman says that the ceiling **lèih deih-mín dōu yáuh gáu chek ge la** *is nine feet from the floor*. Similarly, you might say:
Lèuhn-dēun lèih Hèung-góng (yáuh) yāt-maahn-yāt-chìn gūng-léih.
London is 11,000 km from Hong Kong.

Yáuh *to have* is the verb which appears with numbers most often. Its use in this pattern is optional, although you are more likely to put it in if you are trying to stress that it is *all of 11,000 km*.

The word most often associated with **lèih** is **yúhn** *far, distant*:
Gwóng-jàu lèih Hèung-góng m̀h-haih-géi-yúhn. *Canton is not very far from Hong Kong.*
Néih ūk-kéi lèih Daaih-wuih-tòhng yúhn m̀h yúhn a? *Is your home far from City Hall?*

You will remember from Unit 20 that *to be close to* is a different pattern:
Bā-sí-jaahm hóu káhn Daaih-wuih-tòhng. *The bus stop is very close to City Hall.*

25.11 A LAST LOOK AT DŌU

In the dialogue the salesman is put in a difficult situation – he has to contradict Mr Wong who claims that the ceilings are too low when in fact they are the usual height. What he does is to slip in an otherwise unnecessary **dōu** and that somehow takes the confrontational edge off the contradiction. It is a standard politeness not to disagree too violently with someone else, but rather to show that while you cannot agree with them you do not wish to be offensive about it. In English you might say *that's not quite right* when what you mean is *that's wrong!* – in Cantonese you would add in a **dōu**. So **m̀h haih!** sounds abrupt and rude (*It's not!*), but **dōu m̀h haih** gives the same answer in an acceptably soft way (*I'm afraid that's not the case*).

25.12 BATHROOMS

In Unit 15 you learned that the word for *bathroom* is **sái-sàn-fóng** and now you have met another and newer word: **chùng-lèuhng-fóng**. It seems that this newer term is slowly driving out the older one, but you are bound to come across both of them. There is a difference in their origins: **sái-sàn** *to wash the body* is *to have an all over wash* or *to have a bath*, while **chùng-lèuhng** is really *to have a shower*, but the distinction is becoming blurred.

25.13 AND THAT'S FOR SURE!

Jauh-jàn means *then that would be true*, and it is used at the ends of statements to make them more emphatic. It coincides quite nicely with the English *and that's for sure! and that's the truth!*

 Practice

1 **Name the buildings or rooms which you associate with the following. The first answer would be: gíng-chaat-guhk.**
   a gíng-chaat
   b sái-yì-gèi
   c yeuhk-séui
   d gong-kàhm
   e bei-syù
   f jì-piu
   g lèuhn-pún
   h yàuh-gáan

2 **Make the sentences less aggressive by using dōu, other polite words such as m̀h-gòi, chéng and deui-m̀h-jyuh or perhaps by rephrasing in a softer way.**
   a Máih yūk!
   b Néih góng-cho.
   c Néih m̀h mìhng-baahk.
   d Ngóh m̀h tùhng-yi.
   e Gim-kìuh Daaih-hohk m̀h haih sai-gaai seuhng jeui yáuh-méng ge.

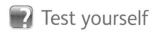
Here are the estate agent's details and plan of a flat which you want to buy. Using Cantonese, explain to your partner what it is like, giving the size of the rooms, the address and other details.

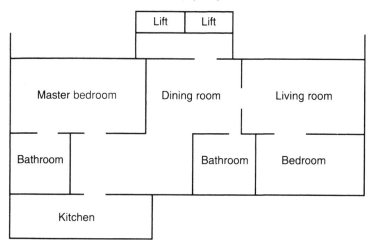

A TWO-BEDROOM FLAT
AT No. 27 CANTON ROAD, 8TH FLOOR
PARKING SPACE INCLUDED IN THE PRICE
ONLY HK$5,500,000!

26 溫習(四) Wàn-jaahp (sei)
Revision (4)

This is the shortest unit in the book – just a few exercises and a couple of passages of Cantonese for you to understand and to help you realize how far you have come in the space of 25 units. As usual you will find translations of these passages in the Key to the exercises, but probably you will not need them.

Of course you are not yet at native-speaker standard, but you should find that you have reached the stage where you know enough to be able to hold a conversation and, more importantly, to find out more for yourself by asking and by working out what some of the things you hear must mean on the basis of what you already know.

Persevere – having come this far you have shown that you are capable of learning Cantonese: it would be a great pity to stop just when you have reached 'critical velocity' for take-off into the cheerful exciting world of Cantonese conversation.

1 Make meaningful sentences with these pairs of words. (We have given simple models in the Key to the exercises at the back of the book.)
- **a** gwún-léih   gìng-léih
- **b** hòi-chí   hòi-chē
- **c** hói-sīn   sàn-sìn
- **d** yāt-làuh   jáu-làuh

2 Read the questions and pick your answers.
- **a** Bīn yeuhng yéh tùhng kèih-tà ge yéh m̀h tùhng júng-leuih a?
  (yàuh-gáan / yàuh-séui / yàuh-piu / yàuh-guhk / yàuh-fai)
- **b** Bīn yeuhng yéh hái sé-jih-làuh léuih-bihn móuh ge nē?
  (dihn-wá / dihn-nóuh / dihn-dāng / dihn-yíng / dihn-nyúhn-lòuh)
- **c** Bīn yeuhng deui ngóh-deih ge sàn-tái hóu nē?
  (dá-bō / dá-gāau / dá-gip / dá-jih / dá-dihn-wá)
- **d** Bīn yeuhng haih jeui gwai nē?
  (bou-jí / baahk-jí / seun-jí / Góng-jí / m̀h-jí)
- **e** Yùh-gwó néih séung heui ngoih-gwok, néih yāt-dihng yiu yáuh bīn yeuhng 'jing' a?
  (bóu-jing / sàn-fán-jing / gíng-yùhn-jing / chìm-jing)

3 Choose suitable final particles to complete the sentences.
- **a** Gàm-yaht ge tìn-hei m̀h hóu, ngóh-deih m̀h heui yàuh-séui _____.
- **b** Nī ga chē gam pèhng, néih dōu m̀h jùng-yi _____? Dím-gáai _____?
- **c** Kéuih m̀h jùng-yi ngóh heui _____? Gám, ngóh jauh m̀h heui _____.
- **d** Jà dihn-dāan-chē hóu ngàih-hím _____. Dím-gáai néih juhng béi néih ge jái jà _____?

4 Hái bīn-douh …

    a sihk-dāk-dóu hói-sīn a?

    b máaih-máh a?

    c daap-dóu bā-sí a?

    d sihk-dāk-dóu ngóh taai-táai jyú ge sung a?

    e gin-dāk-dóu Wòhng Bei-syù a?

5 What are the missing classifiers?

    a yāt _____ deih-jīn

    b yāt _____ wá

    c yāt _____ yiht-séui-lòuh

    d yāt _____ chāan-tói tùhng yí

    e yāt _____ jai-fuhk

    f yāt _____ daaih-mùhn

6 There are deliberate mistakes in each of the following. Can you spot them?

    a Léih Sàang hóu yáuh-chín, kéuih lìhn yāt mān dōu móuh.

    b Ngóh daaih-gwo ngóh màh-mā.

    c Gó chēut dihn-yíng ngóh m̀h tái-gwo.

    d Kéuih hàahng sahp-fàn faai.

    e Kéuih sèui-yìhn haih gìng-léih, yìh-ché sīk dá-jih.

Here are two passages for you to read. Try to answer the questions about them before checking the translations at the back of the book

Passage 1

LÙHNG

 26.01 Hóu noih hóu noih jì-chìhn hái Jùng-gwok yáuh yāt go hóu jùng-yi waahk-wá ge yàhn. Kéuih ge wá waahk-dāk hóu hóu, yàuh-kèih waahk Lùhng, jàn-haih hóu-chíh wúih yūk ge yāt-yeuhng. Yáuh yāt chi, yāt go daaih-gwùn jì-dou kéuih hóu sīk waahk Lùhng jauh hóu hòi-sām gám deui kéuih wah: 'Ngóh jih-géi dōu hóu jùng-yi Lùhng. Yùh-gwó néih háng bòng ngóh waahk yāt tìuh Lùhng, ngóh wúih béi hóu dò chín néih.'

Géi yaht jì-hauh, git-gwó tìuh Lùhng jauh waahk-hóu lak, yìh-ché waahk-dāk hóu hóu, juhng kāp-yáhn-jó hóu dò yàhn làih chàam-gwùn tìm. Daahn-haih jeui hó-sīk jauh haih tìuh Lùhng móuh ngáahn ge. Daaih-gwùn m̀h mìhng-baahk jauh mahn kéuih dím-gáai m̀h waahk ngáahn nē? Kéuih wah, yùh-gwó waahk-jó ngáahn jì-hauh, tìuh Lùhng jauh wúih fèi-jáu ge la!

Dòng-yín kéuih góng ge yéh móuh yàhn wúih sèung-seun lā. Daaih-gwùn hóu nàu, yāt-dihng yiu kéuih waahk-màaih deui ngáahn. Jàn kèih-gwaai, kéuih yāt waahk-yùhn deui ngáahn, tìuh Lùhng jauh yūk-jó géi háh, jàn-haih yàuh jèung jí douh tiu-jó chēut-làih, fèi-jáu-jó lak.

    a Nī go yàhn waahk ge lùhng wúih m̀h wúih hóu-chíh jàn lùhng a?

    b Kéuih dím-gáai m̀h waahk ngáahn nē?

    c 'yūk-jó géi háh' Yìng-màhn haih māt-yéh yi-si a?

Passage 2

PROGRESS

 26.02 Chāt-baat-sahp nìhn jì-chìhn, gó-jahn-sìh Seuhng-hói syun haih yāt go hóu sìn-jeun ge daaih sìhng-síh, daahn-haih Jùng-gwok kèih-tà hóu dò sìhng-síh tùhng-màaih hèung-há deih-fòng dōu juhng haih hóu lohk-hauh ge. Yāt yaht, yáuh yāt go hèung-há-yàhn, Léih Sìn-sàang, yáuh sih yiu heui Seuhng-hói taam kéuih ge pàhng-yáuh Wòhng Daaih Gwok. Wòhng Sìn-sàang jyuh hái yāt gàan yauh daaih yauh leng, chit-beih yauh chàih-chyùhn ge jáu-dim léuih-bihn.

Léih Sàang làih-dou jáu-dim, hái daaih-tòhng dáng Wòhng Sìn-sàang ge sìh-hauh, gin-dóu yāt go lóuh taai-táai maahn-máan gám hàahng-yahp yāt gàan fóng-jái léuih-bihn. Léih Sìn-sàang meih gin-gwo līp, só-yíh kéuih m̀h jì gó ga haih līp làih-ge. Léuhng fàn jūng jì-hauh, fóng-jái ge mùhn hòi-jó lak, yāt go yauh leng yauh hauh-sāang ge síu-jé hàahng-chēut-làih.

> **LANGUAGE TIP**
> **daaih-tòhng** = *lobby, great hall*

Léih Sàang hòi-chí ge sìh-hauh gok-dāk hóu kèih-gwaai, yìhn-hauh kéuih jauh hóu hòi-sām gám wah: 'Sìhng-síh yàhn jàn-haih sìn-jeun lak: hah chi ngóh yāt-dihng daai-màaih taai-táai làih.'

a Léih Sàang haih hèung-há-yàhn, só-yíh fèi-sèuhng-jì sìn-jeun. Ngāam m̀h ngāam?

b Kéuih dím-gáai dá-syun hah chi daai-màaih taai-táai làih Seuhng-hói?

Grammar summary

This summary sets out some of the basic principles of Cantonese grammar, which you can use for quick reference. Where helpful it refers you back to earlier parts of the book where greater detail can be found. The references are in the form [1.3], where the first number shows the unit and the second a heading in the Language discovery sections of that unit. [D] refers to a Dialogue.

The grammar points are arranged in the following order:

1 Adjectives	**8** Final particles	**15** Possessives
2 Adverbs	**9** Money	**16** Potentials
3 Alternatives	**10** Negatives	**17** Questions
4 Classifiers	**11** Nouns	**18** Time
5 Commands	**12** Numbers	**19** Verbs
6 Comparatives / Superlatives	**13** Paired constructions	**20** Verb endings
7 Directions	**14** Passives	**21** Word order

1 ADJECTIVES

a Adjectives go before the nouns they describe (**yāt jek daaih būi** *a large cup*). [1.2]

b Adjectives can also function as verbs. [1.2; 13.3]

c Adjectives can be formed with **hóu**-verb *good to*: (**hóu-sihk** *good to eat, delicious*). [13.8]

d Adjectival clauses and phrases go before the nouns they describe and are linked to them with **ge**: **ngóh hóu séung máaih ge chē** *the car I very much want to buy*. [4.6; 8.9; 17.1]

2 ADVERBS

a A fixed adverb comes immediately before a verb (although the negative **m̀h** can be placed between them):
dōu *all, both, also* [1.6; 4.9; 8.4; 9.5; 22.9; 24.7; 25.11]
jauh *then* [24.9]
joi *again* [6.3]
juhng *in addition* [8.1]
sìn *first* [6.3]
sìn-ji *only then* [10.5]
yauh *both … and* [5.5]

b Adverbs of degree such as **hóu** *very* and **dōu-géi** *quite* go immediately in front of adjectival verbs like **daaih** *big* and auxiliary verbs like **séung** *want to* and **sīk** *know how to* (but again the negative **m̀h** can be placed between them).

c Adverbs of time when something occurs must come before the verb, but not necessarily directly before the verb. [6.9; 8.3; 8.9; 24.4]

d Adverbs of duration of time come after the verb, but not necessarily directly after the verb. [6.11; 10.9; 18.3; 20.4; 24.4]

e Adverbs of place normally come before the verb, although not necessarily directly before the verb, but if the location is the result of the action of the verb then the adverb comes after the verb:

Hái Yìng-gwok Wòhng Sàang móuh ūk.	*Mr Wong has not got a house in Britain.*
Kéuih chóh hái sō-fá-yí seuhng-bihn.	*She seats herself on the sofa.* [4.3; 11.7; 12.7; 25.10]

f Adverbs of manner can be made by joining them to a verb with the verb ending **-dāk**: **Kéuih jáu-dāk hóu faai** *He runs very quickly.* [8.8; 15.2]

g Adverbs can be made from adjectives by the formula <u>hóu</u> adjective <u>gám</u>: **hóu leng gám** *very prettily* [8.10]

3 ALTERNATIVES

a When *or* occurs in a question it is translated by **dihng-haih**: **Néih tìng-yaht heui dihng-haih hauh-yaht heui nē?** *Are you going tomorrow or the day after?* [13.6; 16.7]

b When *or* occurs in a statement it is usually translated by **waahk-jé**: **Kéuih waahk-jé làih waahk-jé m̀h làih** *He'll come or he won't* [16.7], but there is another pattern: **yāt-haih … yāt-haih …** [25.D2]

c When *or* occurs with numbers, indicating an approximate figure, two numbers are given together without other device (although it is possible to separate them with **waahk-jé**): **luhk-chāt yaht** *six or seven days* [10.4; 13.6]

4 CLASSIFIERS

a Whenever nouns are counted or specified with *this, that, which?, each, the whole* the correct classifier must be placed between the number or specifier and the noun. [2.4; 12.recap; 16.3; 17.8; 20.1; 25.2; 25.3]

b The plural classifier and the classifier for uncountable things is **dī**. [4.8; 15.3]

c The classifier can be used to form possessives in place of **ge**. [12.3]

d At the beginning of a sentence the classifier can be used with definite reference (like *the* in English). [4.8]

e The classifier can be doubled in conjunction with the adverb **dōu** to give the meaning *each one of*. [5.9]

f There are a very small number of nouns that do not need a classifier. [8.7; 9.8; 13.2]

g A list of the classifiers dealt with in this book can be found under 'cl' in the English–Cantonese vocabulary. You will undoubtedly meet others as you advance your studies.

5 COMMANDS

a Negative commands (*don't!*) are made with **m̀h-hóu** or its more abrupt form **máih**. [4.12; 16.4]

b Positive commands (*do it!*) use abruptly spoken verbs (**jáu!** *go!*), or, rather less forcefully, the final particle **lā!**, or the verb ending **-jó** with a following object, or some adjectival verbs and verb endings with the comparative **-dī** ending. [3.11; 17.7; 19.1]

6 COMPARATIVES AND SUPERLATIVES

a Comparatives are formed with **-gwo** *surpassing*. The pattern is X adjective-**gwo** Y. *A bit more* is expressed with **síu-síu** and *a lot more* with **hóu-dò**:

Ngóh gòu-gwo néih.	*I am taller than you.*
Ngóh gòu-gwo néih síu-síu.	*I am a bit taller than you.*
Ngóh gòu-gwo néih hóu-dò.	*I am a lot taller than you.* [12.2; 16.9; 18.8]

b Negative comparison uses the pattern X **móuh** Y **gam** adjective: **Néih móuh ngóh gam gòu** *You are not as tall as I am.* [16.8; 16.9]

c If there is only an X and no Y the patterns are:

Ngóh gòu-dī.	*I'm taller.*
Ngóh gòu hóu-dò.	*I'm a lot taller.*
Néih móuh gam gòu.	*You're not so tall.* [16.9]

d Superlatives make use of **jeui** *most*, often adding **lak** after the adjective: **Kéuih jeui gòu lak** *He is tallest.* [8.5; 16.9]

e Equivalence is expressed by X **tùhng / móuh** Y **yāt-yeuhng gam** adjective:

Ngóh tùhng néih yāt- yeuhng gam gòu.	*I'm just as tall as you are.*
Kéuih móuh ngóh yāt-yeuhng gam gòu.	*He's not just as tall as I am.* [13.4; 16.9]

7 DIRECTIONS

a Directions to and from the speaker are usually indicated by the use of **làih** *come* and **heui** *go* [5.3], but other words can also do the job. [3.2; 19.2; 22.2]

b Compass directions are straightforward except that the intermediate directions (NE, SE, SW, NW) are always the reverse of the English order, so EN, ES, WS and WN. [6.intro]

8 FINAL PARTICLES

Particles are words which for the most part have no meaning in themselves, but which add nuance or sentiment or some other gloss to a sentence or phrase. [3.11] Some are capable of relatively clear definition, such as **a** [1.10], **àh?** [3.5], **bo** [5.D1], **jē** [3.9], **làih-ge** [19.7], **lak** [3.6; 25.4], **ma?** [1.3], **mē?** [5.7], **nē?** [1.5; 5.1] and **tìm** [8.1]; but usage of many others is not consistent among native speakers and so defies adequate definition. Unfortunately, all speakers of Cantonese use many particles, but they do not all use the same ones, neither do they all necessarily agree on which particle to use when. Sometimes the ill-defined particles seem to add little or nothing to the meaning and may be treated as 'voiced pauses' ('spoken commas' if you like) and ignored. A list of the final particles dealt with in this book can be found under 'fp' in the English–Cantonese vocabulary.

9 MONEY

There is a formal word for the *dollar* (**yùhn**), but in speech most people use **māan** or **go**. Slang words for *money* come and go so fast that none of them are taught here, except the ubiquitous use of **séui** *water*. [5.10; 13.1; 19.D1; 20.2]

10 NEGATIVES

Negative words come in front of the words they negate. The most common negative is **m̀h** *not*, but it cannot negate the verb **yáuh** *to have*, which is achieved by substituting the verb **móuh** *not to have*. **Meih** means *not yet*. The negative command is **M̀h-hóu!** *Don't!*, and even greater stress can be achieved by the addition of **chìn-kèih**: **Chìn-kèih m̀h-hóu …** *Whatever you do, don't …* [1.9; 3.8; 3.10; 16.4; 18.5; 25.4]

11 NOUNS

Nouns only have one form and do not change according to case, number or gender. The exception is the noun **yàhn** *person* which has a plural form **yàhn-deih**, but this plural form is reserved for the meaning *other people* and as an oblique way of referring to oneself or to the person being addressed – it is not used in such expressions as *three people*, which is **sàam go yàhn**. [1.8; 2.6]

12 NUMBERS

The number system is simple, and involves learning only the numbers zero–10, plus 100, 1,000, 10,000 and 100,000,000. It diverges from Western systems in that large numbers are counted in ten-thousands rather than thousands. The number *two* (**yih**) is not used in front of classifiers, **léuhng** being used instead. [2.6; 6.7; 10.4; 11.2; 13.7; 18.7; 19.9; 24.2]

13 PAIRED CONSTRUCTIONS

bòng … sáu	*to help …* [4.D1]
dím-yéung verb **faat?**	*in what way?* [8.8]
hóu adjective **gám**	*adjective > adverb* [8.10]
hóu-chíh X yāt-yeuhng	*just like X* [4.D1]
hóu-chíh X m̀h-chíh Y	*more like X than Y* [6.D2]
lìhn X dōu …	*even X …* [17.11]
m̀h haih … jauh haih …	*if it's not … then it's …* [24.D2]
m̀h-jí … yìh-ché …	*not only … but also …* [23.2]
sèui-yìhn … daahn-haih …	*although … yet …* [18.D1]
sìn … joi …	*first … then …* [6.3]
sung … béi …	*to give … to …* [4.11]
X móuh Y gam adjective	*X isn't as 'adjective' as Y* [16.8]
yàn-waih … só-yíh …	*because … therefore …* [4.D2]
yāt haih … yāt haih …	*either … or …* [25.D2]
yāt … jauh …	*as soon as … then …* [24.9]
yauh … yauh …	*both … and …* [5.5]
yùh-gwó … jauh …	*if … then …* [4.D2]
yuht … yuht …	*the more … the more …* [19.11]

14 PASSIVES

The passive construction is not common in Cantonese, but you will hear it from time to time. It uses the pattern X **beih** Y verb and the verb usually carries a verb ending of some kind:
Tìuh yú beih jek māau sihk-jó lak *The fish was eaten by the cat.* [12.4; 17.3]

15 POSSESSIVES

a Possessives are formed with **ge**, which is positioned as if it were the English apostrophe *'s*:
Wòhng Síu-jé ge nàahm-pàhng-yáuh *Miss Wong's boyfriend.* [2.2; 17.2]

b They can also be formed with the appropriate classifier (singular or plural) instead of **ge**:

ngóh go jái	*my son*
ngóh dī néui	*my daughters* [12.3]

16 POTENTIALS

Potentials (*can, may, be able*) are formed in three ways:

a with the verbs **hó-yíh**, **sīk** and **wúih**. **Hó-yíh** often implies *permission to* and so is rather like *may* in English, while **sīk** and **wúih** indicate acquired *ability to* and so are like *to know how to*:

Ngóh hó-yíh heui yàuh-séui.	*I may go swimming (Daddy says so).*
Ngóh sīk yàuh-séui.	*I can swim (I can do the breast stroke).* [5.D2; 6.10]

b with the verb ending **-dāk**: **Ngóh yàuh-dāk séui** *I can swim* (= either *may* or *know how to*). [6.10]

c with the positive ending -**dāk-dóu** and / or the negative ending -**m̀h-dóu**: **Néih tái-m̀h-tái-dāk-dóu kéuih a?** *Can you see her?* [18.6]

17 QUESTIONS

Questions do not change basic word orders. There are four main ways of forming them:

a Using a question word such as **bīn? māt-yéh? géi-sí?** The final particle **a?** is frequently used in association with these question words

Néih séung máaih māt-yéh a?	*What do you want to buy?* [2.1; 3.1; 3.3; 8.3; 8.8; 9.7; 20.4]

The answer echoes the form of the question, appearing in the same place in the sentence as the question word:

Ngóh séung máaih dī choi.	*I want to buy some vegetables.*

The question words **dím-gáai?** and **jouh-māt-yéh?** are exceptional in that they are usually answered by **yàn-waih …** *because ….*

b Using the choice-type question form verb–negative–verb, usually backed up by **a?**

Kéuih sīk m̀h sīk góng Jùng-màhn a?	*Does he know how to speak Chinese?* [1.10]

Choice-type questions can be simply answered *yes* or *no* by using the positive or negative form of the verb:

M̀h sīk.	*He doesn't (know how to speak Chinese).*

c Using a question particle such as **àh? mē? nē?** at the end of the sentence [1.3; 1.5; 3.5]:

Néih haih Jùng-gwok-yàhn mē?   *Do you mean to say you're Chinese?*

Type *c* questions are often answered simply by **haih** *yes* or **m̀h haih** *no*:

M̀h haih, ngóh m̀h haih Jùng-gwok-yàhn.   *No, I'm not Chinese.*

Haih, ngóh haih Jùng-gwok-yàhn.   *Yes, I am Chinese.*

d Questions about past events can be asked using **meih** or **móuh** and the verb endings **-jó** and **-gwo**. [18.5]

e 'Question tags' such as **hóu m̀h hóu a?** or **dāk m̀h dāk a?** can be added to a sentence. [2.5; 5.12]

f The use of **dī** in a question can anticipate a plural answer. [15.3]

18 TIME

clock-time: [15.6; 25.7]

days: [8.7; 10.10; 11.5]

weeks: [5.2; 10.8]

months: [17.5; 20.3]

seasons: [8.2]

years: [8.7; 10.10]

For 'time when' and 'duration of time', see **Adverbs**.

19 VERBS

a Verbs only have one form (they do not conjugate) and do not change according to tense or number or person. [1.7]

b Verbs are negated by **m̀h**, **móuh** or **meih** placed before them. There are two exceptions:

  1 the verb **yáuh** *to have* does not have a negative form with **m̀h**: normally the verb **móuh** *not to have* is used as the negative.

  2 the negative of the verb **yiu** *to need* is usually **m̀h-sái** *not need*. [3.8; 3.10; 4.5; 18.5]

c Verbs normally have subjects, which may or may not be stated depending on whether they can be understood from the context. Exceptions are rare, although it is doubtful if there is really any subject to the 'weather sentences' **lohk-syut** *it is snowing* or **lohk-yúh** *it is raining*.

d Verbs do not all take objects, although some verbs such as **sihk** *to eat* and **góng** *to speak* (called 'lonely verbs' in the units) usually require a generalized object if a specific one is not mentioned. [4.2; 9.2; 9.3; 9.12; 15.1; 18.4; 25.1]

e Where there is a series of verbs together it is the first of them which normally is the grammatically operative one, that is, the one which takes the negative or is acted on by an adverb: **Néih gàm-yaht séung m̀h séung heui Bāk-gìng a?** *Do you want to go to Beijing today?*

f Adjectival verbs. All adjectives can be used with verbal function: **Kéuih ge chē hóu daaih** *His car is very large.* [1.2]

20 VERB ENDINGS

a A number of endings can be attached directly to verbs to convey aspects of meaning:

-cho	an error has occurred (**hàahng-cho** *go the wrong way*). [19.4]
-dóu	the action of the verb has been successfully carried out (**sihk-dóu** *managed to eat*). [8.11; 18.6]
-gán	the action of the verb is still going on (**sihk-gán** *eating it now*). [4.4; 11.3]
-gwo	the action has been experienced at some time (**sihk-gwo** *have tasted it in the past*). [6.12]
-háh	the action is carried out briefly (**sihk-háh** *a quick bite*). [5.4]
-héi-làih	the action is what is being talked about (**sihk-héi-làih** *when it comes to eating*). [11.1]
-hòi	the action is opening a gap (**hàahng-hòi** *walk away*). [17.9]
-hóu	the action is satisfactorily finished (**jouh-hóu** *done the job*). [20.8]
-jó	the action has been completed (**sihk-jó** *ate it*). [4.4; 6.12; 24.3]
-jyuh	the action is sustained (**sihk-jyuh** *keep on eating*). [11.3]
-lohk-heui	continue doing (**góng-lohk-heui** *carry on speaking*). [19.D2]
-lohk-làih	the action is happening in a downward direction (**hàahng-lohk-làih** *walking down this way*). [11.10]
-màaih	the action is closing a gap (**hàahng-màaih** *walk closer*). [17.9]
-saai	the action is fully committed (**sihk-saai** *eaten all up*). [15.10]
-sèhng	something is becoming something else (**jouh-sèhng** *make into …*). [8.12]
-séuhng	something is going onto something else (**tip-séuhng** *stick onto …*). [20.9]
-yùhn	the action has ended (**sihk-yùhn** *finished eating*). [6.8]

A list of the verb endings dealt with in this book can also be found under 've' in the English–Cantonese vocabulary.

b **-dāk** has two functions:

1 it enables adverbs of manner to be attached to verbs and may be thought of as meaning *in such a way that* (**sihk-dāk faai** *eats quickly*). [15.2]

2 it adds the notion *able to, can* to the verb (**sihk-dāk** *can be eaten, can eat*). [6.10; 22.8]

21 WORD ORDER

a The basic word order of Cantonese is subject–verb–object, just as in English:
Ngóh jùng-yi néih *I love you.*

b Other word orders generally have in common that they put the stressed part of the sentence first, regardless of whether it is the grammatical object, a time word, a location or whatever:

Bē-jáu ngóh jùng-yi yám.	*I like drinking beer (but not those other drinks).*
Tìng-yaht kéuih m̀h làih.	*She's not coming tomorrow (although she is coming today and the day after tomorrow).*

The Chinese writing system

Alphabetic writing systems attempt to show the noises people make when they speak. By reconverting the symbols on the page into sounds, the reader can put himself in the position of a listener and so understand what the writer is 'saying'.

Ideographic systems, of which Chinese is the main example, do not make any consistent attempt to show the noises of speech. Instead they try to show the ideas in a speaker's head when he speaks. The reader doesn't reconvert the written symbols into noises and then convert the noises into meanings, he goes straight for the jugular, seeing the symbols as meanings without having to go through the medium of noises.

Each syllable of Cantonese is written with one symbol ('character') and that symbol carries the meaning or in a small number of cases shows the function of the syllable. So the character 人 **yàhn** carries the meaning *person*, while the character for the syllable **nē** 呢 is not actually meaningful but does have the function of asking a follow-up question.

There are well over 50,000 different Chinese characters in existence. This body of characters is large because unlike the restricted number of sounds with which the language expresses itself, the number of different meanings is limitless and each meaningful or functional syllable needs its own unique symbol. A well-educated Chinese person will be able to write perhaps 4,000–5,000 characters and recognize maybe 5,000–6,000 without the aid of a dictionary. About 3,500 different characters are used in middle-brow newspapers.

The first characters (early second millennium BC) seem to have been pictures of the objects they represented and some of those pictures in stylized form remain standard today. 羊 **yèuhng** is a *goat* or *sheep* – it is not hard to see how it derives from a picture of a goat's head with horns: and 目 **muhk** is an *eye*, a squared-off vertical version of a picture of a wide-open eye. William Tell fans with arrows through apples in mind will recognize the symbolism of 中 **jùng** *middle*.

Gradually, other ways of creating characters were devised, some of them making use of similarities of sound, so it is not accidental that the characters 由 **yàuh** *from* and 油 **yàuh** *oil* have the same element in common. But such common elements are at best an unreliable guide to pronunciation and sometimes can be downright misleading. It is most sensible to think of characters as being unique symbols for meanings rather than for pronounced sounds.

Chinese writing speaks more directly and more colourfully to the reader than does an alphabetic system. The two simple sounds **Jùng-gwok** tell you that *China* is meant, but the characters for **Jùng-gwok** 中國 mean 'Middle Kingdom' and carry with them additional messages, such as that 'middle' means *central* and hence *most important*, thus reducing other countries (**ngoih-gwok** *outside kingdoms*) to peripheral lesser status.

The sheer volume and complexity of the character base has made the computerization of Chinese a very tough nut to crack. A computer can easily cope with storing the symbols and reproducing them – the problem is how to access them. The traditional Chinese methods used in printing and in dictionaries were slow and sometimes haphazard, and Chinese typewriters were really clumsy – they consisted of a single key picking up characters one at a time from a large bed of moveable type and banging them onto an inked ribbon to make an impression on the paper before dropping them back into their bed. Faster methods, such as accessing through romanization, fall foul of homophones and of the many different dialects which each have their own ways of pronouncing words. At present Chinese computer software tends to offer the user a choice of several different access methods, but there are greater or lesser problems with all of them.

You may well have worked out for yourself by now that the use of unique symbols attached to meanings allows Chinese script to cope with the homophone problem very well. Two or more words may be pronounced the same and so be spelled the same in an alphabetic system, but their characters can be totally different and easily distinguishable one from the other. **Gáu**, as you now know, means *nine* but it can also mean *dog* or *spring onion* or *a long time*, and those are just some of its meanings. The characters, however, are not at all confusing: 九 is *nine*, 狗 is *dog*, 韮 is *spring onion* and 久 is *a long time*, all very distinctive. Similarly 酒 *alcoholic drink* and 走 *to run, leave* are both pronounced **jáu**, but there is no mistaking one character for the other.

The other problem that characters deal with is the large number of Chinese languages and dialects that have developed in China. Many of these are mutually unintelligible, meaning that lack of verbal communication is a divisive force among the language groups. But everyone reads and writes the same characters, because the symbol for *man* is universal throughout the country regardless of how it is pronounced, as is the symbol for *red*, the symbol for *think* and all other symbols, so the eye can understand what the ear cannot distinguish, and the written language unifies what the spoken word divides. It is true that Cantonese does use a certain number of characters that the rest of China does not recognize, but all literate Cantonese can read and write the standard characters as well, so they can always communicate with everyone else.

Learning the thousands of characters necessary to be fully literate in Chinese is a time-consuming business (for Chinese people as well as for foreigners), and that is why you have learned through romanization. A Chinese person, of course, learns to speak at his mother's knee and he does not need romanization with that language teaching method!

Even so, you may like to learn to recognize some common characters. You will find that knowing them gives an extra dimension to learning Chinese, a very satisfying depth of 'feel' for the language which you have to experience to appreciate.

Writing a character is subject to certain rules of stroke order – you cannot write the different strokes in random order or direction. If you do not observe the correct order it is difficult to get the character to balance properly and it will seem very ugly to the reader, while it will probably become illegible if written in any kind of a hurry. The general rule is that you start at the top left-hand corner of the character and work downwards to finish at the bottom right, but there are quite a lot of exceptions to this and you will need to find a teacher or a specialist book to guide you.

Here are some common characters written stroke by stroke for you to practise:

丨 卜 上 　　**seuhng** *above*; **séuhng** *to go up*
丨 冂 口 中 　**jùng** *middle*
一 丁 下 　　　**hah** *below*
人 女 女 　　　**néuih** *female*
丨 冂 田 田 田 男 男 　**nàahm** *male*
一 扌 扌 扩 扩 拉 拉 　**làai** *pull*

It would be a good idea to learn and to be able to recognize some important characters which will guide you and help to keep you out of trouble.

You have already met:

男 **nàahm** *male* and 女 **néuih** *female*.

which should be helpful when you are looking for the:

廁所 **chi-só** *toilet*　　or　　洗手間 **sái-sáu-gaan** (lit. 'wash hands room')

For help in getting around you should find the following characters useful:

香港 **Hèung-góng** *Hong Kong*　　　　九龍 **Gáu-lùhng** *Kowloon*
巴士站 **bā-sí-jaahm** *bus stop*　　　　電車站 **dihn-chè-jaahm** *tram stop*
的士站 **dīk-sí-jaahm** *taxi-rank*　　　地鐵站 **deih-tit-jaahm** *MTR station*
飛機場 **fèi-gèi-chèuhng** *airport*　　　碼頭 **máh-tàu** *pier, jetty*

To avoid jostling:

入口 **yahp-háu** *entrance*　　　出口 **chēut-háu** *exit*
上 **séung** *board (bus) here*　　落 **lohk** *alight from (bus) here*
推 **tèui** *push*　　　　　　　拉 **làai** *pull*

And for staying out of trouble:

注意 **Jyu-yi** *Pay attention to …*　　小心 **Síu-sàm** *Beware of …*
請勿 **Chíng maht** *Please don't …*　不准 **Bāt jéun …** *Prohibited to …*
危險 **Ngàih-hím** *Danger!*

Tìhng *Stop* 　　 **Heui** *Go*

Incidentally, you may write your character text from left to right across the page as English does (that's the modern way), from right to left down the page (that's the traditional way and, of course, means that you start at what would be the end of an English book) or indeed any way you like, because each character is a discrete entity – you can write round in a circle anti-clockwise if that's how the mood takes you. Chinese newspapers quite often print captions to photographs in a different direction from the rest of the text that they illustrate and this produces no confusion, although if an English newspaper were to try it it would be *deedni gnisufnoc yrev*.

Taking it further

Where do you go from here? Very few textbooks go beyond elementary level and some of them use a variety of other romanization systems which are confusingly different from the Yale system that you have learned, so they would not be easy. Of course, if you have mastered everything in this book you should be able to carry on building up vocabulary and fluency through talking with Cantonese-speaking friends, but there are also some useful works to help you to study on your own.

Far and away the best reference book is *Cantonese: a Comprehensive Grammar* by Stephen Matthews and Virginia Yip, 2nd edition published in 2010 by Routledge. Don't be put off by the title or the size of the book – it is a goldmine of information and full of sparklingly colloquial examples to illustrate the wealth of points it makes. And as a bonus it uses a version of the Yale system almost identical with that with which you are now familiar.

If you want to expand your vocabulary, you could do worse than get hold of a copy of *The Right Word in Cantonese* by Kwan Choi Wah, published by the Commercial Press in 1989 and reissued many times since. It has a long list of everyday vocabulary and some supplementary lists designed specifically for convenience in getting by in Hong Kong. It too uses the Yale system and at the front it has a table comparing some of the most common romanization systems, so that you could use that to make sense of other books not written in Yale. To enable you to get help from Chinese people the Chinese characters are given for all terms.

Available dictionaries of Cantonese are few and some of them are not very user-friendly. Surprisingly useful is the least pretentious of them, Philip Yungkin Lee's *Pocket Cantonese Dictionary*, published by Periplus Hong Kong in 2003. It has a Cantonese-English and an English-Cantonese section, uses the Yale romanization system, gives the Chinese characters for all entries, and despite some inconsistencies and quirky translations it is a very handy entry-level reference work. *The Chinese–English Dictionary* by Chik Hon Man and Ng Lam Sim Yuk was published in 2000 by the Chinese University of Hong Kong Press. It shows Mandarin pronunciations as well as the Cantonese ones (which again are in the Yale system), it is well indexed and good on the meanings of individual characters, but it gives very little assistance with the meanings of combinations of characters. Christopher Hutton and Kingsley Bolton's *A Dictionary of Cantonese Slang* (University of Hawai'i Press 2005) contains a wealth of racy colloquialisms romanized in the Yale system.

Other available dictionaries use a variety of different romanizations. Sidney Lau's *A Practical Cantonese–English Dictionary* (Hong Kong Government Printer, 1977) contains lots of good colloquial material, but you can only look up Cantonese words of which you already know the pronunciation, and it uses Lau's own romanization which shows the tones by superscript numbers (e.g. **yuen**[4] = **yùhn**, **booi**[10] = **būi**). Kwan's book tells you how to convert Lau to Yale and it is not too difficult. *The Cantonese Speaker's Dictionary* by Roy T. Cowles (Hong Kong

University Press 1965) is impressively large, but very cumbersome to look up, and it uses the so-called Meyer-Wempe romanization system with rather complicated pronunciation markers. A work which allows you to find the Cantonese for an English word is *A Practical English–Cantonese Dictionary* by Chiang Ker Chiu, published in Singapore by the Chin Fen Book Store in 1956. It also uses a form of the Meyer-Wempe system (with different tone markers), but despite the limitations of its age it can still prove useful, and again the comparison table in Kwan's book will convert Meyer-Wempe to Yale for you.

Sidney Lau's textbooks published by the Hong Kong government are perhaps the most complete course available, with two volumes each of *Elementary Cantonese*, *Intermediate Cantonese* and *Advanced Cantonese*, all of them using his romanization system. They are rather dated and somewhat unexciting in content, but they are generally reliable and would help to build vocabulary and understanding of grammar to a high level.

Online resources for Cantonese have been slow to appear and are often difficult to use and of uncertain reliability, but it is worth periodically searching to check for any interesting developments.

If you find you are making good progress with the spoken language and you are really serious about going on, your next step should probably be to start learning Chinese characters, so that you can get to grips with Chinese on its own terms. Because all formal Chinese nowadays is written using the grammar, vocabulary and character stock of Mandarin, this is quite a tall order, and you will need to explore the availability of Mandarin textbooks when the time comes.

Key to the exercises

PRONUNCIATION GUIDE

1 mid level and mid level; mid rising and low level; low falling and mid rising; high level and low falling; mid rising and mid level; low falling and high level **2** baahn-sih, móuh-cho, chāt-sáu, séui-ngàuh

UNIT 1

Greetings and name order Gwok Méih (Kwok Mei)

Vocabulary builder 1 Wong, Mrs, you

Dialogue 1, 1 Néih hóu ma?, Néih nē?, Néih taai-táai nē? **2** I'm OK / Great/ I'm good, etc. **3** Wòhng Taai-táai

Language discovery 1.4 The first hóu means *very* and the second hóu means *good*, so hóu hóu means *very good* **1.7 a** singular **b** plural

Pronunciation Mr Wong is well and Mrs Wong is also well; Miss Cheung and Miss Wong are well too

Vocabulary builder 2 Japanese person / people, British / English person / people

Dialogue 2, 1 The first word she says is òu **2** All the statements a–d are false **3 a** Kéuih m̀h yiu chē **b** Yiu. Jèung Síu-jé yiu Yaht-bún chē **c** Haih. Kéuih haih Yìng-gwok yàhn

Language discovery 1.8 a person from Hong Kong or Hong Kong people **1.10** Are you selling American cars?

Practice 1 a Kéuih-deih hóu hóu **b** Wòhng Sìn-sàang hóu **c** Jèung Síu-jé dōu hóu **2 a** Jóu-sàhn **b** Ngóh hóu hóu. Néih nē? **c** Joi-gin **3 a** m̀h **b** m̀h **c** haih **d** Méih-gwok chē

Test yourself a Yaht-bún chē m̀h gwai **b** Kéuih m̀h hóu **c** Néih hóu leng **d** Kéuih-deih yiu m̀h yiu chē a? **e** Kéuih dōu (hóu) leng **f** Kéuih-deih haih Méih-gwok-yàhn **g** Wòhng Sìn-sàang maaih chē **h** Yìng-gwok-yàhn m̀h maaih Méih-gwok chē

UNIT 2

The magic of numbers He believed that the larger sum was much luckier sounding!

Vocabulary builder 1 why, you

Dialogue 1, 1 maaih *to sell*, máaih *to buy* **2 a** F **b** F **c** Maybe: they are colleagues **d** F **3 a** M̀h haih, kéuih haih Jùng-gwok yàhn **b** Wòhng Sìn-sàang ge pàhng-yáuh wán kéuih séung maaih chē

Tones matter! máaih-maaih means *trade* (lit. 'buying and selling')

Language discovery 2.1 Mrs Cheung is very bad (lit. 'very not good') **2.2 a** ge chē **b** ngóh-deih ge **c** Wòhng Síu-jé ge **d** kéuih ge

Vocabulary builder 2 those, question, matter

Dialogue 2, 1 nī go sáu-bīu, gó jì bāt **2** Not really; a thin stick-like watch might be awkward to wear and very difficult to read **3 a** Gó jì bāt haih Hòh Sìn-sàang ge **b** Jèung Síu-jé chìh-dī mahn Wòhng Sìn-sàang **c** Jèung Síu-jé mahn Hòh Sìn-sàang gó go sáu-bīu haih m̀h haih kéuih ge

Language discovery 2.4 This type of watch is very handsome **2.6** 32, 38; sàam-sahp-sei, chāt-sahp-chāt, baat-sahp-gáu, sei-sahp, luhk-sahp-ńgh, ńgh-sahp-yih, sahp-luhk, luhk-sahp-chāt, baat-sahp-sàam, gáu-sahp-sei; 44 New Zealanders; eight Brazilian pens

Practice 1 a Ngóh sing … (add whatever your surname is) **b** Haih, kéuih haih Jùng-gwok-yàhn **c** Ngóh m̀h séung máaih chē **d** Dāk-gwok sáu-bīu hóu gwai **e** Nī jì haih kéuih ge **2** Our recorded version: Wòhng Sìn-sàang, ngóh séung heui Yìng-gwok máaih Yìng-gwok chē / Òu, Yìng-gwok chē hóu gwai / Wòhng Sìn-sàang, néih yáuh māt-yéh chē a? / Ngóh ge dōu haih Yìng-gwok chē **3** Sei go Méih-gwok-yàhn; Sàam go Jùng-gwok-yàhn; Ńgh go Yaht-bún-yàhn; Wòhng Sìn-sàang maaih léuhng go sáu-bīu; Yāt go Méih-gwok-yàhn máaih bāt

Test yourself a go **b** yàhn **c** bún **d** m̀h **e** māt **f** bīn **g** dōu **h** mahn

UNIT 3

Chinese families You can't. There is no one term which covers all the ground that *uncle* does in English. Instead there are separate words for many relationships which English lumps together in one catch-all word (such as *uncle*, or *cousin*, or *grandfather*).

Vocabulary builder 1 sisters, mother, brother, be big

Dialogue 1, 1 Either or both of the ngóhs could be left out **2** C should address A as Bàh-bā; D should address B as Màh-mā; D should address A as Bàh-bā; You should address D as Wòhng Síu-jé; You should address B as Wòhng Taai-táai; Probably C since he is responsible enough to take his mother to the doctor's

Language discovery 3.3 They all mean *Why must you sell your car?* **3.7** Ngóh ge Yaht-bún sáu-bīu / Ngóh go Yaht-bún sáu-bīu

Vocabulary builder 2 bus, taxi, Road, a long time

Dialogue 2, 1 It reverses the English order **2** to sit (*please come and sit down* is a standard polite invitation, not always meant to be acted upon) **3 a** M̀h haih **b** M̀h haih **c** Haih **d** M̀h haih **e** Haih **4 a** Hòh Sìn-sàang jyuh hái Seuhng-hói Gāai **b** Jèung Sìn-sàang jyuh hái Fà-yùhn Douh **c** Hòh Sìn-sàang ge láu móuh chē-fòhng **d** Jèung Sìn-sàang séung taam kéuih **e** Yáuh, yáuh hóu-dò bā-sí heui Fà-yùhn Douh **5** Ngóh daap sahp-luhk houh bā-sí heui Fà-yùhn Douh taam ngóh daaih-lóu

Language discovery 3.8 there are

Practice 1 a Hòh Sìn-sàang bàh-bā haih yī-sāng **b** Wòhng Taai-táai hái ūk-kéi jouh māt-yéh a? **c** Ngóh m̀h séung heui tái yī-sāng **d** Ngóh-deih yāt-chàih fàan sé-jih-làuh **2** Wòhng Sìn-sàang, hóu-noih-móuh-gin. Néih hóu ma? Taai-táai nē? Néih-deih yìh-gā hái bīn-douh jyuh a? / Deui-m̀h-jyuh, Wòhng Sìn-sàang, ngóh yiu daap bā-sí heui Fà-yùhn Douh. Ngóh yiu heui taam ngóh bàh-bā, daai kéuih heui tái yī-sāng.

Test yourself a yī-sāng **b** séung … ūk-kéi **c** yī-sāng **d** Yìng-gwok

UNIT 4

Food, glorious food! hóu yám

Dialogue 1, 1 In his second speech he says that his wife is cooking (jyú-gán faahn) in the kitchen, but it's not true, is it? **2** The food was all bought by her in a restaurant she went to nearby **3 a** F **b** ⊦ **c** F **d** F **e** T

Language discovery 4.2 She's gone to Kowloon shopping **4.5** yiu m̀h yiu; Néih yiu m̀h yiu faahn a?

Are you hearing correctly? 1 gùng-yihp, gùng-sì **2** yuht-leuhng, yùhn-leuhng **3** séuhng-tohng, séuhng-dong **4** wuh-leih, wùh-léi **5** daaih-si, daaih-sih

Vocabulary builder 2 salad, then

Dialogue 2, 1 juhng yáuh hóu dò *there's still a lot* **2** Nī dī sung dōu hóu m̀h hóu meih **3 a** Yùh-gwó néih heui, ngóh jauh heui **b** Yàn-waih ngóh haih Faat-gwok-yàhn só-yíh ngóh hóu sīk jyú Faat-gwok-choi **c** Kéuih dím-gáai m̀h séung heui jáu-làuh: haih m̀h haih yàn-waih m̀h séung sihk-yéh a?

Language discovery 4.13 Wòhng Sìn-sàang, Wòhng Taai-táai

Listen and understand Hòh Sìn-sàang tùhng Hòh Taai-táai dōu haih Jùng-gwok yàhn. Kéuih-deih léuhng go yàhn dōu m̀h sīk jyú Jùng-gwok sung. Gàm-yaht Hòh Sìn-sàang chéng-jó yāt go Yìng-gwok pàhng-yáuh fàan ūk-kéi sihk-faahn, Hòh Táai jauh hái fuh-gahn ge jáu-làuh máaih-jó dī sung. Kéuih máaih-jó yāt go lùhng-hā sà-léut, dōu máaih-jó hóu dò sàn-sìn ngàuh-yuhk, tùhng máaih-jó hóu hóu sihk ge Yaht-bún tìhm-bán. *Mr and Mrs Ho are both Chinese. Neither of them knows how to cook Chinese food. Today Mr Ho has invited a British friend back home for a meal. Mrs Ho bought food from the Chinese restaurant nearby. She bought a lobster salad, lots of fresh beef, and some delicious Japanese desserts.*

Practice 1 a Wòhng Sìn-sàang séung dáng Hòh Taai-táai yāt-chàih sihk-faahn **b** Hòh Taai-táai hái chyùh-fóng jyú-gán faahn **c** Hòh Taai-táai mahn Wòhng Sìn-sàang kéuih jyu ge sung hóu-meih ma? **d** Hòh Sìn-sàang yáuh móuh bòng Hòh Taai-táai sáu a? **e** Hòh Taai-táai jyú ge sung hóu-chíh jáu-làuh ge yāt-yeuhng **2 a** Sīk, ngóh sīk jyú ngàuh-yuhk tòng **b** Móuh, ngóh ūk-kéi fuh-gahn móuh jáu-làuh **c** Móuh, ngóh móuh bòng kéuih sáu **d** Ngóh m̀h nàu **e** M̀h haih **3 a** It's not a dessert **b** Since it's fresh, eat it! **c** There's lots **d** NEVER m̀h yáuh! **e** Léuhng not yih

Test yourself a Hái chyùh-fóng yáuh lùhng-hā, dōu yáuh sàang-gwó, yáuh faahn, yáuh tòng, yáuh tìhm-bán. Dōu yáuh Jèung Sìn-sàang **b** Yáuh, yáuh Jèung Sìn-sàang: kéuih haih laahp-saap-túng!

UNIT 5

Colour symbolism Yellow, Yellow

Dialogue 1, 1 Here hóu m̀h hóu a? means How about it?, What do you say? **2 a** Hóu pèhng. M̀h leng **b** Yáuh laahn. Jèung Síu-jé gó gihn dōu yáuh laahn

Language discovery 5.1 Today's Monday, not Sunday … I wonder why there are so many people in that shop?; Let me see whether there's damage to any of the others… **5.2** léuhng go sìng-kèih or léuhng go láih-baai. Of course in front of the classifier *go* the number 'two' must be *léuhng* not *yih* **5.3** to come back, to come in **5.6** The word ga-fē for *brown* is clearly a comparatively recent import. In the traditional colour scheme, red ran into yellow uninterrupted by brown, and browns were classified either as hùhng or wòhng

Dialogue 2, 1 Too many dead prawns **2 a** Kéuih séung máaih hā **b** Dī hā baat-sahp-ńgh mān yāt gàn **c** Kèih-tà dong-háu ge hā chāt-sahp-yih mān yāt gàn jē **3** lit. 'half catty 8 oz' = six of one and half a dozen of the other = They're both the same

Language discovery 5.11 *yes* dāk, *no* m̀h dāk

Listen and understand Láih-baai-yaht ngóh tùhng taai-táai heui-jó yāt gàan daaih-gáam-ga ge pou-táu máaih sāam-kwàhn. Gó-douh dī sāam-kwàhn yauh pèhng yauh leng, fún-sīk yauh sàn, ngàahn-sīk yauh hóu. Ngóh hóu séung máaih, taai-táai m̀h séung. Ngóh mahn kéuih: 'Dím-gáai m̀h séung máaih a?' / (Wife) 'Nī-douh ge sāam-kwàhn gihn gihn dōu haih chi-fo. Ngóh-deih fàan ūk-kéi lā!' / Ngóh taai-táai hóu sīk máaih-yéh. **1** Hóu is *very* here, so hóu séung is *very much wanted to* and hóu sīk is *knows very well how to* **2 a** Tùhng taai-táai heui **b** Séung máaih sāam-kwàhn **c** Yàn-waih gihn gihn dōu haih chi-fo **d** M̀h haih. Kéuih hóu sīk máaih-yéh

Practice 1 a máaih **4 b** làih **6 c** wán **2 d** sīk **1 e** heui **3 f** yuhng **5 2 a** jē / jēk **b** a? **c** lā **d** àh? **e** mē? **3 a** gwai **b** m̀h leng **c** daaih **d** m̀h dāk **e** móuh laahn **f** síu **g** làih or fàan **4 a** Hùhng-sik ge Méih-gwok chē hóu gwai **b** Ngóh bàh-bā sīk yàuh-séui **c** Wòhng Taai-táai heui pou-táu máaih-yéh **d** Kéuih gàm-yaht m̀h séung sihk-faahn **e** Hòh Sàang m̀h sihk Hòh Taai-táai jyú ge sung **5 a** gàan **b** No classifier needed **c** No classifier needed **d** jì **e** jek **f** jek-jek **6 a** Wòhng Táai yiu béi yih-sahp-baat mān **b** Kéuih yiu béi luhk-sahp-sei mān

Test yourself a Néih sīk m̀h sīk yàu-séui a? **b** M̀h-gòi néih tái-háh ngóh ge chē. Haih m̀h haih laahn-jó a? **c** Kéui máaih ge bāt haih jí-sīk ge **d** Néih sai-lóu jyuh ge ūk hái Yaht-bún bīn-douh a? **e** Gàm-yaht haih Sìng-kèih-ńgh, só-yíh ngóh heui Gáu-lùhng máaih léuhng gàn yú

UNIT 6

Finding your way They are always the opposite way round from English, i.e. Cantonese says 'eastnorth' where English says northeast

Vocabulary builder 1 bus, station

Dialogue 1, 1 X hái bīn-douh a? **2 a** T **b** F **c** F **d** F **e** F

Language discovery 6.5 Cantonese language, Japanese language, English language

Listen and understand

Wòhng Táai	Chéng-mahn, gwai sing a?	*Excuse me, may I ask your name?*
Chàhn Sàang	Ngóh sing Chàhn.	*My name is Chan.*
Wòhng Táai	Chàhn Sìn-sàang, néih hóu. Néih sīk m̀h sīk Yìng-gwok-wá a?	*How do you do, Mr Chan. Do you know English?*
Chàhn Sàang	Sīk, sīk. Daahn-haih m̀h dò, sīk hóu síu jē.	*Yes, yes, but not a lot, I only know a little.*

Wòhng Táai	Gám, m̀h-gòi néih wah ngóh tèng, Yìng-gwok-wá ge 'Bye-bye' haih māt-yéh a?	*In that case, please tell me what this English word 'Bye-bye' means.*
Chàhn Sàang	M̀h jì.	*Don't know.*
Wòhng Táai	Óh, 'Bye-bye' hái Gwóng-jàu-wá jīk-haih 'M̀h jì'. M̀h-gòi, m̀h-gòi, néih taai haak-hei lak.	*Oh, bye-bye means 'Don't know' in Cantonese. Thank you, thank you, that's very polite of you.*

Dialogue 2, 1 The trick is to get away from the Cantonese order and go for what it means rather than what it says. We suggest *I really enjoy going to the countryside* **2** where would it be good fun to go?, one of the most famous universities in the world, fishing ports (which are) in the southern part of the UK, so many, and what's more **3 a** M̀h haih Chàhn Sìn-sàang daih-yāt chi, haih Wòhng Sìn-sàang daih-yāt chi **b** Gim-kìuh Daaih-hohk m̀h haih hái Lèuhn-dēun fuh-gahn; yiu daap fó-chè heui **c** Haih **d** Hóu-chíh haih

Language discovery 6.6 The tone of the surname is changed to a mid rising tone. So the surname Wòhng becomes Lóuh Wóng and Chàhn becomes Lóuh Chán **6.12** He has been to Hong Kong; Have you ever been to a doctor?

Practice 1 a Gàm-yaht haih ngóh daih-yāt-chi chóh dihn-chè **b** Háaih, hā, lùhng-hā, ngóh dōu m̀h jùng-yi sihk. Ngóh jí-haih jùng-yi sihk yú jē **c** Hái Bāk-gìng bā-sí dò m̀h dò a? Ngóh m̀h jì **d** Gó gihn gām-sīk ge sāam-kwàhn hóu leng bo. Haih bīn-go ga? **e** Lèuhn-dēun yáuh hóu dò ūk. Ngóh hóu séung máaih yāt gàan, daahn-haih daaih ge taai gwai lak, sai ge dōu m̀h haih géi pèhng **2 b** 1 Yàuh Lèuhn-dēun heui Gim-kìuh Daaih-hohk chàam-gwùn yiu daap chē heung bak hàahng **c** 2 Yàuh nī-douh daap sahp-ńgh-houh bā-sí heui fèi-gèi-chèuhng yiu géi-dō chín a? **d** 4 Nī-douh ge deih-hah-tit-louh m̀h heui fèi-gèi-chèuhng jí heui Daaih-wuih-tòhng **e** 5 Néih yiu gwo sàam go gàai-háu dou Fà-yùhn Douh daap bā-sí heui fèi-gèi-chèuhng **3** Chóh, daap, jà, jyun, lohk, máaih, maaih, séuhng all regularly go in front of chē, and at a pinch you might add móuh, wán, yáuh, yiu, and perhaps some even more far-fetched verbs

Test yourself Hái fèi-gèi-chèuhng daap deih-hah-tit-louh heung dùng hàahng dou Jùng-wàahn lohk chē. Hái Jùng-wàahn heung nàahm hàahng, gwo léuhng go gàai-háu, jyun heung dùng jauh dou lak

UNIT 7

Passage 1 Yesterday mum asked us if we wanted to have salad. We all said we would like that. Mum said: 'Fine, so I'll make a lobster salad for you. Now, I'm going off to buy the lobster now, and you can go and buy some fresh fruit.' We bought lots of fresh fruit and prepared it all in the kitchen too. Mum came back half an hour later. She said: 'Today the lobsters are small and not fresh, so I didn't buy any, I only bought large prawns. You can pretend the prawn salad is lobster salad!'

1 a F **b** Unknown **c** T **d** F **e** F **2 a** Kéuih máaih-jó daaih hā fàan ūk-kéi **b** Ngóh-deih máaih-jó hóu dò sàn-sìn sàang-gwó fàan ūk-kéi **c** M̀h sàn-sìn **d** Sīk, go-go yàhn dōu sīk jíng sà-léut **e** Yáuh **3 a** Néih sihk-gwo ngàuh-yuhk sà-léut ma? **b** Nī jì Méih-gwok bāt haih ngóh jeui séung máaih ge bāt jì-yāt **c** Nī chi haih ngóh daih-yāt chi làih néih sé-jih-làuh **4 a** Deui-m̀h-jyuh, yìh-gā hóu jóu **b** Ngóh hái ūk-kéi **c** Ngóh séung chéng néih sihk-faahn **d** Néih hóu ma?

e Ngóh dōu hóu. Néih taai-táai nē? **f** Kéuih dōu-géi hóu. Néih tùhng m̀h tùhng ngóh fàan sé-jih-làuh a? **g** Hóu. Néih jà m̀h jà-chē heui a? **h** Chóh géi-dō houh bā-sí a? **i** Hóu, Láih-baai-sei ngóh tùhng néih yāt-chàih fàan sé-jih-làuh **5 a** kéuih màh-mā **b** yāt **c** pèhng **d** m̀h **e** hó-yíh **6 a** 2 Ngóh-deih sàam go yàhn nī go Sìng-kèih-luhk daap fèi-gèi heui Yìng-gwok wáan **b** 5 Wòhng Taai-táai tùhng Wòhng Sìn-sàang yāt-chàih làih ngóh ge sé-jih-làuh **c** 4 Néih ge jyú-yi yāt-dihng haih jeui hóu ge **d** 1 Nī gàan daaih-hohk haih sai-gaai yáuh-méng ge daaih-hohk **e** 3 Lèuhn-dēun haih Yìng-gwok jeui dò yàhn ge deih-fòng jì-yāt

Passage 2 Today I went to the office. Mr Ho told me he will be flying back to England on Thursday and so would not be coming into the office after Wednesday. Mr Ho is one of my best friends and I guess that he will not be returning here after he goes back this time. So, what can I give him as a present? I thought about it for a long while without any ideas, and then went to ask Miss Wong and Mrs Cheung. Miss Wong said: 'How about if the three of us were to ask Mr Ho out for a meal?' Mrs Cheung said: 'It would be best if Mrs Ho could come with him too.' I think that women have the best ideas. Do you agree?

UNIT 8

Hong Kong weather typhoon

Dialogue 1, 1 M̀h-hóu sàai sìh-gaan lā! **2 a** dihn-nyúhn-lòuh **b** m̀h saht-yuhng **c** chèuhng-gok **d** móuh yuhng-gwo **3 a** Heui Seuhng-hói Gāai nī dī bā sí **b** Yìh-gā sihk-gán mihn gó go Chàhn Táai **c** Ngóh sìh-sìh dōu heui sihk háaih gó gàan hói-sīn jáu-làuh **d** Hóu pa chóh hái ūk-kéi gó go hóu haak-hei ge síu-jé

Pronouncing trios Sìng-kèih-luhk *Saturday*; Fà-yùhn Douh *Garden Road*; sé-jih-làuh *office*; miht-fó-túng *fire extinguisher*; saai taai-yèuhng *to sunbathe*; Láih-baai-yāt *Monday*; Jèung Síu-jé *Miss Cheung*; dihn-nyúhn-lòuh *electric heater*; m̀h saht-yuhng *impractical*; yám hei-séui *to drink pop*

Vocabulary builder 2 bikini; useful

Dialogue 2, 1 Mrs Cheung **2 a** Kéuih séung máaih láang-hei-gèi **b** Jùng-yi. Kéuih jùng-yi yám bē-jáu **c** Kéuih dōu jùng-yi sihk **d** Tìn-hei taai yiht ge sìh-hauh **e** Sīk **3 a** M̀h dāk **b** Haih léuhng gihn

Language discovery 8.8 It has moved to the front of the sentence **8.10** He's very angry; He told me angrily …

Practice 1 a Ngóh-deih m̀h jì-dou (what your surname is) **b** Ngóh-deih m̀h sīk (how to swim) **c** Ngóh-deih m̀h sīk (how to use Japanese chopsticks) **d** Ngóh-deih m̀h jì-dou (which car is yours) **2 a** 2 **b** 4 **c** 1 **d** 3 **3 a** Jèung Síu-jé haih hóu leng ge Yaht-bún-yàhn **b** Ngóh m̀h séung máaih Chàhn Sìn-sàang pou-táu maaih ge Méih-gwok bāt **c** Ngóh hóu séung sihk Hòh Táai jíng ge lùhng-hā **4 a** 4 **b** 5 **c** 6 **d** 1

Test yourself M̀h-hóu nàu lā! Ngóh m̀h haih wah néih jì nī go miht-fó-túng haih saht-yuhng ge yéh mē?!

UNIT 9

A problem of age sàam seui

Dialogue 1, 1 Because he is asking a repeated question (Did you X? And did you Y?) **2** yāt *one*; chēut cl: for films; yāt chēut dihn-yíng *a movie*; yāt chēut … ge dihn-yíng *a movie which …*; hóu + yáuh-méng *very + famous*; hóu + hóu-tái *very + good to watch*; yāt chēut hóu yáuh-méng hóu hóu-tái ge dihn-yíng *a movie which is very famous and very good to watch* **3** kàhm-yaht tùhng chîhn-yaht dōu …; ngóh yāt-dī dōu …

Language discovery 9.2 to kick **9.4** Néih-deih gok-dàk nī chēut dihn-yíng chi m̀h chi-gīk a? **9.5** We haven't got a bean **9.6** In these two cases the word for *person* changes tone from yàhn to yán

Dialogue 2, 1 often, frequently **2 a** M̀h ngāam. kéuih sèhng-yaht góng-yéh **b** M̀h tùhng-yi

Language discovery 9.7 ńgh-sahp-géi seui *over 50 / in (my) fifties* **9.12** Ngóh sīk góng Gwóng-jàu-wá

Practice 1 a Hòh Sìn-sàang hóu-chíh ńgh-sahp seui gam-seuhng-há **b** Sìh-sìh wahn-duhng deui gihn-hòng hóu hóu **c** Ngóh jí-haih jùng-yi dá-bō, pàh-sàan tùhng yàuh-séui jē **2 a** 2 **b** 5 **c** 3 **d** 1 **e** 4 **3 a** 5, 2, 1 **b** 3, 1 **c** 1 **d** 8, 4 **e** 1, 3 **4 a** Wòhng Sàang sihk-yéh **b** Wòhng Táai jyú-yéh **c** Wòhng Síu-jé máaih-yéh **d** Jèung Sàang góng-yéh **e** Nī sàam go yàhn yám-yéh

Test yourself a Wòhng Sìn-sàang, jóu-sàhn **b** Good morning **c** Néih séung m̀h séung yám bē-jáu a? **d** I don't like beer **e** Òu, gám ga-fē nē? chàh nē? **f** Coffee and tea are both bad for you. I only drink water **g** Deui-m̀h-jyuh, ngóh-deih móuh séui. Ngóh taai-táai wah ngóh jì nī-douh ge séui m̀h hóu-yám. Dím-gáai m̀h yám bē-jáu a? **h** You keep saying I should drink beer. I've already told you I don't like it. You're really very impolite **i** Dī bē-jáu hóu hóu-yám, haih Yìng-gwok bē-jáu. Chéng yám síu-síu lā **j** This person is very impolite. I'm leaving **k** Òu, kéuih jáu lak!

UNIT 10

Dialogue 1, 1 jauh dāk lā! (lit. 'then it'll be OK') **2 a** toothache **b** tóuh **c** sáu (m̀h jà-dāk cannot hold)

Dialogue 2, 1 Way back in Unit 4 you learned that where a sentence starts with the definite article (*The*) a classifier will very often be the easiest way to translate it. Here Mr Wong asks, 'Is the stomach still aching?' **2** Chi means *an occurrence, a time*, and doubled it means *each time, every time*. As soon as you saw it you should have heard a little alarm bell ringing out a message in your head: 'Where is the dōu?' because you learned in Unit 5 that that is part of the pattern 'doubled classifier plus dōu'. And sure enough, read a little further and there it is. 'Every time before I take my medicine Mummy insists that I shake it …' **3 b** Haih, màh-mā chi-chi dōu yiu kéuih yìuh-wàhn dī yeuhk-séui sìn **c** M̀h haih, kéuih gok-dàk (haih) go tóuh m̀h syù-fuhk **d** M̀h haih, kéuih ngāam-ngāam yám-jó sahp fàn jūng jē

Language discovery 10.8 Thursday of last week; Saturday of this week; Wednesday of next week **10.10** Of course, it is hauh-yaht!

Practice 1 a Yī-sāng hái chán-só tái behng-yàhn **b** Wòhng Sìn-sàang haih Jùng-gwok-yàhn **c** Màh-mā hái pou-táu máaih-yéh **d** Hèung-góng-yàhn hái Hèung-góng jyuh **e** Wòhng

Wài-lìhm ge bàh-bā dōu haih sing Wòhng **2** Néih-deih léuhng-go yàhn yám-jó gam dò m̀h ngāam yám ge yéh deui sàn-tái m̀h hóu ge! Néih-deih dōu séung séi àh?! Wòhng Sìn-sàang, néih yám taai dò bē-jáu – m̀h-hóu yám lā! Wòhng Taai-táai néih yám taai dò ga-fē – m̀h-hóu yám lā! **3 a** Chàhn Sàang dá-gán bō **b** Kéuih sihk-gán lùhng-hā **c** Kéuih yám-gán bē-jáu **d** Kéuih áu-gán **e** Kéuih séi-jó lak

Test yourself Nī jek jyù-jái heui-jó máaih-yéh / Nī jek jyù-jái móuh lèih-hòi ūk-kéi / Nī jek jyù-jái sihk-jó ngàuh-yuhk / Nī jek jyù-jái móuh sihk-yéh / Nī jek jyù-jái wah: 'Òu! òu! òu!' jauh heui tái yī-sāng

UNIT 11

Fashion ngàuh = *ox, cattle*; jái = *son, boy*; ngàuh-jái = a very literal translation for *cowboy*, so ngàuh-jái-fu = *cowboy trousers, jeans*

Dialogue 1, 1 Of course not, she wants to try it on **2 a** Néih jì m̀h jì gó ga baahk-sīk ge chē yiu géi-dō chín a? **b** M̀h jì tìng-yaht wúih m̀h wúih lohk-yúh nē? **c** Ngóh dim jì a? **d** Ngóh sīk jyú Gwóng-jàu choi daahn-haih Bāk-gìng choi jauh m̀h sīk la **3 a** gei, bīn **b** ngóh, chàih, faahn **c** daap or chóh, fuhk **d** gwái séi, góng

Language discovery 11.2 a sàam-baak-yih-sahp-yih ga chē **b** yāt-chìn-baat-baak-lìhng-yih jek ngàuh **c** sei-yīk-lìhng-sei-sahp-luhk go Tòhng-yàhn **d** yih-sahp-baat-maahn-sàam-chìn-gáu-baak-yāt-sahp-ńgh mān **11.4** léuhng tìuh fu: Trousers are considered to be one garment, so 'pair' is not appropriate

Dialogue 2, 1 Another translation of tìm would be *what's more*, and in English that often shows exasperation. So you might translate this as: *Some (wretched) person passing by would think it was an empty chair and would want to go and sit down (on me)*. So tìm is not really translatable here; it's more a condiment giving a flavour of exasperation to the sentence **2** Yesterday I thought this chair was very comfortable, but now …! **3 a** sìh-jōng **b** m̀h hòi-sām **c** gihn ngoih-tou hóu leng **d** sō-fá-yí

Language discovery 11.7 You would not be sure whether the keys were in, on top of, under or just somewhere on the ground near the car

Listen and understand 1 Her caller, perhaps a would-be boyfriend but we can't be sure, has asked her out to dinner tomorrow evening. When she says she is busy he suggests the following evening, and she says that is OK, but then she asks what kind of food they are going to have, and she vetoes it because she is a vegetarian who eats only salad. 'And how are we getting to the restaurant?' she says, but when he tells her … well, we think: Wòhng Síu-jè góng daaih wah! Néih tùhng m̀h tùhng-yi a? **2** Wái! / Ngóh séung chéng néih sihk-faahn. / Géi-sìh a? / Tìng-máahn, hóu-m̀h-hóu a? / M̀h dāk, m̀h dāk. Ngóh tìng-máahn hóu mòhng. / Gám, hauh-máahn nē? / Hauh-máahn dāk. Néih chéng ngóh sihk māt-yéh sung a? / Ngóh jeui jūng-yi sihk ngàuh-yuhk, jyū-yuhk …. / Yauh m̀h dāk. Ngóh haih m̀h sihk yuhk ge yàhn. Ngóh jí-haih sihk sà-léut ge jē. Ngóh-deih chóh māt-yéh chē heui jáu-làuh a? / Tìn-hei gám leng, ngóh-deih hó-yíh chóh dihn-chē héui. / Néih móuh chē àh? Òu, … deui-m̀h-jyuh, màh-mā ngāam-ngāam wah ngóh tèng kéuih hauh-máahn hóu mòhng, yiu ngóh bòng kéuih jyú-sung. Daih-yih yaht joi-gin. Joi-gin.

Practice 1 a sahp-luhk go síu-jé **b** yih-baak jèung jí **c** ńgh-chìn-luhk-baak mān **d** yāt-baak-maahn go Jùng-gwok yàhn **e** yāt-maahn-yih-chìn-chāt-baak-ńgh-sahp **f** baat-chìn-lìhng-sàam-sahp-sei **g** sahp-yāt go jūng-tàuh **h** léuhng jek lùhng-hā **3 a** gauh-fún **b** taai pèhng **c** maaih ūk **d** jì-chìhn **e** yiht **f** sài-nàahm

Test yourself Mrs Ho is going to eat lobster on Monday; Miss Ho is going to see a film on Tuesday; and Mr Ho is going climbing on Wednesday

UNIT 12

A little learning In case you'd forgotten, *university* is daaih-hohk 大學 'big learning'. You met it in Unit 6. Tái-syù means *to read* (lit. 'to look at books')

Dialogue 1, 1 Cantonese verbs can be used as nouns (gerunds), e.g. studying. So sihk-yéh means *to eat*, but it can also mean *eating*, as in Kéuih sihk-yéh hóu sàn-fú *Eating is very hard for him* **2 a** yauh chúhng yauh dò **b** sei go jūng-tàuh **c** jùng-hohk **d** gaau-syù sìn-sàang

Language discovery 12.3 She talks about ngóh go jái and that tells you that she only has one son or at least that she is only talking about one son in this instance **12.6** linguistics, sociology

Dialogue 2, 1 *insist on (jumping)* or perhaps more colloquially *go and (jump the red light)* **2 a** jīk-haih **b** tìhng **c** gíng-chaat **d** daaih

Language discovery 12.7 east, south, west, north

Practice 1 a jek is not the correct classifier for students: it should be go-go **b** How can I say this sentence if it is true? **c** Never ever say m̀h yáuh – it is always móuh **d** The classifier is missing. It should read Gó léuhng go Méih-gwok … **e** Must be wrong. How could the father be only 8 years old?! **2 a** Ngóh go jái sái m̀h sái hohk Jùng-màhn a? **b** Kéuih múih máahn dōu yiu jouh géi-dō go jūng-tàuh gùng-fo a? **c** Ngóh go jái hái Lèuhn-dēun yíh-gìng duhk-gwo ńgh nìhn Síu-hohk. Yìng-gwok hohk-sāang sahp-yāt seui sìn-ji duhk Jùng-hohk. Hèung-góng haih m̀h haih yāt-yeuhng a? **d** Hái néih ge hohk-haauh duhk-syù, duhk yāt nìhn yiu géi-dō chín a? **e** Hohk-sāang sái m̀h sái máaih fo-bún tùhng lihn-jaahp-bóu a? **3 1** e **2** a **3** c **4** b **5** d

Test yourself a Ūk ngoih-bihn yáuh hei-chè **b** Wòhng Sàang hái Wòhng Táai jó-sáu-bihn **c** Bouh syù hái sō-fá-yí seuhng-bihn **d** Ngóh gú kéuih-deih máaih-yùhn yéh fàan-làih **e** Hái kéuih chìhn-bihn yáuh hóu dò séui **f** Go miht-fó-túng haih Wòhng Sìn-sàang máaih ge **g** Kéuih-deih go jái hái yí hah-bihn **h** Wòhng Táai yāt-dihng hóu m̀h hòi-sām

UNIT 13

The Cantonese as gamblers *Dog-track* is gáu-chèuhng; *casino* is dóu-chèuhng

Dialogue 1, 1 síu = *few*; síu-jó = *lessened*; lak = fp changed state; síu-jó lak = *have become fewer* **2 a** Dóu tói-bō **b** Yáuh sàam go jéung-bán: sàam-jéung haih ńgh mān jē (Did you remember to put in the classifier?) **3** M̀h syun lā. Jí-haih sung chín béi móuh chín ge yàhn jē

Dialogue 2, 1 Because he hopes to beat Mr Chan at mahjong and win money **2 a** Kéuih heui Ou-mún dóu **b** Kéuih wah wúih **c** M̀h haih, kéuih yèhng síu-síu jē

Language discovery 13.8 delicious (to drink); good looking, attractive; harmonious, melodic, easy on the ear

Sharpen your ears bāt-gok, bāk-gok; séui-hei, sèui-hei; hāt-yī, hāak-yì; taai-bohk, taai-gwok; bāt-hahng, bāk-hàhng; dá-yan, dá-yàhn; gùng-fù, fùng-fu; fó-chē, fo-chē

Practice 1 a Chàhn Táai gàm-máahn hóu m̀h dāk-hàahn **b** Ngóh bàh-bā sèhng-nìhn dōu m̀h dāk-hàahn **c** M̀h-gòi néih wah béi ngóh tèng néih go jái tìng-yaht mòhng m̀h mòhng a? **d** Kéuih Láih-baai-yih hóu mòhng **e** Ngóh jeui m̀h dāk-hàahn ge sìh-hauh haih jiu-jóu **2 a** Dī **b** gāan … jek **c** chèuhng **d** ga **3** mòhng / dāk-hàahn; syù-fuhk / sàn-fú; gaan-jūng / sìh-sìh; yèhng / syù; hohk-sāang / sìn-sàang; jing-fú / síh-màhn; fùng-fu / síu-síu; gáam-síu / jàng-gà

Test yourself a Ngóh gú haih Wòhng Táai yèhng chín **b** M̀h haih, kéuih hóu m̀h hòi-sām **c** Daih-luhk jek máh haih sei-houh (máh) **d** Gáu-houh máh yèhng **e** Haih Wòhng Taai-táai hóu sīk dóu-máh **f** M̀h ngāam, gáu-houh máh hóu-gwo sei-houh máh **g** Gáu-houh máh dōu hóu-gwo sàam-houh máh **h** M̀h haih, jeui hóu go jek máh haih gáu-houh máh **i** Nī chèuhng choi-máh yáuh luhk jek máh **j** Ngóh gú kéuih-deih haih syù dò-gwo yèhng lak

UNIT 14

Passage 1 When Mr Wong's seven-year-old son came to school yesterday he cheerfully told me that his father had bought a new house last week. The house was large and looked nice, with three bedrooms, and there was a front garden and a garage as well. He said: 'Now I have a room to myself, it's really comfortable. But mummy has to share a room with daddy, so I think she must be unhappy. I don't know why daddy won't let mummy use the third bedroom. No one is using that room now, daddy has only put a lot of books in there, that's all.'

1 a Kéuih haih chāt seui **b** Kéuih máaih-jó yāt gàan sàn ūk **c** Ūk chìhn-bihn yáuh fà-yún tùhng-màaih yāt gàan chē-fòhng tìm **d** Haih màh-mā yiu tùhng kéuih yāt-chàih **e** Daih-sàam gàan fan-fóng léuih-bihn yáuh hóu dò syù **f** Móuh **2 a** hèi-mohng **b** tìn-hei **c** láahng-tīn **d** dá-syun **e** dihn-yíng **f** wahn-duhng **g** gèi-yuhk **h** dò-yùh **i** gihn-hòng **j** noih-yùhng **k** hùhng-dāng **l** pìhng-gwàn **3 a** tìng-yaht **b** Láih-baai-yaht *or* Sìng-kèih-yaht **c** chìhn-yaht **d** sèhng-yaht **e** kàhm-yaht **f** Yaht-bún **g** gàm-yaht **h** yaht-yaht **i** hauh-yaht **4 a 1** The first horse is No. 9 **2** The first horse is not No. 9 **b 1** Miss Jung-san happens to be Japanese **2** Miss Jung-san really is Japanese **c 1** He is going to Canton tomorrow **2** He is not going to Canton until tomorrow **d 1** Mrs Chan has been to the USA more than ten times **2** Mrs Chan has been to the USA dozens of times **5 a** syù-fuhk **b** tìhng-chē ge **c** hóu dò chin **6 b** Wòhng Táai séung máaih gó ga chē, yàn-waih ga chē hóu leng **c** Ngóh m̀h mìhng-baahk gó go yàhn láahng-tīn séung máaih láahng-hei-gèi jouh-māt-yéh a? **d** Gó dī hā m̀h sàn-sìn, só-yíh Chàhn Táai m̀h séung máaih **e** Kéuih sihk-gán yéh ge sìh-hauh, m̀h góng-wá **7 a** Máaih gó ga chē yiu géi-dō chín a? **b** Wòhng Sàang Sìng-kèih-géi (*or* géi-sí) lèih-hòi Yaht-bún a? **c** Hái Léih Táai jó-sáu-bihn gó jehk gáu-jái haih bīn-go sung béi kéuih ga? **d** Gó dī yàhn yáuh géi-dō go haih gaau-syù sìn-sàang a?

Passage 2 Mr Ho bets on the horses: If a rich person wants to buy a horse, then he goes and buys one, but that's a very expensive way to 'buy a horse'! In Hong Kong you will often hear poor people saying 'I think I'll buy a horse today.' What's the explanation? Have a guess, what could it mean if a poor person talks about 'buying a horse'? That's right, 'to buy a horse' means 'to bet on a horse', so when poor people say they want to buy a horse that means they want to bet on a horse. / Mr Ho is not very rich. One day his good friend Mr Cheung phoned him up and asked him, 'There's horse racing tonight. I'd like to invite you to go with me to the racecourse to enjoy ourselves. What do you say?' Mr Ho happily said, 'Fine. Fine. Terrific idea!' / After finishing the phone call he told Mrs Ho. She said, 'You have never been horse racing before. This will only be your first time. I wonder if you'll like it?' Mr Ho said, 'Oh, you're right. This will be my first time horse racing. If I don't like it, I'll have to sit there with nothing to do! What can I do about it?' Mrs Ho said, 'You'd best buy a book before you go to the course. If you feel that it's fun watching the horses, then there's no need to read it. Otherwise, you can sit there and read. What do you think?' Mr Ho is a very docile man: he does whatever his wife says. So of course that evening before he went to the racecourse he bought a book. / Luckily, Mr Ho found the racing quite good fun and there was no need to read. But he didn't win a brass farthing; on the contrary he lost a great deal of money. When he went home he angrily said to his wife, 'Next time I go horse racing I won't listen to you! When you bet on a horse you want to bet to win, you shouldn't bet to lose!' / Do you get it? The pun is on máaih-syù which could be either *buy a book* or *bet and lose*, and superstitious gamblers believe that doing the one results in the other.

8 Mr Cheung came home from gambling at the dog track. His son asked him: 'Daddy, how did the gambling go today? Did you win?' 'Won nine races out of ten.' 'Wow! Daddy, you really know how to gamble. You bet on ten races and only lost on one.' 'To tell you the truth, I didn't win a cent. I bet on ten races and the dog track was the winner on each race!' / Here the pun is on gáu-chèuhng which sounds like either 'dog track' or 'nine races'. Mr Cheung's son naturally enough at first heard what he most wanted to hear, that his father had won handsomely.

UNIT 15

Five-star travel The classifier is jèung, because that is mostly used for objects whose functional surface is flat. And that applies to beds too.

Dialogue 1, 1 Ngóh m̀h seun does of course mean *I don't believe you / it*, but just as in English it is a standard way of expressing surprise, and Mrs Lee would not take offence **2 a** Jáu-dim fòhng-gāan léuih-bihn láahng-hei-gèi miht-fó-túng dōu móuh **b** Ǹgh-sīng-kāp jáu-dim haih jeui hóu jeui hóu ge jáu-dim **c** Yáuh-dī ǹgh-sīng-kāp jáu-dim léuih-bihn yáuh chán-só tùhng-màaih wahn-duhng fóng

Dialogue 2, 1 jauh means *just, spot on* and is the pair to 'if' ideas; so, 'If you check in here then that is just right'; bòng basically means *help* and is used for *on behalf of* (see Unit 10, Dialogue 1), so here it is 'weigh them for me'; kèih-tā appeared in Unit 5 and means *other*: 'Do you have any other luggage as well?'; dōu means *both* and refers to the two items of hand luggage; ló-fàan *take back* – the opposite of gàau *hand over*, which came earlier in the Dialogue **2 a** The tourist addresses her as 'Síu-jé' **b** The check-in attendant doesn't think so, addressing the tourist as 'Sìn-sàang' **c** Only two kilos **d** Four **e** The check-in attendant says he can't miss it

Language discovery 15.5 seuhng-jau **15.6** Sìng-kèih-yih hah-jau sei-dím-chāt-go-jih

Practice 1 b Fó-chē faai dihng-haih fēi-gèi faai nē? **c** Kéuih Láih-baai-sàam dihng-haih Láih-baai-sei làih nē? **d** Hòh Sìn-sàang séung heui Hèung-góng dihng-haih Gwóng-jàu nē? **e** Haih Léih Táai móuh chín dihng-haih Chàhn Táai móuh chín nē? **2 a** yaht-táu **b** yāt-dihng (yáuh) **c** láahng-séui **d** hèng **3 b** Wòhng Sàang máaih hā máaih-dāk hóu pèhng **c** Néih hàahng-louh hàahng-dāk faai-gwo Jèung Síu-jé **d** Néih yám yeuhng-jáu yám-dāk dò-gwo ngóh **e** Léih Sìn-sàang jà-chē jà-dāk m̀h-haih-géi-hóu **4 a** jèung **b** jek **c** ga **d** gàan **e** tìuh **f** ga **g** gàan **h** jèung **i** gihn **5 a** Yāt gàn chúhng-gwo yāt bohng **b** Hái Yìng-gwok máaih gihn-hòng bóu-hím hóu gwai **c** Tùhng-màaih chóh-gán fēi-gèi ge sìh-hauh dōu yáuh míhn-seui yèuhng-jáu maaih **d** M̀h-sái. (remember the normal negative of yiu is m̀h-sái) **e** Hái Lèuhn-dēun yáuh sei go fēi-gèi-chèuhng **6 a** sàam-dím-léuhng-go-jih **b** sahp-dím-sahp-yāt-go-jih **c** gáu-dím-bun **d** chāt-dím-sàam-go-gwāt **e** sahp-yih-dím-lìhng-gáu-fàn(-jūng) **f** ńgh-dím-sahp-ńgh-fàn(-jūng); ńgh-dím-sàam(-go-jih); ńgh-dím-yāt-go-gwāt

Test yourself Néih Láih-baai-luhk léuhng-dím-bun dou-jó máh-chèuhng

UNIT 16

Smile even if … jà faai-jí *to use chopsticks*; jà-sáu *to shake hands*

Dialogue 1, 1 No, in her second speech she asks him dī māt-yéh a?, expecting more than one thing in the answer **2** Ngóh gú yàn-waih gó go háau-si-gwùn pa-dou tàuh-wàhn fan-jó hái-douh jē

Language discovery 16.1 whether reactions to road conditions are fast enough

Dialogue 2, 1 And what's more it's still bleeding, see! **2 a** Ngóh wah kéuih hóu chì-sin lak **b** M̀h wúih **c** Yàn-waih dihn-dāan-chē waaih-jó yiu sàu-léih **d** M̀h hòi-sām ge yàhn hóu síu siu bo! Dòng-yín haih hòi-sām ge yàhn siu lā

Language discovery 16.8 He's not as tall as I am; Cars aren't as fast as planes; I don't walk as slowly as you do

Practice 1 a 1 **b** 1 **c** 1 (Generally Chinese people mention themselves first, in contrast to polite Western practice which is to put self last) **d** 1 **2 a** 2 I also think he is Japanese **b** 2 I give away his ten dollars **c** 2 Mrs Lee is going to Japan to get on a plane **d** 2 It is Mr Wong who is going with me to the City Hall to eat **e** 2 Whose wife is ill? **3 a** dá-màh-jeuk **b** dóu-pē-páai **c** chàu jéung-bán **d** tèng gwóng-bo **e** chùng hùhng-dāng **f** tái dihn-yíng **4** Wòhng Sàang gòu-gwo Chàhn Táai tùhng Wòhng Táai, móuh Léih Sàang Léih Táai gam gòu, daahn-haih tùhng Chàhn Sàang yāt-yeuhng gam gòu. Léih Sàang gòu-gwo Wòhng Táai hóu-dò. Léih Sàang jeui gòu **5 a** Waaih-yàhn **b** Ngh-wuih **c** Sàu-léih **d** yāt-sìh or yáuh-sìh

Test yourself a Mr Lee **b** Mrs Chan **c** Mr Chan **d** Mrs Lung **e** Mr Lung **f** Mrs Lee

UNIT 17

Uniforms hói-gwàn 海軍 luhk-gwàn 陸軍 and hùng-gwàn 空軍

Dialogue 1, 1 The verb ending -gán indicates that a state of affairs is ongoing. Here it reinforces yìh-gā *now* to ask what the applicant is 'currently working at' **2** If you translate yuhng làih sàn-chíng literally as *use [it] to come to apply*, you should be able to get the 'feel' of làih. It is showing a sense of purpose, so you can think of it as meaning *in order to: use [it] in order to apply* **3** You could have spun a coin and got the answer – what isn't tails is heads, and the correct answer is tàuh **4** You should not need to guess. The answer is 'Just one.' The singular classifier jèung is used in the first line of the dialogue

Language discovery 17.1 this photograph which is being used for applying for immigration

Dialogue 2, 1 Remember (yùh-gwó) … jauh … from Unit 4? Here yùh-gwó is missing but jauh gives it away, and it means *if [you] want us to believe you are coppers, then that would be hard*, or more fluently *How can you expect us to believe you are coppers?* **2** Sìn-sàang, m̀h-gòi néih gàau bún wuh-jiu tùhng-màaih chìm-jing béi ngóh lā. Néih géi-sí séung lèih-hòi Hèung-góng a? Nàh, jing-fú kwài-dihng m̀h jéun daai sáu-chēung yahp-làih Hèung-góng: m̀h-gòi néih gàau-béi daih-sei-sahp-yāt-houh gwaih-tói ge gíng-chaat Sà-jín lā **3** The missing word is séi *to die.* **a** My wife says that Mr Chan was driving too fast the day before yesterday, he crashed into a bus and was injured, and he may perhaps die **b** I think the Japanese your elder brother speaks is really funny. Yesterday when I heard him speaking it I (could have) died laughing **c** Mummy said that if I'm not good she will beat me to death. I don't believe it and I'm not scared of her either

Language discovery 17.11 She doesn't fancy even rice

Practice 1 a Wòhng Sàang pàh-gán sàan **b** Kéuih hái sēung-yàhn-chòhng seuhng-bihn fan-gaau **c** Kéuih tiu-gòu **d** Kéuih làai-jyuh jek gáu **e** Kéuih chóh hái sō-fá-yí seuhng-bihn **f** Kéuih kéih hái yāt jèung yí seuhng-bihn **2 a** gíng-chaat **b** sìn-sàang **c** sī-gēi **d** fuhk-mouh-yùhn **e** yī-sāng **3 a** Yāt nìhn yáuh sàam-baak-luhk-sahp-ńgh yaht **b** Tìng-yaht haih Láih-baai-yaht **c** Sei-yuht yáuh sàam-sahp yaht **d** Sàam go sìng-kèih móuh yāt go yuht gam dò yaht **e** Sàam nìhn noih-dī **4 a** Kéuih hái Chàhn Táai jó-bihn gó go síu-jé haih Wòhng Sàang sahp-chāt seui ge néui **b** Néih hái Méih-gwok léuih-yàuh máaih ge Yaht-bún chē haih bīn yāt ga chē a? **c** Néih nī go gauh ge miht-fó-túng m̀h gau daaih. Máaih yāt go daaih-dī ge, hóu m̀h hóu a?

Test yourself a sìn-ji: She said she would come back on Monday, but she didn't return until Wednesday **b** jì-hauh: After you had left I rang your wife **c** lìhn: Last month Mrs Wong didn't even sell one car: her manager was very unhappy about it **d** dōu: He plays mahjong every day, so he has no time to go shopping with me **e** jeuk sāam-kwàhn: It's not very convenient to wear a dress when swimming

UNIT 18

Crime Tái-háh is casual or of no vital importance – 'Oh look, the bus is coming!' But Tái-jyuh is urgent and demands your attention – 'Look out, there's a bus coming at you!'

Dialogue 1, 1 a No, she hasn't **2 a** Haih, yàn-waih kéuih yaht-táu m̀h dāk-hàahn heui máaih-yéh bo **b** Haih Náu-yeuk

Language discovery 18.3 dou gàm-nín wàih-jí, dou kàhm-yaht wàih-jí

Dialogue 2, 1 M̀h yiu!; Dōu m̀h yiu! **2** The thief is saying, 'I have no money to give you to be fined with.' Béi *give* was introduced in Unit 4

Language discovery 18.6 tái-dāk-dóu, daap-dāk-dóu, gú-dāk-dóu

Practice 1 a Gàm-yaht haih Sìng-kèih-géi a? **b** Lèuhn-dēun Fèi-gèi-chèuhng hái sìhng-síh bīn-bihn a? **c** Gwai-sing-a? **d** Dī hā géi-dō chín yāt gàn a? **e** Néih chāt-dím-jūng dihng-haih baat-dím-jūng heui nē? **2** Wòhng Sàang jeui daaih (Remember that daaih is used for comparative age, not for size) **3 a** faai-dī! **b** fong-ga **c** seuhng-bihn **d** suhk-sīk **e** yihng-jàn **f** yī-sāng **g** ngoih-tou **h** ngāam-ngāam **4 a** fàahn-wìhng **b** fòng-mihn **c** sàu-léih **d** yahm-hòh **e** míhn-seui **f** fòng-bihn **5 a** bāk-bihn **b** néuih-yán **c** gó-douh **d** yahp-bihn **e** gauh-nín **f** hauh-yaht **g** gá **h** néui **i** yeh-máahn **6 a** bihn-fuhk **b** chèuhn-lòh-chē **c** gá ge **d** daahn-haih **e** m̀h jéun

Test yourself Of course your version may not be the same as ours, but we suggest the following: **a** Ngóh haih Wòhng Taai-táai, wán Wòhng Sìn-sàang tèng dihn-wá **b** Ngóh haih Wòhng Taai-táai, wán Wòhng Sìn-sàang tèng dihn-wá **c** Néih chì-sin lak! Ngóh jauh haih néih taai-táai. Chì-sin, jàn-haih chì-sin lak! **d** Ngóh yuhng ngóh sàn ge sáu-tàih-dihn-wá-gèi **e** Ngóh yuhng-jó máaih-sung ge chín làih máaih ge

UNIT 19

Money Pound sterling (£)

Dialogue 1, 1 Hóu ak is polite acceptance: *Certainly, sir.* Ngóh jì-dou is *I know*, and lak shows change of state, lit. 'I have changed to knowing'. So we might translate it as *Understood* **2 a** M̀h haih, kéuih hóu m̀h hòi-sàm **b** M̀h wúih, kéuih hàang-dāk hóu maahn bo!

Vocabulary builder 2 You were remembering noih-hóng-yàhn from Unit 15. You learned ngoih-bihn (outside) in Unit 12, and noih has the opposite meaning (inside), as in noih-yùhng (contents) which you met in Unit 9. So now you have the pair, *outsider* and *insider*

Dialogue 2, 1 In a Chinese restaurant **2 a** M̀h haih. Kéuih móuh góng Méih-gwok maaih ge haih māt-yéh bo **b** Kéuih ge gūng-sī m̀h jouh Bà-sài sàang-yi ge la **c** Yàn-waih kéuih pa yùh-gwó tèng gam nàahn-tèng ge wá kéuih jauh wúih móuh-saai waih-háu ge-lak

Language discovery 19.9 *unripe* and *ripe* respectively

Practice 1 a Yáuh luhk-sahp fàn **b** Haih yih-sahp-ńgh **c** Haih baak-fahn-ji-ńgh-sahp suhk **d** Haih sahp-yih-dím **e** Haih pou-táu làih-ge **2 a** Hái sìhng-síh **b** Gok-dāk sàn-fú **c** Geuk-jai yuhng-làih tìhng-chē ā-ma **d** Jóu-chàan haih yāt yaht daih-yāt chi sihk yéh. Haih yaht-táu sihk ge **3 a** 2 **b** 1 **c** 2 **d** 2 **e** 2 **4 a** 2 You and I may not go there **b** 1 I cannot drive on the outlying islands **c** 1 I'll come in the afternoon **d** 1 I like eating fruit and salad **e** 1 When are you going to Japan and what do you intend to do there?

Test yourself a Chàhn Sàang jeui daaih **b** Néuih-ge haih baak-fahn-jī-luhk-sahp **c** Nàahm-ge dòng-yín haih baak-fahn-jī-sei-sahp lā **d** Haih Chàhn Táai gòu **e** Kéuih-deih yáuh sàam go jái

UNIT 20

Money again jèung, of course

Dialogue 1, 1 to register **2 a** Hùng-yàuh gwai hóu dò **b** Wúih, wúih daaih hóu dò **c** Chìu-gwo, yiu yah-sei mān gam dò

Language discovery 20.3 Yāt-yuht yāt-houh, Ńgh-yuht yah-sàam-houh

Dialogue 2, 1 Because he is taking money (See Unit 5, 5.12) **2 a** Kéuih sihk-yùhn léuhng gūng-gàn hā jì-hauh gok-dāk hóu m̀h shyù-fuhk **b** Gauh-nín ngóh hái Lèuhn-dēun ge sìh-hauh, sèhng-yaht lohk-yúh **c** Jà-gán chē ge sìh-hauh, ngóh m̀h jùng-yi kìng-gái **d** Wùih-gwài-chìhn, hái Hèung-góng jyuh ge Yìng-gwok-yàhn dò-gwo yìh-gā **e** Jèung Sìn-sàang gauh-nín heui Tòih-wàan, gàm-nín Ńgh-yuht sìn-ji wúih fàan-làih

Practice 1 2+5+52+10+24+7 = 100 **2 a** Mr Wong hates taking medicine **b** Don't open your eyes wide and stare at me! **c** Materials which are not up to standard are treated as seconds **d** It is, of course, illegal to gamble in a gambling den **e** We should pay more attention to the study conditions of our children **3 a** Luhk-yuht sei-houh **b** Yāt-gáu-gáu-chāt-nìhn Chāt-yuht yāt-houh **c** Yih-lìhng-lìhng-sei-nìhn Ńgh-yuht sahp-ńgh-houh **d** Sahp-yih-yuht sahp-yāt-houh Láih-baai-yaht hah-jau luhk-dím-sàam-go-jih **e** Chēut-nín Baat-yuht sà-ah-yāt-houh **4 a** Yìng-gwok **b** Lèuhn-dēun **c** chìu-gwo yāt-maahn Yìng-bóng **d** yihn-gām **5 a** chēut-gāai / hàahng-gāai **b** daaih-yeuk **c** hùng-yàuh **d** gìng-léih **e** ló-tái

Test yourself a Jèung Táai yèhng-jó yāt-maahn-baat-chìn-yih-baak mān. Hòh Sàang yèhng-jó yāt-maahn-sàam-chìn-luhk-baak-ńgh-sahp mān. Wòhng Sàang yèhng-jó yāt-maahn-lìhng-gáu-baak-yih-sahp mān. Léih Táai yèhng-jó gáu-chìn-yāt-baak mān. Chàhn Sàang yèhng-jó yih-chìn-chāt-baak-sàam-sahp mān jē **b** Ńgh-sahp-yih-go-bun

UNIT 21

Passage 1 Several hundred years ago in a place in the north of China there lived a rich man called Wong. He had lots of horses, all of them tall, mighty and handsome, and he loved them very much. One day a handsome but rather old horse went missing. Mr Wong's friends all felt it was a great pity and they thought that he would be angry and very unhappy, but quite on the contrary he was not only not angry but believed that the horse would come back very soon. After a few days the horse really did come back. His friends said Mr Wong was very fortunate, but he just smiled and said: 'That old horse knows what's what, [I knew] he could find the way home, that's all.'

Passage 2 Long ago there was a doctor in Canton. One day he wrote a letter of great importance to a doctor in another city. At that time China did not have a post office and he was very busy and had no time to take the letter there, so he told his son to take it for him. He said to his son: 'This letter is very important, it must get there quickly! Let's see, the more legs the quicker: your two legs won't be as quick as four legs. You had better use my horse to go. Hurry up!' / The young man set off and his father awaited his return. He knew that a horse would need about eight hours to get to that place and back. Who could have guessed that it was two days before his son returned. He said cheerfully to his father: 'I'm back, dad. Was I quick? I thought and thought and thought up a very fast method. You said the more legs the quicker and that two legs were not as fast as four … so I walked leading the horse along … if two legs aren't as fast as four, then six legs were bound to be faster than four legs, right?'

1 Séung-làih-séung-heui 'think coming think going' means *to rack your brains, to think and think* **a** walking up and down **b** running to and fro **c** We bargained and bargained but couldn't agree a price **2 a** An average horse weighs about 1,000 lbs (yāt-chìn bohng) **b** On average a horse dies at about 20 years of age (yih-sahp seui) **c** A horse can only stay healthy if it exercises for at least half an hour a day (bun go jūng-tàuh) **d** A horse must eat at least 20 lbs of food a day (yih-sahp bohng) **3** 10 a.m. Call taxi; 10.30 a.m. To Manager Wong's office; 12.15 p.m. Lunch in City Hall with Miss Cheung; 3.30 p.m. Get air ticket from travel company; 6.45 p.m. Drinks with Miss Ho at Hong Kong Hotel; 7.30 p.m. Cinema with Miss Ho **4 a** chà-m̀h-dō **b** hahm-baahng-laahng **c** daahn-haih **d** ngāam-ngāam **e** yáuh-sìh **f** jouh-māt-yéh **5 a** Kéuih yàuh-séui, só-yíh m̀h yiht m̀h sàn-fú **b** Kéuih gàm-yaht m̀h jà laahp-saap-chē, kéuih jà kèih-tà chē a **c** Kéuih yih-sahp nìhn jì-chìhn haih yāt go yáuh yāt-chìn-maahn mān ge yáuh-chín yàhn **6** Wòhng Sìn-sàang ge sàn chē: **a** hóu leng **b** leng-haih-leng, daahn-haih móuh Jèung Sàang ge sàn chē gam leng **c** m̀h-haih-géi-leng **d** m̀h gau daaih **e** taai gwai la **f** haih sai-gaai seuhng jeui leng ge chē **g** leng-gwo ngóh ga chē hóu-dò **h** tùhng Jèung Sàang ge sàn chē yāt-yeuhng gam daaih yāt-yeuhng gam gwai **7 a** wái (or go, but that is not really polite enough) **b** lìhn **c** lóuh **d** géi … noih **e** daaih **8 a** Wòhng Sàang A-geuk yiu béi dò-dī (B-geuk kéuih m̀h sái béi) **b** B-geuk haih Léih Sàang yiu béi baat-baak mān **c** Jèung Sàang A-geuk yiu béi sàam-baak mān, B-geuk yiu béi ńgh-baak mān, jīk-haih wah kéuih B-geuk yiu béi dò yih-baak mān **d** Béi jeui síu ge haih Chàhn Sàang: béi jeui dò ge haih Léih Sàang **9 a** Ngóh màhh-mā dá-dihn-wá (ge sìh-hauh) góng-dāk dōu-géi maahn **b** Nī dī ga-fē m̀h gau yiht **c** Néih séung yám bē-jáu dihng-haih séui nē? **d** Néih gó jì seuhng-go-yuht máaih ge bāt móuh ngóh nī jì gam gwai. or Néih seuhng-go-yuht máaih ge gó jì bāt … **e** Kéuih giu ngóh wah béi néih jì néih yiu géi-dò dím jūng làih **f** Wòhng Sìn-sàang lìhn lùhng-hà dōu m̀h jùng-yi sihk **g** Nī dī syù yáuh sàam-fahn-jì-yih haih Jùng-màhn syù **h** Kéuih yuht-làih-yuht-yáuh-chín **10** In July, August and September the weather in Hong Kong is very hot. When it's hot people like to travel by taxi, because cabs are plentiful and comfortable. Why comfortable? Because they all have air-conditioning. Four or five people can get in a taxi and it's not very expensive, in fact, very cheap. Ordinary cars are blue or green, white, red, black or yellow, every colour under the sun, but taxis are different, they are all painted red and silver.

UNIT 22

Water water buffalo

Dialogue 1, 1 yáuh gáu go jih sihk aan-jau means *there are 45 minutes for lunch.* Remember that yāt go jih is *five minutes* **2 a** baat go bun jūng-tàuh **b** yāt-chìn-lìhng-ńgh-sahp mān

Dialogue 2, 1 dinosaur **2 a** Kéuih jyuh hái gó go sìhng-síh chìu-gwo yah-ńgh nín lak **b** Ngóh meih yám-gwo Faat-gwok jáu **c** Yùh-gwó néih séung sàn-chíng hái gó gàan gūng-sī jouh-gūng, néih yāt-dihng sìn yiu sé fùng seun béi gìng-léih **d** Ngóh-deih yiu-chíng néih gaau Gwóng-jàu-wá jì-chìhn, ngóh-deih séung tèng-háh néih góng síu-síu Gwóng-jàu wá sìn

Language discovery 22.8 You really must eat those prawns; Mrs Wong says you simply must go to visit her

Practice 1 a M̀h haih, ngóh m̀h haih Méih-gwok-yàhn **b** Haih, kéuih-deih yuht-làih-yuht-waaih **c** Haih, ngóh meih sihk-gwo jóu-chāan **d** M̀h haih, kéuih hóu jùng-yi fàan-gùng

e Haih, yāt-yeuhng gam jùng-yi **2 a** mēi **b** béi **c** fàan **d** dyún **3 a** -gán **b** -jyuh **c** -gwo **d** -saai **e** -hòi

Test yourself a Chāt-maahn-lìhng-yih-baak-mān **b** Haih Chàhn Sàang ló ge chín dò (Hòh Sàang yāt-guhng jí-haih ló yih-maahn-sei jē) **c** Wòhng Táai gàm-yaht bāt-gwo yuhng-jó yah-sei-go-bun jē **d** Ngóh ūk-kéi yāt-guhng yáuh sahp-ńgh go yàhn (Ṁh-hóu ṁh gei-dāk ngóh lā!)

UNIT 23

Different restaurants, different food Tòhng refers to the Tong (Mandarin: Tang) dynasty AD 618–906, which Cantonese people think of as a particularly splendid period in their history

Dialogue 1, 1 Jùng-gwok-choi **2 a** Ṁh haih, haih gwai-gwo **b** Yàn-waih kéuih hái Faat-gwok hòi chāan-tēng **c** yāt-làuh

Language discovery 23.6 Ngóh góng Gwóng-jàu-wá góng-dāk hóu ṁh hóu; Deui-ṁh-jyuh, ngóh jí-haih sīk góng síu-síu jē; Ngóh góng ge Gwóng-jàu-wá móuh néih Yìng-màhn gam hóu

Dialogue 2, 1 It shows disillusionment: *I didn't realize before but in fact you are nostalgic when it comes to food too* **2 a** Ṁh haih, hóu gauh, jauh-faai chaak ge lak **b** Haih gàm-yaht gà-ga ge jē **c** Hóu jùng-yi, giu-jó yú tùhng-màaih hā tìm

Language discovery 23.8 Ṁh haih, móuh yàhn gin-gwo lùhng bo!

Practice 1 a yāt-làuh **b** gìng-jai **c** làai-yàhn **d** jai-fuhk **e** sàn-séui **2 a** Yàuh ngàhn-hòhng heui Hòh Sàang ūk-kéi jí yáuh léuhng gūng-léih jē **b** Ngàhn-hòhng hái Hòh Sàang ūk-kéi dùhng-bihn **3 a** Yiu tìhng-chē bo! **b** Làahm-sīk gà wòhng-sīk haih luhk-sīk **c** Làahm-sīk gà hùhng-sīk haih jí-sīk **d** Hóu gauh ge dihn-yíng haih hāk-baahk-sīk ge **4** 'Nī tìuh yú jàn-haih leng, yāt-dihng hóu hóu-meih. Bīn-wái háng béi yāt-maahn mān a?' **5 a** Wàh! Nī-douh dī hói-sīn jàn haih hóu-meih, yauh sàn-sìn yauh jíng-dāk leng. Sīk-hèung-meih dōu haih yāt-làuh ge **b** All our fish are live here, of course they're fresh **c** Ṁh-gòi màaih-dāan lā **d** Thank you. $2,890 **e** Māt-yéh wá?! Gam dò gé! Jàn-haih ṁh pèhng a! **f** You should know that it's very hard to buy live fish now. Added to that, our restaurant presents you with chopsticks, one pair for each customer **g** Ngóh meih máaih-gwo gam gwai ge faai-jí a. Hóu lā. Ṁh pèhng, daahn-haih dōu dái. Nī-douh haih sàam-chìn mān **h** Thank you

Test yourself a Kéuih haih sei-sahp bohng **b** Haih yauh-sáu **c** Kéuih yìh-gā luhk seui **d** Kéuih jí-haih gàau-jó baat-sahp mān béi fuhk-mouh-yùhn jē!

UNIT 24

Hobbies Syù-fóng (lit. 'book room' or 'writing room') is a *study, private library*. Syù-póu (lit. 'book shop') is just that, a *bookshop*

Dialogue 1, 1 secretary (lit. 'secret writer') **2 a** How about ṁh jùng-yi? **b** Of course not. Ga-kèih means *leave* in the sense of *holiday* **c** chēut-làih wán is *come out to look for it* and chēut-làih wáan means *come out to play*

Language discovery 24.1 a Gó dī syù néih séung tái bīn bún a? Bīn bún ngóh dōu m̀h séung tái **b** Néih jùng-yi jouh māt-yéh gūng-jok a? Ngóh māt-yéh gūng-jok dōu m̀h jùng-yi jouh **c** Néih gàm-máahn chéng géi-dō go yàhn-haak làih sihk-faahn a? Géi-dō dōu m̀h chéng **24.5** ngóh-wah or ngóh-tái

Dialogue 2, 1 Mrs Wong says, 'You should urge your son not to play so many computer games.' Note how closely the Cantonese resembles a direct command (e.g. Don't do that!) **2 a** Seuhng-go-sìng-kèih ngóh gin-dóu yāt go néih ge jái, m̀h haih Wài-lìhm jauh haih Wài-lìhm sai-lóu lak **b** Ngóh bàh-bā sèhng-yaht dōu hóu mòhng, m̀h haih tek jūk-kàuh jauh haih tái-syù lak **c** Ngóh m̀h chìng-chó: kéuih m̀h haih Láih-baai-yāt heui Bāk-gìng jauh haih Láih-baai-sàam heui Bà-sài lak

Practice 1 a a shadow **b** kàhm-yaht **2 b** Ngóh hái ūk-kéi ge sìh-hauh, m̀h daai móu **c** Nàahm-yán luhk-sahp-ńgh seui sìn-ji hó-yíh ló teui-yàu-gām **d** Ngóh gàm-jìu-jóu yāt tái bou-jí jauh jì-dou ngóh-deih gūng-sī ge chìhng-fong hóu ngàih-hím **e** Chàhn Sìn-sàang yuht yám bē-jáu yuht jùng-yi yám or Chàhn Sìn-sàang yuht-làih-yuht-jùng-yi yám bē-jáu **3 a** Yāt go sai-mān-jái séung làai gáu, daahn-haih jek gáu m̀h séung hàahng **b** Yāt go nàahm-yán tèui-jyuh yāt ga waaih-jó ge chē. Kéuih taai-táai jà-jyuh gó ga waaih chē **c** Yáuh yàhn hòi faai chē chùhng-gwo hùhng-dāng **d** Gíng-chaat yuhng sáu-chēung dá-séi-jó yāt go yáuh chēung ge waaih yàhn **4 a** chìhn-bihn **b** bāk-bihn **c** nī-douh **d** yauh-sáu-bihn **e** chēut-bihn

Test yourself a Chéng-mahn, yáuh móuh bā-sí heui gèi-chèuhng a? **b** Yàuh Daaih-wuih-tòhng heui gèi-chèuhng yiu géi-dō chín a? **c** Yiu chóh géi-noih (bā-sí) a? **d** Bā-sí yáuh móuh chi-só a? **e** Yih-ńgh-yāt-houh bàan-gèi géi-dō-dím-jūng héi-fèi a? **f** Yih-ńgh-yāt-houh bàan-gèi géi-sí dou Lèuhn-dēun a?

UNIT 25

Housing in Hong Kong Sàan-déng ge láu gwai-gwo Sàn-gaai ge hóu dò

Dialogue 1, 1 Ngóh-deih jauh kyut-dihng m̀h wahn lak *We decided not to move them after all* **2 a** Kéuih haih jih-géi yāt-go-yàhn jyuh ge **b** Syut-gwaih yāt-dihng yáuh: Hèung-góng gam yiht, móuh syut-gwaih m̀h dāk bo! **c** Kéuih luhk go yuht chìhn yìh-jó màhn lak

Language discovery 25.3 rice bowls, soup bowls, tea bowls; big bowls, little bowls **25.4 a** yìh-gā kéuih m̀h làih lak **b** dím-gáai m̀h tái lak? **c** Sìng-kèih-sei jì-hauh jauh m̀h wúih lohk lak

Dialogue 2, 1 'Sir, we're there.' Clearly they have gone up in the lift **2** Yāt gàan ūk certainly does mean *house*, but ūk is also used in a more general way to mean *housing, dwelling, residence, the premises* **3** criminals, miscreants, baddies **4** Think back to tái-m̀h-dóu 'look but not succeeding' *unable to see*. In this case jeuhk, which amongst other things means *to catch fire*, is doing the same job as dóu: 'lying down but not sparking', *unable to get to sleep*

Language discovery 25.9 (camera) film, a store, boss, brandy

Practice 1 a gíng-chaat-guhk **b** chyùh-fóng **c** chán-só or yì-yún **d** haak-tēng **e** sé-jih-làuh **f** ngàhn-hòhng **g** dóu-chèuhng **h** yàuh-gúk **2 a** M̀h-gòi néih m̀h-hóu yūk a **b** Néih góng-dāk dōu m̀h-haih-géi-ngāam bo **c** Néih yáuh-dī m̀h-haih-géi-mìhng-baahk ah **d** Ngóh dōu m̀h hó-yíh (or m̀h wúih) tùhng-yi **e** Deui-m̀h-jyuh, Gim-kìuh Daaih-hohk dōu m̀h haih sai-gaai seuhng jeui yáuh-méng ge

Test yourself (Suggested answer) Taai-táai, gó chàhng láu yauh daaih yauh leng. Jyú-yàhn-fóng hóu daaih, yáuh tou-fóng chi-só tùhng chùng-lèuhng-fóng; juhng yáuh daih-yih gàan fan-fóng tùhng-màaih daih-yih go chùng-lèuhng-fóng tìm. Haak-tēng tùhng chyùh-fóng dōu-géi daaih. Yáuh léuhng ga līp, juhng yáuh chē-wái bàau-kwut hái ūk-ga léuih-bihn. Deih-jí hóu hóu, jīk-haih Gwóng-jàu Douh yah-chāt-houh baat láu. Ga-chìhn hóu pèhng: bāt-gwo yiu ńgh-baak-ńgh-sahp-maahn mān Góng-jí jē. Ngóh hóu séung máaih!

UNIT 26

1 a Gìng-léih ge gùng-jok jauh haih yiu gwún-léih-hóu kéuih ge gūng-sī **b** Hòi-chí hòi-chē jì-chìhn néih yiu jyu-yi māt-yéh a? **c** Sàn-sìn ge hói-sìn hóu hóu-sihk **d** Hèung-góng yáuh hóu dò yāt-làuh ge jáu-làuh **2 a** yàuh-séui **b** dihn-yíng **c** dá-bō **d** Góng-jí **e** chìm-jing **3 a** la **b** àh … a **c** mē / àh … lā **d** bo … nē **4 a** hái hói-sìn jáu-gā **b** hái máh-chèuhng **c** hái bā-sí-jaahm **d** hái ngóh ūk-kéi **e** hái sé-jih-làuh **5 a** jèung **b** fūk **c** ga **d** tou **e** tou **f** douh **6 a** It doesn't make sense: how can he be rich if he hasn't got even $1? **b** How can you be older than your mother? **c** M̀h does not go with -gwo: it should be meih tái-gwo **d** It should be hàahng-dāk sahp-fān faai **e** Yìh-ché does not go with sèui-yìhn: change yìh-ché to daahn-haih

Passage 1 a Chì-sin! Nī go sai-gaai kèih-saht bīn-douh yáuh lùhng a? **b** Yàn-waih kéuih pa tìuh lùhng wúih fēi-jáu la **c** shook itself a few times **Translation**: A very long time ago in China there was a man who loved painting. His pictures were superb, especially when he was painting dragons, they looked just as though they could move. Once a high official, getting to know that he was good at painting dragons, said to him with great delight: 'I myself love dragons too. If you were willing to paint a dragon for me I would pay you very well.' / A few days later sure enough the dragon was done and very well painted at that. It attracted a lot of people who came to look at it. But alas the dragon had no eyes. The official was mystified and asked why he did not paint the eyes. The painter replied that if he did so the dragon would fly away. / Of course no one could believe what he said. The official was very angry and insisted on him putting the eyes in. Strange as it may seem, as soon as he had painted them the dragon gave a few shakes and really did jump out from the paper and fly away.

Passage 2 a M̀h ngāam. Sèung-fáan kéuih hóu lohk-hauh la **b** Kéuih hēi-mohng Léih Táai yahp-jó fóng-jái chēut-làih jì-hauh wúih hauh-sāang-jó ge lak **Translation**: Seventy or 80 years ago Shanghai was considered a very advanced city, but many other cities and rural areas of China were still very backward. / One day a certain Mr Lee came up from the country with matters about which he needed to see his friend Wong Tai Kwok in Shanghai. Mr Wong lived in a large and beautiful hotel with all possible facilities. / When Mr Lee got to the hotel and was waiting in the lobby for Mr Wong, he saw an elderly lady slowly walk into a tiny room. He had never seen a lift, so he didn't know that that was what it was. A couple of minutes later the doors of the little room opened and out walked a beautiful young lady. / Mr Lee at first thought it very strange, but afterwards he said gleefully: 'The city folks really are advanced: next time I'll be sure to bring my wife with me.'

Cantonese–English vocabulary

Numbers in brackets indicate the unit in which the entry is introduced.

Abbreviations

app	=	appendix
cl	=	classifier
fp	=	final particle
ve	=	verb ending

ā	丫	*fp: triumphantly scoring a point*	(8)
a-	呀	*prefix for names/relationships*	(22)
a!	呀!	*fp: emphatic, exclamatory*	(12)
a?	呀?	*fp: finishes a question*	(1)
àai!	唉!	*alas!*	(19)
aan-jau	晏晝	*midday; lunch*	(22)
àh?	吖?	*fp: that's right, isn't it?*	(3)
ái	矮	*short, squat, low*	(22)
A-jàu	亞洲	*Asia*	(19)
ak	呃	*fp: 'that will be quite alright'*	(19)
ā-ma!	丫嗎!	*fp: you should realize*	(5)
a-múi	阿妹	*younger sister*	(3)
áu	嘔	*vomit*	(10)
Aù-jàu	歐洲	*Europe*	(19)
Aù-lòh (Aù-yùhn)	歐羅（歐元）	*Euro (€)*	(19)
bá	把	*cl: for umbrellas, tools, etc.*	(8)
baahk-faahn	白飯	*boiled / steamed rice*	(25)
baahk-jí	白紙	*blank paper*	(20)
baahk-sīk	白色	*white*	(5)
baahn-faat	辦法	*method, way, means*	(18)
baak	百	*hundred*	(11)
baak-fahn-jì-sàam	百分之三	*three per cent*	(19)
baak-fo-gūng-sī	百貨公司	*department store*	(8)
bàan	班	*cl: group of, gang of*	(17)
bāan-gèi	班機	*scheduled flight*	(15)
baat	八	*eight*	(2)
bàau	包	*wrap up*	(20)
bàau-gwó	包裹	*parcel*	(20)
bàau-kwut	包括	*include*	(25)
baau-tàai	爆呔	*have a puncture*	(16)
bàh-bā	爸爸	*father*	(3)
baht-lāan-déi	拔蘭地	*brandy*	(25)
baih!	嘥!	*oh dear! oh heck! alas!*	(17)
bāk	北	*north*	(6)
bāk-bihn	北邊	*north side*	(12)
Bāk-bìng-yèuhng	北冰洋	*Arctic Ocean*	(19)
Bāk-gìng	北京	*Beijing (Peking)*	(1)
Bāk-gìng-choi	北京菜	*Peking food*	(23)
Bà-sài	巴西	*Brazil*	(1)
bā-sí	巴士	*bus*	(3)

bā-sí-jaahm	巴士站	*bus stop*	(6)
bāt	筆	*pen*	(2)
bāt-gwo	不過	*but, however*	(17)
bāt-gwo	不過	*only*	(20)
bāt-yùh	不如	*it would be better if*	(19)
behng	病	*illness*	(10)
behng-yàhn	病人	*patient, sick person*	(10)
béi	俾	*give*	(4)
béi-gaau	比較	*compare, comparatively*	(19)
béi-gìn-nèih	比堅尼	*bikini*	(8)
beih	被	*by (passive)*	(12)
beih-bīk	被逼	*forced to*	(11)
beih-gò	鼻哥	*nose*	(9)
bei-maht	秘密	*secret*	(24)
bei-syù	秘書	*secretary*	(22)
bē-jáu	啤酒	*beer*	(4)
bihn-faahn	便飯	*pot luck*	(4)
bihn-fuhk	便服	*plain clothes*	(17)
bihn-yì	便衣	*plain clothes*	(17)
biht-yàhn	別人	*other people*	(24)
bīn?	邊?	*which?*	(2)
bīn-douh?	邊度?	*where?*	(3)
bìng-bām-bō	乒乓波	*table-tennis*	(9)
bīn-go?	邊個?	*who? which one?*	(2)
bin-nyúhn	變暖	*warm up*	(23)
bīn-syu?	邊處?	*where?*	(3)
bíu-gaak	表格	*form, table*	(20)
bíu-yihn	表現	*perfom, performance*	(22)
bō	波	*ball*	(9)
bo!	噃!	*fp: let me tell you*	(5)
bohng	磅	*pound (weight)*	(12)
bòng	幫	*on behalf of, for the benefit of*	(10)
bòng … sáu	幫 … 手	*help*	(4)
bòng-báan	幫辦	*inspector*	(17)
bòng-chan	幫襯	*patronize, give custom*	(23)
bō-sí	波士	*boss*	(25)
bóu	補	*compensate*	(22)
bou-dou	報到	*check in, register*	(15)
bou-douh	報導	*report, to report*	(18)
bóu-fàan-sou	補返數	*make up for*	(10)
bouh	部	*area, part, portion*	(6)
bouh	部	*cl: for books*	(12)
bóu-hím	保險	*insurance*	(15)
bouh-mùhn	部門	*department*	(19)
bou-jí	報紙	*newspaper*	(18)
bóu-jing	保證	*guarantee*	(20)
bou-líu	布料	*material, fabric*	(11)
bóu-òn	保安	*security, keep secure*	(25)
bùi	杯	*cl: a cup of, glass of*	(25)
būi	杯	*cup, glass*	(25)
bui-jek	背脊	*back (of body)*	(9)
bun	半	*half*	(4)
bún	本	*cl: for books*	(12)
bún-chìhn	本錢	*capital*	(13)

bún-deih	本地	*local, indigenous*	(18)
bun-sàang-suhk	半生熟	*medium (cooked steak)*	(19)
chà	差	*not up to scratch, lacking*	(19)
chà-m̀h-dō	差唔多	*almost*	(12)
chàai-lóu	差佬	*policeman*	(12)
chàai-yàhn	差人	*policeman*	(12)
chaak	拆	*demolish, tear down*	(23)
chāak-yihm	測驗	*test; evaluation*	(12)
chàam-gà	參加	*take part in*	(11)
chàam-gwùn	參觀	*visit a place*	(6)
chàan	餐	*cl: for meals*	(4)
chāan	餐	*meal*	(4)
cháang-jāp	橙汁	*orange juice*	(4)
cháang-sīk	橙色	*orange (colour)*	(5)
chāan-páai	餐牌	*menu*	(23)
chāan-tēng	餐廳	*restaurant*	(23)
cháau-faahn	炒飯	*fried rice*	(25)
chàh	查	*investigate, check*	(19)
chàh	茶	*tea*	(4)
Chàhn	陳	*surname: Chan*	(1)
chàhng	層	*cl: for a flat, apartment; storey, deck*	(3)
chàh-wú	茶壺	*tea-pot*	23
chàh-wún	茶碗	*tea bowl*	(25)
chàih-chyùhn	齊全	*complete, all embracing*	(23)
chàn-ngáahn	親眼	*with one's own eyes*	(18)
chán-só	診所	*clinic*	(10)
chāt	七	*seven*	(2)
chàuh-fáan	囚犯	*prisoner*	18
chàuh-fún	籌款	*fund raising*	(13)
chàu-jéung	抽獎	*lucky draw*	(13)
chàu-tīn	秋天	*autumn*	(8)
che	斜	*steep*	(16)
chē	車	*car*	(1)
chē-fòhng	車房	*garage*	(3)
chèh-deui-mihn	斜對面	*diagonally opposite*	(12)
chek	呎	*foot (length)*	(25)
chek	赤	*red; naked*	(19)
chek-geuk-yī-sāng	赤腳醫生	*barefoot doctor*	(19)
chek-jih	赤字	*in the red, deficit*	(19)
Chek-laahp-gok	赤鱲角	*Chek Lap Kok (airport)*	(6)
che-lóu	斜路	*steep road*	(16)
chéng	請	*invite*	(4)
chéng	請	*please*	(3)
chéng-mahn	請問	*please may I ask*	(6)
chē-sìh	車匙	*car-key*	(16)
chē-tàai	車呔	*car-tyre*	(16)
chèuhng	場	*cl: for performances, bouts, games*	(13)
chèuhng	長	*long*	(22)
chèuhng-gok	牆角	*corner*	(8)
chèuhng-maht	長襪	*stockings*	(11)
chèuhng-sai	詳細	*detailed, fine, minute*	(22)
chèuhn-lòh-chē	巡邏車	*patrol car*	(17)
chèuih-bín	隨便	*as you please, feel free*	(4)

chéui-sìu	取消	*cancel*	(10)
chéun	蠢	*stupid*	(22)
chēung-lím-bou	窗簾布	*curtains*	(25)
chèun-tīn	春天	*spring*	(8)
chēut	齣	*cl: for films and plays*	(9)
chēut	出	*out*	(17)
chēut-bihn	出邊	*outside*	(12)
chēut-gāai	出街	*go out into the street*	(18)
chēut-háu	出口	*exit*	(6)
chēut-nín	出年	*next year*	(8)
chē-wái	車位	*parking space*	(25)
chi	次	*time, occasion*	(6)
chi-fo	次貨	*seconds*	(5)
chi-gīk	刺激	*exciting*	(9)
chìh-dī	遲啲	*later*	(2)
chìh-gāng	匙羹	*spoon*	(23)
chìhn-bihn	前邊	*front*	(12)
chìhn-geí-nìhn	前幾年	*a few years ago*	(18)
chìhng-fong	情況	*situation, circumstances*	(16)
chìhn-máahn	前晚	*evening of the day before yesterday*	(11)
chìhn-nín	前年	*year before last*	(10)
chìhn-yaht	前日	*day before yesterday*	(9)
chìh-sihn	慈善	*charity*	(13)
chīm-jing	簽證	*visa*	(15)
chín	淺	*light (coloured); shallow*	(25)
chín	錢	*money*	(5)
chìn	千	*thousand*	(11)
chìng-chó	清楚	*clear, clearly*	(18)
chìng-git	清潔	*cleaning*	(25)
chìn-kèih	千祈	*whatever you do, don't*	(16)
chín-làahm-sīk	淺藍色	*light blue*	(25)
chì-sin	黐線	*crazy*	(16)
chi-só	廁所	*toilet*	(10)
chit-beih	設備	*facilities, equipment*	(15)
chit-gai	設計	*design*	(11)
chìu-gwo	超過	*exceed*	(19)
chìuh-sāp	潮濕	*humid*	(8)
cho	錯	*ve: error*	(19)
chóh	坐	*sit*	(3)
chóh	坐	*travel by*	(6)
chóh-gāam	坐監	*in prison*	(18)
chóh-hòi-dī	坐開啲	*sit further away*	(17)
chóh-màaih-dī	坐埋啲	*sit closer*	(17)
chòhng	床	*bed*	(15)
choi	菜	*vegetables; food, cuisine*	(4)
choi-chē	賽車	*motor racing*	(16)
choi-chē-sáu	賽車手	*racing driver*	(16)
choi-dōu	菜刀	*kitchen chopper*	(23)
chòih-gáam	裁減	*cut, reduce*	(19)
choi-máh	賽馬	*race horses*	(13)
chò-kāp	初級	*elementary, first grade*	(24)
chòuh	嘈	*noisy*	(22)
chúhng	重	*heavy*	(12)
chúhng-leuhng	重量	*weight*	(15)

chùng	衝	rush, dash against	(12)
chùng-lèuhng	沖涼	have a shower	(25)
chùng-lèuhng-fóng	沖涼房	bathroom, shower room	(25)
chyúh-chūk	儲蓄	savings; to save	(19)
chyùh-fóng	廚房	kitchen	(4)
chyùhn	全	whole, entire	(12)
chyùhn-bouh	全部	all, the whole lot	(23)
chyùhn-jān	傳真	fax	(22)
chyùhn-jān-gèi	傳真機	fax machine	(22)
chyùhn-kàuh	全球	global	(23)
chyùhn-túng	傳統	traditional	(22)
chyú-léih	處理	deal with, handle	(22)
chyùn-suhk	全熟	very well done (steak)	(19)
dá	打	hit	(9)
dá go dyún-seun	打個短訊	send a text message	(22)
daahn-haih	但係	but	(6)
daahn-sing	彈性	flexible	(22)
daai	帶	lead, guide	(2)
daai	戴	wear	(11)
daaih	大	big	(3)
daaih-dong	大檔	gambling den	(13)
daaih-fōng	大方	tasteful, sophisticated	(11)
daaih-gáam-ga	大減價	sale	(5)
daaih-hohk	大學	university	(6)
daaih-lóu	大佬	older brother	(3)
daaih-máh-louh	大馬路	main road	(15)
daaih-mùhn-háu	大門口	main doorway	(20)
Daaih-sài-yèung	大西洋	Atlantic Ocean	(19)
daaih-sèng	大聲	loud, in a loud voice	(11)
daaih-tòhng	大堂	lobby	(26)
daaih-wah-gwái	大話鬼	liar	(9)
daaih-wuih-tòhng	大會堂	city hall	(6)
Daaih-yàhn	大人	Your Honour, Your Excellency	(18)
daaih-yeuk	大約	approximately	(20)
dāan-chē	單車	bicycle	(16)
dāan-yàhn-chòhng	單人床	single bed	(15)
daap	搭	travel by	(3)
daap-līp	搭軨	ride in a lift	(25)
daap-m̀h-dóu	搭唔倒	unable to catch	(18)
daap-dāk-dóu	搭得倒	able to catch	(18)
dá-bō	打波	play ball	(9)
dá-dihn-wá	打電話	make a phone call	(10)
dá-fó	打火	strike fire	(24)
dá-fó-gèi	打火機	cigarette lighter	(24)
dá-fùng	打風	typhoon	(8)
dá-gāau	打交	fight	(18)
dá-gip	打劫	rob	(18)
dahk-biht	特別	special	(23)
Dahk-biht hàhng-jing kèui	特別行政區	Special Administrative Region (SAR)	(20)
dahk-daaih	特大	XL, extra-large	(12)
dahk-faai	特快	express	(20)
Dahk-kèui	特區	SAR (Special Administrative Region)	(20)
Dahk-sáu	特首	Chief Executive of SAR	(20)

dá-hòh-bāau	打荷包	purse snatching, to pick pockets	(18)
dái	抵	worth it	(15)
daih-	第	prefix for ordinal numbers	(6)
daih-mēi	第尾	last in order	(22)
daih-yāt	第一	the first	(6)
daih-yih	第二	the second, the next	(6)
dá-jih	打字	type	(22)
dá-jih-gèi	打字機	typewriter	(24)
dāk	得	can	(6)
dāk	得	OK	(5)
dāk	得	ve: in such a way	(15)
Dāk-gwok	德國	Germany	(1)
dāk-hàahn	得閒	at leisure	(13)
Dāk-màhn	德文	German language	(12)
dá-léhng-tàai	打領呔	tie a necktie	(10)
dá-màh-jeuk	打麻雀	play Mahjong	(13)
dáng	等	let, allow	(5)
dáng	等	wait	(4)
dàng	瞪	stare, open the eyes	(17)
dāng	燈	light, lamp	(12)
dàng-daaih-deui-ngáahn	瞪大對眼	take a good look	(17)
dáng-dáng	等等	etcetera	(15)
dáng-ngóh-béi	等我俾	let me pay	(5)
dá-sou	打掃	sweep	(25)
dá-syun	打算	intend	(8)
dá-yan	打印	print	(22)
dá-yan-gèi	打印機	printer	(22)
dehng-fóng	定房	book a room	(24)
dehng-tói	定枱	book a table	(24)
deih-fòng	地方	place	(6)
deih-há	地下	ground floor, the ground, the floor	(3)
deih-hah-tit-louh	地下鐵路	underground railway	(6)
deih-jí	地址	address	(20)
deih-jīn	地氈	carpet	(25)
Deih-jùng-hói	地中海	Mediterranean Sea	(19)
deih-léih	地理	geography	(12)
deih-mín	地面	floor	(25)
deih-tit	地鐵	underground railway	(6)
deih-tit-jaahm	地鐵站	underground station	(6)
déng	頂	cl: for hats	(11)
deui	對	cl: pair of	(9)
deui	兌	exchange money	(19)
deui	對	with regard to, towards	(9)
deui-m̀h-jyuh	對唔住	sorry	(1)
deui-mihn	對面	opposite	(12)
deui-wuhn-léut	兌換率	exchange rate	(19)
dī	啲	cl: for plurals and uncountables	(4)
dihn	電	electricity	(16)
dihn-chè	電車	tram	(6)
dihn-dāan-chē	電單車	motorbike	(16)
dihn-dāng	電燈	electric light	(9)
dihn-faahn-bōu	電飯煲	electric rice cooker	(9)
dihng-haih	定係?	or?	(13)
dihn-jí	電子	electronic	(25)

dihn-nóuh	電腦	*computer*	(9)
dihn-nyúhn-lòuh	電暖爐	*electric heater*	(8)
dihn-sih	電視	*television*	(9)
dihn-sih-gèi	電視機	*television set*	(15)
dihn-tòih	電台	*radio station*	(13)
dihn-wá	電話	*telephone*	(9)
dihn-yàuh	電郵	*email*	(22)
dihn-yàuh	電油	*petrol, gas*	(16)
dihn-yíng	電影	*film (cinema)*	(9)
dihp	碟	*cl: a dish of*	(23)
diht-jeuih	秩序	*order*	(12)
dīk-sí	的士	*taxi*	(3)
dīk-sih-gōu	的士高	*discotheque*	(24)
dím	點	*spot, dot, point*	(23)
dím(-yéung)?	點（樣）？	*how? in what way?*	(5)
dím-gáai?	點解？	*why?*	(4)
dím-sām	點心	*dim sum*	(4)
díp	碟	*dish, plate*	(23)
dit	跌	*fall, fall down*	(19)
diuh-tàuh	掉頭	*turn to face the other way*	(16)
dò	多	*many, much*	(3)
dò-dī	多啲	*a little more*	(15)
dò-jeh	多謝	*thank you*	(5)
dò-jeh-saai	多謝晒	*thank you very much*	(15)
dong	當	*regard as*	(4)
dong-háu	檔口	*street stall*	(5)
dòng-yín	當然	*of course*	(13)
dou	到	*arrive, arrive at, reach*	(6)
dóu	賭	*gamble on, bet on*	(13)
dóu	倒	*ve: successfully*	(8)
dōu	都	*all, both*	(4)
dōu	都	*also*	(1)
dóu-bō	賭波	*bet on football*	(13)
dóu-chèuhng	賭場	*casino*	(13)
dóu-chín	賭錢	*gamble with money*	(13)
dóu-gáu	賭狗	*bet on dogs*	(13)
dōu-géi	都幾	*quite*	(3)
dóu-gú-piu	賭股票	*gamble on shares*	(13)
douh	度	*cl: for doors*	(20)
douh	道	*road, street*	(3)
dóu-máh	賭馬	*bet on horses*	(13)
dóu-ngoih-wuih	賭外匯	*gamble on foreign exchange*	(13)
dóu-pē-páai	賭啤牌	*gamble at cards*	(13)
dou-yìh-gā-wàih-jí	到而家爲止	*up to now*	(18)
dò-yùh	多餘	*surplus*	(9)
duhk-laahp	獨立	*independent*	(22)
duhk-séi	毒死	*poison, be poisoned*	(17)
duhk-syù	讀書	*study*	(12)
dùng	東	*east*	(6)
dùng-bāk	東北	*northeast*	(6)
dùng-bihn	東邊	*east side*	(12)
dùng-nàahm	東南	*southeast*	(6)
dùng-tīn	冬天	*winter*	(8)
dyún	短	*short*	(22)

dyún-maht	短襪	socks	(11)
dyún-seun	短訊	text message	(22)
faahn	犯	offend, commit crime	(18)
faahn	飯	rice, food	(4)
fáahn-duhk	販毒	peddle drugs	(17)
faahn-tēng	飯廳	dining room	(25)
fàahn-wìhng	繁榮	prosperous	(13)
faahn-wún	飯碗	rice bowl	(25)
faai	塊	cl: for carpets, land plots	(25)
faai	快	fast, quick, quickly	(15)
faai-dī	快啲	get a move on!	(17)
faai-jí	筷子	chopsticks	(6)
faai-lohk	快樂	happy	(23)
fàan	返	return	(3)
fàan sé-jih-làuh	返寫字樓	go to the office	(3)
fàan-gùng	返工	go to work	(22)
fāan-tāan	番攤	fantan	(13)
fáan-ying	反應	reaction	(16)
Faat-gwok	法國	France	(1)
faat-gwùn	法官	judge, magistrate	(18)
Faat-màhn	法文	French language	(12)
faat-muhng	發夢	have a dream	(25)
faat-ok-muhng	發噩夢	have a nightmare	(25)
faat-sàng	發生	happen, occur, transpire	(18)
fahn	份	cl: newspapers	(18)
fahn-jí	份子	element, member	(12)
faht-chín	罰錢	fine, be fined	(18)
fai-yuhng	費用	cost, fee	(15)
fàn (-jūng)	分（鐘）	minute (clock)	(10)
fan-m̀h-jeuhk(-gaau)	瞓唔著（覺）	unable to get to sleep	(25)
fan-fóng	瞓房	bedroom	(14)
fan-gaau	瞓覺	sleep	(16)
fan-lihn	訓練	training, to train	(24)
fàn-míhn	分娩	give birth	(22)
fā-yéung	花樣	pattern	(11)
Fà-yùhn-Douh	花園道	Garden Road	(3)
fà-yún	花園	flower garden	(2)
feì	飛	fly	(24)
fēi	飛	ticket	(15)
feì-faat	非法	illegal	(13)
fèi-gèi	飛機	aircraft	(6)
fèi-gèi-chèuhng	飛機場	airport	(6)
fèi-gèi-piu	飛機票	air ticket	(15)
fèih	肥	fat, obese	(22)
Fèi-jàu	非洲	Africa	(19)
fèi-lám	菲林	film (for camera)	(25)
fèi-sèung (jì)	非常（之）	extraordinary, extraordinarily	(22)
fō	科	subject, discipline	(12)
fó-buhn	伙伴	partner	(19)
fo-bún	課本	textbook	(12)
fó-chè	火車	railway train	(6)
fó-chè-tàuh	火車頭	railway engine	(19)
fó-gei	伙記	waiter, junior employee	(4)

fō-geih	科技	science and technology	(24)
fòhng-gāan	房間	room	(15)
fō-hohk	科學	science	(12)
fòng-bihn	方便	convenient	(17)
fong-ga	放假	take a holiday	(9)
fong-gùng	放工	finish work	(22)
fòng-mihn	方面	aspect	(12)
fu	副	cl: for spectacles	(11)
fu	褲	trousers	(11)
fú	苦	bitter	(23)
fuh-gahn	附近	nearby	(4)
fuh-jaak	負責	responsible	(22)
fuhk-mouh	服務	service	(15)
fuhk-mouh-yùhn	服務員	waiter; one who serves	(15)
fūi-sīk	灰色	grey	(5)
fūk	幅	cl: for paintings, curtains	(17)
fūk-leih	福利	benefits, welfare	(22)
fùng	封	cl: for letters	(19)
fùng	風	wind	(8)
fùng-fu	豐富	rich, abundant	(13)
fùng-séui	風水	geomancy, Feng Shui	(22)
fún-sīk	款式	style	(5)
fùn-yìhng	歡迎	welcome	(22)
ga	架	cl: for vehicles, machinery	(3)
gá	假	false	(17)
ga?	㗎?	fp = ge + a?	(2)
gāai	街	street	(3)
Gáai-fong-gwān	解放軍	People's Liberation Army (PLA)	(17)
gāai-háu	街口	street corner	(6)
gaai-siuh	介紹	introduce	(4)
gáam-sàn	減薪	reduce wages	(19)
gáam-síu	減少	reduce, cut down	(9)
gàan	間	cl: for houses and rooms	(3)
gáan-dàan	簡單	simple	(20)
gaan-jip	間接	indirectly	(22)
gaan-jūng	間中	occasionally	(10)
gàau	交	hand over	(15)
gáau-m̀h-dihm	攪唔掂	can't be done, can't cope	(19)
gáau-dihm	攪掂	fix, cope with	(19)
gaau-syù	教書	teach	(12)
gàau-tùng	交通	traffic, communication	(12)
gàau-tùng-dāng	交通燈	traffic lights	(12)
gaau-yuhk	教育	education	(12)
ga-chìhn	價錢	price	(11)
ga-chìhn-páai	價錢牌	price tag	(11)
ga-fē	咖啡	coffee	(4)
ga-fē-sīk (fē-sīk)	咖啡色（啡色）	brown	(5)
gà-ga	加價	increase price	(23)
gahn or káhn	近	close to	(20)
gāi	雞	chicken	(23)
gà-jē	家姐	older sister	(3)
ga-kèih	假期	holiday	(22)
gam	咁	so	(4)

gám	敢	dare	(18)
gám	噉	so, in that case	(3)
gàm-jìu-jóu	今朝早	this morning	(4)
gàm-máahn	今晚	this evening, tonight	(11)
gàm-nín	今年	this year	(8)
gam-noih	咁耐	so long a time	(18)
gam-seuhng-há	咁上下	approximately	(9)
gàm-sìh-gàm-yaht	今時今日	nowadays	(22)
gām-sīk	金色	gold, golden	(5)
gàm-yaht	今日	today	(4)
gám-yéung	噉樣	in that case, so	(3)
gán	緊	ve: -ing	(4)
gàn	斤	catty	(5)
Gà-nàh-daaih	加拿大	Canada	(1)
gàn-jyuh	跟住	following, accordingly	(19)
gán-yiu	緊要	important	(21)
ga-sái	駕駛	driving, to drive	(16)
gau	夠	enough	(16)
gáu	狗	dog	(13)
gáu	九	nine	(2)
gauh	舊	old (not new), used	(8)
gauh-nín	舊年	last year	(8)
gau-jai-gām	救濟金	relief money	(18)
gau-jūng	夠鐘	time's up	(13)
Gáu-lùhng	九龍	Kowloon	(1)
Gau-mehng a!	救命呀!	Help! Save me!	(18)
gà-yàhn	家人	family member(s)	(3)
gà-yahp	加入	join, recruit into	(17)
ge!	嘅!	fp: that's how it is!	(3)
ge	嘅	links adjectives to nouns	(4)
ge	嘅	shows possession; -'s	(2)
gé	嘅	fp: puzzlement, surprise	19
gei	寄	post a letter, mail	(20)
géi	幾	quite, rather, fairly	(3)
géi	幾	several	(9)
géi?	幾?	how many? how much?	(9)
gèi-chèuhng	機場	airport	(6)
Gèi-chèuhng Faai-sin	機場快綫	Airport Express Line	(6)
gei-dāk	記得	remember	(9)
géi-dō?	幾多?	how much? how many?	(5)
gèi-fùh	幾乎	almost but not quite	(18)
géi-gam … lak!	幾咁 … 嘞!	how very …!	(18)
gèi-hei	機器	machine, machinery	(24)
géi-nihm	紀念	memorial, to commemorate	(20)
géi-noih?	幾耐?	how long?	(20)
gèi-piu	機票	air ticket	(15)
géi-sí? or géi-sìh?	幾時?	when?	(8)
gèi-wuih	機會	chance, opportunity	(22)
gèi-yuhk	肌肉	muscle	(9)
ge-la	嘅喇	fp: strong emphasis	(5)
ge-lak	嘅嘞	fp: anticipated result; 'this will be'	(19)
géng	頸	neck	(9)
géng-hot	頸渴	thirsty	(22)
géui-baahn	舉辦	run, hold, conduct	(15)

geuk	腳	foot, leg	(9)
geuk-jai	腳掣	footbrake	(16)
geuk-jí	腳趾	toe	(9)
gihn	件	cl: most clothing items	(5)
gihn-hòng	健康	healthy	(9)
gím-chàh	檢查	check, inspect	(25)
gím-hung	檢控	accuse	(12)
Gim-kìuh	劍橋	Cambridge	(6)
gin	見	see, meet	(8)
gìn-chìh	堅持	insist, insist on	(25)
gíng-chaat	警察	policeman	(12)
gìng-gwo	經過	pass by, via	(11)
gìng-jai	經濟	economy, economic	(13)
gìng-léih	經理	manager	(15)
gíng-yùhn-jing	警員証	warrant card	(17)
git-chūk	結束	come to an end	(19)
git-gwó	結果	result	(16)
giu	叫	tell to do	(17)
go	個	cl: for people and many objects	(2)
gó	嗰	that, those	(2)
gó-douh	嗰度	there	(5)
gói	改	alter	(8)
gói-bin	改變	change, alter	(24)
gó-jahn-sìh	嗰陣時	at that time	(10)
gok-dāk	覺得	feel	(9)
gò-kehk	歌劇	opera	(24)
gòn	乾	dry	(22)
góng	講	speak	(9)
góng daaih-wah	講大話	tell lies	(9)
Góng-baih	港幣	Hong Kong dollar	(19)
Góng-jí (Góng-yùhn)	港紙（港元）	Hong Kong dollars	(19)
gong-kàhm	鋼琴	piano	(24)
góng-siu	講笑	joke	(16)
gòn-jehng	乾淨	clean	(15)
gón-jyuh	趕住	hurrying	(15)
gó-syu	嗰處	there	(5)
gòu	高	high, tall	(10)
gòu-yíh-fù-kàuh	高爾夫球	golf	(9)
gú	估	guess	(2)
gú-m̀h-dóu	估唔倒	unable to guess	(18)
gú-dāk-dóu	估得倒	able to guess	(18)
gù-duhk	孤獨	solitary	(24)
gu-haak	顧客	customer, client	(23)
guhk	局	bureau, office, department	(16)
guih	劫	tired	(24)
gùng-faai	公筷	communal chopsticks	(24)
gùng-fo	功課	homework	(12)
gūng-gàn	公斤	kilogram	(12)
gùng-guhng	公共	public	(12)
gùng-gwàan	公關	public relations	(15)
gùng-héi	恭喜	congratulations	(23)
gùng-jok	工作	work	(22)
gūng-léih	公里	kilometre	(23)
gūng-sī	公司	company	(8)

gùng-yàhn	工人	*worker, servant*	(25)
gùng-yàhn-fóng	工人房	*servant's room*	(25)
gú-piu	股票	*stocks and shares*	(13)
gwàai	乖	*well behaved, obedient, 'good boy'*	(13)
gwàan-haih	關係	*relationship, relevance, connection*	(13)
gwa-houh	掛號	*register*	(10)
gwai	貴	*expensive*	(1)
gwái	鬼	*devil, ghost*	(10)
gwai-gwok	貴國	*your country*	(23)
gwaih-tói	櫃台	*counter*	(15)
gwái-lóu	鬼佬	*Westerner, 'devil chap'*	(10)
gwai-sing-a?	貴姓呀?	*what is your name?*	(1)
gwàn-deui	軍隊	*army*	(17)
gwàn-fuhk	軍服	*military uniform*	(17)
gwa-ngāu	掛鈎	*peg*	(19)
gwàn-yàhn	軍人	*soldier, military personnel*	(17)
gwāt(-jung)	骨（鐘）	*quarter (clock)*	(15)
gwo	過	*than*	(12)
gwo	過	*ve: past, across, by*	(6)
gwo-bóng	過磅	*weigh*	(15)
gwo-chúhng	過重	*overweight*	(15)
gwok-gà	國家	*country, state*	(19)
gwòng(-máahng)	光（猛）	*bright*	(25)
gwóng-bo	廣播	*broadcast*	(13)
Gwóng-dùng	廣東	*Guangdong (province)*	(23)
Gwóng-dùng-choi	廣東菜	*Cantonese food*	(23)
Gwóng-jàu	廣州	*Guangzhou (Canton)*	(1)
Gwóng-jàu-wá	廣州話	*Cantonese language*	(23)
gwo-nìhn	過年	*Chinese New Year*	(23)
gwo-sìh	過時	*overtime*	(22)
gwún	管	*control, be in charge of*	(12)
gwùn	官	*official, officer*	(16)
gwún-léih	管理	*management, manage*	(25)
hà!	哈！	*ha ha!*	(23)
hā	蝦	*prawn, shrimp*	(5)
hàahm	鹹	*salty*	(23)
hàahng	行	*walk*	(15)
hàahng-gāai	行街	*go out into the streets*	(15)
hàahng-hòi-jó	行開咗	*not here*	(17)
hàahng-louh	行路	*walk along*	(15)
hàahng-sàan	行山	*walk in the country, hiking*	(15)
háaih	蟹	*crab*	(5)
hàaih	鞋	*shoes*	(11)
haak-hei	客氣	*polite*	(4)
hāak-sīk	黑色	*black*	(5)
haak-tēng	客廳	*living room, lounge*	(25)
hàan	慳	*stingy; to save*	(8)
háau	考	*examine, test*	(16)
háau-si	考試	*examination*	(16)
háh	吓	*ve: briefly, have a little*	(5)
hah-(yāt)-chi	下（一）次	*next time*	(15)
hah-bihn	下邊	*under, underside*	(12)
hah-go-láih-baai	下個禮拜	*next week*	(10)

hah-go-yuht	下個月	next month	(17)
hah-jau	下晝	afternoon, p.m.	(15)
hahm-baah(ng)-laahng	冚吧（唥）呤	all told	(20)
hàhng	行	journey, go towards	(6)
Hàhng-jing jéung-gwùn	行政長官	Chief Executive of SAR	(20)
hàhng-léih	行李	luggage	(15)
hàhng-yàhn	行人	pedestrian	(16)
hah-pàh	下巴	chin	(9)
hahp-kwài-gaak	合規格	qualify, meet requirements	(17)
hahp-léih	合理	reasonable	(23)
hah-tīn	夏天	summer	(8)
hái	喺	at, in, on	(2)
hái-douh	喺度	at the indicated place	(11)
haih	係	be	(1)
hāk-sīk (hāak-sīk)	黑色	black	(5)
háng	肯	willing	(22)
háu	口	mouth	(10)
háu-bouh	口部	mouth	(9)
hauh-bihn	後邊	back	(12)
hauh-lòih	後來	later, afterwards	(25)
hauh-máahn	後晚	evening of the day after tomorrow	(11)
hauh-nín	後年	year after next	(10)
hauh-sāang	後生	young	(12)
hauh-sāang-jái	後生仔	youngster	(12)
hauh-yaht	後日	day after tomorrow	(10)
Héi faai!	起筷！	Lift your chopsticks!	(4)
hei-chè	汽車	vehicle, car	(12)
héi-fèi	起飛	take off (aircraft)	(15)
hei-hauh	氣候	climate	(23)
héi-làih	起嚟	ve: when it comes to it	(11)
hèi-mohng	希望	hope, to hope	(10)
héi-sàn	起身	get up	(10)
hei-séui	汽水	pop, soda	(4)
héi-yáuh-chí-léih	豈有此理	how could that be?	(16)
hèng	輕	light (in weight)	(15)
heui	去	go, go to	(2)
heung	向	towards	(6)
hèung	香	fragrant	(23)
Hèung-góng	香港	Hong Kong	(1)
hèung-há	鄉下	countryside	(6)
hèung-pín-chàh	香片茶	jasmine tea	(25)
héung-sauh	享受	enjoy	(15)
hing-cheui	興趣	interest	(13)
hìng-daih	兄弟	brothers	(3)
Hòh	何	surname: Ho	(1)
hohk	學	learn, study	(12)
hohk-haauh	學校	school	(12)
hohk-sāang	學生	pupil, student	(12)
hòhng-noih-yàhn	行內人	insider, expert	(15)
hói	海	sea	(17)
hòi	開	open	(19)
hòi	開	run / start a business	(23)
hòi	開	ve: open a gap	(17)
hòi-chē	開車	start / drive a car	(16)

hòi-chí	開始	begin, start	(23)
hói-gwàn	海軍	navy	(17)
hòi-sām	開心	happy	(8)
hói-sīn	海鮮	seafood	(5)
hói-sīn jáu-làuh / gā	海鮮酒樓 / 家	seafood restaurant	(5, 23)
hói-tāan	海灘	beach	(8)
hó-nàhng	可能	possible that, possibility	(16)
hó-sīk	可惜	it's a pity that, unfortunately	(11)
hóu	好	good, nice	(1)
hóu	好	ve: satisfactorily	(20)
hóu	好	very	(1)
hóu-chíh	好似	just like	(4)
hóu-chói	好彩	lucky, fortunately	(12)
hóu-dò	好多	a lot more	(16)
hóu-gám	好感	favourable impression	(23)
houh	號	number; day of the month	(3, 20)
hòuh-jí	毫子	ten cents	(20)
hóu-meih	好味	delicious	(4)
hóu-noih-móuh-gin	好耐冇見	long time no see	(3)
hóu-sihk	好食	good to eat, delicious	(4)
hóu-tái	好睇	good-looking, attractive	(13)
hóu-tèng	好聽	harmonious, melodic	(13)
hóu-wáan	好玩	good fun, enjoyable	(13)
hóu-yám	好飲	delicious (to drink)	(13)
hó-yíh	可以	may, can	(6)
hùhng-dāng	紅燈	red light	(12)
hùhng-luhk-dāng	紅綠燈	traffic lights	(12)
hùhng-sīk	紅色	red	(5)
hùng	空	empty	(11)
hùng-gwàn	空軍	air force	(17)
hùng-hei	空氣	air, fresh air	(24)
húng-lùhng	恐龍	dinosaur	(22)
hùng-yàuh	空郵	airmail	(20)
hyun	勸	advise, urge, plead with	(24)
hyut	血	blood	(16)
jà faai-jí	揸筷子	use chopsticks	(6)
jà fèi-gèi	揸飛機	fly a plane	(6)
jaahm-sìh	暫時	temporary	(20)
jaahp-gwaan	習慣	accustomed to; habit	(24)
jaahp-háu	閘口	gate, gateway	(15)
jaahp-jùng	集中	concentrated, centralized	(23)
jaak	窄	narrow	(16)
jaan	讚	praise	(11)
jáan	盞	cl: for lamps and lights	(12)
jáau(-fàan)-chín	找（返）錢	give change	(20)
jà-chē	揸車	drive a vehicle	(6)
jái	仔	son	(10)
jài	擠	put, place	(8)
jai-douh	制度	system	(22)
jai-fuhk	制服	uniform	(17)
jái-néui	仔女	children	(22)
jàm	斟	pour	(25)
jàm-báan	砧板	chopping board	(23)

jàng	憎	*hate*	(24)
jàng-gà	增加	*increase*	(13)
jàn-haih	真係	*truly*	(4)
jà-sáu	揸手	*shake hands*	(16)
jāt-déi	質地	*quality*	(5)
jáu	酒	*alcoholic drink*	(4)
jáu	走	*run, run away*	(3)
jáu-dim	酒店	*hotel*	(15)
jáu-gā	酒家	*Chinese restaurant*	(23)
jauh	就	*then*	(4)
jauh-faai	就快	*soon*	(23)
jauh-jàn	就真	*that's for sure!*	(25)
jáu-làuh	酒樓	*Chinese restaurant*	(4)
jáu-lóng	走廊	*passage, corridor*	(8)
jáu-naahn	走難	*flee disaster; take refuge*	(6)
jáu-wúi	酒會	*reception, cocktail party*	(11)
jē	啫	*fp: only, and that's all*	(3)
jē	遮	*umbrella*	(8)
jek	隻	*cl: for animals, crockery, ships, one of a pair*	(5, 6, 16, 25)
jēk	唧	*fp: only, and that's all*	(3)
jeuhn(-leuhng)	儘量	*so far as possible*	(19)
jeui	最	*most*	(6)
jeui-gahn	最近	*recently*	(19)
jeuih	罪	*crime*	(18)
jeuih-mìhng	罪名	*charge, accusation*	(18)
jeuih-on	罪案	*criminal case*	(13)
jeui-síu	最少	*at least*	(18)
jeuk	雀	*bird*	(24)
jeuk	著 or 着	*wear*	(11)
jéun	准	*permit*	(17)
jèun	樽	*cl: a bottle of; bottle*	(10)
jeun-bouh	進步	*progress*	(24)
jèung	張	*cl: for sheet-like objects*	(2)
Jèung	張	*surname: Cheung*	(1)
jéung-bán	獎品	*prize*	(13)
jèung-lòih	將來	*future*	(24)
jèun-tip	津貼	*allowance, grant*	(22)
ji	至	*only then*	(10)
jí	紙	*paper*	(20)
jì	枝	*cl: for stick-like objects*	(2)
jì	知	*know a fact*	(6)
jí(-haih)	只（係）	*only*	(4)
jì-chìhn	之前	*before*	(10)
jì-dou	知道	*know a fact*	(8)
jì-fòng	脂肪	*body fat*	(9)
jih	字	*characters; five minutes*	(15)
jì-hauh	之後	*after*	(6)
jih-géi	自己	*self*	(24)
jihk-jip	直接	*direct, directly*	(22)
jihk-sìng-gèi	直昇機	*helicopter*	(6)
jihm-jím	漸漸	*gradually*	(8)
jihng	靜	*quiet*	(22)
jih-òn	治安	*law and order*	(18)

jih-yuhn	自願	*voluntarily, willing*	(18)
jīk-haih	即係	*that is to say, that is precisely*	(5)
jīk-yùhn	職員	*staff, employee, clerk*	(19)
jī-máh	之嘛	*fp: only*	(12)
jí-muih	姊妹	*sisters*	(3)
ji-nàhng dihn-wá	智能電話	*smartphone*	(24)
jing	証	*certificate, pass*	(17)
jíng	整	*make, prepare*	(4)
jíng-chē	整車	*repair a car*	(16)
jing-fú	政府	*government*	(12)
jing-haih	正係	*just happens to be*	(11)
Jìng-yuht	正月	*First lunar month*	(17)
jín-láahm	展覽	*show, exhibition*	(11)
jì-noih	之內	*within*	(6)
jì-piu	支票	*cheque*	(19)
jí-sīk	紫色	*purple*	(5)
jìu-jóu	朝早	*morning*	(4)
jì-yāt	之一	*one of the …*	(6)
jí-yiu	只要	*so long as, provided that*	(9)
jó	咗	*ve: completion*	(4)
jó	左	*left*	(10)
jó-(sáu-)bihn	左（手）邊	*left side*	(12)
joh	座	*cl: for massive things*	(25)
johng	撞	*run into, knock into*	(16)
johng-chē	撞車	*have a car-crash*	(16)
joi	再	*again*	(4)
joi-chi	再次	*another time, a second time*	(18)
joi-gin	再見	*goodbye*	(1)
jok-áu	作嘔	*retch, about to vomit*	(10)
jóu	早	*early*	(4)
jóu-chāan	早餐	*breakfast*	(19)
jouh	做	*do*	(3)
jouh-gùng	做工	*work*	(22)
jouh-māt-yéh?	做乜嘢？	*why? for what reason?*	(3)
jouh-sàang-yi	做生意	*do business*	(4)
jóu-sàhn	早晨	*good morning*	(1)
jó-yìuh-yauh-báai	左搖右擺	*shaking from side to side*	(10)
juhng	重	*even more; furthermore*	(8)
juhng	重	*still, yet*	(3)
juhng-meih	重未	*still not yet*	(16)
jūk	粥	*congee, rice gruel*	(4)
jūk-kàuh	足球	*soccer*	(9)
jūk-kéi	捉棋	*play chess*	(24)
júng	種	*cl: kind of*	(2)
jūng	鐘	*clock*	(15)
jung-fā	種花	*cultivate flowers*	(24)
jùng-gāan	中間	*in the middle of, in between*	(12)
Jùng-gwok	中國	*China*	(1)
Jùng-gwok-choi	中國菜	*Chinese food*	(23)
Jùng-gwok-wá	中國話	*Chinese language*	(18)
Jùng-gwok-yàhn	中國人	*Chinese person*	(10)
jùng-hohk	中學	*secondary school*	(12)
júng-leuih	種類	*type, kind, species*	(23)
Jùng-màhn	中文	*Chinese language*	(12)

jūng-tàuh	鐘頭	*hour*	(4)
Jùng-wàahn	中環	*Central District*	(6)
jùng-yi	中意	*like, fond of*	(6)
Jùng-yì	中醫	*Chinese medicine*	(10)
jyú	煮	*cook*	(4)
jyù	豬	*pig*	(10)
jyú-choi	主菜	*main course*	(4)
jyuh	住	*live, dwell*	(3)
jyuh	住	*ve: sustain*	(11)
jyù-jái	豬仔	*piglet*	(10)
jyun	轉	*turn, change*	(6)
jyūn-gā	專家	*expert, specialist*	(24)
jyú-sihk-lòuh	煮食爐	*cooking stove*	(25)
jyú-yàhn-fóng	主人房	*master bedroom*	(25)
jyu-yi	注意	*pay attention to*	(15)
jyú-yi	主意	*idea*	(6)
jyù-yuhk	豬肉	*pork*	(4)
kàhm-máahn	擒晚	*last night, yesterday evening*	(11)
kàhm-yaht	擒日	*yesterday*	(4)
káhn	近	*near, close to*	(20)
kàhn-lihk	勤力	*hard-working*	(22)
kā-lāai-ōu-kēi	卡啦OK	*karaoke*	(24)
kāp	吸	*inhale, to smoke*	(18)
kāp-duhk	吸毒	*take drugs*	(18)
kāp-yáhn	吸引	*attract*	(13)
kàuh	球	*ball*	(9)
kàu-tùng	溝通	*communicate*	(24)
kéih	企	*stand*	(17)
kèih-gwaai	奇怪	*strange*	(24)
kèih-saht	其實	*in fact, in reality*	(19)
kèih-tà	其他	*other*	(5)
kèuhng-gàan	強姦	*rape, to rape*	(18)
kéuih	佢	*he, she, it*	(1)
kìng-gái	傾偈	*chat*	(11)
kwaang	逛	*cruise*	(25)
kwaang-gūng-sī	逛公司	*go window shopping*	(25)
kwàhn	裙	*skirt*	(11)
kwài-dihng	規定	*regulate, lay down a rule*	(17)
kyùhn	權	*right, powers, authority*	(17)
kyut-dihng	決定	*decide*	(25)
kyut-faht	缺乏	*lack*	(24)
la	嗕	*fp: that's how the case stands now*	(3)
lā	啦	*fp: urging agreement or co-operation*	(3)
làahm-kàuh	籃球	*basketball*	(9)
làahm-sīk	藍色	*blue*	(5)
laahn	爛	*broken, damaged*	(5)
láahn-doh	懶惰	*lazy*	(22)
láahng	冷	*cold*	(8)
láahng-hei-gèi	冷氣機	*air conditioner*	(8)
láahng-tīn	冷天	*winter, cold weather*	(8)
laahp-saap	垃圾	*rubbish*	(4)
laahp-saap-túng	垃圾桶	*rubbish bin*	(4)

Laahp-yuht	臘月	*Twelfth lunar month*	(17)
laaht	辣	*spicy hot*	(23)
laaht-taat	辣撻	*dirty*	(15)
làai	拉	*arrest*	(17)
làai	拉	*pull*	(17)
láam-kàuh	欖球	*rugby, American football*	(9)
làih	嚟	*come*	(3)
láih-baai	禮拜	*week*	(5)
láih-fuhk	禮服	*tuxedo, evening dress*	(11)
làih-ge/ga?	嚟嘅 / 㗎?	*fp: for identification*	(19)
lak	嘞	*fp: that's how the case stands now*	(3)
lā-ma	啦嗎	*fp: contradicting*	(17)
láu	樓	*flat, apartment*	(3)
làuh	流	*flow*	(16)
làuh	留	*remain*	(24)
làuh-dái	樓底	*ceiling*	(25)
làuh-fàan	留返	*leave behind*	(24)
làuh-tài	樓梯	*staircase*	(25)
léhng-tàai	領呔	*necktie*	(8)
leih	脷	*tongue*	(9)
Léih	李	*surname: Li / Lee*	(1)
lèih	離	*distant from*	(25)
lèih-dóu	離島	*outlying island*	(6)
lèih-hòi	離開	*leave, depart from*	(9)
léih-yàuh	理由	*reason*	(25)
lēk	叻	*smart, clever*	(22)
leng	靚	*pretty, beautiful*	(1)
Lèuhn-Dēun	倫敦	*London*	(6)
lèuhn-dou	輪到	*turn of*	(16)
léuhng	兩	*two*	(2)
léuhng-tái	兩睇	*two ways of looking at it*	(16)
lèuhn-pún	輪盤	*roulette*	(13)
léuih-bihn	裏邊	*inside*	(9)
léuih-yàuh	旅遊	*tourism, travel*	(15)
léung	両	*ounce*	(5)
lihk-sí	歷史	*history*	(12)
Lìhm-jing Gùng-chyúh	廉政公署	*ICAC*	(18)
Líhm-syù	臉書	*Facebook*	(24)
lìhn … dōu …	連 ⋯ 都	*even*	(17)
lihng	令	*cause*	(18)
lìhng	零	*zero*	(11)
lihn-jaahp	練習	*practise*	(24)
lihn-jaahp-bóu	練習簿	*exercise book*	(12)
lìhn-juhk	連續	*in succession, consecutively*	(19)
līp	軨	*lift, elevator*	(25)
lō	囉	*fp: agreement with previous speaker*	(15)
ló	攞	*take*	(15)
lohk	落	*descend; alight*	(6)
lohk-hauh	落後	*backward, old-fashioned*	(22)
lohk-heui	落去	*ve: continue*	(19)
lohk-làih	落嚟	*ve: downward*	(11)
lohk-yúh	落雨	*rain*	(8)
lòih-wóhng	來往	*coming and going; current (account)*	(19)
ló-tái	裸體	*naked, nude*	(17)

lóuh	老	old, elderly	(6)
Lóuh	老	prefix for names: 'Old'	(6)
lóuh-baak-sing	老百姓	The Chinese people	(11)
louh-bīn	路邊	roadside	(17)
louh-háu	路口	road junction	(6)
louh-mín	路面	road surface	(15)
lóuh-saht	老實	honest	(13)
lóuh-sì	老師	teacher	(12)
louh-tòih	露台	balcony	(25)
lóuh-yàhn	老人	elderly, the aged	(18)
luhk	六	six	(2)
luhk-dāng	綠燈	green light	(12)
luhk-gwàn	陸軍	army	(17)
luhk-sīk	綠色	green	(5)
lùhng	龍	dragon	(23)
lùhng-hā	龍蝦	lobster	(4)
lùhng-jéng-chàh	龍井茶	dragon well tea	(25)
ma?	嗎?	fp: makes questions	(1)
maahn	慢	slow	(16)
maahn	萬	ten thousand	(11)
máahn	晚	evening	(6)
máahn-chāan	晚餐	dinner, supper	(22)
máahn-faahn	晚飯	dinner	(23)
Maahn-léih chèuhng-sìhng	萬里長城	Great Wall of China	(11)
maaih	賣	sell	(1)
máaih	買	buy	(2)
màaih	埋	ve: close up to	(17)
máaih-choi	買菜	food shopping	(23)
màaih-dāan	埋單	make out the bill	(23)
máaih-máh	買馬	bet on horses	(14)
máaih-sung	買餸	food shopping	(23)
máaih-yéh	買嘢	shopping	(4)
māau	貓	cat	(24)
máh	馬	horse	(13)
máh-chèuhng	馬場	racecourse	(13)
màh-fàahn	麻煩	trouble, troublesome	(10)
máh-louh	馬路	road	(6)
màh-mā	媽媽	mother	(3)
mahn	問	ask a question	(2)
màhn-gín	文件	document	(22)
Máh-nìhn	馬年	Year of the Horse	(23)
mahn-tàih	問題	problem	(15)
máh-tàu	碼頭	pier, jetty	(6)
maht-fu	襪褲	tights	(11)
máih	咪	don't!	(4)
mān	蚊	dollar	(5)
māt-yéh?	乜嘢?	what? what kind of?	(2)
màu-dài	踎低	squat down, crouch	(10)
màuh-saat	謀殺	murder, to murder	(18)
mauh-yihk	貿易	trade	(19)
mē? (= māt-yéh?)	咩?	what? what kind of?	(2)
mē?	咩?	fp: do you mean to say that …?	(5)
meih	未	not yet	(10)

méih	尾	*tail, end*	(17)
mèih-bō-lòuh	微波爐	*microwave oven*	(25)
Méih-gām (Méih-yùhn)	美金（美元）	*American dollars*	(19)
Méih-gwok	美國	*USA*	(1)
Méih-jàu	美洲	*America (continent)*	(19)
m̀h	唔	*not*	(1)
m̀h gán-yiu	唔緊要	*never mind*	(2)
m̀h haih ... jauh haih ...	唔係……就係	*if not this, then that*	(24)
m̀h-cho	唔錯	*not bad*	(11)
m̀h-dāk	唔得	*no can do*	(5)
m̀h-dihm	唔掂	*can't cope, can't manage*	(19)
m̀h-gin-jó	唔見咗	*lost*	(24)
m̀h-gòi	唔該	*thank you*	(2)
m̀h-gòi-saai	唔該晒	*thank you very much*	(15)
m̀h-gwaai-dāk	唔怪得	*no wonder*	(23)
m̀h-haih-géi	唔係幾	*not very*	(3)
m̀h-haih-hóu	唔係好	*not very*	(3)
m̀h-hóu	唔好	*don't*	(4)
m̀h-hóu-yi-sì	唔好意思	*I'm sorry; embarrassed*	(4)
m̀h-jí	唔只	*not only*	(18)
m̀h-jì	唔知	*I don't know; I wonder*	(11)
m̀h-sái	唔駛	*no need to*	(4)
m̀h-síu-dāk	唔少得	*not less than*	(15)
m̀h-syù-fuhk	唔舒服	*unwell, uncomfortable*	(10)
mihn	麵	*noodles*	(4)
míhn-fai	免費	*free of charge*	(5)
mìhng-baahk	明白	*understand*	(12)
mìhng-seun-pín	明信片	*postcard*	(20)
míhn-seui	免税	*tax free, duty free*	(15)
miht-fó-túng	滅火筒	*fire extinguisher*	(8)
mòhng	忙	*busy*	(10)
móhng(seuhng) kau(-maht)	網上購物	*online shopping*	(24)
móhng-kàuh	網球	*tennis*	(9)
móhng-seuhng	網上	*online*	(24)
móu	帽	*hat, cap*	(11)
móuh	冇	*have not*	(3)
móuh-cho	冇錯	*there's no mistake, quite right*	(19)
mòuh-gān	毛巾	*towel*	(15)
móuh-mahn-tàih	冇問題	*no problem!*	(15)
muhk-dīk	目的	*purpose, aim, goal, target*	(24)
muhn	悶	*bored*	(24)
mùhn	門	*door*	(20)
mùhn-háu	門口	*doorway*	(20)
múih	每	*each, every*	(12)
mùih-hei	煤氣	*town gas*	(25)
nàahm	男	*male*	(9)
nàahm	南	*south*	(6)
nàahm-bihn	南邊	*south side*	(12)
nàahm-chi(-só)	男廁所	*gentlemen's toilet*	(17)
Nàahm-fèi	南非	*South Africa*	(1)
nàahm-gùng-yàhn	男工人	*male servant*	(25)
nàahm-hohk-sāang	男學生	*boy pupils / students*	(17)
nàahm-pàhng-yáuh	男朋友	*boyfriend*	(17)

nàahm-sing pàhng-yáuh	男性朋友	*friend who is male*	(17)
nàahm-yán	男人	*man, adult male*	(9)
nàahn	難	*difficult*	(17)
nàahn-sihk	難食	*unpalatable*	(17)
nàahn-tái	難睇	*ugly*	(17)
nàahn-tèng	難聽	*unpleasant to hear*	(17)
naauh-jūng	鬧鐘	*alarm clock*	(15)
nàh!	嗱！	*there! here it is, look!*	(5)
nám	諗	*think about*	(20)
nàu	嬲	*angry*	(4)
Náu-yeuk	紐約	*New York*	(18)
nē?	呢？	*fp: for rhetorical questions*	(5)
nē?	呢？	*fp: repeats same question*	(1)
néih, néih-deih	你，你哋	*you*	(1)
néih-tái	你睇	*in your opinion*	(24)
néih-wah	你話	*in your opinion*	(24)
néui	女	*daughter*	(17)
néuih	女	*female*	(17)
néuih-chi(-só)	女廁（所）	*ladies' toilet*	(17)
néuih-gíng	女警	*policewoman*	(17)
néuih-hohk-sāang	女學生	*girl pupils / students*	(17)
néuih-pàhng-yáuh	女朋友	*girlfriend*	(17)
néuih-sing pàhng-yáuh	女性朋友	*friend who is female*	(17)
néuih-sìu-fòhng-yùhn	女消防員	*firewoman*	(17)
néuih-yán	女人	*woman, adult female*	(9)
ngáahn	眼	*eye*	(9)
ngaahng	硬	*hard, unyielding*	(11)
ngáahn-géng	眼鏡	*spectacles*	(11)
ngàahn-sīk	顏色	*colour*	(5)
ngāam	啱	*correct*	(9)
ngāam-ngāam	啱啱	*exactly, precisely*	(11)
ngāam-ngāam	啱啱	*moment ago*	(10)
ngàh	牙	*tooth*	(10)
ngàhn-chín	銀錢	*dollar*	(20)
ngàhn-hòhng	銀行	*bank*	(19)
ngàhn-sīk	銀色	*silver-coloured*	(5)
ngái	矮	*short, squat, low*	(22)
ngàih-hím	危險	*danger*	(24)
ngàuh	牛	*cow, ox*	(4)
ngàuh-jái-fu	牛仔褲	*jeans*	(11)
ngàuh-náaih	牛奶	*milk (cow's)*	(4)
ngàuh-yuhk	牛肉	*beef*	(4)
ńgh	五	*five*	(2)
ńgh-sīng-kāp	五星級	*five star, top class*	(15)
ngh-wuih	誤會	*misunderstand*	(16)
ngóh	我	*I, me*	(1)
Ngòh-gwok-wá	俄國話	*Russian language*	(12)
Ngòh-màhn	俄文	*Russian language*	(12)
ngoih-bihn	外邊	*outside*	(12)
ngoih-gwok	外國	*foreign country*	(18)
ngoih-hóng-yàhn	外行人	*layman, outsider*	(19)
ngoih-tou	外套	*jacket*	(11)
ngoih-wuih	外匯	*foreign exchange*	(13)
nī	呢	*this, these*	(2)

nī-douh	呢度	*here*	(5)
nī-géi-nìhn	呢幾年	*these last few years*	(24)
nī-géi-yaht	呢幾日	*these last few days*	(24)
nī-go-yuht	呢個月	*this month*	(17)
nìhn	年	*year*	(8)
nìhn-méih	年尾	*end of the year*	(22)
nìng	擰	*bring*	(16)
nī-páai	呢排	*recently*	(24)
nī-syu	呢處	*here*	(5)
noih	耐	*long time*	(3)
noih-hóng-yàhn	内行人	*insider, expert*	(15)
noih-yùhng	内容	*contents*	(9)
nyúhn	暖	*warm*	(15)
óh!	哦！	*oh, now I understand!*	(4)
ok-muhng	噩夢	*nightmare*	(25)
òn-chyùhn	安全	*safe*	(25)
òu!	噢！	*oh! (surprise)*	(1)
Ou-jàu	澳洲	*Australia*	(1)
Ou-mún	澳門	*Macau*	(1)
pa	怕	*fear*	(8)
paak-wái	泊位	*park a car*	(16)
páau-máh	跑馬	*horse racing*	(19)
pàhng-yáuh	朋友	*friend*	(2)
pàh-sàan	爬山	*climb mountains, walk in the hills*	(9)
pèhng	平	*cheap*	(5)
pèih-dáai	皮帶	*leather belt*	(11)
pei-yùh	譬如	*for example*	(16)
pē-páai	啤牌	*playing cards*	(13)
pìhng-gwàn	平均	*average*	(12)
pìhng-yàuh	平郵	*surface mail*	(20)
po-cháan	破產	*go bankrupt*	(22)
póu-néi-chàh	普洱茶	*pu-er tea*	(25)
póu-pin	普遍	*common (widespread)*	(18)
pou-táu	舖頭	*shop*	(5)
póu-tùng	普通	*common*	(18)
Póu-tùng-wá	普通話	*Putonghua (Mandarin)*	(18)
póu-tùng-yàhn	普通人	*ordinary chap*	(18)
pùih	陪	*keep company with*	(25)
pun	判	*judge, sentence*	(18)
saai	晒	*ve: completely*	(15)
sàai	嘥	*waste*	(8)
saai-taai-yèuhng	曬太陽	*sunbathe*	(8)
sàam	三	*three*	(2)
sāam	衫	*clothing*	(8)
sāam-kwàhn	衫裙	*dress*	(5)
sàan	山	*mountain, hill*	(9)
saan-bouh	散步	*stroll, go walking*	(24)
Sàan-déng	山頂	*The Peak, hilltop*	(25)
sàang	生	*raw, 'rare'; unripe*	(19)
Sàang	生	*Mr (short for Sìn-sàang)*	(4)
sàang-gwó	生果	*fruit*	(4)

sàang-yaht	生日	*birthday*	(23)
sàang-yi	生意	*business*	(4)
saan-séui	散水	*scatter away*	(17)
sàan-séui	山水	*scenery*	(22)
sahp	十	*ten*	(2)
sahp-fàn	十分	*totally*	(18)
sahp-go-baat-go	十個八個	*nine or ten*	(10)
saht-joih	實在	*in fact, really*	(11)
saht-yuhng	實用	*practical*	(8)
sai	細	*small*	(5)
sái	駛	*drive a vehicle*	(16)
sái	洗	*wash*	(15)
sài	西	*west*	(6)
sài-bāk	西北	*northwest*	(6)
sài-bihn	西邊	*west side*	(12)
sài-chāan	西餐	*Western food*	(23)
sai-gaai	世界	*world*	(6)
sài-jōng	西裝	*suit (Western)*	(11)
sai-lóu	細佬	*younger brother*	(3)
sai-mān-jái	細蚊仔	*children*	(22)
sài-nàahm	西南	*southwest*	(6)
sái-sàn	洗身	*bathe*	(15)
sái-sàn-fóng	洗身房	*bathroom*	(15)
sái-sáu-gaan	洗手間	*washroom, toilet*	(App)
sái-wún-gèi	洗碗機	*dishwasher*	(25)
Sài-yàhn	西人	*Westerner*	(9)
Sài-yì	西醫	*Western medicine*	(10)
sái-yì-gèi	洗衣機	*washing machine*	(25)
sà-jín	沙展	*sergeant*	(17)
sà-léut	沙律	*salad*	(4)
sàm	深	*deep*	(25)
sàm-gèi	心機	*mind, thoughts*	(22)
sàn	新	*new*	(5)
sàn-chíng	申請	*apply*	(17)
sàn-fán-jing	身份證	*identity card*	(17)
sàn-fú	辛苦	*hard, distressing*	(12)
sàn-fún	新款	*new style*	(11)
Sàn-gaai	新界	*New Territories*	(25)
sàng-wuht	生活	*live; livelihood*	(18)
sàng-wuht fòng-sīk	生活方式	*life-style*	(24)
sàn-màhn	新聞	*news*	(13)
Sàn-sài-làahn	新西蘭	*New Zealand*	(1)
sàn-séui	薪水	*salary*	(22)
sàn-sìn	新鮮	*fresh*	(4)
sàn-tái	身體	*body*	(9)
sāp	濕	*wet*	(22)
sāt-baaih	失敗	*loss, failure*	(12)
sau	瘦	*thin, skinny*	(22)
sáu	手	*hand, arm*	(9)
sáu-bīu	手錶	*wristwatch*	(2)
sáu-chēung	手槍	*handgun, pistol*	(17)
sáu-dói	手袋	*handbag, purse*	(11)
sàu-dóu	收倒	*receive*	(19)
sàu-faat	收發	*receive and send*	(22)

sauh(-dóu)	受（倒）	suffer	(24)
sáu-jai	手掣	handbrake	(16)
sáu-jí	手指	finger	(9)
sáu-juhk-fai	手續費	handling charge	(20)
sáu-jūk	手足	brothers (secret society)	(17)
sàu-léih	修理	repair	(16)
sáu-maht	手襪	gloves	(11)
sáu-sàn	搜身	conduct a body search	(17)
sáu-sìn	首先	first of all	(20)
sáu-tàih	手提	portable	(15)
sáu-tàih dihn-nóuh	手提電腦	laptop / notebook	(24)
sáu-tàih-dihn-wá	手提電話	mobile phone	(15)
sáu-yaht	首日	first day	(20)
sàu-yàm-gèi	收音機	radio receiver	(24)
sé	寫	write	(19)
sèh	蛇	snake	(23)
séh-gàau móhng-jaahm	社交網站	social media	(24)
sèhng	成	ve: become	(8)
sèhng-	成	whole	(9)
sèhng-yaht	成日	all day	(9)
séh-wúi	社會	society	(12)
séh-wúi-hohk	社會學	sociology	(12)
sei	四	four	(2)
séi	死	die, dead	(5)
Sei-chyùn	四川	Sichuan (Szechwan)	(23)
Sei-chyùn-choi	四川菜	Sichuan food	(23)
séi-jái	死仔	deadbeats, bastards	(17)
sé-jih-làuh	寫字樓	office	(2)
sé-jih-tói	寫字枱	desk	(15)
sé-mìhng	寫明	written clearly	(19)
séng	醒	wake up	(16)
séuhng	上	board, get onto	(6)
séuhng	上	go up	(17)
séuhng	上	ve: onto	(8)
seuhng-(yāt)-chi	上（一）次	last time	(15)
séuhng-bàan	上班	go to work, go on shift	(22)
seuhng-bihn	上邊	on top of	(12)
séuhng-chē	上車	get onto a vehicle	(17)
seuhng-go-láih-baai	上個禮拜	last week	(10)
seuhng-go-yuht	上個月	last month	(17)
Seuhng-hói	上海	Shanghai	(1)
seuhng-jau	上晝	morning, a.m.	(15)
séuhng-móhng	上網	surf the internet, go online	(22)
séuhng-móhng dehng-fóng	上網定房	book a room online	(24)
séuhng-móhng dehng-tói	上網定枱	book a table online	(24)
séuhng-sàan	上山	go up the hill	(17)
seuhng-sī	上司	superior officer, boss	(17)
seuhng-sou	上訴	appeal to a higher court	(18)
seui	歲	year of age	(9)
séui	水	water; money	(4, 19)
séui-gwó	水果	fresh fruit	(22)
seuih-fóng	睡房	bedroom	(25)
séui-ngàuh	水牛	water-buffalo	(22)
séui-pèih	水皮	useless	(22)

séui-sīn-chàh	水仙茶	*narcissus tea*	(25)
sèui-teui	衰退	*go into decline*	(19)
sèui-yìhn	雖然	*although*	(18)
seun	信	*believe*	(4)
seun	信	*letter*	(19)
seun-fūng	信封	*envelope*	(20)
séung	想	*would like to*	(2)
sèung	傷	*wound, injury*	(16)
sēung	雙	*cl: pair of*	(16)
sēung	雙	*double*	(9)
sèung-fáan	相反	*on the contrary*	(11)
séung-gèi	相機	*camera*	(17)
séung-jeuhng	想像	*imagine*	(18)
sèung-lèuhng	雙粮	*double salary*	(22)
seung-pín	相片	*photograph*	(17)
sèung-seun	相信	*believe, trust*	(19)
sèung-yàhn-chòhng	雙人床	*double bed*	(15)
seun-jí	信紙	*letter paper*	(20)
sēut-sāam	恤衫	*shirt*	(11)
si	試	*try*	(11)
sī-gēi	司機	*driver*	(12)
sih	事	*matter, business*	(2)
sih-dō	士多	*store, corner shop*	(25)
sìh-gaan	時間	*time*	(3)
sìh-hauh	時候	*time*	(8)
sih-hou	嗜好	*hobby, pastime*	(24)
sìh-jōng	時裝	*fashion*	(11)
sihk	食	*eat*	(4)
Sihk faahn!	食飯！	*have a meal; Tuck in!*	(4)
síh-kèui	市區	*urban area*	(6)
sihk-faahn	食飯	*eat, have a meal*	(4)
Sihk-jó faahn meih a?	食咗飯未呀？	*Have you eaten?*	(1)
Sihk-jó lak	食咗嘞	*I have eaten*	(1)
sihk-maht	食物	*food*	(23)
síh-màhn	市民	*citizen*	(12)
síhn	鱔	*eel*	(5)
sìhng-jīk	成績	*result, score, report*	(16)
sìhng-laahp	成立	*established, to establish*	(18)
sìhng-síh	城市	*city, town*	(18)
sìh-sìh	時時	*always, often*	(8)
sīk	識	*know how to*	(4)
sīk-hahp	適合	*suitable to, fitting*	(13)
sīk-hèung-meih	色香味	*appearance, aroma and flavour*	(23)
sìn	先	*first*	(6)
sing	姓	*surname*	(1)
sìng	升	*rise, go up*	(19)
sing-gaak	性格	*temperament, disposition*	(24)
sìng-gong-gèi	升降機	*lift, elevator*	(25)
sìng-kèih	星期	*week*	(5)
sìn-jeun	先進	*advanced*	(22)
sìn-ji	先至	*only then*	(10)
Sìn-sàang	先生	*Mr*	(1)
sìn-sàang	先生	*teacher*	(12)
siu	笑	*smile*	(16)

síu	少	few, little	(4)
Síu-	小	prefix for names: 'Little'	(22)
síu-bā	小巴	minibus	(6)
sìu-fòhng-guhk	消防局	fire brigade	(17)
sìu-fòhng-yùhn	消防員	fireman	(17)
síu-hohk	小學	primary school	(12)
Síu-jé	小姐	Miss	(1)
síu-sàm	小心	careful	(16)
síu-sìh	小時	hour	(25)
sìu-sīk	消息	news, information	(23)
síu-síu	少少	somewhat	(5)
sìu-yé	宵夜	midnight snack	(22)
si-yuhng-kèih	試用期	probationary period	(22)
só	鎖	lock	(25)
sō-fá-yí	梳化椅	sofa, easy chair	(11)
sou-hohk	數學	mathematics	(12)
sou-máh	數碼	digital	(17)
só-yíh	所以	therefore	(4)
suhk	熟	cooked; ripe	(19)
suhk (-yù)	屬（於）	belong to	(23)
suhk-sīk	熟識	familiar with	(15)
sung	送	deliver, send	(6)
sung	餸	food	(4)
syù	書	book	(12)
syù	輸	lose	(13)
syù-faat	書法	calligraphy	(24)
syù-fuhk	舒服	comfortable	(10)
syùhn	船	ship, boat	(6)
syùn	酸	sour	(23)
syun	算	regarded as, reckoned	(8)
syún-sāt	損失	loss	(23)
syut-gōu	雪糕	ice cream	(8)
syut-gwaih	雪櫃	refrigerator	(15)
táahm	淡	bland, tasteless	(23)
taai	太	too	(4)
Táai	太	Mrs (short for Taai-táai)	(4)
Taai-gwok	泰國	Thailand	(18)
Taai-pìhng-yèuhng	太平洋	Pacific Ocean	(19)
Taai-táai	太太	Mrs	(1)
taai-yèuhng-ngáahn-géng	太陽眼鏡	sunglasses	(11)
taam	探	visit a person	(3)
tàam-wù	貪污	corruption	(18)
tái	睇	look at	(5)
tái-m̀h-dóu	睇唔倒	unable to see	(18)
tái-dāk-dóu	睇得倒	able to see	(18)
tàih	提	mention	(25)
tái-hei	睇戲	see a play, go to the cinema	(9)
tàih-séng	提醒	remind	(24)
Tái-jyuh!	睇住！	Look out! Mind your step!	(18)
tái-syù	睇書	read	(12)
tái-yī-shāng	睇醫生	see the doctor	(3)
tàuh	頭	head	(9)
tàuh-jéung	頭獎	first prize	(13)

tàuh-jyu	投注	*stake, bet*	(13)
tàuh-sìn	頭先	*just now*	(10)
tàuh-tung	頭痛	*headache*	(10)
tàuh-wàhn	頭暈	*dizzy*	(10)
tàuh-yāt	頭一	*the first*	(22)
tau-jì	透支	*overdraft, to overdraw*	(19)
tàu-yéh	偷嘢	*steal*	(18)
tek	踢	*kick*	(9)
tèng	聽	*listen*	(6)
tèui	推	*push*	(17)
teui-yàu	退休	*retire*	(22)
teui-yàu-gām	退休金	*pension*	(22)
tìhm	甜	*sweet*	(23)
tìhm-bán	甜品	*dessert*	(4)
tìhng	停	*stop*	(11)
tìhng-chē	停車	*stop a car*	(16)
tìhn-sé	填寫	*fill in a form*	(20)
tìm	添	*fp: as well, what's more, also*	(8)
tìng-máahn	聽晚	*tomorrow night*	(11)
tìng-yaht	聽日	*tomorrow*	(8)
tìn-hei	天氣	*weather*	(8)
tìn-màhn-tòih	天文台	*observatory*	(8)
Tìn-sīng máh-tàuh	天星碼頭	*Star Ferry Pier*	(6)
tip-séuhng	貼上	*stick on*	(20)
tit-Gwùn-yàm-chàh	鐵觀音茶	*iron Guan-Yin tea*	(25)
tiu	跳	*jump*	(10)
tiu-gòu	跳高	*jump high; high jump*	(10)
tìuh	條	*cl: for long flexible things*	(8)
tiuh-gín	條件	*conditions, terms*	(22)
tiu-móuh	跳舞	*dance*	(24)
Tòhng-chāan	唐餐	*Chinese food*	(23)
Tòhng-yàhn	唐人	*Chinese people*	(10)
tói	枱	*table*	(19)
tói-bō	枱波	*billiards, snooker*	(9)
tòih	抬	*carry, lift*	(16)
Tòih-wàan	台灣	*Taiwan*	(1)
tòng	湯	*soup*	(4)
tòng-wún	湯碗	*soup bowl*	(25)
tou	套	*cl: set of, suit of*	(8)
tou-fóng	套房	*en suite*	(25)
tóuh	肚	*stomach, belly*	(9)
tóuh-ngoh	肚餓	*hungry*	(22)
T-sēut	T恤	*T-shirt*	(11)
tùhng	同	*same, alike*	(24)
tùhng	同	*with, and*	(3)
tùhng-màaih	同埋	*and*	(2)
tùhng-sih	同事	*colleague*	(16)
tùhng-yi	同意	*agree*	(8)
tung	痛	*pain*	(10)
tùng-yùhng	通融	*stretch a point*	(15)
ūk	屋	*house*	(3)
ūk-ga	屋價	*house price*	(25)
ūk-kéi	屋企	*home*	(3)

wá	話	language, speech	(4)
wà!	嘩！	wow!	(5)
waahk-gwái-geuk	畫鬼腳	draw a ghost's leg	(21)
waahk-jé	或者	or, perhaps	(16)
waahk-wá	畫畫	paint, draw	(24)
wàahn-gíng	環境	environment	(23)
waaih	壞	bad	(12)
waaih	壞	go wrong, break down	(16)
wàaih-gauh	懷舊	nostalgia, nostalgic	(23)
wàaih-yìh	懷疑	suspect	(17)
wáan	玩	play	(6)
wah	話	say	(6)
wah … jì / tèng	話 … 知 / 聽	tell someone something	(6)
wahn(-syù)	運（輸）	transport	(11)
wahn-duhng	運動	physical exercise	(9)
wahn-fai	運費	transportation costs	(25)
wái	位	cl: (polite) for people	(17)
wai!	喂！	hey!	(17)
wái!	喂！	hello! (on the phone)	(10)
waih-háu	胃口	appetite	(19)
wàih-kéih	圍棋	Go, 'surrounding chess'	(24)
Wài-lìhm	威廉	William	(10)
wán	搵	look for	(2)
wàn-jaahp	溫習	revise lessons	(12)
wihng-chìh	泳池	swimming pool	(15)
wohk	鑊	wok	(23)
wohk-cháan	鑊鏟	wok slice	(23)
Wòhng	王	surname: Wong	(1)
wòhng-ngàuh	黃牛	brown cow	(12)
wòhng-sīk	黃色	yellow	(5)
wuh-háu	戶口	bank account	(19)
wuh-jiu	護照	passport	(15)
wuh-lyùhn-móhng	互聯網	internet	(22)
wuhn	換	exchange	(25)
wuh-sih	護士	nurse	(10)
wúi	會	meeting; club, society	(13)
wúih	會	able to	(5)
wúih	會	it is likely that (future possibility)	(8)
Wùih-gwài	回歸	Hong Kong Handover (1997)	(20)
wù-jòu	污糟	dirty	(15)
wún	碗	bowl	(23)
wún-gwaih	碗櫃	cupboard	(25)
wù-yíhm	污染	pollution	(23)
yah-	廿	twenty-	(13)
yahm-hòh	任何	any	(17)
yàhn	人	person	(1)
yàhn-deih	人哋	other people	(App)
yàhn-haak	人客	customer	(19)
Yàhn-jái	人仔	Renminbi, RMB	(19)
Yàhn-màhn-baih	人民幣	Renminbi, RMB	(19)
yàhn-sou	人數	number of people	(13)
yàhn-yùhn	人員	personnel, staff	(25)
yahp	入	enter	(5)

yahp-bihn	入邊	inside	(12)
yahp-dihn-yàuh	入電油	refuel, put petrol in	(16)
yahp-háu	入口	entrance	(6)
yaht	日	day	(6)
Yaht-bún	日本	Japan	(1)
Yaht-màhn	日文	Japanese language	(12)
yaht-táu	日頭	daytime	(15)
yah-yāt-dím	廿一點	blackjack, pontoon	(13)
yám	飲	drink	(4)
yám-chàh	飲茶	drink tea, have dim sum	(4)
Yan-douh-yèuhng	印度洋	Indian Ocean	(19)
yàn-waih	因爲	because	(4)
yāt	一	one	(2)
yāt … jauh	一 ⋯ 就	as soon as	(24)
yāt-bùn	一般	general, the general run of, common	(12)
yāt-chai (or yāt-chit)	一切	every single one of	(22)
yāt-chàih	一齊	together	(3)
yāt-chit (or yāt-chai)	一切	every single one of	(22)
yāt-dī	一啲	a little bit	(9)
yāt-dihng	一定	certainly	(3)
yāt-go-jih	一個字	five minutes	(15)
yāt-go-yàhn	一個人	alone	(18)
yāt-guhng	一共	altogether	(20)
Yāt-gwok-léuhng-jai	一國兩制	One country, two systems	(20)
yāt-háh	一下	once, a little bit	(15)
yāt-haih … yāt-haih …	一係 ⋯ 一係	either … or …	(25)
yāt-heung	一向	all along, up to now	(19)
yāt-jahn(-gāan)	一陣（間）	in / for a moment	(24)
yāt-jihk	一直	straight	(6)
yāt-làuh	一流	first rate	(23)
yāt-sìh	一時	momentarily, briefly	(16)
yāt-sìhng	一成	one tenth	(19)
yāt-yeuhng	一樣	same	(11)
Yāt-yuht	一月	January	(17)
yauh	又	furthermore	(5)
yauh	右	right	(10)
yáuh	有	have	(2)
yáuh	有	there is / are	(3)
yàuh	由	from	(6)
yàuh	遊	tour, to tour	(15)
yauh … yauh …	又 ⋯ 又	both … and …	(5)
yauh-(sáu-)bihn	右（手）邊	right side	(12)
yáuh-behng	有病	ill	(10)
yáuh-chín	有錢	rich	(13)
yáuh-dī	有啲	some, a little bit	(10)
yàuh-fai	郵費	postage	(20)
yàuh-gáan	郵簡	airletter form	(20)
yàuh-gúk	郵局	post office	(20)
yáuh-gwàan	有關	relevant	(19)
yàuh-haak	遊客	tourist, traveller	(15)
yàuh-hei	遊戲	games	(24)
yàuh-hei-gèi	游戲機	games machine	(24)
Yàuh-jing-júng-gúk	郵政總局	General Post Office	(20)
yàuh-kèih(-haih)	尤其（係）	especially	(12)

yáuh-māt-yéh-sih-a?	有乜嘢事呀？	for what purpose? why?	(2)
yáuh-méng	有名	famous	(6)
yàuh-piu	郵票	postage stamp	(20)
yàuh-sàm	有心	kind of you	(1)
yàuh-séui	游水	swim	(5)
yàuh-séui hói-sīn	游水海鮮	swimming seafood	(23)
yàuh-séui-fu	游水褲	swimming trunks	(8)
yáuh-sih	有事	something is wrong	(16)
yáuh-sìh	有時	sometimes	(13)
yàuh-túng	郵筒	pillar box	(20)
yáuh-yàhn	有人	somebody	(11)
yáuh-yāt-dī	有一啲	somewhat, a little bit	(10)
yáuh-yuhng	有用	useful	(8)
yéh	嘢	thing, object	(8)
yeh-	廿	twenty-	(13)
yeh-máahn	夜晚	nighttime	(15)
yèhng	贏	win	(13)
yeuhk	藥	medicine	(10)
yeuhk-séui	藥水	medicine (liquid)	(10)
yeuhng	樣	kind, sort, type	(13)
yéuhng	養	rear, keep (pets, livestock)	(24)
yèuhng-jáu	洋酒	liquor (non-Chinese)	(15)
yèuhng-mòuh-sāam	羊毛衫	sweater	(11)
Yèuhng-nìhn	羊年	Year of the Sheep	(23)
yéuhng-sìhng	養成	inculcate, form, breed	(24)
yeuhng-yeuhng	樣樣	all kinds of	(13)
yeuhn-yuht	閏月	intercalary month	(17)
yí	椅	chair	(11)
yí!	咦！	hello, what's this?	(5)
yì-gwaih	衣櫃	wardrobe	(15)
yih	二	two	(2)
yìh-ché	而且	moreover	(9)
yìh-gā	而家	now	(2)
yíh-gìng	已經	already	(8)
yíh-jái	耳仔	ear	(9)
yìh-màhn	移民	immigrate, emigrate	(17)
yìh-màhn-yùhn	移民員	immigration officer	(17)
yìhm-juhng	嚴重	serious, desperate	(10)
yihn-gām	現金	cash, ready money	(19)
yihng-jān	認真	serious, sincere	(16)
yihng-sīk	認識	recognize; understand	(23)
yìhn-hauh	然後	afterwards	(10)
yiht	熱	hot	(8)
yiht-séui-lòuh	熱水爐	water heater, boiler	(25)
yíh-wàih	以爲	assume, think	(11)
yīk	億	hundred million	(11)
yì-laaih	依賴	rely on	(24)
yì-lìuh	醫療	medical	(22)
yíng(-séung)	影（相）	photograph	(17)
Yìng-bóng	英鎊	pound sterling	(19)
Yìng-gwok	英國	UK	(1)
yíng-héung	影響	influence	(19)
Yìng-màhn	英文	English language	(12)
yī-sāng	醫生	doctor	(3)

yi-sì	意思	*meaning*	(17)
yiu	要	*must, need to*	(3)
yiu	要	*want*	(1)
yìu-chéng	邀請	*invite*	(23)
yùh-wàhn	搖勻	*shake up*	(10)
yi-yih	意義	*meaning, significance*	(23)
yì-yún	醫院	*hospital*	(10)
yú	魚	*fish*	(5)
yuh-beih	預備	*prepare*	(4)
yùh-góng	漁港	*fishing port*	(6)
yùh-gwó	如果	*if*	(4)
yùh-gwó-m̀h-haih	如果唔係	*otherwise*	(12)
yuh-jì	預知	*predict*	(24)
yuhk	肉	*meat*	(4)
yúh-mòuh-kàuh	羽毛球	*badminton*	(9)
yúhn	遠	*distant, far*	(25)
yùhn	元	*dollar*	(13)
yùhn	完	*ve: ended*	(6)
yuhng	用	*spend, use*	(4)
yùhn-gūng	員工	*staff, employees*	(19)
yùhng-yih	容易	*easy*	(20)
yùhn-lòih	原來	*originally*	(20)
yùhn-yàn	原因	*reason*	(23)
yuht	月	*moon, month*	(17)
yuht … yuht …	越 … 越	*the more … the more …*	(19)
yuht-git-dāan	月結單	*monthly statement*	(19)
yuht-méih	月尾	*end of the month*	(17)
yúh-yìhn-hohk	語言學	*linguistics*	(12)
yūk	郁	*make a movement*	(17)

English–Cantonese vocabulary

Numbers in brackets indicate the unit in which the entry is introduced.

Abbreviations

app	=	appendix
cl	=	classifier
fp	=	final particle
ve	=	verb ending

a little bit	**yāt-dī**	一啲	(9)
a little more	**dò-dī**	多啲	(15)
a lot more	**hóu-dò**	好多	(16)
able to	**wúih**	會	(5)
able to catch	**daap-dāk-dóu**	搭得倒	(18)
able to guess	**gú-dāk-dóu**	估得倒	(18)
able to see	**tái-dāk-dóu**	睇得倒	(18)
accuse	**gím-hung**	檢控	(12)
accustomed to; habit	**jaahp-gwaan**	習慣	(24)
address	**deih-jí**	地址	(20)
advanced	**sìn-jeun**	先進	(22)
advise, urge, plead with	**hyun**	勸	(24)
Africa	**Fèi-jàu**	非洲	(19)
after	**jì-hauh**	之後	(6)
afternoon, p.m.	**hah-jau**	下晝	(15)
afterwards	**yìhn-hauh**	然後	(10)
again	**joi**	再	(4)
agree	**tùhng-yi**	同意	(8)
air conditioner	**láahng-hei-gèi**	冷氣機	(8)
air force	**hùng-gwàn**	空軍	(17)
air ticket	**fèi-gèi-piu**	飛機票	(15)
air ticket	**gèi-piu**	機票	(15)
air, fresh air	**hùng-hei**	空氣	(24)
aircraft	**fèi-gèi**	飛機	(6)
airletter form	**yàuh-gáan**	郵簡	(20)
airmail	**hùng-yàuh**	空郵	(20)
airport	**fèi-gèi-chèuhng**	飛機場	(6)
airport	**gèi-chèuhng**	機場	(6)
Airport Express Line	**Gèi-chèuhng Faai-sin**	機場快綫	(6)
alarm clock	**naauh-jùng**	鬧鐘	(15)
alas!	**àai!**	唉！	(19)
alcoholic drink	**jáu**	酒	(4)
alight, descend	**lohk**	落	(6)
all along, up to now	**yāt-heung**	一向	(19)
all day	**sèhng-yaht**	成日	(9)
all kinds of	**yeuhng-yeuhng**	樣樣	(13)
all told	**hahm-baah(ng)-laahng**	冚吧（唪）唥	(20)
all, both	**dōu**	都	(4)
all, the whole lot	**chyùhn-bouh**	全部	(23)
allowance, grant	**jèun-tip**	津貼	(22)

almost	chà-m̀h-dō	差唔多	(12)
almost but not quite	gèi-fùh	幾乎	(18)
alone	yāt-go-yàhn	一個人	(18)
already	yíh-gìng	已經	(8)
also	dōu	都	(1)
alter	gói	改	(8)
although	sèui-yìhn	雖然	(18)
altogether	yāt-guhng	一共	(20)
always	sìh-sìh	時時	(8)
America (continent)	Méih-jàu	美洲	(19)
American dollars	Méih-gām (Méih-yùhn)	美金（美元）	(19)
and	tùhng-màaih	同埋	(2)
angry	nàu	嬲	(4)
another time, a second time	joi-chi	再次	(18)
any	yahm-hòh	任何	(17)
apartment, flat	láu	樓	(3)
appeal to a higher court	seuhng-sou	上訴	(18)
appearance, aroma and flavour	sīk-hèung-meih	色香味	(23)
appetite	waih-háu	胃口	(19)
apply	sàn-chíng	申請	(17)
approximately	daaih-yeuk	大約	(20)
approximately	gam-seuhng-há	咁上下	(9)
Arctic Ocean	Bāk-bìng-yèuhng	北冰洋	(19)
area, part, portion	bouh	部	(6)
army	gwàn-deui, luhk-gwàn	軍隊，陸軍	(17)
arrest	làai	拉	(17)
arrive, arrive at, reach	dou	到	(6)
as soon as	yāt … jauh	一……就	(24)
as you please, feel free	chèuih-bín	隨便	(4)
Asia	A-jàu	亞洲	(19)
ask a question	mahn	問	(2)
aspect	fòng-mihn	方面	(12)
assume, think	yíh-wàih	以為	(11)
at least	jeui-síu	最少	(18)
at leisure	dāk-hàahn	得閒	(13)
at that time	gó-jahn-sìh	嗰陣時	(10)
at the indicated place	hái-douh	喺度	(11)
at, in, on	hái	喺	(2)
Atlantic Ocean	Daaih-sài-yèung	大西洋	(19)
attract	kāp-yáhn	吸引	(13)
Australia	Ou-jàu	澳洲	(1)
autumn	chàu-tīn	秋天	(8)
average	pìhng-gwàn	平均	(12)
back	hauh-bihn	後邊	(12)
back (of body)	bui-jek	背脊	(9)
backward, old-fashioned	lohk-hauh	落後	(22)
bad	waaih	壞	(12)
badminton	yúh-mòuh-kàuh	羽毛球	(9)
balcony	louh-tòih	露台	(25)
ball	bō	波	(9)
ball	kàuh	球	(9)
bank	ngàhn-hòhng	銀行	(19)
bank account	wuh-háu	戶口	(19)

barefoot doctor	chek-geuk-yī-sāng	赤腳醫生	(19)
basketball	làahm-kàuh	籃球	(9)
bathe	sái-sàn	洗身	(15)
bathroom, shower room	chùng-lèuhng-fóng	沖涼房	(25)
bathroom	sái-sàn-fóng	洗身房	(15)
be	haih	係	(1)
beach	hói-tāan	海灘	(8)
because	yàn-waih	因爲	(4)
bed	chòhng	床	(15)
bedroom	fan-fóng	瞓房	(25)
bedroom	seuih-fóng	睡房	(14)
beef	ngàuh-yuhk	牛肉	(4)
beer	bē-jáu	啤酒	(4)
before	jì-chìhn	之前	(10)
begin, start	hòi-chí	開始	(23)
Beijing (Peking)	Bāk-gìng	北京	(1)
believe	seun	信	(4)
believe, trust	sèung-seun	相信	(19)
belong to	suhk(-yù)	屬（於）	(23)
benefits, welfare	fūk-leih	福利	(22)
bet on dogs	dóu-gáu	賭狗	(13)
bet on football	dóu-bō	賭波	(13)
bet on horses	dóu-máh	賭馬	(13)
bet on horses	máaih-máh	買馬	(14)
bicycle	dāan-chē	單車	(16)
big	daaih	大	(3)
bikini	béi-gìn-nèih	比堅尼	(8)
billiards, snooker	tói-bō	枱波	(9)
bird	jeuk	雀	(24)
birthday	sàang-yaht	生日	(23)
bitter	fú	苦	(23)
black	hāak-sīk	黑色	(5)
black	hāk-sīk (hāak-sīk)	黑色	(5)
blackjack, pontoon	yah-yāt-dím	廿一點	(13)
bland, tasteless	táahm	淡	(23)
blank paper	baahk-jí	白紙	(20)
blood	hyut	血	(16)
blue	làahm-sīk	藍色	(5)
board, get onto	séuhng	上	(6)
body	sàn-tái	身體	(9)
body fat	jì-fōng	脂肪	(9)
boiled / steamed rice	baahk-faahn	白飯	(25)
book	syù	書	(12)
book a room online	séuhng-móhng dehng-fóng	上網定房	(24)
book a table online	séuhng-móhng dehng-tói	上網定枱	(24)
bored	muhn	悶	(24)
boss	bō-sí	波士	(25)
both … and …	yauh … yauh …	又 ⋯ 又	(5)
both, all	dōu	都	(4)
bowl	wún	碗	(23)
boy pupils / students	nàahm-hohk-sāang	男學生	(17)
boyfriend	nàahm-pàhng-yáuh	男朋友	(17)
brandy	baht-lāan-déi	拔蘭地	(25)
Brazil	Bà-sài	巴西	(1)

breakfast	jóu-chāan	早餐	(19)
bright	gwòng(-máahng)	光（猛）	(25)
bring	nìng	擰	(16)
broadcast	gwóng-bo	廣播	(13)
broken, damaged	laahn	爛	(5)
brothers	hìng-daih	兄弟	(3)
brothers (secret society)	sáu-jūk	手足	(17)
brown	ga-fē-sīk (fē-sīk)	咖啡色（啡色）	(5)
brown cow	wòhng-ngàuh	黃牛	(12)
bureau, office, department	guhk	局	(16)
bus	bā-sí	巴士	(3)
bus stop	bā-sí-jaahm	巴士站	(6)
business	sàang-yi	生意	(4)
busy	mòhng	忙	(10)
but	daahn-haih	但係	(6)
but, however	bāt-gwo	不過	(17)
buy	máaih	買	(2)
by (passive)	beih	被	(12)
calligraphy	syù-faat	書法	(24)
Cambridge	Gim-kìuh	劍橋	(6)
camera	séung-gèi	相機	(17)
can	dāk, hó-yíh	得，可以	(6)
can't be done, can't cope	gáau-m̀h-dihm	攪唔掂	(19)
can't cope, can't manage	m̀h-dihm	唔掂	(19)
Canada	Gà-nàh-daaih	加拿大	(1)
cancel	chéui-sìu	取消	(10)
Cantonese food	Gwóng-dùng-choi	廣東菜	(23)
Cantonese language	Gwóng-jàu-wá	廣州話	(23)
capital	bún-chìhn	本錢	(13)
car	chē	車	(1)
careful	síu-sàm	小心	(16)
car-key	chē-sìh	車匙	(16)
carpet	deih-jīn	地氈	(25)
carry, lift	tòih	抬	(16)
car-tyre	chē-tàai	車呔	(16)
cash, ready money	yihn-gām	現金	(19)
casino	dóu-chèuhng	賭場	(13)
cat	māau	貓	(24)
catty	gàn	斤	(5)
cause	lihng	令	(18)
ceiling	làuh-dái	樓底	(25)
Central District	Jùng-wàahn	中環	(6)
certainly	yāt-dihng	一定	(3)
certificate, pass	jing	証	(17)
chair	yí	椅	(11)
chance, opportunity	gèi-wuih	機會	(22)
change, alter	gói-bin	改變	(24)
charge, accusation	jeuih-mìhng	罪名	(18)
charity	chìh-sihn	慈善	(13)
chat	kìng-gái	傾偈	(11)
cheap	pèhng	平	(5)
check, inspect	gím-chàh	檢查	(25)
check-in, register	bou-dou	報到	(15)

Chek Lap Kok (airport)	**Chek-laahp-gok**	赤鱲角	(6)
cheque	**jì-piu**	支票	(19)
chicken	**gāi**	雞	(23)
Chief Executive of SAR	**Dahk-sáu**	特首	(20)
Chief Executive of SAR	**Hàhng-jing jéung-gwùn**	行政長官	(20)
children	**jái-néui**	仔女	(22)
children	**sai-mān-jái**	細蚊仔	(22)
chin	**hah-pàh**	下巴	(9)
China	**Jùng-gwok**	中國	(1)
Chinese characters	**jih**	字	(15)
Chinese food	**Jùng-gwok-choi**	中國菜	(23)
Chinese food	**Tòhng-chāan**	唐餐	(23)
Chinese language	**Jùng-gwok-wá**	中國話	(18)
Chinese language	**Jùng-màhn**	中文	(12)
Chinese medicine	**Jùng-yì**	中醫	(10)
Chinese New Year	**gwo-nìhn**	過年	(23)
Chinese people	**Tòhng-yàhn**	唐人	(10)
Chinese people	**Jùng-gwok-yàhn**	中國人	(10)
Chinese restaurant	**jáu-gā**	酒家	(23)
Chinese restaurant	**jáu-làuh**	酒樓	(4)
chopping board	**jàm-báan**	砧板	(23)
chopsticks	**faai-jí**	筷子	(6)
cigarette lighter	**dá-fó-gèi**	打火機	(24)
citizen	**síh-màhn**	市民	(12)
city hall	**daaih-wuih-tòhng**	大會堂	(6)
city, town	**sìhng-síh**	城市	(18)
cl: (polite) for people	**wái**	位	(17)
cl: a bottle of; bottle	**jèun**	樽	(10)
cl: a cup of, glass of	**bùi**	杯	(25)
cl: a dish of	**dihp**	碟	(23)
cl: for a flat, apartment; storey, deck	**chàhng**	層	(3)
cl: for animals, crockery, ships, one of a pair	**jek**	隻	(5, 6, 16, 25)
cl: for books	**bouh**	部	(12)
cl: for books	**bún**	本	(12)
cl: for carpets, land plots	**faai**	塊	(25)
cl: for doors	**douh**	度	(20)
cl: for films and plays	**chēut**	齣	(9)
cl: for hats	**déng**	頂	(11)
cl: for houses and rooms	**gàan**	間	(3)
cl: for lamps and lights	**jáan**	盞	(12)
cl: for letters	**fùng**	封	(19)
cl: for long flexible things	**tìuh**	條	(8)
cl: for massive things	**joh**	座	(25)
cl: for meals	**chàan**	餐	(4)
cl: for paintings, curtains	**fūk**	幅	(17)
cl: for people and many objects	**go**	個	(2)
cl: for performances, bouts, games	**chèuhng**	場	(13)
cl: for plurals and uncountables	**dī**	啲	(4)
cl: for sheet-like objects	**jèung**	張	(2)
cl: for spectacles	**fu**	副	(11)
cl: for stick-like objects	**jì**	枝	(2)
cl: for umbrellas, tools, etc.	**bá**	把	(8)
cl: for vehicles, machinery	**ga**	架	(3)

cl: group of, gang of	bàan	班	(17)
cl: kind of	júng	種	(2)
cl: most clothing items	gihn	件	(5)
cl: newspapers	fahn	份	(18)
cl: pair of	deui	對	(9)
cl: pair of	sēung	雙	(16)
cl: set of, suit of	tou	套	(8)
clean	gòn-jehng	乾淨	(15)
cleaning	chìng-git	清潔	(25)
clear, clearly	chìng-chó	清楚	(18)
climate	hei-hauh	氣候	(23)
climb mountains, walk the hills	pàh-sàan	爬山	(9)
clinic	chán-só	診所	(10)
clock	jūng	鐘	(15)
close to	gahn or káhn	近	(20)
clothing	sāam	衫	(8)
coffee	ga-fē	咖啡	(4)
cold	láahng	冷	(8)
colleague	tùhng-sih	同事	(16)
colour	ngàahn-sīk	顏色	(5)
come	làih	嚟	(3)
come to an end	git-chūk	結束	(19)
comfortable	syù-fuhk	舒服	(10)
coming and going; current (account)	lòih-wóhng	來往	(19)
common	póu-tùng	普通	(18)
common (widespread)	póu-pin	普遍	(18)
communal chopsticks	gùng-faai	公筷	(24)
communicate	kàu-tùng	溝通	(24)
company	gūng-sī	公司	(8)
compare, comparatively	béi-gaau	比較	(19)
compensate	bóu	補	(22)
complete, all embracing	chàih-chyùhn	齊全	(23)
computer	dihn-nóuh	電腦	(9)
concentrated, centralized	jaahp-jùng	集中	(23)
conditions, terms	tiuh-gín	條件	(22)
conduct a body search	sáu-sàn	搜身	(17)
congee, rice gruel	jūk	粥	(4)
congratulations	gùng-héi	恭喜	(23)
contents	noih-yùhng	内容	(9)
control, be in charge of	gwún	管	(12)
convenient	fòng-bihn	方便	(17)
cook	jyú	煮	(4)
cooked; ripe	suhk	熟	(19)
cooking stove	jyú-sihk-lòuh	煮食爐	(25)
corner	chèuhng-gok	牆角	(8)
correct	ngāam	啱	(9)
corridor, passage	jáu-lóng	走廊	(8)
corruption	tàam-wù	貪污	(18)
cost, fee	fai-yuhng	費用	(15)
counter	gwaih-tói	櫃台	(15)
country, state	gwok-gà	國家	(19)
countryside	hèung-há	鄉下	(6)
cow, ox	ngàuh	牛	(4)
crab	háaih	蟹	(5)

crazy	chì-sin	黐線	(16)
crime	jeuih	罪	(18)
criminal case	jeuih-on	罪案	(13)
cruise	kwaang	逛	(25)
cultivate flowers	jung-fā	種花	(24)
cup, glass	būi	杯	(25)
cupboard	wún-gwaih	碗櫃	(25)
curtains	chēung-lím-bou	窗簾布	(25)
customer	yàhn-haak	人客	(19)
customer, client	gu-haak	顧客	(23)
cut, reduce	chòih-gáam	裁減	(19)
damaged, broken,	laahn	爛	(5)
dance	tiu-móuh	跳舞	(24)
danger	ngàih-hím	危險	(24)
dare	gám	敢	(18)
daughter	néui	女	(17)
day	yaht	日	(6)
day after tomorrow	hauh-yaht	後日	(10)
day before yesterday	chìhn-yaht	前日	(9)
day of the month	houh	號	(20)
daytime	yaht-táu	日頭	(15)
dead, die	séi	死	(5)
deadbeats, bastards	séi-jái	死仔	(17)
deal with, handle	chyú-léih	處理	(22)
decide	kyut-dihng	決定	(25)
deep	sàm	深	(25)
delicious	hóu-meih	好味	(4)
delicious (to drink)	hóu-yám	好飲	(13)
deliver, send	sung	送	(6)
demolish, tear down	chaak	拆	(23)
department	bouh-mùhn	部門	(19)
department store	baak-fo-gūng-sī	百貨公司	(8)
descend; alight	lohk	落	(6)
design	chit-gai	設計	(11)
desk	sé-jih-tói	寫字枱	(15)
dessert	tìhm-bán	甜品	(4)
detailed, fine, minute	chèuhng-sai	詳細	(22)
devil, ghost	gwái	鬼	(10)
diagonally opposite	chèh-deui-mihn	斜對面	(12)
die, dead	séi	死	(5)
difficult	nàahn	難	(17)
digital	sou-máh	數碼	(17)
dim sum	dím-sām	點心	(4)
dining room	faahn-tēng	飯廳	(25)
dinner	máahn-faahn	晚飯	(23)
dinner, supper	máahn-chāan	晚餐	(22)
dinosaur	húng-lùhng	恐龍	(22)
direct, directly	jihk-jip	直接	(22)
dirty	laaht-taat	辣撻	(15)
dirty	wù-jòu	污糟	(15)
discotheque	dīk-sih-gōu	的士高	(24)
dish, plate	díp	碟	(23)
dishwasher	sái-wún-gèi	洗碗機	(25)

distant from	lèih	離	(25)
distant, far	yúhn	遠	(25)
dizzy	tàuh-wàhn	頭暈	(10)
do	jouh	做	(3)
do business	jouh-sàang-yi	做生意	(4)
doctor	yī-sāng	醫生	(3)
document	màhn-gín	文件	(22)
dog	gáu	狗	(13)
dollar	māan	蚊	(5)
dollar	ngàhn-chín	銀錢	(20)
dollar	yùhn	元	(13)
don't	m̀h-hóu	唔好	(4)
don't!	máih!	咪!	(4)
door	mùhn	門	(20)
doorway	mùhn-háu	門口	(20)
dot, spot, point	dím	點	(23)
double	sēung	雙	(9)
double bed	sèung-yàhn-chòhng	雙人床	(15)
double salary	sèung-lèuhng	雙粮	(22)
dragon	lùhng	龍	(23)
dragon well tea	lùhng-jéng-chàh	龍井茶	(25)
draw a ghost's leg	waahk-gwái-geuk	畫鬼腳	(21)
dress	sāam-kwàhn	衫裙	(5)
drink	yám	飲	(4)
drink tea, have dim sum	yám-chàh	飲茶	(4)
drive a vehicle	jà-chē	揸車	(6)
drive a vehicle	sái	駛	(16)
driver	sī-gēi	司機	(12)
driving, to drive	ga-sái	駕駛	(16)
dry	gòn	乾	(22)
each, every	múih	每	(12)
ear	yíh-jái	耳仔	(9)
early	jóu	早	(4)
east	dùng	東	(6)
east side	dùng-bihn	東邊	(12)
easy	yùhng-yih	容易	(20)
eat	sihk	食	(4)
eat, have a meal	sihk-faahn	食飯	(4)
economy, economic	gìng-jai	經濟	(13)
education	gaau-yuhk	教育	(12)
eel	síhn	鱔	(5)
eight	baat	八	(2)
either … or …	yāt-haih … yāt-haih …	一係 ······ 一係	(25)
elderly, the aged	lóuh-yàhn	老人	(18)
electric heater	dihn-nyúhn-lòuh	電暖爐	(8)
electric light	dihn-dāng	電燈	(9)
electric rice cooker	dihn-faahn-bōu	電飯煲	(9)
electricity	dihn	電	(16)
electronic	dihn-jí	電子	(25)
element, member	fahn-jí	份子	(12)
elementary, first grade	chò-kāp	初級	(24)
elevator, lift	sìng-gong-gèi	升降機	(25)
email	dihn-yàuh	電郵	(22)

embarrassed, I'm sorry	m̀h-hóu-yi-sì	唔好意思	(4)
emigrate, immigrate	yìh-màhn	移民	(17)
empty	hùng	空	(11)
en suite rooms	tou-fóng	套房	(25)
end of the month	yuht-méih	月尾	(17)
end of the year	nìhn-méih	年尾	(22)
English language	Yìng-màhn	英文	(12)
enjoy	héung-sauh	享受	(15)
enough	gau	夠	(16)
enter	yahp	入	(5)
entrance	yahp-háu	入口	(6)
envelope	seun-fūng	信封	(20)
environment	wàahn-gíng	環境	(23)
especially	yàuh-kèih(-haih)	尤其（係）	(12)
established, to establish	sìhng-laahp	成立	(18)
etcetera	dáng-dáng	等等	(15)
Euro (€)	Aù–lòh (Aù-yùhn)	歐羅（歐元）	(19)
Europe	Aù-jàu	歐洲	(19)
even	lìhn … dōu …	連……都	(17)
even more; furthermore	juhng	重	(8)
evening	máahn	晚	(6)
evening dress, tuxedo	láih-fuhk	禮服	(11)
evening of day after tomorrow	hauh-máahn	後晚	(11)
evening of day before yesterday	chìhn-máahn	前晚	(11)
every, each	múih	每	(12)
every single one of	yāt-chit (or yāt-chai)	一切	(22)
exactly, precisely	ngāam-ngāam	啱啱	(11)
examination	háau-si	考試	(16)
examine, test	háau	考	(16)
exceed	chìu-gwo	超過	(19)
exchange	wuhn	換	(25)
exchange money	deui	兌	(19)
exchange rate	deui-wuhn-léut	兌換率	(19)
exciting	chi-gīk	刺激	(9)
exercise book	lihn-jaahp-bóu	練習簿	(12)
exit	chēut-háu	出口	(6)
expensive	gwai	貴	(1)
expert, specialist	jyūn-gā	專家	(24)
express	dahk-faai	特快	(20)
extraordinarily	fèi-sèuhng (jì)	非常之	(22)
eye	ngáahn	眼	(9)
Facebook	Líhm-syù	臉書	(24)
facilities, equipment	chit-beih	設備	(15)
fall, fall down	dit	跌	(19)
false	gá	假	(17)
familiar with	suhk-sīk	熟識	(15)
family member(s)	gà-yàhn	家人	(3)
famous	yáuh-méng	有名	(6)
fantan	fāan-tāan	番攤	(13)
fashion	sìh-jōng	時裝	(11)
fast, quick, quickly	faai	快	(15)
fat, obese	fèih	肥	(22)
father	bàh-bā	爸爸	(3)

favourable impression	hóu-gám	好感	(23)
fax	chyùhn-jān	傳真	(22)
fax machine	chyùhn-jān-gèi	傳真機	(22)
fear	pa	怕	(8)
feel	gok-dāk	覺得	(9)
female	néuih	女	(17)
Feng Shui, geomancy	fùng-séui	風水	(22)
few years ago	chìhn-geí-nìhn	前幾年	(18)
few, little	síu	少	(4)
fight	dá-gāau	打交	(18)
fill in a form	tìhn-sé	填寫	(20)
film (cinema)	dihn-yíng	電影	(9)
film (for camera)	fèi-lám	菲林	(25)
fine, be fined	faht-chín	罰錢	(18)
finger	sáu-jí	手指	(9)
finish work	fong-gùng	放工	(22)
fire brigade	sìu-fòhng-guhk	消防局	(17)
fire extinguisher	miht-fó-túng	滅火筒	(8)
fireman	sìu-fòhng-yùhn	消防員	(17)
firewoman	néuih-sìu-fòhng-yùhn	女消防員	(17)
first	sìn	先	(6)
first day	sáu-yaht	首日	(20)
First lunar month	Jìng-yuht	正月	(17)
first of all	sáu-sìn	首先	(20)
first prize	tàuh-jéung	頭獎	(13)
first rate	yāt-làuh	一流	(23)
fish	yú	魚	(5)
fishing port	yùh-góng	漁港	(6)
five	ńgh	五	(2)
five minutes	yāt-go-jih	一個字	(15)
five star, top class	ńgh-sīng-kāp	五星級	(15)
fix, cope with	gáau-dihm	攪掂	(19)
flat, apartment	láu	樓	(3)
flee disaster; take refuge	jáu-naahn	走難	(6)
flexible	daahn-sing	彈性	(22)
floor	deih-mín	地面	(25)
flow	làuh	流	(16)
flower garden	fà-yún	花園	(2)
fly	fèi	飛	(24)
fly a plane	jà fèi-gèi	揸飛機	(6)
following, accordingly	gàn-jyuh	跟住	(19)
food	sihk-maht	食物	(23)
food	sung	餸	(4)
food shopping	máaih-choi	買菜	(23)
food shopping	máaih-sung	買餸	(23)
foot (length)	chek	呎	(25)
foot, leg	geuk	腳	(9)
footbrake	geuk-jai	腳掣	(16)
for example	pei-yùh	譬如	(16)
for what purpose? why?	yáuh-māt-yéh-sih-a?	有乜嘢事呀？	(2)
forced to	beih-bīk	被逼	(11)
foreign country	ngoih-gwok	外國	(18)
foreign exchange	ngoih-wuih	外匯	(13)
form, table	bíu-gaak	表格	(20)

four	sei	四	(2)
fp = ge + a?	ga?	㗎?	(2)
fp: contradicting	lā-ma	啦嗎	(17)
fp: expected result; 'this will be'	ge-lak	嘅嘞	(19)
fp: puzzlement, surprise	gé	嘅	19
fp: 'that will be quite alright'	ak	呃	(19)
fp: agreement with speaker	lō	囉	(15)
fp: as well, what's more, also	tìm	添	(8)
fp: do you mean to say that ...?	mē?	咩?	(5)
fp: emphatic, exclamatory	a!	呀!	(12)
fp: finishes a question	a?	呀?	(1)
fp: for identification	làih-ge/ga?	嚟嘅／㗎?	(19)
fp: for rhetorical questions	nē?	呢?	(5)
fp: let me tell you	bo!	噃!	(5)
fp: makes questions	ma?	嗎?	(1)
fp: only	jī-máh	之嘛	(12)
fp: only, and that's all	jē	啫	(3)
fp: only, and that's all	jēk	唧	(3)
fp: repeats same question	nē?	呢?	(1)
fp: strong emphasis	ge-la	嘅喇	(5)
fp: that's how it is now	la	嚹	(3)
fp: that's how it is now	lak	嘞	(3)
fp: that's how it is!	ge!	嘅!	(3)
fp: that's right, isn't it?	àh?	吖?	(3)
fp: triumphantly scoring a point	ā?	丫?	(8)
fp: urging agreement or co-operation	lā	啦	(3)
fp: you should realize	ā-ma!	丫嗎!	(5)
fragrant	hèung	香	(23)
France	Faat-gwok	法國	(1)
free of charge	míhn-fai	免費	(5)
French language	Faat-màhn	法文	(12)
fresh	sàn-sìn	新鮮	(4)
fresh air	hùng-hei	空氣	(24)
fresh fruit	séui-gwó	水果	(22)
fried rice	cháau-faahn	炒飯	(25)
friend	pàhng-yáuh	朋友	(2)
friend who is female	néuih-sing pàhng-yáuh	女性朋友	(17)
friend who is male	nàahm-sing pàhng-yáuh	男性朋友	(17)
from	yàuh	由	(6)
front	chìhn-bihn	前邊	(12)
fruit	sàang-gwó	生果	(4)
fund raising	chàuh-fún	籌款	(13)
furthermore	yauh	又	(5)
future	jèung-lòih	將來	(24)
gamble at cards	dóu-pē-páai	賭啤牌	(13)
gamble on foreign exchange	dóu-ngoih-wuih	賭外匯	(13)
gamble on shares	dóu-gú-piu	賭股票	(13)
gamble on, bet on	dóu	賭	(13)
gamble with money	dóu-chín	賭錢	(13)
gambling den	daaih-dong	大檔	(13)
games	yàuh-hei	遊戲	(24)
games machine	yàuh-hei-gèi	游戲機	(24)

garage	chē-fòhng	車房	(3)
Garden Road	Fà-yùhn-Douh	花園道	(3)
gate, gateway	jaahp-háu	閘口	(15)
General Post Office	Yàuh-jing-júng-gúk	郵政總局	(20)
general run of, common	yāt-bùn	一般	(12)
gentlemen's toilet	nàahm-chi(-só)	男廁所	(17)
geography	deih-léih	地理	(12)
geomancy, Feng Shui	fùng-séui	風水	(22)
German language	Dāk-màhn	德文	(12)
Germany	Dāk-gwok	德國	(1)
get a move on!	faai-dī	快啲	(17)
get onto a vehicle	séuhng-chē	上車	(17)
get up	héi-sàn	起身	(10)
ghost, devil	gwái	鬼	(10)
girl pupils / students	néuih-hohk-sāang	女學生	(17)
girlfriend	néuih-pàhng-yáuh	女朋友	(17)
give	béi	俾	(4)
give birth	fàn-míhn	分娩	(22)
give change	jáau(-fàan)-chín	找（返）錢	(20)
global	chyùhn-kàuh	全球	(23)
gloves	sáu-maht	手襪	(11)
go bankrupt	po-cháan	破產	(22)
go into decline	sèui-teui	衰退	(19)
go out into the street	chēut-gāai	出街	(18)
go out into the streets	hàahng-gāai	行街	(15)
go to the office	fàan sé-jih-làuh	返寫字樓	(3)
go to work	fàan-gùng	返工	(22)
go to work, go on shift	séuhng-bàan	上班	(22)
go up	séuhng	上	(17)
go up the hill	séuhng-sàan	上山	(17)
go window shopping	kwaang-gūng-sī	逛公司	(25)
go wrong, break down	waaih	壞	(16)
Go, 'surrounding chess'	wàih-kéih	圍棋	(24)
go, go to	heui	去	(2)
gold, golden	gām-sīk	金色	(5)
golf	gòu-yíh-fù-kàuh	高爾夫球	(9)
good fun, enjoyable	hóu-wáan	好玩	(13)
good morning	jóu-sàhn	早晨	(1)
good to eat, delicious	hóu-sihk	好食	(4)
good, nice	hóu	好	(1)
goodbye	joi-gin	再見	(1)
good-looking, attractive	hóu-tái	好睇	(13)
government	jing-fú	政府	(12)
gradually	jihm-jím	漸漸	(8)
Great Wall of China	Maahn-léih chèuhng-sìhng	萬里長城	(11)
green	luhk-sīk	綠色	(5)
green light	luhk-dāng	綠燈	(12)
grey	fūi-sīk	灰色	(5)
ground floor, ground, floor	deih-há	地下	(3)
Guangdong (province)	Gwóng-dùng	廣東	(23)
Guangzhou (Canton)	Gwóng-jàu	廣州	(1)
guarantee	bóu-jing	保證	(20)
guess	gú	估	(2)
ha ha!	hà!	哈！	(23)

half	bun	半	(4)
hand over	gàau	交	(15)
hand, arm	sáu	手	(9)
handbag, purse	sáu-dói	手袋	(11)
handbrake	sáu-jai	手掣	(16)
handgun, pistol	sáu-chēung	手槍	(17)
handling charge	sáu-juhk-fai	手續費	(20)
happen, occur, transpire	faat-sàng	發生	(18)
happy	faai-lohk	快樂	(23)
happy	hòi-sām	開心	(8)
hard, distressing	sàn-fú	辛苦	(12)
hard, unyielding	ngaahng	硬	(11)
hard-working	kàhn-lihk	勤力	(22)
harmonious, melodic	hóu-tèng	好聽	(13)
hat, cap	móu	帽	(11)
hate	jàng	憎	(24)
have	yáuh	有	(2)
have a car-crash	johng-chē	撞車	(16)
have a dream	faat-muhng	發夢	(25)
have a meal; Tuck in!	Sihk faahn!	食飯！	(4)
have a nightmare	faat-ok-muhng	發噩夢	(25)
have a puncture	baau-tàai	爆呔	(16)
have not	móuh	冇	(3)
Have you eaten?	Sihk-jó faahn meih a?	食咗飯未呀？	(1)
he, she, it	kéuih	佢	(1)
head	tàuh	頭	(9)
headache	tàuh-tung	頭痛	(10)
healthy	gihn-hòng	健康	(9)
heavy	chúhng	重	(12)
helicopter	jihk-sìng-gèi	直昇機	(6)
hello! (on the phone)	wái!	喂！	(10)
hello, what's this?	yí!	咦！	(5)
help	bòng … sáu	幫 … 手	(4)
Help! Save me!	Gau-mehng a!	救命呀！	(18)
here	nī-douh	呢度	(5)
here	nī-syu	呢處	(5)
hey!	wai!	喂！	(17)
high, tall	gòu	高	(10)
history	lihk-sí	歷史	(12)
hit	dá	打	(9)
hobby, pastime	sih-hou	嗜好	(24)
holiday	ga-kèih	假期	(22)
home	ūk-kéi	屋企	(3)
homework	gùng-fo	功課	(12)
honest	lóuh-saht	老實	(13)
Hong Kong	Hèung-góng	香港	(1)
Hong Kong dollars	Góng-baih	港幣	(19)
Hong Kong dollars	Góng-jí (Góng-yùhn)	港紙（港元）	(19)
Hong Kong Handover (1997)	Wùih-gwài	回歸	(20)
hope, to hope	hèi-mohng	希望	(10)
horse	máh	馬	(13)
horse racing	páau-máh	跑馬	(19)
hospital	yì-yún	醫院	(10)
hot	yiht	熱	(8)

hotel	jáu-dim	酒店	(15)
hour	jūng-tàuh	鐘頭	(4)
hour	síu-sìh	小時	(25)
house	ūk	屋	(3)
house price	ūk-ga	屋價	(25)
how could that be?	héi-yáuh-chí-léih?	豈有此理？	(16)
how long?	géi-noih?	幾耐？	(20)
how many? how much?	géi?	幾？	(9)
how much? how many?	géi-dō?	幾多？	(5)
how very … !	géi-gam … lak!	幾咁 … 嘞！	(18)
how? in what way?	dím(-yéung)?	點（樣）？	(5)
humid	chìuh-sāp	潮濕	(8)
hundred	baak	百	(11)
hundred million	yīk	億	(11)
hungry	tóuh-ngoh	肚餓	(22)
hurrying	gón-jyuh	趕住	(15)
I don't know; I wonder	m̀h-jì	唔知	(11)
I have eaten	Sihk-jó lak	食咗嘞	(1)
I, me	ngóh	我	(1)
ICAC	Lìhm-jing Gùng-chyúh	廉政公署	(18)
I'm sorry; embarrassed	m̀h-hóu-yi-sì	唔好意思	(4)
ice cream	syut-gōu	雪糕	(8)
idea	jyú-yi	主意	(6)
identity card	sàn-fán-jing	身份證	(17)
if	yùh-gwó	如果	(4)
if not this, then that	m̀h haih …jauh haih …	唔係……就係	(24)
ill	yáuh-behng	有病	(10)
illegal	feì-faat	非法	(13)
illness	behng	病	(10)
imagine	séung-jeuhng	想像	(18)
immigrate, emigrate	yìh-màhn	移民	(17)
important	gán-yiu	緊要	(21)
in fact, in reality	kèih-saht	其實	(19)
in fact, really	saht-joih	實在	(11)
in prison	chóh-gāam	坐監	(18)
in succession, consecutively	lìhn-juhk	連續	(19)
in that case, so	gám-yéung	嗽樣	(3)
in the middle of, in between	jùng-gāan	中間	(12)
in the red, deficit	chek-jih	赤字	(19)
in your opinion	néih-tái	你睇	(24)
in your opinion	néih-wah	你話	(24)
in / for a moment	yāt-jahn(-gāan)	一陣（間）	(24)
include	bàau-kwut	包括	(25)
increase	jàng-gà	增加	(13)
increase price	gà-ga	加價	(23)
inculcate, form, breed	yéuhng-sìhng	養成	(24)
independent	duhk-laahp	獨立	(22)
Indian Ocean	Yan-douh-yèuhng	印度洋	(19)
indirectly	gaan-jip	間接	(22)
influence	yíng-héung	影響	(19)
inhale, to smoke	kāp	吸	(18)
inside	léuih-bihn	裏邊	(9)
inside	yahp-bihn	入邊	(12)

insider, expert	hòhng-noih-yàhn	行內人	(15)
insider, expert	noih-hóng-yàhn	內行人	(15)
insist, insist on	gìn-chìh	堅持	(25)
inspector	bòng-báan	幫辦	(17)
insurance	bóu-hím	保險	(15)
intend	dá-syun	打算	(8)
intercalary month	yeuhn-yuht	閏月	(17)
interest	hing-cheui	興趣	(13)
internet	wuh-lyùhn-móhng	互聯網	(22)
introduce	gaai-siuh	介紹	(4)
investigate, check	chàh	查	(19)
invite	chéng	請	(4)
invite	yìu-chéng	邀請	(23)
iron Guan-Yin tea	tit-Gwùn-yàm-chàh	鐵觀音茶	(25)
it is likely that (future possibility)	wúih	會	(8)
it would be better if	bāt-yùh	不如	(19)
it's a pity that, unfortunately	hó-sīk	可惜	(11)
jacket	ngoih-tou	外套	(11)
January	Yāt-yuht	一月	(17)
Japan	Yaht-bún	日本	(1)
Japanese language	Yaht-màhn	日文	(12)
jasmine tea	hèung-pín-chàh	香片茶	(25)
jeans	ngàuh-jái-fu	牛仔褲	(11)
join, recruit into	gà-yahp	加入	(17)
joke	góng-siu	講笑	(16)
journey, go towards	hàhng	行	(6)
judge, magistrate	faat-gwùn	法官	(18)
judge, sentence	pun	判	(18)
jump	tiu	跳	(10)
jump high; high jump	tiu-gòu	跳高	(10)
just happens to be	jing-haih	正係	(11)
just like	hóu-chíh	好似	(4)
just now	tàuh-sìn	頭先	(10)
karaoke	kā-lāai-ōu-kēi	卡啦OK	(24)
keep company with	pùih	陪	(25)
kick	tek	踢	(9)
kilogram	gūng-gàn	公斤	(12)
kilometre	gūng-léih	公里	(23)
kind of you	yáuh-sàm	有心	(1)
kind, sort, type	yeuhng	樣	(13)
kitchen	chyùh-fóng	廚房	(4)
kitchen chopper	choi-dōu	菜刀	(23)
know a fact	jì	知	(6)
know a fact	jì-dou	知道	(8)
know how to	sīk	識	(4)
Kowloon	Gáu-lùhng	九龍	(1)
lack	kyut-faht	缺乏	(24)
ladies' toilet	néuih-chi(-só)	女廁（所）	(17)
lamp, light	dāng	燈	(12)
language, speech	wá	話	(4)
laptop / notebook	sáu-tàih dihn-nóuh	手提電腦	(24)

last in order	daih-mēi	第尾	(22)
last month	seuhng-go-yuht	上個月	(17)
last night, yesterday evening	kàhm-máahn	擒晚	(11)
last time	seuhng-(yāt)-chi	上（一）次	(15)
last week	seuhng-go-láih-baai	上個禮拜	(10)
last year	gauh-nín	舊年	(8)
later	chìh-dī	遲啲	(2)
later, afterwards	hauh-lòih	後來	(25)
law and order	jih-òn	治安	(18)
layman, outsider	ngoih-hóng-yàhn	外行人	(19)
lazy	láahn-doh	懶惰	(22)
lead, guide	daai	帶	(2)
learn, study	hohk	學	(12)
leather belt	pèih-dáai	皮帶	(11)
leave behind	làuh-fàan	留返	(24)
leave, depart from	lèih-hòi	離開	(9)
left	jó	左	(10)
left(-hand) side	jó-(sáu-)bihn	左（手）邊	(12)
let, allow	dáng	等	(5)
let me pay	dáng-ngóh-béi	等我俾	(5)
letter	seun	信	(19)
letter paper	seun-jí	信紙	(20)
liar	daaih-wah-gwái	大話鬼	(9)
life-style	sàng-wuht fòng-sīk	生活方式	(24)
Lift your chopsticks!	Héi faai!	起筷！	(4)
lift, elevator	līp	軠	(25)
light (coloured); shallow	chín	淺	(25)
light (in weight)	hèng	輕	(15)
light, lamp	dāng	燈	(12)
light blue	chín-làahm-sīk	淺藍色	(25)
like, fond of	jùng-yi	中意	(6)
likely that	wúih	會	(8)
linguistics	yúh-yìhn-hohk	語言學	(12)
links adjectives to nouns	ge	嘅	(4)
liquor (non-Chinese)	yèuhng-jáu	洋酒	(15)
listen	tèng	聽	(6)
live, dwell	jyuh	住	(3)
live; livelihood	sàng-wuht	生活	(18)
living room, lounge	haak-tēng	客廳	(25)
lobby	daaih-tòhng	大堂	(26)
lobster	lùhng-hā	龍蝦	(4)
local, indigenous	bún-deih	本地	(18)
lock	só	鎖	(25)
London	Lèuhn-Dēun	倫敦	(6)
long	chèuhng	長	(22)
long time	noih	耐	(3)
long time no see	hóu-noih-móuh-gin	好耐冇見	(3)
look at	tái	睇	(5)
look for	wán	搵	(2)
Look out! Mind your step!	Tái-jyuh!	睇住！	(18)
lose	syù	輸	(13)
loss	syún-sāt	損失	(23)
loss, failure	sāt-baaih	失敗	(12)
lost	m̀h-gin-jó	唔見咗	(24)

loud, in a loud voice	daaih-sèng	大聲	(11)
lucky draw	chàu-jéung	抽獎	(13)
lucky, fortunately	hóu-chói	好彩	(12)
luggage	hàhng-léih	行李	(15)
Macau	Ou-mún	澳門	(1)
machine, machinery	gèi-hei	機器	(24)
main course	jyú-choi	主菜	(4)
main doorway	daaih-mùhn-háu	大門口	(20)
main road	daaih-máh-louh	大馬路	(15)
make a movement	yūk	郁	(17)
make a phone call	dá-dihn-wá	打電話	(10)
make out the bill	màaih-dāan	埋單	(23)
make up for	bóu-fàan-sou	補返數	(10)
make, prepare	jíng	整	(4)
male	nàahm	男	(9)
male servant	nàahm-gùng-yàhn	男工人	(25)
man, adult male	nàahm-yán	男人	(9)
management, manage	gwún-léih	管理	(25)
manager	gìng-léih	經理	(15)
many, much	dò	多	(3)
master bedroom	jyú-yàhn-fóng	主人房	(25)
material, fabric	bou-líu	布料	(11)
mathematics	sou-hohk	數學	(12)
matter, business	sih	事	(2)
may, can	hó-yíh	可以	(6)
meal	chāan	餐	(4)
meaning	yi-sì	意思	(17)
meaning, significance	yi-yih	意義	(23)
meat	yuhk	肉	(4)
medical	yì-lìuh	醫療	(22)
medicine	yeuhk	藥	(10)
medicine (liquid)	yeuhk-séui	藥水	(10)
Mediterranean Sea	Deih-jùng-hói	地中海	(19)
medium (cooked steak)	bun-sàang-suhk	半生熟	(19)
meeting; club, society	wúi	會	(13)
memorial, to commemorate	géi-nihm	紀念	(20)
mention	tàih	提	(25)
menu	chāan-páai	餐牌	(23)
method, way, means	baahn-faat	辦法	(18)
microwave oven	mèih-bō-lòuh	微波爐	(25)
midday; lunch	aan-jau	晏晝	(22)
midnight snack	sìu-yé	宵夜	(22)
military uniform	gwàn-fuhk	軍服	(17)
milk (cow's)	ngàuh-náaih	牛奶	(4)
mind, thoughts	sàm-gèi	心機	(22)
minibus	síu-bā	小巴	(6)
minute (clock)	fàn(-jūng)	分（鐘）	(10)
Miss	Síu-jé	小姐	(1)
misunderstand	ngh-wuih	誤會	(16)
mobile phone	sáu-tàih-dihn-wá	手提電話	(15)
moment ago	ngāam-ngāam	啱啱	(10)
momentarily, briefly	yāt-sìh	一時	(16)
money	chín	錢	(5)

monthly statement	yuht-git-dāan	月結單	(19)
moon, month	yuht	月	(17)
moreover	yìh-ché	而且	(9)
morning	jìu-jóu	朝早	(4)
morning, a.m.	seuhng-jau	上晝	(15)
most	jeui	最	(6)
mother	màh-mā	媽媽	(3)
motor racing	choi-chē	賽車	(16)
motorbike	dihn-dāan-chē	電單車	(16)
mountain, hill	sàan	山	(9)
mouth	háu	口	(10)
mouth	háu-bouh	口部	(9)
Mr	Sìn-sàang	先生	(1)
Mrs	Taai-táai	太太	(1)
murder, to murder	màuh-saat	謀殺	(18)
muscle	gèi-yuhk	肌肉	(9)
must, need to	yiu	要	(3)
naked, nude	ló-tái	裸體	(17)
naked; red	chek	赤	(19)
narcissus tea	séui-sīn-chàh	水仙茶	(25)
narrow	jaak	窄	(16)
navy	hói-gwàn	海軍	(17)
near, close to	káhn	近	(20)
nearby	fuh-gahn	附近	(4)
neck	géng	頸	(9)
necktie	léhng-tàai	領呔	(8)
never mind	m̀h gán-yiu	唔緊要	(2)
new	sàn	新	(5)
new style	sàn-fún	新款	(11)
New Territories	Sàn-gaai	新界	(25)
New York	Náu-yeuk	紐約	(18)
New Zealand	Sàn-sài-làahn	新西蘭	(1)
news	sàn-màhn	新聞	(13)
news, information	sìu-sīk	消息	(23)
newspaper	bou-jí	報紙	(18)
next month	hah-go-yuht	下個月	(17)
next time	hah-(yāt)-chi	下（一）次	(15)
next week	hah-go-láih-baai	下個禮拜	(10)
next year	chēut-nín	出年	(8)
nightmare	ok-muhng	噩夢	(25)
nighttime	yeh-máahn	夜晚	(15)
nine	gáu	九	(2)
nine or ten	sahp-go-baat-go	十個八個	(10)
no can do	m̀h-dāk	唔得	(5)
no need to	m̀h-sái	唔駛	(4)
no problem!	móuh-mahn-tàih	冇問題	(15)
no wonder	m̀h-gwaai-dāk	唔怪得	(23)
noisy	chòuh	嘈	(22)
noodles	mihn	麵	(4)
north	bāk	北	(6)
north side	bāk-bihn	北邊	(12)
northeast	dùng-bāk	東北	(6)
northwest	sài-bāk	西北	(6)

nose	**beih-gò**	鼻哥	(9)
nostalgia, nostalgic	**wàaih-gauh**	懷舊	(23)
not	**m̀h**	唔	(1)
not bad	**m̀h-cho**	唔錯	(11)
not here	**hàahng-hòi-jó**	行開咗	(17)
not less than	**m̀h-síu-dāk**	唔少得	(15)
not only	**m̀h-jí**	唔只	(18)
not up to scratch, lacking	**chà**	差	(19)
not very	**m̀h-haih-géi**	唔係幾	(3)
not very	**m̀h-haih-hóu**	唔係好	(3)
not yet	**meih**	未	(10)
now	**yìh-gā**	而家	(2)
nowadays	**gàm-sìh-gàm-yaht**	今時今日	(22)
number…	**… houh**	……號	(3)
number of people	**yàhn-sou**	人數	(13)
nurse	**wuh-sih**	護士	(10)

observatory	**tìn-màhn-tòih**	天文台	(8)
occasionally, intermittent	**gaan-jūng**	間中	(10)
of course	**dòng-yín**	當然	(13)
offend, commit crime	**faahn**	犯	(18)
office	**sé-jih-làuh**	寫字樓	(2)
official, officer	**gwùn**	官	(16)
often	**sìh-sìh**	時時	(8)
oh dear! oh heck! alas!	**baih!**	嚟!	(17)
oh! (surprise)	**òu!**	噢!	(1)
oh, now I understand!	**óh!**	哦!	(4)
OK	**dāk**	得	(5)
old (not new), used	**gauh**	舊	(8)
old, elderly	**lóuh**	老	(6)
older brother	**daaih-lóu**	大佬	(3)
older sister	**gà-jē**	家姐	(3)
on behalf of, for the benefit of	**bòng**	幫	(10)
on the contrary	**sèung-fáan**	相反	(11)
on top of	**seuhng-bihn**	上邊	(12)
once, a little bit	**yāt-háh**	一下	(15)
one	**yāt**	一	(2)
One country, two systems	**Yāt-gwok-léuhng-jai**	一國兩制	(20)
one of the …	**… jì-yāt**	……之一	(6)
one tenth	**yāt-sìhng**	一成	(19)
online	**móhng-seuhng**	網上	(24)
online shopping	**móhng(seuhng) kau(-maht)**	網上購物	(24)
only	**bāt-gwo**	不過	(20)
only	**jí(-haih)**	只（係）	(4)
only then	**(sìn-)ji**	（先）至	(10)
open	**hòi**	開	(19)
opera	**gò-kehk**	歌劇	(24)
opposite	**deui-mihn**	對面	(12)
or, perhaps	**waahk-jé**	或者	(16)
or?	**dihng-haih**	定係	(13)
orange (colour)	**cháang-sīk**	橙色	(5)
orange juice	**cháang-jāp**	橙汁	(4)
order	**diht-jeuih**	秩序	(12)
ordinary chap	**póu-tùng-yàhn**	普通人	(18)

originally	yùhn-lòih	原來	(20)
other	kèih-tà	其他	(5)
other people	biht-yàhn	別人	(24)
other people	yàhn-deih	人哋	(App)
otherwise	yùh-gwó-m̀h-haih	如果唔係	(12)
ounce	léung	両	(5)
out	chēut	出	(17)
outlying island	lèih-dóu	離島	(6)
outside	chēut-bihn	出邊	(12)
outside	ngoih-bihn	外邊	(12)
overdraft, to overdraw	tau-jì	透支	(19)
overtime	gwo-sìh	過時	(22)
overweight	gwo-chúhng	過重	(15)
Pacific Ocean	Taai-pìhng-yèuhng	太平洋	(19)
pain	tung	痛	(10)
paint, draw	waahk-wá	畫畫	(24)
paper	jí	紙	(20)
parcel	bàau-gwó	包裹	(20)
park a car	paak-wái	泊位	(16)
parking space	chē-wái	車位	(25)
partner	fó-buhn	伙伴	(19)
pass by, via	gìng-gwo	經過	(11)
passage, corridor	jáu-lóng	走廊	(8)
passport	wuh-jiu	護照	(15)
patient, sick person	behng-yàhn	病人	(10)
patrol car	chèuhn-lòh-chē	巡邏車	(17)
patronize, give custom	bòng-chan	幫襯	(23)
pattern	fā-yéung	花樣	(11)
pay attention to	jyu-yi	注意	(15)
peddle drugs	fáahn-duhk	販毒	(17)
pedestrian	hàhng-yàhn	行人	(16)
peg	gwa-ngāu	掛鉤	(19)
Peking food	Bāk-gìng-choi	北京菜	(23)
pen	bāt	筆	(2)
pension	teui-yàu-gām	退休金	(22)
People's Liberation Army (PLA)	Gáai-fong-gwān	解放軍	(17)
perform, performance	bíu-yihn	表現	(22)
permit	jéun	准	(17)
person	yàhn	人	(1)
personnel, staff	yàhn-yùhn	人員	(25)
petrol, gas	dihn-yàuh	電油	(16)
photograph	seung-pín	相片	(17)
photograph	yíng(-séung)	影（相）	(17)
physical exercise	wahn-duhng	運動	(9)
piano	gong-kàhm	鋼琴	(24)
pier, jetty	máh-tàu	碼頭	(6)
pig	jyù	豬	(10)
piglet	jyù-jái	豬仔	(10)
pillar box	yàuh-túng	郵筒	(20)
place	deih-fòng	地方	(6)
plain clothes	bihn-fuhk, bihn-yì	便服，便衣	(17)
play	wáan	玩	(6)
play ball	dá-bō	打波	(9)

play chess	jūk-kéi	捉棋	(24)
play Mahjong	dá-màh-jeuk	打麻雀	(13)
playing cards	pē-páai	啤牌	(13)
plead with, advise, urge,	hyun	勸	(24)
please	chéng	請	(3)
please may I ask	chéng-mahn	請問	(6)
poison, be poisoned	duhk-séi	毒死	(17)
policeman	chàai-lóu	差佬	(12)
policeman	chàai-yàhn, gíng-chaat	差人，警察	(12)
policewoman	néuih-gíng	女警	(17)
polite	haak-hei	客氣	(4)
pollution	wù-yíhm	污染	(23)
pop, soda	hei-séui	汽水	(4)
pork	jyù-yuhk	豬肉	(4)
portable	sáu-tàih	手提	(15)
possible that, possibility	hó-nàhng	可能	(16)
post a letter, mail	gei	寄	(20)
post office	yàuh-gúk	郵局	(20)
postage	yàuh-fai	郵費	(20)
postage stamp	yàuh-piu	郵票	(20)
postcard	mìhng-seun-pín	明信片	(20)
pot luck	bihn-faahn	便飯	(4)
pound (weight)	bohng	磅	(12)
pound sterling	Yìng-bóng	英鎊	(19)
pour	jàm	斟	(25)
practical	saht-yuhng	實用	(8)
practise	lihn-jaahp	練習	(24)
praise	jaan	讚	(11)
prawn, shrimp	hā	蝦	(5)
predict	yuh-jì	預知	(24)
prefix for names / relationships	a-	呀	(22)
prefix for names: 'Little'	Síu-	小	(22)
prefix for names: 'Old'	Lóuh	老	(6)
prefix for ordinal numbers	daih-	第	(6)
prepare	yuh-beih	預備	(4)
pretty, beautiful	leng	靚	(1)
price	ga-chìhn	價錢	(11)
price tag	ga-chìhn-páai	價錢牌	(11)
primary school	síu-hohk	小學	(12)
print	dá-yan	打印	(22)
printer	dá-yan-gèi	打印機	(22)
prisoner	chàuh-fáan	囚犯	(18)
prize	jéung-bán	獎品	(13)
probationary period	si-yuhng-kèih	試用期	(22)
problem	mahn-tàih	問題	(15)
progress	jeun-bouh	進步	(24)
prosperous	fàahn-wìhng	繁榮	(13)
public	gùng-guhng	公共	(12)
public relations	gùng-gwàan	公關	(15)
pu-er tea	póu-néi-chàh	普洱茶	(25)
pull	làai	拉	(17)
pupil, student	hohk-sāang	學生	(12)
purple	jí-sīk	紫色	(5)
purpose, aim, goal, target	muhk-dīk	目的	(24)

purse snatching, to pick pockets	dá-hòh-bāau	打荷包	(18)
push	tèui	推	(17)
put, place	jài	擠	(8)
Putonghua (Mandarin)	Póu-tùng-wá	普通話	(18)
qualify, meet requirements	hahp-kwài-gaak	合規格	(17)
quality	jāt-déi	質地	(5)
quarter (clock)	gwāt(-jung)	骨（鐘）	(15)
quiet	jihng	靜	(22)
quite	dōu-géi	都幾	(3)
quite, rather, fairly	géi	幾	(3)
race horses	choi-máh	賽馬	(13)
racecourse	máh-chèuhng	馬場	(13)
racing driver	choi-chē-sáu	賽車手	(16)
radio receiver	sàu-yàm-gèi	收音機	(24)
radio station	dihn-tòih	電台	(13)
railway engine	fó-chè-tàuh	火車頭	(19)
railway train	fó-chè	火車	(6)
rain	lohk-yúh	落雨	(8)
rape, to rape	kèuhng-gàan	強姦	(18)
raw, 'rare'; unripe	sàang	生	(19)
reaction	fáan-ying	反應	(16)
read	tái-syù	睇書	(12)
rear, keep (pets, livestock)	yéuhng	養	(24)
reason	léih-yàuh	理由	(25)
reason	yùhn-yàn	原因	(23)
reasonable	hahp-léih	合理	(23)
receive	sàu-dóu	收倒	(19)
receive and send	sàu-faat	收發	(22)
recently	jeui-gahn	最近	(19)
recently	nī-páai	呢排	(24)
reception, cocktail party	jáu-wúi	酒會	(11)
recognize; understand	yihng-sīk	認識	(23)
red	hùhng-sīk	紅色	(5)
red light	hùhng-dāng	紅燈	(12)
red; naked	chek	赤	(19)
reduce wages	gáam-sàn	減薪	(19)
reduce, cut down	gáam-síu	減少	(9)
refrigerator	syut-gwaih	雪櫃	(15)
refuel, put petrol in	yahp-dihn-yàuh	入電油	(16)
regard as	dong	當	(4)
regarded as, reckoned	syun	算	(8)
register	gwa-houh	掛號	(10)
regulate, lay down a rule	kwài-dihng	規定	(17)
relationship, connection	gwàan-haih	關係	(13)
relevant	yáuh-gwàan	有關	(19)
relief money	gau-jai-gām	救濟金	(18)
rely on	yì-laaih	依賴	(24)
remain	làuh	留	(24)
remember	gei-dāk	記得	(9)
remind	tàih-séng	提醒	(24)
Renminbi, RMB	Yàhn-jái	人仔	(19)
Renminbi, RMB	Yàhn-màhn-baih	人民幣	(19)

repair	**sàu-léih**	修理	(16)
repair a car	**jíng-chē**	整車	(16)
report, to report	**bou-douh**	報導	(18)
responsible	**fuh-jaak**	負責	(22)
restaurant	**chāan-tēng**	餐廳	(23)
result	**git-gwó**	結果	(16)
result, score, report	**sìhng-jīk**	成績	(16)
retch, about to vomit	**jok-áu**	作嘔	(10)
retire	**teui-yàu**	退休	(22)
return	**fàan**	返	(3)
revise lessons	**wàn-jaahp**	溫習	(12)
rice bowl	**faahn-wún**	飯碗	(25)
rice, food	**faahn**	飯	(4)
rich	**yáuh-chín**	有錢	(13)
rich, abundant	**fùng-fu**	豐富	(13)
ride in a lift	**daap-līp**	搭軚	(25)
right	**yauh**	右	(10)
right side	**yauh-(sáu-)bihn**	右（手）邊	(12)
right, powers, authority	**kyùhn**	權	(17)
ripe, cooked	**suhk**	熟	(19)
rise, go up	**sìng**	升	(19)
road	**máh-louh**	馬路	(6)
road junction	**louh-háu**	路口	(6)
road surface	**louh-mín**	路面	(15)
roadside	**louh-bīn**	路邊	(17)
rob	**dá-gip**	打劫	(18)
room	**fòhng-gāan**	房間	(15)
roulette	**lèuhn-pún**	輪盤	(13)
rubbish	**laahp-saap**	垃圾	(4)
rubbish bin	**laahp-saap-túng**	垃圾桶	(4)
rugby, American football	**láam-kàuh**	欖球	(9)
run / start a business	**hòi**	開	(23)
run into, knock into	**johng**	撞	(16)
run, hold, conduct	**géui-baahn**	舉辦	(15)
run, run away	**jáu**	走	(3)
rush, dash against	**chùng**	衝	(12)
Russian language	**Ngòh-gwok-wá**	俄國話	(12)
Russian language	**Ngòh-màhn**	俄文	(12)
safe	**òn-chyùhn**	安全	(25)
salad	**sà-léut**	沙律	(4)
salary	**sàn-séui**	薪水	(22)
sale	**daaih-gáam-ga**	大減價	(5)
salty	**hàahm**	鹹	(23)
same	**yāt-yeuhng**	一樣	(11)
same, alike	**tùhng**	同	(24)
savings; to save	**chyúh-chūk**	儲蓄	(19)
say	**wah**	話	(6)
scatter away	**saan-séui**	散水	(17)
scenery	**sàan-séui**	山水	(22)
scheduled flight	**bāan-gèi**	班機	(15)
school	**hohk-haauh**	學校	(12)
science	**fō-hohk**	科學	(12)
science and technology	**fō-geih**	科技	(24)

sea	hói	海	(17)
seafood	hói-sīn	海鮮	(5)
seafood restaurant	hói-sīn jáu-làuh / gā	海鮮酒樓 / 家	(5, 23)
secondary school	jùng-hohk	中學	(12)
seconds	chi-fo	次貨	(5)
secret	bei-maht	秘密	(24)
secretary	bei-syù	秘書	(22)
security, keep secure	bóu-òn	保安	(25)
see a play, go to the cinema	tái-hei	睇戲	(9)
see the doctor	tái-yī-shāng	睇醫生	(3)
see, meet	gin	見	(8)
self	jih-géi	自己	(24)
sell	maaih	賣	(1)
send a text message	dá go dyún-seun	打個短訊	(22)
sergeant	sà-jín	沙展	(17)
serious, desperate	yìhm-juhng	嚴重	(10)
serious, sincere	yihng-jān	認真	(16)
servant's room	gùng-yàhn-fóng	工人房	(25)
service	fuhk-mouh	服務	(15)
seven	chāt	七	(2)
several	géi	幾	(9)
shake hands	jà-sáu	揸手	(16)
shake up	yìuh-wàhn	搖勻	(10)
shaking from side to side	jó-yìuh-yauh-báai	左搖右擺	(10)
Shanghai	Seuhng-hói	上海	(1)
ship, boat	syùhn	船	(6)
shirt	sēut-sāam	恤衫	(11)
shoes	hàaih	鞋	(11)
shop	pou-táu	舖頭	(5)
shopping	máaih-yéh	買嘢	(4)
short	dyún	短	(22)
short, squat, low	ái or ngái	矮	(22)
show, exhibition	jín-láahm	展覽	(11)
shower	chùng-lèuhng	沖涼	(25)
shows possession; -'s	ge	嘅	(2)
Sichuan (Szechwan)	Sei-chyùn	四川	(23)
Sichuan food	Sei-chyùn-choi	四川菜	(23)
silver-coloured	ngàhn-sīk	銀色	(5)
simple	gáan-dàan	簡單	(20)
single bed	dāan-yàhn-chòhng	單人床	(15)
sisters	jí-muih	姊妹	(3)
sit	chóh	坐	(3)
sit closer	chóh-màaih-dī	坐埋啲	(17)
sit further away	chóh-hòi-dī	坐開啲	(17)
situation, circumstances	chìhng-fong	情況	(16)
six	luhk	六	(2)
skirt	kwàhn	裙	(11)
sleep	fan-gaau	瞓覺	(16)
slow	maahn	慢	(16)
small	sai	細	(5)
smart, clever	lēk	叻	(22)
smartphone	ji-nàhng dihn-wá	智能電話	(24)
smile	siu	笑	(16)
snake	sèh	蛇	(23)

so	gam	咁	(4)
so, in that case	gám	噉	(3)
so far as possible	jeuhn(-leuhng)	儘量	(19)
so long a time	gam-noih	咁耐	(18)
so long as, provided that	jí-yiu	只要	(9)
soccer	jūk-kàuh	足球	(9)
social media	séh-gàau móhng-jaahm	社交網站	(24)
society	séh-wúi	社會	(12)
sociology	séh-wúi-hohk	社會學	(12)
socks	dyún-maht	短襪	(11)
sofa, easy chair	sō-fá-yí	梳化椅	(11)
soldier, military personnel	gwàn-yàhn	軍人	(17)
solitary	gù-duhk	孤獨	(24)
some, a little bit	yáuh-dī	有啲	(10)
somebody	yáuh-yàhn	有人	(11)
something is wrong	yáuh-sih	有事	(16)
sometimes	yáuh-sìh	有時	(13)
somewhat	síu-síu	少少	(5)
somewhat, a little bit	yáuh-yāt-dī	有一啲	(10)
son	jái	仔	(10)
soon	jauh-faai	就快	(23)
sophisticated, tasteful	daaih-fōng	大方	(11)
sorry	deui-m̀h-jyuh	對唔住	(1)
soup	tòng	湯	(4)
soup bowl	tòng-wún	湯碗	(25)
sour	syùn	酸	(23)
south	nàahm	南	(6)
South Africa	Nàahm-fèi	南非	(1)
south side	nàahm-bihn	南邊	(12)
southeast	dùng-nàahm	東南	(6)
southwest	sài-nàahm	西南	(6)
speak	góng	講	(9)
special	dahk-biht	特別	(23)
Special Administrative Region (SAR)	Dahk-biht hàhng-jing kèui; Dahk-kèui	特別行政區；特區	(20)
species, type, kind	júng-leuih	種類	(23)
spectacles	ngáahn-géng	眼鏡	(11)
spend, use	yuhng	用	(4)
spicy hot	laaht	辣	(23)
spoon	chìh-gāng	匙羹	(23)
spot, dot, point	dím	點	(23)
spring	chèun-tīn	春天	(8)
squat down, crouch	màu-dài	踎低	(10)
staff, employee, clerk	jīk-yùhn	職員	(19)
staff, employees	yùhn-gūng	員工	(19)
staircase	làuh-tài	樓梯	(25)
stake, bet	tàuh-jyu	投注	(13)
stand	kéih	企	(17)
Star Ferry Pier	Tìn-sīng máh-tàuh	天星碼頭	(6)
stare, open the eyes	dàng	瞪	(17)
start / drive a car	hòi-chē	開車	(16)
steal	tàu-yéh	偷嘢	(18)
sleep	che	斜	(16)
steep road	che-lóu	斜路	(16)

stick on	tip-séuhng	貼上	(20)
still not yet	juhng-meih	重未	(16)
still, yet	juhng	重	(3)
stingy; to save	hàan	慳	(8)
stockings	chèuhng-maht	長襪	(11)
stocks and shares	gú-piu	股票	(13)
stomach, belly	tóuh	肚	(9)
stop	tìhng	停	(11)
stop a car	tìhng-chē	停車	(16)
store, corner shop	sih-dō	士多	(25)
straight	yāt-jihk	一直	(6)
strange	kèih-gwaai	奇怪	(24)
street	gāai	街	(3)
street corner	gāai-háu	街口	(6)
street stall	dong-háu	檔口	(5)
street, road	douh	道	(3)
stretch a point	tùng-yùhng	通融	(15)
strike fire	dá-fó	打火	(24)
stroll, go walking	saan-bouh	散步	(24)
student, pupil	hohk-sāang	學生	(12)
study	duhk-syù	讀書	(12)
stupid	chéun	蠢	(22)
style	fún-sīk	款式	(5)
subject, discipline	fō	科	(12)
suffer	sauh(-dóu)	受（倒）	(24)
suit (Western)	sài-jōng	西裝	(11)
suitable to, fitting	sīk-hahp	適合	(13)
summer	hah-tīn	夏天	(8)
sunbathe	saai-taai-yèuhng	曬太陽	(8)
sunglasses	taai-yèuhng-ngáahn-géng	太陽眼鏡	(11)
superior officer, boss	seuhng-sī	上司	(17)
surf the internet	séuhng-móhng	上網	(22)
surface mail	pìhng-yàuh	平郵	(20)
surname	sing	姓	(1)
surname: Chan	Chàhn	陳	(1)
surname: Cheung	Jèung	張	(1)
surname: Ho	Hòh	何	(1)
surname: Li/Lee	Léih	李	(1)
surname: Wong	Wòhng	王	(1)
surplus	dò-yùh	多餘	(9)
suspect	wàaih-yìh	懷疑	(17)
sweater	yèuhng-mòuh-sāam	羊毛衫	(11)
sweep	dá-sou	打掃	(25)
sweet	tìhm	甜	(23)
swim	yàuh-séui	游水	(5)
swimming pool	wihng-chìh	泳池	(15)
swimming seafood	yàuh-séui hói-sīn	游水海鮮	(23)
swimming trunks	yàuh-séui-fu	游水褲	(8)
system	jai-douh	制度	(22)
table	tói	枱	(19)
table-tennis	bìng-bām-bō	乒乓波	(9)
tail, end	méih	尾	(17)
Taiwan	Tòih-wàan	台灣	(1)

take	ló	攞	(15)
take a good look	dàng-daaih-deui-ngáahn	瞪大對眼	(17)
take a holiday	fong-ga	放假	(9)
take drugs	kāp-duhk	吸毒	(18)
take off (aircraft)	héi-fèi	起飛	(15)
take part in	chàam-gà	參加	(11)
tasteful, sophisticated	daaih-fōng	大方	(11)
tax free, duty free	míhn-seui	免税	(15)
taxi	dīk-sí	的士	(3)
tea	chàh	茶	(4)
tea bowl	chàh-wún	茶碗	(25)
teach	gaau-syù	教書	(12)
teacher	lóuh-sì	老師	(12)
teacher	sìn-sàang	先生	(12)
tea-pot	chàh-wú	茶壺	(23)
telephone	dihn-wá	電話	(9)
television	dihn-sih	電視	(9)
television set	dihn-sih-gèi	電視機	(15)
tell lies	góng daaih-wah	講大話	(9)
tell someone something	wah … jì / tèng	話……知 / 聽	(6)
tell to do	giu	叫	(17)
temperament, disposition	sing-gaak	性格	(24)
temporary	jaahm-sìh	暫時	(20)
ten	sahp	十	(2)
ten cents	hòuh-jí	毫子	(20)
ten thousand	maahn	萬	(11)
tennis	móhng-kàuh	網球	(9)
test; evaluation	chāak-yihm	測驗	(12)
text message	dyún-seun	短訊	(22)
textbook	fo-bún	課本	(12)
Thailand	Taai-gwok	泰國	(18)
than	gwo	過	(12)
thank you	dò-jeh	多謝	(5)
thank you	m̀h-gòi	唔該	(2)
thank you very much	dò-jeh-saai	多謝晒	(15)
thank you very much	m̀h-gòi-saai	唔該晒	(15)
that is to say, that is precisely	jīk-haih	即係	(5)
that, those	gó	嗰	(2)
that's for sure!	jauh-jàn	就真	(25)
The Chinese people	lóuh-baak-sing	老百姓	(11)
the first	daih-yāt	第一	(6)
the first	tàuh-yāt	頭一	(22)
the more … the more …	yuht … yuht …	越 … 越	(19)
The Peak, hilltop	Sàan-déng	山頂	(25)
the second, the next	daih-yih	第二	(6)
then	jauh	就	(4)
there	gó-douh	嗰度	(5)
there	gó-syu	嗰處	(5)
there is/are	yáuh	有	(3)
there! here it is, look!	nàh!	嗱!	(5)
there's no mistake, quite right	móuh-cho	冇錯	(19)
therefore	só-yíh	所以	(4)
these last few days	nī-géi-yaht	呢幾日	(24)
these last few years	nī-géi-nìhn	呢幾年	(24)

thin, skinny	sau	瘦	(22)
thing, object	yéh	嘢	(8)
think about	nám	諗	(20)
thirsty	géng-hot	頸渴	(22)
this evening, tonight	gàm-máahn	今晚	(11)
this month	nī-go-yuht	呢個月	(17)
this morning	gàm-jìu-jóu	今朝早	(4)
this year	gàm-nín	今年	(8)
this, these	nī	呢	(2)
thousand	chìn	千	(11)
three	sàam	三	(2)
three per cent	baak-fahn-jì-sàam	百分之三	(19)
ticket	fēi	飛	(15)
tie a necktie	dá-léhng-tàai	打領呔	(10)
tights	maht-fu	襪褲	(11)
time	sìh-gaan	時間	(3)
time	sìh-hauh	時候	(8)
time, occasion	chi	次	(6)
time's up	gau-jūng	夠鐘	(13)
tired	guih	劫	(24)
today	gàm-yaht	今日	(4)
toe	geuk-jí	腳趾	(9)
together	yāt-chàih	一齊	(3)
toilet, washroom	chi-só	廁所	(10)
tomorrow	tìng-yaht	聽日	(8)
tomorrow night	tìng-máahn	聽晚	(11)
tongue	leih	脷	(9)
too	taai	太	(4)
tooth	ngàh	牙	(10)
totally	sahp-fàn	十分	(18)
tour, to tour	yàuh	遊	(15)
tourism, travel	léuih-yàuh	旅遊	(15)
tourist	yàuh-haak	遊客	(15)
towards	heung	向	(6)
towel	mòuh-gān	毛巾	(15)
town gas	mùih-hei	煤氣	(25)
trade	mauh-yihk	貿易	(19)
traditional	chyùhn-túng	傳統	(22)
traffic lights	gàau-tùng-dāng	交通燈	(12)
traffic lights	hùhng-luhk-dāng	紅綠燈	(12)
traffic, communication	gàau-tùng	交通	(12)
training, to train	fan-lihn	訓練	(24)
tram	dihn-chè	電車	(6)
transport	wahn(-syù)	運（輸）	(11)
transportation costs	wahn-fai	運費	(25)
travel by	chóh	坐	(6)
travel by	daap	搭	(3)
trouble, troublesome	màh-fàahn	麻煩	(10)
trousers	fu	褲	(11)
truly	jàn-haih	真係	(4)
try	si	試	(11)
T-shirt	T-sēut	T恤	(11)
turn of	lèuhn-dou	輪到	(16)
turn to face the other way	diuh-tàuh	掉頭	(16)

turn, change	jyun	轉	(6)
tuxedo, evening dress	láih-fuhk	禮服	(11)
Twelfth lunar month	Laahp-yuht	臘月	(17)
twenty-	yah- or yeh-	廿	(13)
two	léuhng	兩	(2)
two	yih	二	(2)
two ways of looking at it	léuhng-tái	兩睇	(16)
type	dá-jih	打字	(22)
type, kind, species	júng-leuih	種類	(23)
typewriter	dá-jih-gèi	打字機	(24)
typhoon	dá-fùng	打風	(8)
ugly	nàahn-tái	難睇	(17)
UK	Yìng-gwok	英國	(1)
umbrella	jē	遮	(8)
unable to catch	daap-m̀h-dóu	搭唔倒	(18)
unable to get to sleep	fan-m̀h-jeuhk(-gaau)	瞓唔著（覺）	(25)
unable to guess	gú-m̀h-dóu	估唔倒	(18)
unable to see	tái-m̀h-dóu	睇唔倒	(18)
uncomfortable	m̀h-syù-fuhk	唔舒服	(10)
under, underside	hah-bihn	下邊	(12)
underground railway	deih-(hah-)tit(-louh)	地（下）鐵（路）	(6)
underground station	deih-tit-jaahm	地鐵站	(6)
understand	mìhng-baahk	明白	(12)
unfortunately, it's a pity that	hó-sīk	可惜	(11)
uniform	jai-fuhk	制服	(17)
university	daaih-hohk	大學	(6)
unpalatable	nàahn-sihk	難食	(17)
unpleasant to hear	nàahn-tèng	難聽	(17)
unripe, raw, 'rare'	sàang	生	(19)
unwell	m̀h-syù-fuhk	唔舒服	(10)
up to now	dou-yìh-gā-wàih-jí	到而家爲止	(18)
urban area	síh-kèui	市區	(6)
USA	Méih-gwok	美國	(1)
use chopsticks	jà faai-jí	揸筷子	(6)
useful	yáuh-yuhng	有用	(8)
useless	séui-pèih	水皮	(22)
ve: become	sèhng	成	(8)
ve: briefly, have a little	háh	吓	(5)
ve: close up to	màaih	埋	(17)
ve: completely	saai	晒	(15)
ve: completion	jó	咗	(4)
ve: continue	lohk-heui	落去	(19)
ve: downward	lohk-làih	落嚟	(11)
ve: ended	yùhn	完	(6)
ve: error	cho	錯	(19)
ve: in such a way	dāk	得	(15)
ve: -ing	gán	緊	(4)
ve: onto	séuhng	上	(8)
ve: open a gap	hòi	開	(17)
ve: past, across, by	gwo	過	(6)
ve: satisfactorily	hóu	好	(20)
ve: successfully	dóu	倒	(8)

ve: sustain	jyuh	住	(11)
ve: when it comes to it	héi-làih	起嚟	(11)
vegetables; food, cuisine	choi	菜	(4)
vehicle, car	hei-chè	汽車	(12)
very	hóu	好	(1)
very well done (steak)	chyùn-suhk	全熟	(19)
visa	chīm-jing	簽證	(15)
visit a person	taam	探	(3)
visit a place	chàam-gwùn	參觀	(6)
voluntarily, willing	jih-yuhn	自願	(18)
vomit	áu	嘔	(10)
wait	dáng	等	(4)
waiter, junior employee	fó-gei	伙記	(4)
waiter; one who serves	fuhk-mouh-yùhn	服務員	(15)
wake up	séng	醒	(16)
walk	hàahng	行	(15)
walk along	hàahng-louh	行路	(15)
walk in the country	hàahng-sàan	行山	(15)
want	yiu	要	(1)
wardrobe	yì-gwaih	衣櫃	(15)
warm	nyúhn	暖	(15)
warm up	bin-nyúhn	變暖	(23)
warrant card	gíng-yùhn-jing	警員証	(17)
wash	sái	洗	(15)
washing machine	sái-yì-gèi	洗衣機	(25)
washroom, toilet	sái-sáu-gaan	洗手間	(App)
waste	sàai	嘥	(8)
water heater, boiler	yiht-séui-lòuh	熱水爐	(25)
water; money	séui	水	(4; 19)
water-buffalo	séui-ngàuh	水牛	(22)
wear	daai	戴	(11)
wear	jeuk	著 or 着	(11)
weather	tìn-hei	天氣	(8)
week	láih-baai, sìng-kèih	禮拜，星期	(5)
weigh	gwo-bóng	過磅	(15)
weight	chúhng-leuhng	重量	(15)
welcome	fùn-yìhng	歡迎	(22)
well behaved, 'good boy'	gwàai	乖	(13)
west	sài	西	(6)
west side	sài-bihn	西邊	(12)
Western food	sài-chāan	西餐	(23)
Western medicine	Sài-yì	西醫	(10)
Westerner	Sài-yàhn	西人	(9)
Westerner, 'devil chap'	gwái-lóu	鬼佬	(10)
wet	sāp	濕	(22)
what is your name?	gwai-sing-a?	貴姓呀？	(1)
what? what kind of?	mē? (= māt-yéh?)	咩？	(2)
what? what kind of?	māt-yéh?	乜嘢？	(2)
whatever you do, don't	chìn-kèih	千祈	(16)
when?	géi-sí? or géi-sìh?	幾時？	(8)
where?	bīn-douh?	邊度？	(3)
where?	bīn-syu?	邊處？	(3)
which?	bīn?	邊？	(2)

white	baahk-sīk	白色	(5)
who? which one?	bīn-go?	邊個？	(2)
whole	sèhng-	成	(9)
whole, entire	chyùhn	全	(12)
why?	dím-gáai?	點解？	(4)
why? for what reason?	jouh-māt-yéh?	做乜嘢？	(3)
William	Wài-lìhm	威廉	(10)
willing	háng	肯	(22)
win	yèhng	贏	(13)
wind	fùng	風	(8)
winter	dùng-tīn	冬天	(8)
winter, cold weather	láahng-tīn	冷天	(8)
with one's own eyes	chàn-ngáahn	親眼	(18)
with regard to, towards	deui	對	(9)
with, and	tùhng	同	(3)
within	jì-noih	之內	(6)
wok	wohk	鑊	(23)
wok slice	wohk-cháan	鑊鏟	(23)
woman, adult female	néuih-yán	女人	(9)
work	gùng-jok	工作	(22)
work	jouh-gùng	做工	(22)
worker, servant	gùng-yàhn	工人	(25)
world	sai-gaai	世界	(6)
worth it	dái	抵	(15)
would like to	séung	想	(2)
wound, injury	sèung	傷	(16)
wow!	wà!	嘩！	(5)
wrap up	bàau	包	(20)
wristwatch	sáu-bīu	手錶	(2)
write	sé	寫	(19)
written clearly	sé-mìhng	寫明	(19)
XL, extra-large	dahk-daaih	特大	(12)
year	nìhn	年	(8)
year after next	hauh-nín	後年	(10)
year before last	chìhn-nín	前年	(10)
year of age	seui	歲	(9)
Year of the Horse	Máh-nìhn	馬年	(23)
Year of the Sheep	Yèuhng-nìhn	羊年	(23)
yellow	wòhng-sīk	黃色	(5)
yesterday	kàhm-yaht	擒日	(4)
you	néih, néih-deih	你，你哋	(1)
young	hauh-sāang	後生	(12)
younger brother	sai-lóu	細佬	(3)
younger sister	a-múi	阿妹	(3)
youngster	hauh-sāang-jái	後生仔	(12)
your country	gwai-gwok	貴國	(23)
Your Honour, Your Excellency	Daaih-yàhn	大人	(18)
zero	lìhng	零	(11)

"Global scale" of the Common European Framework of Reference for Languages: learning, teaching, assessment (CEFR)

Advanced	**CEFR LEVEL C2**	Can understand with ease virtually everything heard or read. Can summarise information from different spoken and written sources, reconstructing arguments and accounts in a coherent presentation. Can express him/herself spontaneously, very fluently and precisely, differentiating finer shades of meaning even in more complex situations.
Advanced	**CEFR LEVEL C1**	Can understand a wide range of demanding, longer texts, and recognise implicit meaning. Can express him/herself fluently and spontaneously without much obvious searching for expressions. Can use language flexibly and effectively for social, academic and professional purposes. Can produce clear, well-structured, detailed text on complex subjects, showing controlled use of organisational patterns, connectors and cohesive devices.
Intermediate	**CEFR LEVEL B2** (A Level)	Can understand the main ideas of complex text on both concrete and abstract topics, including technical discussions in his/her field of specialisation. Can interact with a degree of fluency and spontaneity that makes regular interaction with native speakers quite possible without strain for either party. Can produce clear, detailed text on a wide range of subjects and explain a viewpoint on a topical issue giving the advantages and disadvantages of various options.
Intermediate	**CEFR LEVEL B1** (Higher GCSE)	Can understand the main points of clear standard input on familiar matters regularly encountered in work, school, leisure, etc. Can deal with most situations likely to arise whilst travelling in an area where the language is spoken. Can produce simple connected text on topics which are familiar or of personal interest. Can describe experiences and events, dreams, hopes and ambitions and briefly give reasons and explanations for opinions and plans.
Beginner	**CEFR LEVEL A2:** (Foundation GCSE)	Can understand sentences and frequently used expressions related to areas of most immediate relevance (e.g. very basic personal and family information, shopping, local geography, employment). Can communicate in simple and routine tasks requiring a simple and direct exchange of information on familiar and routine matters. Can describe in simple terms aspects of his/her background, immediate environment and matters in areas of immediate need.
Beginner	**CEFR LEVEL A1**	Can understand and use familiar everyday expressions and very basic phrases aimed at the satisfaction of needs of a concrete type. Can introduce him/herself and others and can ask and answer questions about personal details such as where he/she lives, people he/she knows and things he/she has. Can interact in a simple way provided the other person talks slowly and clearly and is prepared to help.